S0-AIM-073

THE
CRUISING GUIDE
TO THE
Northern
LEEWARD ISLANDS
Anguilla to Montserrat
14TH
Edition

ANGUILLA
ST. MARTIN & ST. MAARTEN
SABA
SINT EUSTATIUS (STATIA)
ST. CHRISTOPHER (ST. KITTS)
NEVIS
REDONDA
MONTSERRAT

Chris Doyle

THE CRUISING GUIDE TO THE
NORTHERN LEEWARD ISLANDS
Anguilla to Monserrat

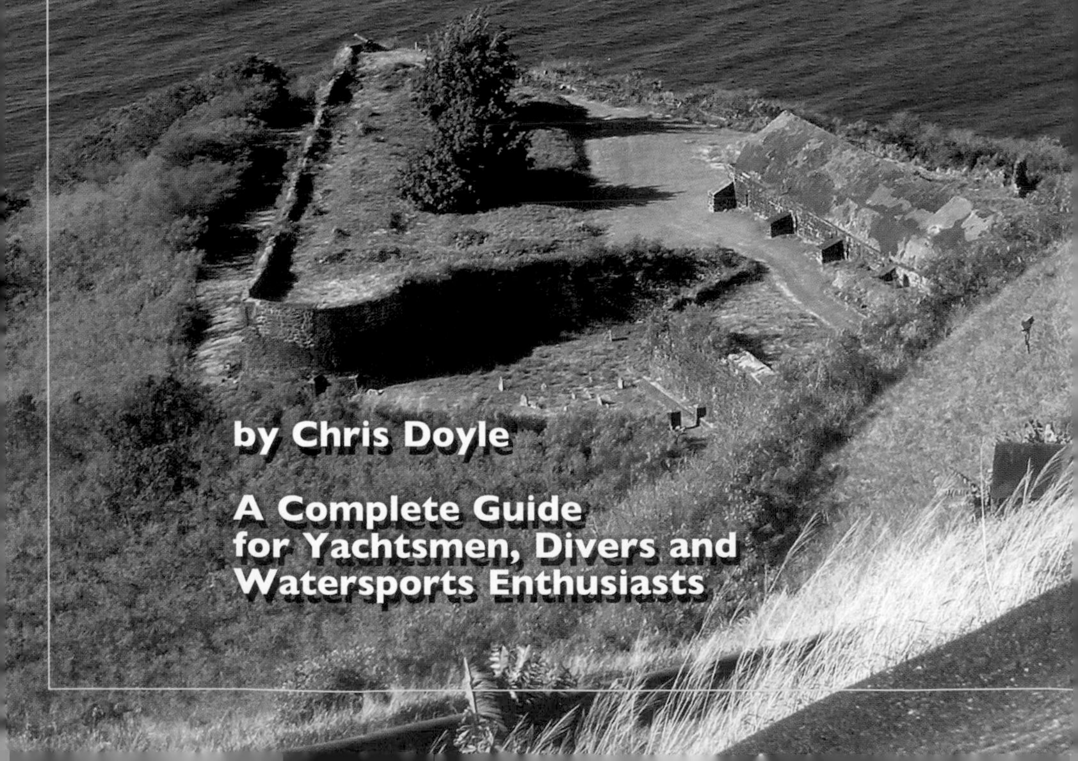

by Chris Doyle

**A Complete Guide
for Yachtsmen, Divers and
Watersports Enthusiasts**

Brimstone Hill Fortress, St. Kitts

© Copyright 2015 by Cruising Guide Publications, Inc. and Chris Doyle

All rights reserved. No portion of this publication may be reproduced in any form, including office duplication equipment, without the written permission of the publisher.

Published by
Cruising Guide Publications, Inc.
P. O. Box 1017, Dunedin, FL 34697-1017
(727) 733-5322   Fax (727) 734-8179
(800) 330-9542
info@cruisingguides.com
Website: **www.cruisingguides.com**

Author: Chris Doyle
Editor: Nancy Scott, Ashley Scott, Chelsea Scott
Book Design/Layout: Carol Dioca-Bevis - Carol Design
Cover Design/Layout: Carol Dioca-Bevis - Carol Design
Photography: Chris Doyle, Paul Tobais, Anne Purvis
Color Charts: Chris Doyle
Marketing and Advertising Sales: Maureen Larroux
Advertising Coordinator: Ashley Scott, Pat Kozemski

This guide is intended for use with official navigational charts. Every effort has been made to describe conditions accurately, however, the publisher makes no warranty, expressed or implied, for any errors or for any omissions in this publication. The skipper must use this guide only in conjunction with charts and other navigational aids and not place undue credence in the accuracy of this guide. This guide is not to be used for navigational purposes.

Fourteenth Edition (2016 - 2017)
Printed in China
ISBN 9780-9914550-5-8

In Memory of Philip Walwyn, the legendary St. Kitts Yachtsman and boat builder. This photo is Kate, which he built to the 12-meter rule, circa 1902.

Paul Tobias

TABLE OF CONTENTS

continued on page viii

TABLE OF CONTENTS (con't)

LIST OF SKETCH CHARTS

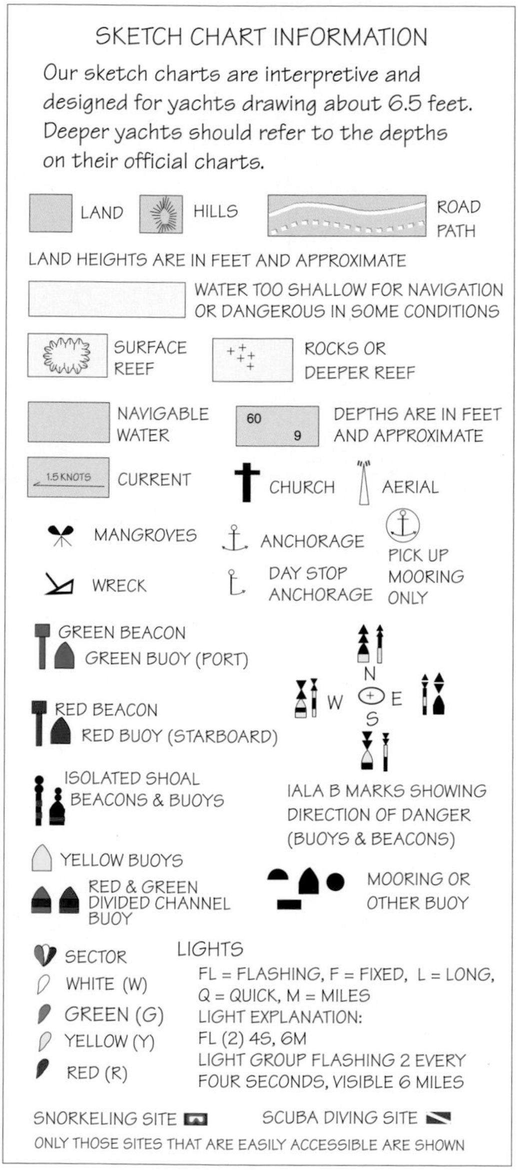

SKETCH CHART INFORMATION

Our sketch charts are interpretive and designed for yachts drawing about 6.5 feet. Deeper yachts should refer to the depths on their official charts.

LAND   HILLS   ROAD   PATH

LAND HEIGHTS ARE IN FEET AND APPROXIMATE

WATER TOO SHALLOW FOR NAVIGATION OR DANGEROUS IN SOME CONDITIONS

SURFACE REEF   ROCKS OR DEEPER REEF

NAVIGABLE WATER   60   9   DEPTHS ARE IN FEET AND APPROXIMATE

1.5 KNOTS   CURRENT   CHURCH   AERIAL

MANGROVES   ANCHORAGE   PICK UP MOORING ONLY

WRECK   DAY STOP ANCHORAGE

GREEN BEACON
GREEN BUOY (PORT)

N   W   E   S

RED BEACON
RED BUOY (STARBOARD)

ISOLATED SHOAL BEACONS & BUOYS   IALA B MARKS SHOWING DIRECTION OF DANGER (BUOYS & BEACONS)

YELLOW BUOYS

RED & GREEN DIVIDED CHANNEL BUOY   MOORING OR OTHER BUOY

SECTOR
WHITE (W)
GREEN (G)
YELLOW (Y)
RED (R)

LIGHTS

FL = FLASHING, F = FIXED, L = LONG, Q = QUICK, M = MILES

LIGHT EXPLANATION:

FL (2) 4S, 6M

LIGHT GROUP FLASHING 2 EVERY FOUR SECONDS, VISIBLE 6 MILES

SNORKELING SITE   SCUBA DIVING SITE

ONLY THOSE SITES THAT ARE EASILY ACCESSIBLE ARE SHOWN

NOTICE

No warranty, expressed or implied, is made by the publisher with respect to accuracy. This guide and these charts are the work of one individual. There may be errors and omissions – so undue credence should not be placed in this guide. This guide should be used with navigational charts and other navigational aids. This guide should not be used for navigation.

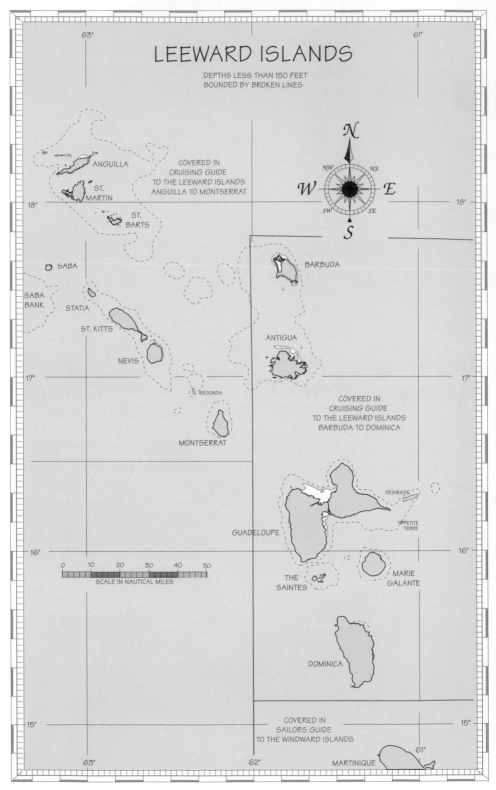

LEEWARD ISLANDS

DEPTHS LESS THAN 150 FEET
BOUNDED BY BROKEN LINES

COVERED IN
CRUISING GUIDE
TO THE LEEWARD ISLANDS
ANGUILLA TO MONTSERRAT

ANGUILLA

ST. MARTIN

ST. BARTS

SABA

SABA BANK

STATIA

ST. KITTS

NEVIS

REDONDA

MONTSERRAT

BARBUDA

ANTIGUA

COVERED IN
CRUISING GUIDE
TO THE LEEWARD ISLANDS
BARBUDA TO DOMINICA

GUADELOUPE

DESIRADE

PETITE TERRE

THE SAINTES

MARIE GALANTE

DOMINICA

COVERED IN
SAILORS GUIDE
TO THE WINDWARD ISLANDS

MARTINIQUE

0 10 20 30 40 50
SCALE IN NAUTICAL MILES

N
NW NE
W E
SW SE
S

Banana Bay, Nevis   Chris Doyle

The Leeward Islands

HE LEEWARD ISLANDS were so called by the British because they were downwind of the Windward Islands, (St. Lucia to Grenada) making it easier to sail to them from the Windwards. (The Dutch on the other hand used to call Saba, Statia and Sint Maarten the Windward Islands because from Aruba, Bonaire and Curacao, their other possessions, they were to Windward.) The Leeward Islands are generally considered to include all the islands from Anguilla to Dominica, though under the British colonial administration Dominica was switched from the Windwards to the Leewards

I wrote my first guide to this area for Cruising guide Publications 26 years ago. Since then marine services and shoreside businesses of direct interest to yachts have increased annually. The Leewards book was always big (the last editions all contained around 520 pages), and to continue giving the same level of coverage it was clear the guide would have to grow and thus become too big and heavy for comfortable use. (I stopped carrying it around when I updated quite a few years ago). So we decided to break The Cruising Guide to the Leeward Islands into two books, Anguilla to Montserrat and Barbuda to Dominica.

This decision will please some people and not others, but ultimately the value of a book depends on how good the information is, how easy it is to use, and whether it is handy enough to take ashore when necessary. For all these reasons splitting the book was inevitable to maintain the same standards.

1

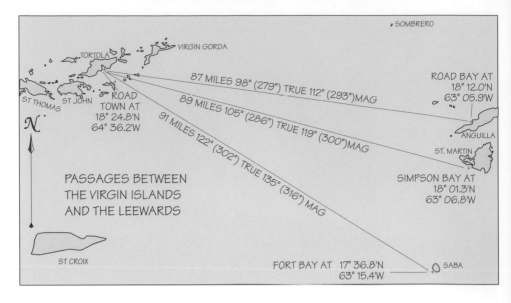

BETWEEN THE LEEWARD ISLANDS AND THE VIRGIN ISLANDS

The Virgin Islands lie around 80-90 miles from Anguilla, St. Martin and Saba, the closest of the Leeward Islands. A current from half a knot to a knot and a half usually flows in a westerly to north westerly direction. The trade winds blow from the easterly quadrant. All this makes it really easy to sail from the Leewards to the Virgin Islands; it is downwind and down current. If you plan to overnight and arrive in the morning, don't forget the current can significantly increase your speed.

The return trip is tough, with both wind and current on the nose. Unless the wind is way in the northeast, you are unlikely to be able to lay even Saba on one tack, so unless you like heavy weather beating, avoid strong Christmas winds.

Approaching cold fronts can be preceded by calm days, which could be a weather opportunity if you have a big engine.

The Virgin Islands are covered in *Cruising Guide to the Virgin Islands*, by Nancy and Simon Scott, available from www.CruisingGuides.com.

Non-Americans planning to visit the USVI, need to know they must not arrive for the first time on a boat without a visa. They will be heavily fined for illegal entry.

It is best by far to get a visa, which will normally give you a 6-month stamp on entry. Your home country is the easiest place to get one but, if you are already in the Caribbean, you can make an appointment online (allow a few months) and go in person to Barbados or Trinidad.

Some people manage to skirt this using a visa waiver (if your nationality allows it). Visa waivers only work as long as you first enter on a commercial carrier. You apply online for an ESTA under the visa waiver program (https://esta.cbp.dhs.gov/esta/). Once approved you must enter on a commercial carrier, and you will need to know which carrier in order to fill in the form.

Most people choose and take a ferry, make sure they get stamped in through immigration and return by ferry. In theory they are then free to enter and leave by yacht for 90 days. I have been told this only clears you in for the Virgin Islands and not the US mainland. It is also not the proper way. You are supposed to get a visa.

Heading to Guadeloupe ?

L'AMER

Waterfront

The Restaurant in Deshaies ...

FUN AND FRIENDLY WITH EXCELLENT FOOD

FOR THE SAILOR :
Baywide WIFI, clothes washing-machine, 8H to 11H and 3PM to 6PM.
Drinking water in emergency.

BREAKFAST 8AM
LUNCH
12PM TO 3PM
DINNER
7PM TO 9.30PM

RESTO BAR
L'AMER
DESHAIES

L'AMER
DESHAIES
TOWN DOCK

OPEN EVERY DAY

BAR OPEN ALL DAY

DESHAIES - GUADELOUPE F.W.I.
0590 68 30 30 / 0690 50 03 22
www.l-amer.fr / laurent.lelou@l-amer.fr

Take Out   f   WiFi   Free WIFI at the restaurant and at the anchor,
Ask for the code.

PLANNING
YOUR CRUISE

Road Bay, Anguilla

Chris Doyle

Introduction

THE islands from Anguilla through to Montserrat can be divided into two distinct groups. St. Martin, St. Barts, and Anguilla lie clustered together in the northeast and have much in common. They are older islands that have been eroded over time to no more than gentle hills. They all have an abundance of spectacular white-sand beaches that melt into pale blue water, of the kind one can see in almost any Caribbean tourist brochure.

This, along with stable governments, and a sunny climate, have led them into a startling economic and social rebirth. As a result of this I call them the Renaissance Islands. They are major destinations for discriminating visitors who want fun and amenities, but enjoy them tinged with a certain degree of character and without too many high-rises. St. Martin has the most visitors, and two or three cruise ships can often be seen on the dock in Philipsburg. It also has the best and most protected anchorages, and is the Caribbean's major base for power superyachts; many of the world's most majestic private craft gather here for the winter. It is also a popular bareboating and cruising base. Sailors appreciate the easy sailing conditions among islands that are close to one another and offer a wide choice of anchorages.

A few miles to the southeast of St. Martin is St. Barts, which is more exclusive, with high-end shopping targeted towards wealthy visitors, beautiful views and hikes, and many fine restaurants.

In the other direction (northeast of St. Martin) is Anguilla, the flattest of the three, also the most laid back and peaceful. It is popular with discerning holiday makers who have discriminating palates and gourmet restaurants abound.

By complete contrast, Saba, Statia, St. Kitts, Nevis and Montserrat, are newer volcanic islands. They form a line, just far enough from the Renaissance islands for a few hours of perfect Caribbean open water sailing. They are all small, steeply mountainous, and surrounded by deep water. The peaks of their mountains often lie in the clouds so I call them The Islands that Brush the Clouds. Most lack natural secure harbors, which has meant that access has not always been easy. As a result each has developed in a certain degree of isolation and they are individually distinctive. All offer fascinating cruising for the adventurous who like to explore ashore and are not afraid of coping with sometimes difficult anchorages and occasionally uncomfortable nights. Tall mountains with dense forests provide a complete change of scene from the Renaissance Islands.

St. Kitts and Nevis has a burgeoning yachting industry. The giant Christophe Harbour in the south of St. Kitts has been dredged out of an old salt pond, creating a really secure harbor for almost any condition. In the north Telca, a much smaller marina has been built right under Brimstone Hill. Behind, St. Kitts Marine Works is a giant yacht haul out and yacht storage area.

We wish you fair winds and fine cruising in this delightful and varied area!

5

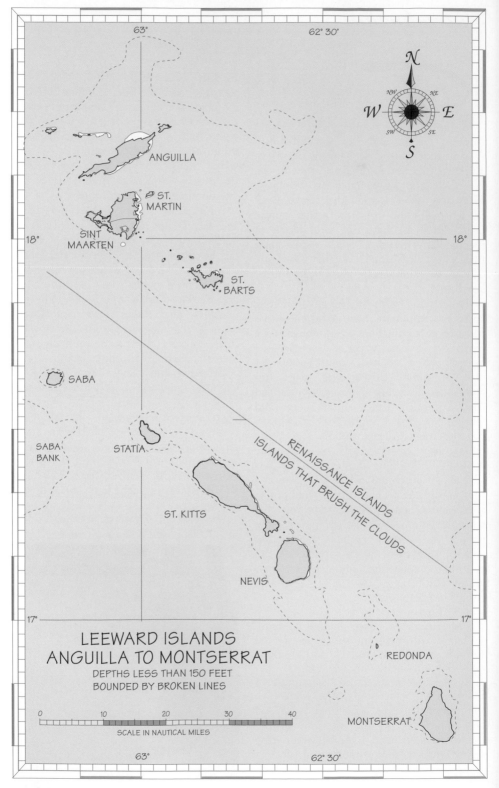

63°   62° 30'

N

NW   NE

W   E

SW   SE

S

ANGUILLA

ST. MARTIN

SINT MAARTEN

18°   18°

ST. BARTS

SABA

SABA BANK   STATIA

RENAISSANCE ISLANDS
ISLANDS THAT BRUSH THE CLOUDS

ST. KITTS

NEVIS

17°   17°

LEEWARD ISLANDS
ANGUILLA TO MONTSERRAT
DEPTHS LESS THAN 150 FEET
BOUNDED BY BROKEN LINES

REDONDA

0   10   20   30   40

SCALE IN NAUTICAL MILES

MONTSERRAT

63°   62° 30'

Marigot Bay, St. Martin Chris Doyle

Planning Your Cruise

CURRENCY

In St. Barts and French St. Martin the currency is the Euro. Anguilla, St. Kitts and Nevis, and Montserrat share a British heritage and a common currency. They all use the Eastern Caribbean (EC) dollar at a fixed rate of around 2.67 EC to one dollar US. Saba and Statia use the US dollar. Sint Maarten uses a Caribbean guilder (florin) but US dollars are more often used.

You do not have to worry about this as US dollars are accepted in all these islands. So much so that even in EC dollar countries, taxi drivers frequently quote in US, as do restaurants. Asking "what kind of dollars" avoids a lot of confusion. If you do end up with some EC or florins, spend it all before you go home. If you take it back home to change, your bank will laugh at you.

TOURIST SEASON

People flock to the Caribbean to escape the chill, so the winter months (November to mid-April) are the fullest. Hotels and charter companies offer discounts for the rest of the year. The best sailing is between mid-April and early June. It is generally dry with easy breezes; too late for northerly swells, too early for hurricanes, and one can get it at bargain rates. Restaurant and bar prices stay the same the year round. During the very slowest months (September and October), some small hotels and yacht services close down, and everyone goes on holiday.

WHAT TO BRING

What does one really need for sand, sun and a little hiking? Bathing things, a few shirts and pairs of shorts, and a simple dress or light slacks and open necked shirts for the evening. Include your camera, lots of sunblock, a long loose shirt and trousers, plus a hat and socks against sunburn. Bring ample prescription drugs if you need them and keep them in your carry-on bag. Snorkelers and divers will want to bring their favorite masks and fins. Divers may

7

also want to bring regulators and BCs, though it is probably easier to rent tanks and weight belts in the islands than to carry them with you.

LANGUAGE

English is spoken widely throughout the area. Speaking French is a bonus in the French islands.

LOCAL CUSTOMS

Islanders can be quite conservative at heart, and particular about dress. Unless you are in the heart of an all holiday district in St. Martin, people generally wear clothes away from the beach, rather than beachwear. In the major towns people dress much as you would if you were going to your local town.

Greetings such as "good morning" or "good afternoon" are important. It is considered rude to approach people with a question or to transact business without first greeting them.

Everyone likes to be tipped, but it is not always expected. In restaurants where no service charge is added, a 10% tip is normal. If service has already been included (as it is by law in the French territories), a little extra is appreciated, but not mandatory. I would tip taxi drivers if they give extra service, such as carrying your bags.

WATER SKIING

Local laws require that a water ski vessel have two persons on board and water skiing or speeding on a jet ski or aquatic scooter within 100 yards of the beach, or in harbors where yachts are anchored, is strictly forbidden.

GREEN FLASH

As the sun goes down it hangs, a huge orb on the horizon. Watch it sink slowly, and pay attention: as the top of the sun disappears over the horizon the last vestige turns bright green. It barely lasts a second and only happens on a clear horizon in excellent visibility. To photograph it with a reasonable chance of success, you will need a telephoto and auto drive. If you are unable to see it, try using binoculars.

HAZARDS

Dengue fever and chickungunya, viruses spread by infected Aedes mosquitoes, don't kill many people, but are serious, and in the case of chickungunya, can have long-lasting effects. It is best to avoid them. Dengue has been with us for years, with occasional outbreaks. Chickungunya arrived in 2013, spread like wildfire, and has now died down in most islands, as many people caught it and became immune. Happily the risk to those living on the water seems to be significantly less than to those on land, but it is still out there, and one should be particularly careful in the summer wet season when there are more mosquitoes. Aedes mosquitoes have stripy legs, generally bite by day and are particularly voracious at dawn and dusk. So buy plenty of bug repellent, and use it liberally especially at happy hour and wearing long sleeve shirts and pants will help.

Scorpions and centipedes also live on the islands, can give a bad sting, but are not generally deadly. You are unlikely to see one, but it is worth looking before you sit down in the scrub on the edge of the beach.

A much more real danger is the manchineel tree (*Hippomane mancinella*) which grows abundantly along some beaches. This pretty tree with its yellow-green apples is toxic and the sap can

manchineel

Chris Doyle

BUDGET MARINE

ANTIGUA · ARUBA · BONAIRE · CURAÇAO · GRENADA · ST. MAARTEN · ST. MARTIN · ST. THOMAS · TORTOLA · TRINIDAD

AB Inflatables are available through all Budget Marine locations and agents. Please visit our website at www.budgetmarine.com for further information.

IAB

www.abinflatables.com

PLANNING YOUR CRUISE

produce a rash like poison ivy. It is all right to take shade under the tree, but avoid brushing through the leaves or standing under it in the rain. Putting a manchineel branch on a beach fire will quickly scatter your barbecue guests. Any sap in your eye is likely to cause blindness, which luckily often turns out to be temporary (about three days). The worst danger comes from eating the apples. They can cause blisters from stem to stern and could be deadly.

SEA SAFETY

Swimming and snorkeling are among the great pleasures of being in the Leewards and they are quite safe provided one uses common sense. The most serious threat to life and limb comes from speeding dinghies and fishing boats – you need to be on guard against these, especially in harbor.

Accidental drowning deaths are rare and are usually caused when someone gets carried away by currents that can build up once you get away from the beach. Be cautious about swimming far from the beach and look over the side to check for current before you dive off the yacht.

You are likely to see plenty of sea urchins. They are black spiny creatures, best avoided because their prickles can easily penetrate skin and break off on contact. This is quite painful, especially for the first few hours. If you do bump into one, you can try removing the spine, but it is tricky as they break easily. It is easier to treat them with hot lime juice that will help dissolve them.

Caribbean sharks and barracudas have been much maligned in popular adventure stories. They have yet to attack anyone in these waters unless harassed, and so are not considered a danger here. Barracudas are very curious and have a habit of following you around. Some people advocate not wearing reflective jewelry as it resembles trolling spinners. On the other hand, diving tank stems are brightly reflective and none have yet been attacked. Moray eels also suffer from bad press, but they are in fact short sighted and timid and will

Golden Rock, Nevis

Chris Doyle

not come out and bother you. It would be pushing your luck to stick your hand into holes among rocks or coral.

Some corals are poisonous and all are delicate, so look and do not touch them. Coral scratches can become infected, and if you get one, scrub it well with soap and fresh water. Stinging jellyfish do exist but are not very common; occasionally the swimmer may feel a mild tingling from a small variety of jellyfish known as "sea ants."

If you swim at night, keep in mind that no dinghy operator can see you, nor can your companions if something goes awry, and that so few people swim at night that little is known about possible dangers.

If you want to scare yourself, look for horrors in any good book on dangerous marine creatures. However, you are unlikely to come to much harm, provided you watch where you put your hands and feet and keep an eye on sea conditions and passing craft.

DRUGS

Many US states and European countries have been liberalizing drug laws. This trend has not reached the Caribbean, and the penalties for being found with illegal drugs in most countries are so severe it would be foolish to risk it (confiscation of the your yacht would just be the first step). Luckily we have an alternative, if your mind needs bending, try a rum punch!

SUNTAN

Sunburn is a major cause of sickness and ruined holidays. Tropical sun is dangerously burning. Cool breezes, seawater, and even

Open All Year

Tapas Lunch from 12 Noon Everyday

A La Carte Dinner from 6pm except Sunday

+1 (268) 464 5283 | +1 (268) 562 4510

reservations@sheer-rocks.com

www.sheer-rocks.com

SheeRRockS
Antigua | West Indies
Restaurant | Bar | Lounge | Plunge Pool | Tapas | Daybeds

cloudy days can make you oblivious to being roasted while you play. On boats, reflected sun off the sea adds to the problem. Use broad-spectrum block out SPF 30+ and keep covered most of the day. Loose, long-sleeved cotton clothing, hats, and sunglasses are a must, as are light cotton socks to protect the tops of your feet. Be especially careful of your back and the backs of your legs when snorkeling.

PHOTOGRAPHY

The islands are so photogenic that it can be difficult to stop taking pictures. Luckily, with modern digital photography, there is no need to, just bring plenty of storage. Colors often look better before 1000 and after 1500.

If you are using an SLR, polarizing filters will bring out the water colors. You get to see the effect by twisting the filter as you look through the viewfinder.

FISHING

Trolling for dinner gives you something to do as you sail between the islands and those you catch yourself will be fresher than supermarket fare. You need about 100 yards of 80 - 100-lb test line, something to wind it on, a wire leader, swivel, hook, and lure. It is easiest to buy the whole set up from a fishing tackle store. Rig the line with a clip so you can see if you have caught anything, or check it every few minutes.

Ciguatera fish poisoning exists in this area and is said to be particularly bad around Redonda Rock. Common symptoms are a bad stomach upset followed later by various neurological symptoms, such as tingling sensations and pains in the joints. It can be serious.

Local sailors consider tuna, dolphin, sailfish, wahoo, and marlin generally safe. Most of us also eat small Spanish mackerel, and kingfish (4lbs or less). Barracuda, especially large ones, are best avoided in this area.

Spearfishing can be very damaging to the fragile reef ecology and, in addition, the presence of ciguatera (mentioned above) makes the eating of reef fish in this area an unpredictable enterprise. It is also illegal in most islands.

Chartering

Sandy Island, Anguilla

Chris Doyle

This is an ideal area for chartering, with easy access to St. Martin from the USA and Europe.

The waters surrounding St. Martin, St. Barts, and Anguilla offer satisfyingly crisp, yet short, passages and the anchorages include sandy coves and unspoiled beaches, yet there is plenty of action ashore for those who seek it.

For a little more adventure, the islands from Saba to Nevis sit tantalizingly on the horizon on a clear day. If you decide to take the challenge a good half-day ocean passage will transport you into this quite different world of mountains, rainforest and different cultures.

St. Martin has many bareboat bases and is the Caribbean capital of large powered luxury superyachts, many of which charter. Charters on such boats are usually arranged through brokers. A 10% tip of the charter price to the crew is normal.

www.doyleguides.com has links to charter company websites.

Charter Companies in St. Martin
(see also overseas agents)

Anchorage Multicoques, 0590-51-90-37, F: 0590-51-11-12, sxm@anchorage-multicoques.com, catamaran charter, bare and skippered.

Anyway Marine, 0590-87-91-41/29-35-93, F: 0590-29-34-76, anyway@wanadoo.fr.

Dream Yacht Charters, 0590-27-13-41, stmartin@dreamyachtcharter.com All kinds, including by the cabin.

Harel Yachts, 0599-29-43-85, 0690-76-22-22, 721-556-1396, herveharel@orange.fr. Skippered and bareboat charters, mainly cats.

It a time when sound advice is priceless... Ours is free.

Boats look new and crews seem friendly online, but a picture never tells the whole story, so why risk your vacation on the unknown?

For over 30 years Ed Hamilton & Co has used their firsthand knowledge to arrange Bareboat and Crewed Yacht Charters Worldwide.

See why Ed Hamilton & Co has been named one of Conde Nast Traveler's Top Travel Agents for 9 years running and remains the most respected Caribbean brokerage in the industry.

www.ed-hamilton.com
800-621-7855

Ed Hamilton &Co.
Yacht Charter Agents

Bareboat & Crewed Charters Worldwide

PLANNING YOUR CRUISE

International Yacht Collection, 721-544-2515/524-6006, mark@IYC.com, superyacht agent.

No Limits Charters and the Maritime School of the West Indies, 0599-51-04-95, 0690-62-99-55, info@nolimitsyachts.com crewed charters and serious maritime school for yacht-master courses.

PYC, 721-581-5305, piesxm@gmail.com, Skippered and day charters.

Reve Marine, 0690-40-10-05, revemarine@stmartin.com, power boats.

Sunsail, 0590-29-50-50, F: 0590-87-31-58, VHF: 74, stmartinbase@sunsail.com, laure-ramel@tuimarine.com, bareboat and skippered charters, one-way charters from Antigua.

St. Martin Yacht Charters, 0590-51-90-37/0690-33-43-38, info@stmartinyc.com, bareboat and skippered.

Tradewind Yachts, 721-544-3045, info@trade-winds.com, Skippered, time share.

The Moorings, 0590-87-32-55, F: 0590-87-32-54 customer@domaccess.com, bareboats and crewed yachts, one way charters available.

VPM Best Sail, 0590 29-41-35, F: 0590 29 42 75, saintmartin@vpm-bestsail.com, All kinds of charter, multihulls and monohulls.

Charter Companies in St. Barts

Nautica FWI, 0590-27-56-50, F: 0590-27-56-52, nfyachts@wanadoo.fr or nfyachts @compuserve.com. All kinds of charters from superyachts to bareboat.

Ocean Must, 0590-27-62-25, F: 0590-27-95-17, VHF: 10, oceanmust@wanadoo.fr. Small power bareboats, day trips, and skippered boats, deepsea fishing.

Master Ski Pilou, 0590-27-91-79, 0690-27-55-70, lepilou@wanadoo.fr, skippered power boats, 40-65 feet.

Maho Bay Sint Maarten

Anne Purvis

👣 **Barefoot Yacht Charters** *Celebrating 25 years of excellence*

We'll take you to places you've never dreamed of ...

La Soufrière Volcano, St.Vincent

BAREBOAT YACHT CHARTERS | LUXURY FULLY CREWED & HONEYMOON CHARTERS | ASA SAILING SCHOOL

· *Full-Service Marine Centre & Yacht Management Facility · Restaurant & Bar · Ocean-view Apartments · Sail Loft · Surf Shop · Internet Café · Water-sports Centre · Boutique*

👣 **Barefoot Yacht Charters**

Blue Lagoon, St Vincent & The Grenadines, W.I. | Tel.: 1.784.456.9526 / 9334 | Fax: 1.784.456.9238
E-mail: barebum@vincysurf.com | www.barefootyachts.com

PLANNING YOUR CRUISE

USA and Overseas Charter Agents

Barefoot Yacht Charters, 784-456-9526, F: 784-456-9238, barebum@carib-surf.com.

Ed Hamilton & Co, 800-622-7855/ 207-549-7855, F: 207-882-7851.

Horizon Yacht Charters, 877-494-8787, 284-494-8787, F: 284-494-8989, info@horizoncharters.com.

Nicholson's Yachts Worldwide, 800-662- 6066/ 617-225-0555, F: 617-225-0190, info@nicholsonyachts.coms.

Sunsail (USA), 800-327-2276, 410-280-2553, F: 410-280-2406.

Sunsail (UK), (2392) 222-300, Fax: (2392) 222-333.

The Moorings 888-952-8420, sales@moorings.com.

The Sint Maarten

We have many great regattas in the Caribbean, but only a few evolve into superstar status, pulling in hundreds of boats from all over the world like a giant magnet. The Sint Maarten Heineken Regatta is one of those. It began in 1980 with a modest 12 entries and now draws over 200 boats and thousands of sailors for a giant event of epic proportions.

The motto has always been one of serious racing and serious fun, the latter in the form of lively parties, a two pronged approach that offers something to everyone. The party side involves four days of serious partying that starts at 1700, carries onto midnight or well after and typically features several groups a night. It attracts far more than the racing crowd, many of whom will party early and then crash to get enough rest for next race. It brings in enough enthusiasts to keep the title sponsor Heineken Beer happy and willing to build stages and bring in high level stage management and top level artists, which all can experience for free. The result is outstanding and open to everyone whether they are racing or not. So for many, and for different reasons, The Sint Maarten Heineken Regatta has become a pivotal part of their Caribbean calendar, and it attracted 52 nationalities at the last entry. It takes place on the first full weekend in March.

With an event this huge there are lots of classes. At the last regatta about nine CSA classes, five bareboat classes (and for anyone without a boat this is definitely the regatta to enter a bareboat), four multihull classes, three lottery classes, (more on that later) and the occasional specialty classes depending on demand. To make all this go smoothly takes a tremendous amount of dedicated and unpaid work which falls on volunteers, both locals and visitors who come specially to help at this event.

Originally the event moved to different

Heineken Regatta

parts of the island but as the event got bigger this caused organizational problems with both the fun and the racing, so more recently the racing has been largely centralized in Simpson Bay, while the parties continue to cover the entire island.

The regatta sets a huge umbrella to attract all and recently there has been an upsurge in participation in the lottery class. This class is so called because almost anyone can join, it eliminates the need for complicated rating certificates, and it relies on inspired and not so inspired rating guesswork so the results are only partially a result of a crew sailing the boat speed. But cruisers love it as they do not have to get measured, and can still join in the fun.

Every day after racing between 1500 and 1700 and on Sunday at 1330, the St. Maarten Heineken Regatta makes a spectator bridge splash. All regatta participants are asked to make a show when they come through the bridge, by dancing on the deck, dressing up and getting the crowd crazy. Judges are seated on the deck of the Sint Maarten Yacht Club, and score the boats on originality, effort and the best crowd response.

The St. Maarten Heineken Regatta consists of two events, a one day warm up (Gill Commodore's Cup) and three days of the real thing (the St. Maarten Heineken Regatta). This first day of racing gives the arriving, bareboat and cruising crews a chance to get their act together, before the main event. Simpson Bay is a large bay for anchoring and the Lagoon authority makes things easy by offering increased bridge openings during the course of the event. Cruisers can anchor in the lagoon or even in Marigot and take a quick dinghy ride to the action in Simpson Bay. More information at www.heinekenregatta.com

Check it out and become an aficionado!

Photos courtesy the Sint Maarten Heineken Regatta

ISLAND READING

MAGAZINES AND NEWSPAPERS:

All at Sea, available in most islands, is a fine, free, nautical newspaper, full of local and international stories of interest to yachtspeople. Useful information includes the bridge opening times into Simpson Bay.

Caribbean Compass, published in the Windward Islands, is available in the Leewards. This free paper is excellent and you can download it online at www.caribbeancompass.com

Every island has its own glossy tourist magazines, with information on restaurants and nightlife. These are free and available at tourist offices and in most hotels.

BOOKS

Photo

Leeward Anchorages, Chris Doyle, has larger (8.5 by 11 inches) aerial photos of most anchorages in the Leewards with brief descriptions. Safe passages, markers, buoys, and hazards included. Cruising Guide Publications. ISBN 0944428-82-7

Snorkeling and Diving

The Complete Diving Guide: The Caribbean, Volume 2 (out of print), Anguilla to Guadeloupe; and Volume 3: Dominica to Tobago. Colleen Ryan and Brian Savage, with shore sections by Chris Doyle. These are ancient but are still the only comprehensive dive guides to this area. Dives that can be done from your yacht are described. ISBN, Vol 2: 0-944428-48-7, Vol 3: 0-944428-42-8. Complete Dive Guide Publications are available through Cruising Guide Publications. (1-800-330-9542) *Volume 1: Puerto Rico and the Virgin Islands* is also available.*

Scuba Diving from Your Yacht. Free book-let given out by the Scuba Shop in Oyster Pond, St. Martin. Call: 011-5995-70823. Describes easy to use scuba sites in St. Martin and St. Barts for those diving from their own boats.

Reef Creatures, Reef Fish, and *Reef Coral*, a series by Paul Humann. The best identification books for snorkelers and divers. Beautiful color photographs. The only identification source for many creatures. Widely available in dive shops. ISBNs: Creatures, 1878348531; Fish, 1878348574; Coral, 187834854X*

Plants

200 Tropical Plants, John M. Kingsbury. This is a good general purpose plant identification book for visitors. Good color photographs and a very wide coverage. Bullbrier Press, ISBN 0961261021

Birds

Birds of the Eastern Caribbean, Peter Evans. Good coverage of all the birds you are likely to see in the Leewards with many color photographs, Macmillan Caribbean, ISBN 0333521552

Birds of the West Indies, James Bond. Thorough treatment of all Caribbean birds and it includes many line drawings and color plates. Collins, ISBN 0-61-8002-1-03

Birds of the West Indies, Herbert Raffaele et al. Excellent artist's color plates for easy identification. Princetown University Press, 069111319X

*Available from Cruising Guide Publications 1-800-330-9542/ 1-727-733-5322
www.cruisingguides.com

Saban cottage with a view

Chris Doyle

CRUISING
INFORMATION

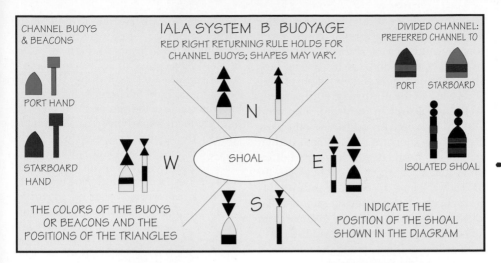

NAVIGATION

Island hops in this area are short so, except on very hazy days, you will see the island you are heading to before you leave the one you have come from.

The equatorial current flows in a northwesterly direction. Sometimes it may be imperceptible; at other times you may find a knot or more. It can intensify around the ends of the islands, and is offset for a few hours on the rising tide. When you are crossing channels, it is worth watching your GPS or taking back bearings to assess the extent of the set. The daily tidal range is only about one and a half feet.

BUOYAGE SYSTEM

There are not many navigational buoys in this area. Those that exist are mainly for commercial traffic and mark channels into the larger harbors. The IALA "B" buoyage system is in use throughout the Caribbean. Red buoys are left on starboard and green buoys on port as you go into harbor (the red-right-returning rule). Occasionally, a shoal surrounded by deep water will be marked with a yellow and black buoy on which mounted triangles indicate the direction of the shoal. (See above diagram.)

WEATHER

The weather is generally sunny, breezy, and perfect for sailing. One gets a few showers and rainy days, with more of these in the summer. The winds are nearly always northeast to southeast at 7 to 25 knots. In the winter months the winds get stronger and more northeasterly. In the summer they are more gentle and southeasterly. There are very occasional calms. Rain usually arrives in short intense squalls that can be seen coming from afar. Sometimes they lay you flat with gusts of over 40 knots; usually they do not. There is no way to tell before they arrive.

During the winter, high-pressure systems often build to the northeast of the Caribbean. If a high pressure system becomes strong it generates brisk northeast to easterly winds of 20-25 knots, sometimes 25-30 knots. Such winds are known locally as "Christmas winds." Sometimes they blow for weeks, and it is blustery but, except in the summer hurricanes, there are no storms or gales. Christmas winds scoop enough moisture off the sea to produce frequent showers, though for the most part conditions are sunny.

These high-pressure systems are offset by cold fronts that sweep southeast from the US. These usually stall and dissipate before they reach this area, but a few do make it, and you need to know what to expect. Before the cold front the weather is usually very pleasant and calm, with light variable winds, often from the south to west. If the cold front gets stalled, these conditions can last several days. The cold front arrives with a buildup of a big cloud bank to the northwest, northwesterly swells, and a shift in the wind. The wind is likely to switch to northwest and blow at about 16 knots for some hours. It then switches to north or northeast and often blows at 20-25 knots (with stronger gusts in rain showers) for a day or two. Northwesterly swells, occasionally severe, are normal. If a cold front is coming you want to move to an anchorage that is protected from the north and northwest. I have made the mistake of being caught out twice at night in exposed anchorages. Luckily the anchor held, but it is neither pleasant nor conducive to a good night's sleep.

A combination of factors can give rise to unusual winds and weather. It is rare, but I have seen the wind blow from both the north and the northwest for some days, and I have seen squalls produce quite strong westerly winds for a few hours.

Cruising is good year round, but winter swells and the hurricane season can affect your planning. Northerly or northwesterly swells roll down from time to time in the winter months. They usually come as a result of cold fronts and storms north of the Leewards. Out at sea they are of no consequence, but along the coast normally tranquil anchorages may become uncomfortable or dangerous. Such swells are most frequent from November to January, though they can come any time. In the exposed islands of Saba and Statia you may have to put to sea, even at night, if bad swells arrive. In other places you have to be selective about where you anchor overnight.

The hurricane season is from June until October. The months of June, July and October each average one hurricane every three years for the whole western Atlantic, including the Caribbean Sea and the Gulf of Mexico. Both August and September, average around five a year. A hurricane as late as December is possible, but unlikely. Hurricanes frequently start far south, but head northwest to pass through the Leewards. Luckily, storm forecasts are good and one usually gets several days advance notice. Hurricane winds can come from any direction, turning normal anchorages into deadly lee shores. They can also produce swells far from their centers. In this area only St. Martin has good hurricane holes (Port

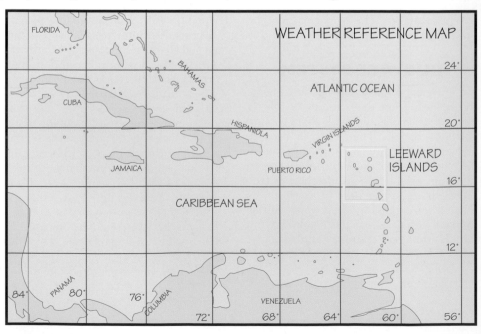

WEATHER REFERENCE MAP

FLORIDA

BAHAMAS

CUBA

ATLANTIC OCEAN

HISPANIOLA

JAMAICA

PUERTO RICO

VIRGIN ISLANDS

LEEWARD ISLANDS

CARIBBEAN SEA

PANAMA

COLUMBIA

VENEZUELA

84° 80° 76° 72° 68° 64° 60° 56°

24° 20° 16° 12°

Gustavia sunset   Chris Doyle

Christophe in St. Kitts looks excellent, but it is both private and new and I am not sure it will be open as a hurricane hole.)

You need a storm plan when planning a cruise in the summer, especially in August and September. In Saint Martin, Simpson Bay Lagoon, Anse Marcel, and Oyster Pond are used for refuge, though nothing is certain and even in these protected anchorages yachts can be lost.

In the hurricane season it is essential to listen to the forecasts, or better get a daily check of the weather on the internet. Cruisingguides.com and doyleguides.com give links to weather. During the hurricane season check with sites like Boat US hurricane page or Storm Carib.

For northerly swells and lesser weather systems, ZBVI is the best radio station, and can often be reached throughout this area, except in St. Kitts and Nevis where it clashes with a powerful religious station; helpful to those who prefer to pray about the weather rather than listen to forecasts. Wind Guru is one of the easiest links to use outside the hurricane season, it gives you a one week forecast of both winds and swells.

Listen closely when you hear about a tropical disturbance, tropical wave, or upper level trough. These are poorly organized weather systems associated with rain squalls

of varying intensity, but they can develop. Get to shelter for a tropical depression (an organized weather system with rain and sustained winds of up to 35 knots), a Tropical Storm (lots of rain and sustained winds of 35 to 63 knots), or a hurricane (sustained winds of more than 64 knots).

Seasons are not well differentiated, but the wettest time of the year is from August to November and the driest is from February to June. Temperatures are 70 to 85 degrees Fahrenheit (20-29 Celsius) year round.

Visibility is often more than 30 miles. Strong winds can put enough water in the atmosphere to cut visibility to 15 miles, but occasional hazier days are caused by dust from Africa. Sometimes reddish traces may be found on the cabin and decks. Even in hazy conditions, visibility is usually 5 to 15 miles.

CUSTOMS AND IMMIGRATION

This area includes many different countries, each with its own customs and immigration formalities to be dealt with on arrival and departure. These are not difficult. When you approach a new country, hoist that country's courtesy flag on the starboard side and directly underneath hoist the yellow flag. Proceed to, and anchor in, a port of clearance. Once you have cleared, take down the yellow flag.

Carry your boat papers, passports, and a blue or black pen (red and green are unacceptable) when you visit customs and immigration. Details are given under island and harbor headings. Typically, you are asked to fill in forms supplied by the officer. In the French islands, you do your entry on a customs computer, many of which are located in marinas or shops. The French islands are all part of France, so if you are going directly from one to another, you should not need to clear out or in again.

In some islands you can pre-clear online with systems that remember all your details from previous visits. St. Barts has its own system on portdegustavia.fr. Anguilla, St. Kitts and Nevis, and Montserrat are on sailclear.com

The customs officers have to wear uniforms and sit in offices all day. They, like you, would probably prefer to be having fun, so if you arrive looking too relaxed they will refuse to deal with you. At a minimum, wear flip-flops, a presentable t-shirt and shorts.

Customs have been known to arrive long after official opening hours, so if you need to get going in the morning, clear out the day before. Those with pets on board will be able to walk them ashore in the Dutch islands. The French islands will allow them ashore, provided they have a rabies certificate. Anguilla, St. Kitts and Nevis, and Montserrat are free of rabies and will not allow animals off the boat without enough red tape to bury your pet.

COMMUNICATIONS

I still remember the old days, waiting in line at a public phone and then trying to balance a notebook on my knee using one hand to hold the phone and the other to write some incoming information, only I can barely hear because a car has just pulled into the parking lot with its stereo going at full blast.

Now GSM phones are available throughout the Caribbean and work well on yachts. Some companies cover many islands, but roaming charges are so prohibitive, that it often pays to buy a new SIM (about $10 US) when you get to a new country. It is easiest for the cruiser to buy prepaid card SIMs, which you can top up as needed. Some services do not charge roaming for incoming calls, so if you have two phones you can keep one for incoming calls and thus maintain the same number.

Digicel has very wide coverage including the French islands, though to use it in Montserrat you need a 4G phone. Lime works for all the English speaking islands.

Carte Orange works in all the French islands, with roaming in the English-speaking islands. In St. Martin you can get by on both sides with a Carte Orange, but if you need a phone in Saba and Statia, you will need to get a Telcel or Chippie SIM. You can buy it in Sint Maarten, where it will also work. If you are buying a phone, get a four-band, unlocked phone for the greatest flexibility.

You can store numbers in your GSM phone either in the phone or on the SIM card. Selection is normally through the contacts setup menu. Copy your numbers to both, so they will be on the phone when you change SIMs, and on the SIM when you drop your phone in the sea. (As long as you can recover the phone, and wash and dry the SIM it should work fine. I cannot say the same of the phone.) Special call packages are often available.

Satellite phones connect well throughout the Caribbean. Because you are tuning to a satellite and not a fixed tower, you may lose your connection more often than with GSM, especially on long calls. They will often not be suitable for local Caribbean calls, as these can incur high roaming charges. In the directory in the back of this book, we list both the area code and the phone number for each listing we give. You will also need the information on our phone info box below.

Most phone companies offer digital packages on SIMs, and with a smart phone, or other device you can use these to bring internet onboard. While nominally 2, 3 or 4G they can be pretty slow. Orange is also expensive, so much so that when using it, you will want to disable any automatic program updates. The little Huawei mobile WiFi USB adaptors are handy as they act

RADIO
For Local News, Views & Weather Forecasts

AM Band

ANTIGUA BROADCASTING SERVICE AM 620: Weather 0750

ZBVI (VIRGIN ISLANDS) AM 780
Good weather forecast at 0730 and 0805 daily except Sunday when it is at 0945
Updates on most hours and half hours

FM Band

ANGUILLA RADIO 1000

ANTIGUA BROADCASTING SERVICE 90.5: Weather 0750

RADIO ST. BARTH: 98.7. Weather at 0730, 1230 and 1730

GEM RADIO IN ST. MARTIN: 88.9. In the other islands look for Gem between 92 and 95. Weather usually on the hour and half hour

ISLAND 92 (91.9) ST. MARTIN: Weather and bridge times 0900, Monday to Friday. Upgrades are given where necessary at 1000 and on weekends. Frequent updates for hurricanes. Marine Trades Calender weekdays at 0945
All at Sea marine program weekdays at 0845

VOICE OF ST. MARTIN (PJD3) 102.7 MHz: General St. Martin channel, occasional news and weather. If you have a TV, try channel 09 for news and weather.

VHF

CHANNEL 10 IN ST. MARTIN has daily cruisers net at 0730.
This is also used as the cruisers calling channel.

SSB & Ham

Caribbean Weather Net: 8104 USB at 0830 (Safety and Security Net 0815)
Caribbean Emergency Weather Net: 3815 kHz LSB at 1835
NMN Offshore forecast: 4426, 6501 & 8764 USB at 0530, 1130 & 2330
Southbound 11 12359 USB at 1600
Cocktail and Weather Net: 7086 LSB at 1630 (not normally Sunday)
Weather Fax for radio information: http://weather.noaa.gov/fax/marine.shtml
For more detailed SSB and shortwave listings go to: Caribbeancompass.com and click on "selected shortwave weather reports."

Internet

Cruisingguides.com, Doyleguides.com, and Caribbeancompass.com
all give links to local weather.

as a hot spot, so everyone on board can get access at the same time.

Various companies offer WiFi internet coverage bringing broad-band high-speed internet access right into your boat. To take full advantage of such WiFi you will need a booster aerial. Whatever you buy needs to operate on the IEEE 802.11 b and/or g standard, and have an output power of at least 100mw.

Most bars, restaurants and cafés offer free internet and in this age of smart phones and internet pads, many people just take their device ashore to hook up.

VHF radio is still widely used in this area, both by vessels and shore-side stations such as charter companies, dive shops, and restaurants. It is still a good form of local

PHONE INFO

Country Codes
Zone A NANP
(North American Numbering Plan)
USA............................1-(area code)
island area codes
Anguilla........................1-(264)
Antigua........................1-(268)
Barbados.....................1-(246)
Dominica.....................1-(767)
Grenada ....1-(473)
Montserrat ....1-(664)
Sint Maarten ....1-(721)
St. Lucia......................1-(758)
St. Vincent ....1-(784)
St. Kitts ....1-(869)
Trinidad......................1-(868)

Country Codes
Zone B
Guadeloupe.................590
Martinique...................596
Saba, Statia.................599
UK.................................44
Australia.......................61
Austria 43
Germany 49
Denmark 45
France 33
Italy..............................39
Sweden 46
Switzerland 41

NANP Zone A.
Within this group dial:
1 + (area code) + (7 - digit number).
If you are dialing the same area code you are calling from, you can usually just dial the last 7 digits.
To dial overseas,
dial 011 (or +) country code and number

NANP Zone B. Within the same country dial the area code and number. To dial oveseas dial 00 (or +) country code, area code and number.

Both areas:
If an overseas area code starts with a 0, omit it when dialing.

Notes
French St. Martin, St. Barts, and Guadeloupe work like one country with one area code. When calling from overseas, the number is + 590 590 + 6 digits (regular phones) or +590 690 + 6 digits (mobile phones). When calling internally dial: 0590 + 6 digits or (mobile) 0690 + 6 digits.
Calling within French territories is not considered overseas. Just dial the area code and number
Calling within the Dutch islands is not considered overseas, just dial 0 and the last 7 digits. If you are calling within one island, just dial the last 7 digits.
SIM phones are sometimes smart enough to recognize where you are. When this happens you need only dial as you would if your phone was from the country you are in. (For example in NANP countries just dial the last 7 digits). The converse side of this is if you are dialing the same area code as your phone, but you are in a different island, you may well have to dial + (country code) + (phone number).
If you are in a French island using an overseas SIM, do not dial 00 to get out of the country, dial + instead.

SATELLITE PHONES
GLOBALSTAR set up for the Americas, works like any NANP Zone A phone.
IRIDIUM works like any NANP Zone B phone
INMARSAT works like any NANP Zone B phone, but the # key is used after all numbers.

communication, though completely open to the listening public, and you cannot beat the price.

Channel 16 is for emergency and raising other stations only. As soon as you have made contact, switch to another channel. In St. Martin, shore stations stand by on channel 10, so keep this one for making contact only.

SECURITY ABOARD

This is a reasonably secure area, but it depends on where you are anchored. I hear of more thefts, especially dinghy thefts, in Grand Case and Marigot in St. Martin than most other places. It does not stop me visiting, but I would take sensible precautions.

Lock your outboard onto your dinghy and lock the dinghy onto the dock when you go ashore. At night, hoist the dinghy, or lock it to the boat and remove the outboard and lock that onto the stern rail. Lock your yacht when you leave it alone. Do not leave valuables unattended on the beach or in the dinghy. If you are in a restaurant with a bag, keep it close. Do not leave things and wander off to the toilet or talk to friends.

While you are unlikely to have a problem, a few precautions will lessen the impact in case you are unlucky. Avoid bringing large amounts of cash and use credit cards, which are replaceable. Visa and MasterCard are much more widely accepted than American Express. Valuable jewelry is best left at home, and it is advisable to take holiday insurance on expensive cameras and binoculars. Be a little cautious about walking at night down small side streets or away from town.

MOORINGS

Marine park moorings are usually available in Ile Pinel in St. Martin, Isle Forchue and Colombier in St. Barts, and in Saba, and Statia. Port authority moorings are available in Nevis.

It would be nice to be able to say that all official moorings are well maintained and will hold your boat. Unfortunately this is not always the case, and boats using official moorings have both gone adrift and become total wrecks.

Always use moorings with caution. The water is lovely and clear, so snorkel and check the condition as far as you can. Watch out for frayed rope, unseized shackles, and make sure it is attached to something secure. The two places where there have been the most problems are Statia and Nevis.

GARBAGE

There are garbage facilities in just about every community, so just bag it all up and take it to one of these. Under no circumstance should you throw plastic bags over the side. Some turtles feed on jelly fish and if they eat plastic bags by mistake they will die. Better they live and eat those jelly fish!

ENVIRONMENTAL NOTES

The coastal water in this area is generally spectacularly clean and clear. Let us keep it that way. Care should be taken while anchoring. Anchors can do great harm to coral, which is very slow growing. Never anchor on living coral. If you are not sure of the nature of the bottom, snorkel before you anchor and take a look.

When anchoring, let out anchor chain or line equivalent to at least five times the depth of the water. Try to arrive in good light when you can find a patch of sand to anchor on; dragging across the seabed and plowing up seagrass is harmful.

Stow trash and dispose of it properly, do not throw things overboard. Coral reefs require clean, nutrient-poor water to thrive. An excess of nutrients encourages the growth of algae, which smothers the coral. Most detergents, soaps, and shampoos are now phosphate free, but even the new ones can be somewhat harmful. Bleach on the other hand will kill everything, including fish, so be very parsimonious in the use of these products, especially when anchored near rocks or reefs.

Avoid wearing gloves when diving or snorkeling, and be careful not to touch or stand on coral.

Take care about what you buy. When you buy straw work, woven mats, cloth, clothing, woodcraft, coconut-craft, jewelry made from seeds and conch shells, and other renewable resources, you are supporting the local economy without damaging the environment. Please do not buy anything made from coral or turtle shell. Reefs are badly damaged by coral collectors, and all the local turtles are endangered.

COMMON SEABIRDS

Birds are often your companions at sea. Sometimes, when there is a school of fish, a huge mixed flock will be wheeling and fishing together. If you are fishing this is a good omen, sail over and join in.

Some of the birds you are likely to meet are shown here. The tropic bird is identifiable by its long tail and fluttery flight.

The magnificent frigate bird is sometimes known as the scissor bird (look at the tail in flight) and also the man-o-war bird because it chases other birds that have caught fish and tries to harass them into dropping their catch, whereupon it will grab it in the air or on the surface of the water. The frigate has the largest wingspan for its weight of any bird and is very agile in the air, but this comes at a cost, for it cannot dive or land for more than a moment in the sea, as it becomes waterlogged. So it either catches fish on or near the surface or lets others do the diving.

Boobies are one of the most common seabirds; you meet them everywhere. They are excellent divers, and some seem to have learned that flying fish fly in front of yachts, so they hang strategically close by. The ones shown here are brown boobies, but there is also a masked booby with a lot more white and the juveniles, too, have much more white.

The royal tern is with us year round, but the laughing gull, like many of you, comes mainly in the winter. As you can see from the photos, terns and gulls look different, although they are around the same size so in flight at a distance you have to look quite hard to tell them apart.

The pelican is of course hard to mistake for anything else. They often fly in formation and have a car-wreck approach to diving, for which they are equipped with their own form of protective air bag.

Tropic bird

Royal tern

Pelican

Magnificent frigate birds

Laughing gulls

Brown boobies

29

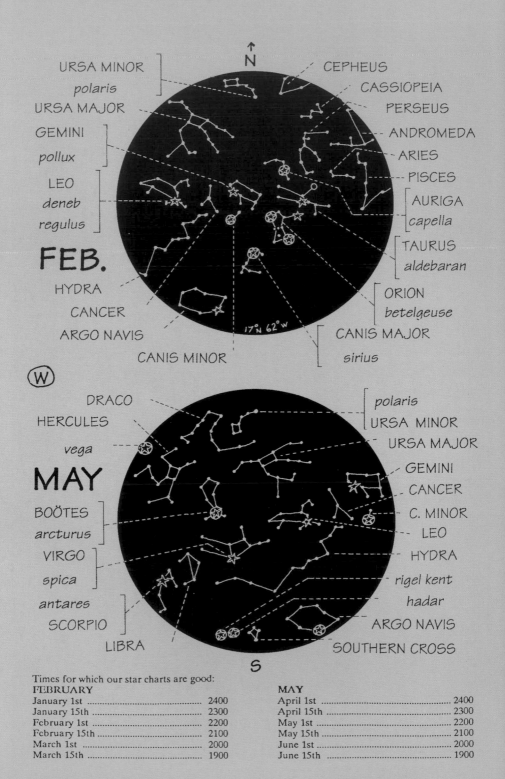

N

URSA MINOR
polaris
URSA MAJOR

GEMINI
pollux

LEO
deneb
regulus

FEB.

HYDRA
CANCER
ARGO NAVIS

CANIS MINOR

17°N 62°W

CEPHEUS
CASSIOPEIA
PERSEUS
ANDROMEDA
ARIES
PISCES
AURIGA
capella
TAURUS
aldebaran
ORION
betelgeuse
CANIS MAJOR
sirius

W

DRACO
HERCULES
vega

MAY

BOÖTES
arcturus

VIRGO
spica

antares
SCORPIO
LIBRA

polaris
URSA MINOR
URSA MAJOR
GEMINI
CANCER
C. MINOR
LEO
HYDRA
rigel kent
hadar
ARGO NAVIS
SOUTHERN CROSS

S

Times for which our star charts are good:

FEBRUARY		MAY	
January 1st	2400	April 1st	2400
January 15th	2300	April 15th	2300
February 1st	2200	May 1st	2200
February 15th	2100	May 15th	2100
March 1st	2000	June 1st	2000
March 15th	1900	June 15th	1900

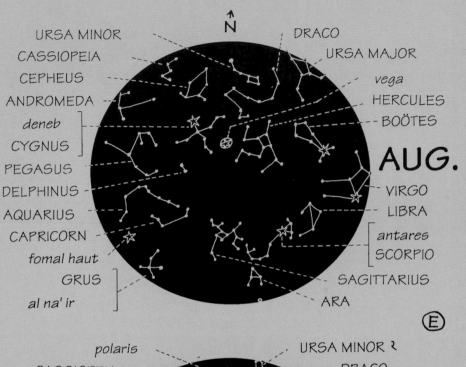

URSA MINOR
CASSIOPEIA
CEPHEUS
ANDROMEDA
deneb
CYGNUS
PEGASUS
DELPHINUS
AQUARIUS
CAPRICORN
fomal haut
GRUS
al na' ir

N

DRACO
URSA MAJOR
vega
HERCULES
BOÖTES

AUG.

VIRGO
LIBRA
antares
SCORPIO
SAGITTARIUS
ARA

A

Ⓔ

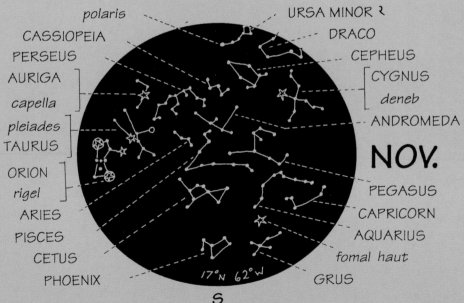

polaris
CASSIOPEIA
PERSEUS
AURIGA
capella
pleiades
TAURUS
ORION
rigel
ARIES
PISCES
CETUS
PHOENIX

URSA MINOR ♎
DRACO
CEPHEUS
CYGNUS
deneb
ANDROMEDA

NOV.

PEGASUS
CAPRICORN
AQUARIUS
fomal haut
GRUS

17°N 62°W

S

DISTANCE TABLE ANGUILLA TO ANTIGUA

MILEAGE CHART

Approximate mileage for planning purposes only. Distances in nautical miles and rounded off to a mile. I used the shortest routes while avoiding traversing The Narrows between St. Kitts and Nevis. Going through The Narrows cuts the distance significantly in some cases, see below:

Distances going through The Narrows

St. Kitts, Christophe Harbour to Jolly Harbour 46
St. Kitts, Christophe Harbour to English Harbour 54
Nevis, Oualie Bay to Jolly Harbour 43
Nevis, Oualie Bay to English Harbour 52
Nevis, Oualie Bay to St. Barts, Gustavia 44

	Antigua, English Harbour	Antigua, Jolly Harbour	Montserrat, Little Bay	Nevis, Charlestown	Nevis, Oualie Bay	St. Kitts, Christophe Harbour	St. Kitts, Basseterre	St. Kitts, Marine Works	Statia, Oranjestad	Saba (Fort bay)	St. Barts, Gustavia	St. Barts, Anse du Colombier	St. Barts, Isle Forchue	Sint Maarten, Simpson Bay	Sint Maarten, Philipsburg	St. Martin, Oyster Pond	St. Martin, Tintemarre	St. Martin, Grand Case	St. Martin, Marigot	Anguilla, Rendezvous Bay	Anguilla, Road Bay
Anguilla, Rendezvous Bay																					010
St. Martin, Marigot																				007	013
St. Martin, Grand case																			004	005	014
St. Martin, Tintemarre																		004	008	008	017
St. Martin, Oyster pond																	005	008	012	012	021
Sint Maarten, Philipsburg																004	009	012	014	014	019
Sint Maarten, Simpson Bay															005	009	012	010	009	016	016
St. Barts, Isle Forchue														013	009	008	009	011	016	022	027
St. Barts, Anse du Colombier													003	015	012	009	011	013	019	023	024
St. Barts, Gustavia												003	005	017	014	013	015	020	023	026	030
Saba (Fort bay)											029	029	028	028	029	030	035	038	033	035	033
Statia, Oranjestad										017	027	029	035	034	034	039	044	042	044	035	038
St. Kitts, Marine Works									012	029	035	043	044	045	048	050	054	057	060	052	047
St. Kitts, Basseterre								008	012	023	040	045	046	048	051	054	058	060	064	060	059
St. Kitts, Christophe Harbour							004	009	016	028	040	045	049	053	054	058	060	061	065	069	066
Nevis, Oualie Bay						004	009	016	029	043	046	053	054	055	059	060	065	069	068	069	071
Nevis, Charlestown					004	006	010	017	029	046	049	054	055	060	061	067	068	078	080	077	074
Montserrat, Little Bay				033	038	039	043	049	061	067	077	084	086	088	091	097	104	106	115	098	093
Antigua, Jolly Harbour			024	045	049	052	054	062	067	076	085	089	090	096	099	128	133	136	115	105	103
Antigua, English Harbour		012	028	053	057	059	062	069	077	084	093	114	117	126	125	133	138	145	116	106	105
Guadeloupe, Deshaies	041	046	042	070	075	076	080	086	098	114	115	116	128	125	126	133	136	138	128	115	145

GPS

SATELLITE NAVIGATION
in the Leeward Islands

The GPS positions
given here have ID numbers
that are shown on our sketch charts.
You can download all these
waypoints directly to your GPS
by visiting www.doyleguides.com,
where I have posted
the waypoints and a
link to the appropriate software.

ID	LATITUDE	LONGITUDE	COMMENT
LANG01	N18°13.30'	W063°04.50'	Crocus Bay
LANG02	N18°12.00'	W063°05.90'	Road Bay
LANG03	N18°09.40'	W063°10.70'	Anguillita
LANG04	N18°15.70'	W063°10.70'	Prickly Pear Cays
LANG05	N18°16.00'	W063°15.00'	Dog Island
LANG06	N18°16.00'	W062°57.00'	Scrub I passage S approach
LSTM01	N18°00.40'	W063°03.30'	Philipsburg
LSTM02	N18°01.30'	W063°06.80'	Simpson Bay
LSTM03	N18°04.90'	W063°06.10'	Marigot near unlit buoys
LSTM04	N18°03.50'	W063°09.30'	Point Basse Terre
LSTM05	N18°06.80'	W063°03.80'	Grande Case
LSTM06	N18°06.20'	W062°59.90'	Orient Bay entrance
LSTM07	N18°03.00'	W063°00.40'	Oyster Pond entrance
LSTM08	N18°07.40'	W063°02.50'	Anse Marcel approach
LSTM09	N18° 06.00'	W063° 04.70'	Friars Bay
LSTB01	N17°55.50'	W062°52.80'	Anse de Colombier
LSTB02	N17°54.30'	W062°52.00'	Gustavia (N. entrance)
LSTB03	N17°51.00'	W062°50.00'	South approach to St. Barts
LSTB04	N17°57.30'	W062°54.70'	Ile Forchue
LSTB05	N17°55.00'	W062°56.00'	West approach St. Barts
LSTB06	N17°52.40	W062°49.10'	Approaches to Grand Saline
LSTB07	N17° 54.7'	W062° 50.00'	Approach Bay St. Jean
LSAB01	N17°36.80'	W063°15.40'	Fort Bay
LSAB02	N17°39.00'	W063°15.50'	Saba NW approach
LSAB03	N17°37.00'	W063°13.00'	Saba SE approach
LSTA01	N17°29.00'	W062°59.50'	Oranjestad
LSTA02	N17°32.00'	W063°00.00'	Statia N approach
LSTA03	N17°27.40'	W062°58.00'	Statia S approach
LSKT01	N17°24.60'	W062°52.60'	Off northwest coast St. Kitts
LSKT02	N17°17.00'	W062°43.00'	Basseterre
LSKT03	N17°15.80'	W062°37.50'	North approach to The Narrows
LSKT04	N17°21.40'	W062°51.60.'	Sandy Point Town
LSKT05	N17°15.00'	W062°40.00.'	Approach to White House Bay
LSKT06	N17°20.30'	W062°50.10.'	St. Kitts Marine Works
LSKT07	N17°26.00'	W062°49.50.'	Approach to Dieppe Bay
LNVS01	N17°08.60'	W062°38.00'	Charlestown
LNVS02	N17°05.00'	W062°39.00'	Nevis SW approach
LNVS03	N17°12.00'	W062°37.30'	Nevis approaches Oualie, Tamarind
LMTS01	N16°48.40'	W062°12.80'	Little Bay
LMTS02	N16°44.3'	W062°14.50'	Old Road Bay
LMTS03	N16°50.00'	W062°10.00'	NE Montserrat
LMTS04	N16°41'00'	W062°15.00'	SW Montserrat
LMTS05	N16°47'00'	W062°07.50'	East Montserrat
LMTS06	N16°38.50'	W062°09.00'	South Montserrat

These should not be used for navigation without first checking the data out against current DMA or BA charts.

Professional Yachts

DURING THE WINTER season, the Leewards are a major cruising area for some of the largest yachts in the world.

Below is a list of people who will organize everything when you don't have the time to look for individual services.

Anguilla

BWA Yachting, Sue Ruan, 721-554-8918/554-2436

Axa Yacht Services, Gabi Gumbs 264-584-3826

LH Enterprises, Lesley Lloyd, 264-581-5683, enterprises@anguillanet.com

Simone Connor, 264-476-6534, mysandy-island@hotmail.com

St. Martin

St. Martin is perhaps the Caribbean's largest megayacht base. You will find everything you need to support your yacht here. Most marinas have a full line of services for superyachts and these include:

Marina Fort St. Louis, 0590 51 11 11, F: 0590 51 11 12, VHF:16, marinafortlouis@domaccess.fr

Palapa Marina, 721-545-2735, F: 721-545-2510, VHF: 68, office@palapamarina.com

Yacht Club Port de Plaisance 721-544-4565, F: 599-544-4566, VHF: 16/78, info@yachtclubportdeplaisance.com

Simpson Bay Marina, 599-544-2309, F: 721-544-3378, VHF: 16/79A, sbm@igymarinas.com

Yacht Club Isle de Sol, 721-544-2408, F: 721 544-2906, IDS@igymarinas.com.

You can also find superyacht agents who will arrange everything for you:

BWA Yachting, 721-554-8918/554-2436, .frye@BWAyachting.com

Dockside Management, 721-542-4096/559-1948, F: 721-544-4097, US: 305-677-0055, office@docksidemanagement.net

International Yacht Collection, 721-544-2515/ 721-524-1524 mark@iyc.com

Mega Yacht Services, 721-544-4440, Cell: 721-520-1530, harrison@megayachtservice.com

Shore Support, 721-587-0007/544-5009, 0690-75-58-08, simon@shoresupport.net

Yacht Assistance, 0590-51-04-95, 0690-62-99-55, info@yachtassistance.com

St. Barts

The Port of Gustavia has dock space for yachts less than 60 meters. Two agencies specialize in superyacht services:

Nautica FWI, 0590-27-56-50, F: 590-27-56-52, nfyachts@wanadoo.fr

St. Barth Services, 0590-27-56-26, 0690-50-06-25, F: 0590-27-56-81, brice@stbarthservices.com

Statia

Fuel can be taken on in Statia. Contact the Port Authority, 599-318-2888, VHF:16, 14

St. Kitts/Nevis

Big yachts can fuel in Port Zante or, if there is space, in the cruise ship dock by arrangement with the port authority. Christophe Harbour is now open for large yachts and they can provide anything you need.

Christophe Harbour, 869-466-4577/8738

Delisle Walwyn, 869-662-4872/465-2631, VHF: 16

Port Zante, 869-466-5021, F: 869-466-5020, VHF:#68, info@portzante.com

Serviciz, 869-762-8130/663-8130, F: 464-4188, rickie@serviciz.com

St. Kitts Yacht Services, 869-662-4400, F: 869-465-0712, info@stkittsyachtservices.com

Nevis Yacht Services, 869-469-6545/667-7466/664-9171, info@nevisyachtservices.com

Scuba Diving

NEARLY EVERYONE WHO dives successfully is hooked. Few sports attract such dedicated adherents. Yet those who have not dived have little appreciation of what it is all about. This is not surprising because the world underwater is totally alien from life on land and language does a poor job of describing it. A major difference is in locomotion. One is weightless underwater and movement more closely resembles flying or drifting in outer space than walking or running.

We find ourselves gliding into a brand new environment with a fluidity and ease known only in our dreams. And as soon as we relax enough to look around, we realize that life under the sea is very strange indeed. The background color is in the restful blue-green spectrum, yet painted on top of this are some of the brightest colors imaginable:

sponges that look like ancient urns glow a luminous blue and there are huge schools of fish in brilliant reds, mauves, yellows and blues. It is a topsy-turvy world full of wonders. Tall soft waving plants that are really colonies of tiny animals, little squids moving by a kind of jet propulsion, and rays gliding with elegant ease. Best of all it has been barely touched by man so most of the fish are not frightened. Indeed, the tiny damselfish, which can easily fit in the palm of a hand, regards a diver as another big fish and will charge headlong to protect its territory with such gallant determination that is hard not to laugh. If we put an upside down hand out among the cleaning shrimp, they will crawl aboard and clean our skin. We can swim close by schools of fish whose very numbers are astonishing.

Diving is easy. Anyone who just wants to give diving a go can do so very quickly with a 'resort course.' It will take one whole morning or afternoon. First you get a one

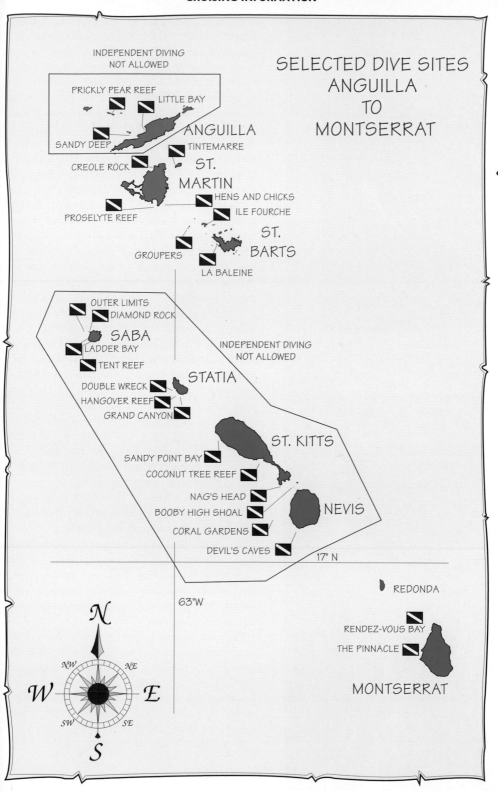

SELECTED DIVE SITES
ANGUILLA
TO
MONTSERRAT

INDEPENDENT DIVING
NOT ALLOWED

PRICKLY PEAR REEF
LITTLE BAY
ANGUILLA
SANDY DEEP
TINTEMARRE
CREOLE ROCK
ST.
MARTIN
HENS AND CHICKS
PROSELYTE REEF
ILE FOURCHE
ST.
BARTS
GROUPERS
LA BALEINE

OUTER LIMITS
DIAMOND ROCK
SABA
LADDER BAY
TENT REEF
INDEPENDENT DIVING
NOT ALLOWED
DOUBLE WRECK
STATIA
HANGOVER REEF
GRAND CANYON
ST. KITTS
SANDY POINT BAY
COCONUT TREE REEF
NAG'S HEAD
BOOBY HIGH SHOAL
NEVIS
CORAL GARDENS
DEVIL'S CAVES
17° N

63°W

REDONDA

RENDEZ-VOUS BAY
THE PINNACLE
MONTSERRAT

N
NW NE
W E
SW SE
S

Wrasse

Eagle ray

hour talk that tells you in simple language what diving is all about. Then you try out the equipment in shallow water and, lastly, you go for your first dive. A resort course only qualifies you to dive under the close supervision of an instructor at the same dive shop.

The next step from the resort course is the Scuba Diver course put out by PADI. This two-and-a-half day course certifies you to dive with any dive master at any shop to a depth of 40 feet. It is a good introduction and, being short, it is easy to do on holiday. You can complete your training on your next holiday, as this course counts as credit towards being an independent open water diver. A full diving course in the islands takes about four or five days and includes a couple of hours of instruction each day, followed by a dive, during which you increase your practical skills.

The islands from Anguilla to Montserrat offer a tremendous variety of diving. The nature of the land is often reflected beneath the sea. Islands like Saba and Statia that are rugged and dramatic onshore have breathtaking walls, pinnacles and rocks below. Islands with a more gentle form such as Anguilla and St. Martin have huge forests of coral below and the diving is easy and relaxing. Cruising divers are especially lucky because they can try a dive in each island, sampling a smorgasbord of the area's very best dives.

Most places you can dive from your yacht with your own or rented equipment, but there are exceptions and park regulations.

In Anguilla, Saba, Statia, St. Kitts, and Nevis diving is forbidden except with a local dive shop. Most of St. Barts is a marine park and while you are welcome to dive, you should first go to the marine park office and pay your diving fees.

We try to give information for those dive sites that are suitable for diving straight from your boat or dinghy, and many of these are marked on our sketch charts. For more information, check the Complete Dive Guide series that describes all the dives in great detail, including underwater plans.

Sometimes sea conditions make sites

unsuitable; divers must judge for themselves. Those diving in St. Martin and St. Barts should contact the Scuba Shop in Oyster Pond. The owners put out a free booklet with maps describing sites suitable for yachts.

We include some sites that are out of reach of most yacht dinghies. In these cases it is best to go with a local dive shop. I strongly recommend that newly qualified divers and those who have not dived recently do their first dive with a dive shop.

Coral reefs are particularly fragile and it is essential that all of us sports divers take the greatest care to preserve this natural wonderland. Coral reefs are made up of colonies of small creatures called polyps that bond together to make up the huge structures we see. Many are sensitive to handling, and a small amount of damage can lead to the introduction of invasive sponges, which could slowly destroy a large clump of coral. Unlike plants, corals grow extremely slowly, so any damage is long lasting.

A diver can damage coral by kicking it with fins, grabbing it, or bumping into it. Underwater photographers can also damage it by lying on it or supporting themselves on the coral while taking pictures. There are several things that can help. Never wear gloves when you dive, they decrease your sensitivity and you will be tempted to grab onto coral.

When you first go down, try to descend onto a sand patch beside the reef. This way you will be kicking sand rather than reef while you get your balance and buoyancy under control. Avoid the illegal practice of taking underwater souvenirs, be they live shells, hard coral or seafans. Nature is good at recycling, even shells that look dead often contain critters which have moved in and are living inside.

It is very beautiful underwater and the fish and sea creatures are unafraid and, in many cases, downright curious. Enjoy it and help keep it wonderful.

A list of dive shops is given in the *Directory* at the back of this book.

Green turtle

Lion Fish

anchorages of the
RENAISSANCE
ISLANDS

anguilla • st. martin • sint maarten • st. barthelemy (st. bart

Sandy Ground Beach, Anguilla

Chris

Anchorages of The Renaissance Islands

IN THE LESSER ANTILLES there are two kinds of islands, both volcanic. The relatively young ones, which are mountainous and steep, form a gentle arc from Grenada to Saba. The older islands were once like the youngsters, but have eroded to nearly flat and at some time sank below sea level where they acquired limestone cappings before being uplifted and resurfacing. St. Martin, St. Barts, and Anguilla are of the older type and they lie together on a large bank, 30 miles to the north of Statia and Saba. They are less mountainous than their volcanic cousins and consequently drier. The relatively shallow water has allowed for the growth of corals, shells, and algae, which over millions of years have been transformed into long, white, sandy beaches.

The early success of plantations on these islands was short lived. Rainfall was inadequate for agricultural crops and the thin soil was quickly depleted. As a consequence, their economies and populations declined until quite recent times. With the coming of the leisure age, they have begun a renaissance that promises to far exceed any past splendor. A major contributing factor has been the pleasant dry climate that worked against these islands earlier. St. Martin led the way, with its duty free status, tolerant French/Dutch administration, and the easy access provided by a large airport. Hotels and condominiums have rapidly replaced the dry scrub behind the beaches and the population has more than tripled over the last 40 years. As St. Martin boomed, those wanting a quieter, more exclusive kind of island have visited St. Barts and Anguilla.

Politically, St. Martin is divided in two. The northern part is French (Saint Martin) and the southern part Dutch (Sint Maarten); to make life easy we refer to the whole island as St. Martin. Sint Maarten is self-governing, but Holland still handles foreign affairs. St. Martin and St. Barts are French, and are like communes in France. Anguilla is still British, though largely self-governing.

Attractions for yachtspeople include short but invigorating passages between the islands and a wide variety of anchorages. One can suit one's mood with either peaceful hideaways or bustling ports with restaurants, shops, and nightlife. St. Martin in particular offers first-rate duty free provisioning, some of the Caribbean's largest chandleries, and many efficient yacht services.

RENAISSANCE ISLANDS

Tintamarre Island

Chris Doyle

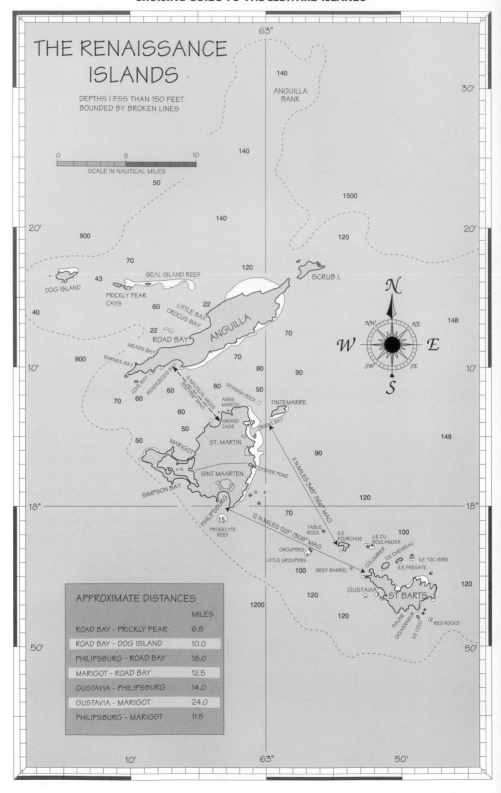

THE RENAISSANCE ISLANDS

DEPTHS LESS THAN 150 FEET
BOUNDED BY BROKEN LINES

63°

140
ANGUILLA BANK

30'

140

0   5   10
SCALE IN NAUTICAL MILES

50

140

1500

20'

140

50

800

120

20'

70

SEAL ISLAND REEF

120

SCRUB I.

DOG ISLAND
43
PRICKLY PEAR CAYS
22
LITTLE BAY
CROCUS BAY

60

40

22
ROAD BAY
ANGUILLA

70

148

10'

800

MEADS BAY

BARNES BAY

COVE BAY
RENDEZVOUS BAY
80
SPANISH ROCK
80
90
10'

70

60

60
5 NAUTICAL MILES
352° 172° MAG

TINTEMARRE

50

ANSE MARCEL

60
50
GRAND CASE
ORIENT BAY

148

50
MARIGOT
ST. MARTIN

90

SINT MAARTEN
OYSTER POND

11 N.MILES 345° 1166° MAG

SIMPSON BAY

120

18'
PHILIPSBURG
(15)
70
12 N.MILES 128° 1308° MAG
TABLE ROCK
ILE FOURCHUE
100
18'

PROSELYTE REEF
ILE DU BOULANGER
COLUMBIER
ILE CHEVREAU
ILE TOC VERS
ILE FREGATE

GROUPERS
LITTLE GROUPERS
100
BEEF BARREL
120

100
GUSTAVIA
ST BARTS
120

APPROXIMATE DISTANCES

	MILES
ROAD BAY – PRICKLY PEAR	6.5
ROAD BAY – DOG ISLAND	10.0
PHILIPSBURG – ROAD BAY	18.0
MARIGOT – ROAD BAY	12.5
GUSTAVIA – PHILIPSBURG	14.0
GUSTAVIA – MARIGOT	24.0
PHILIPSBURG – MARIGOT	11.5

1200
120
120
SALINE
GOUVERNEUR
ILE COCO
RED ROCKS

50'
50'

10'
63°
50'

Crocus Bay   Chris Doyle

Anguilla

NGUILLA IS A LOW island surrounded by soft, powdery, white sand beaches and banks of coral. For the most part it has a wonderful sense of peace and the people are outstandingly friendly and honest. The population of 12,000 relies on tourism as the major industry. Anguilla has an American medical school.

The tourist boom has bought with it a rash of building, with styles varying from rectangular concrete boxes to the elaborately grandiose in many flavors. Here and there, but getting rarer, you come across a traditional old Anguillan house; they stand out as very pleasing to the eye in their simplicity and elegance.

The two main visitor activities in Anguilla are beaches and eating out. As a consequence Anguilla has so many really excellent restaurants that mentioning them all would take a book; I have stuck to those close to the anchorages.

In 1967, Britain lumped Anguilla with St. Kitts and Nevis and made them an autonomous state. This awkward parceling conveniently filed them away for the British Colonial Office, but ignored both the social and geographical realities. Anguillans were dead set against this arrangement and wanted to remain with England. They rebelled against the rule of St. Kitts' Premiere Bradshaw who told them he "would show them who was boss" and threatened to "turn Anguilla into a desert." An amazing armed rebellion followed in which there were only minor casualties and no fatalities. The Anguillan rebels would open fire on the police station – manned from St. Kitts – at all hours of the night or day until the police were quite unnerved. A large armed crowd then gave the police an ultimatum to leave the island and they blocked the runway to stop rein-

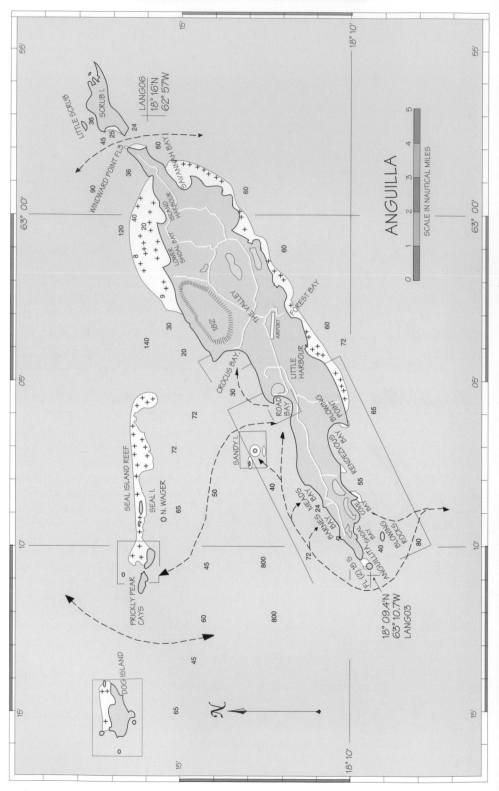

ANGUILLA

SCALE IN NAUTICAL MILES

0 1 2 3 4 5

LITTLE SCRUB

SCRUB I.

LANG06
18° 16'N
62° 57'W

WINDWARD POINT Fl.3

SAVANNAH BAY

ISLAND HARBOUR

LOWER SHOAL BAY

THE VALLEY

AIRPORT

FOREST BAY

LITTLE HARBOUR

CROCUS BAY.

ROAD BAY

SANDY I.

SEAL ISLAND REEF

SEAL I.

O. N. WAGER

PRICKLY PEAR CAYS

DOG ISLAND

BLOWING POINT

RENDEZVOUS BAY

COVE BAY

BARNES MEADS BAY

ANGUILLITA SHOAL

BOORS

ROCKS

BLOWING

Fl.(2) 15 s

18° 09.4'N
63° 10.7'W
LANG03

N

Anguilla

Regulations

Yachts should proceed directly to Road Bay, the main port of entry. Blowing Point is also a permissible point of entry, but it is commercial and not recommended for yachts. The Fisheries Department does not allow anchoring in certain areas; we note these in our harbor descriptions. Yachts anchoring outside Road Bay need a cruising permit and all yachts will need to pay charges. We give full customs details under Road Bay. The waters all around Anguilla are protected; nude bathing, spearfishing and the collecting of coral or live shells are forbidden. Beach fires are not allowed. In the marine park areas, water skiing, fishing, pumping bilges or heads, and the taking of anything (except pictures) is banned. The marine park is open from 0600-1900. Yachts may not overnight in the park. Divers must go with an authorized local dive operator.

Telephones

The area code for Anguilla is 264. Cable and Wireless and Digicel cell phones work here. If you don't have one and need to make a call, talk to An at Syd-An's; she can help.

Shopping Hours

Normal shopping hours are 0800-1200 and 1300-1600.

Transport

Anguilla's airport takes all inter-island airlines, but is not jumbo-jet sized. American Airlines has direct flights to Puerto Rico and other airlines have good linkage to neighboring islands. Easy connections can be made via St. Martin. There is also a ferry service that runs about every 45 minutes between Blowing Point and St. Martin.

The easiest way to get around in Anguilla is to use a taxi from the stand next to customs. Taxi rates are calculated by dividing Anguilla into zones. If you stay in the same zone, fares are usually $10 US. The farthest destination is $36 US. These rates are for one or two people. (Four for the tour.) Extra people are charged $3 for regular runs, $5 for island tours.

Example rates in $US are:	
Road Bay to The Valley	$15
Road Bay to the airport	$15
Tours, 2 hours up to 4 people	$80

Rental cars are easily available. You will need to buy a local license for about $20 US. Drive on the left. Stephen (264-772-5194), and Maurice (264-476-0505/235-2676), are Sandy Ground taxis, Maurice has cars to rent. Booker (532-3548) and Kitch (772-7742) are often there. Bikes are available from Aslin (264-235-8931).

Holidays

- January 1
- Good Friday and Easter Monday (Easter Sunday is March 27, 2016; April 16, 2017)
- May 1 (Labor Day)
- Second Saturday in June (Queen's Birthday)
- Whit Monday (50 days after Easter Sunday, May 16, 2016; June 5, 2017)
- Last Friday in May (Anguilla Day)
- First Monday and Tuesday, Thursday and Friday in August (Carnival, August Thursday and Constitution Day)
- December (mid/variable) (Separation Day)
- December 25-26

forcements from arriving.

The Anguillans, fearing an armed invasion from St. Kitts, decided to take the offensive and invade St. Kitts themselves. A small boatload of men went there, aided by two American mercenaries. The invasion was a complete fiasco. A big hole got blown in the ground near the defense force headquarters and there was a shootout at a police station. There were no casualties. However, after that no one in St. Kitts really wanted to mess with the Anguillans. Several Americans thought up fancy schemes to help the Anguillans finance their island and, in 1969, Britain, under the mistaken impression the island had been taken over by the Mafia, invaded. Armed men waded ashore onto the beaches to be met by goats and curious small boys. After the embarrassment died down, Anguillans got what they wanted and are again administered by the British.

Road Bay, the main anchorage in Anguilla, is a charming village set on a lovely beach. The sail to and from St. Martin is usually a pleasant haul over turquoise water. From Road Bay you can visit

other anchorages along Anguilla's south and north coasts, as well as making day stops offshore at Sandy Island, Dog Island, and Prickly Pear Cays. There may be fees involved (see *Road Bay*).

You must clear into Anguilla, and the place to do this is Road Bay. Customs can be found at Blowing Point, but the anchorage is tiny and rolly and best left to commercial craft and ferries. From Road Bay you can get a cruising permit to explore other anchorages, some of which are in the marine park.

The Anguilla Sailing Association runs the annual Anguilla Regatta (second weekend in May). It is fun, with Anguilla racing boats, visiting yachts, and the 12-meter fleet from St. Martin. They also organize the Anguilla Youth Sailing Club, which teaches local kids to sail in a fleet of dinghies, some of which you are likely to see out on the water. The sailing program is open to everyone, with scholarships for those who cannot afford it. In this endeavor they have had support from local businesses all over Anguilla, including those in Sandy Ground.

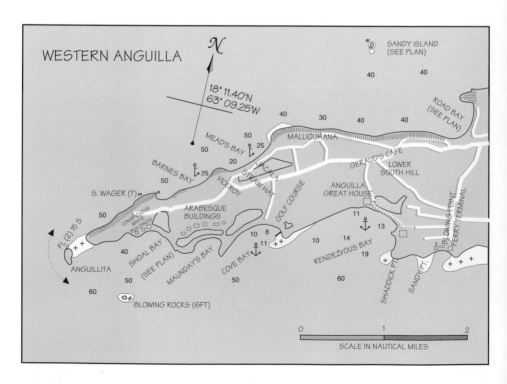

Sunset Bar, Viceroy   Chris Doyle

APPROACHING ROAD BAY FROM THE SOUTHWEST

From St. Martin, Anguilla appears low-lying and rather uniform. Toward the western end there are some very white ultra-modern buildings that almost glow in the sunlight behind Shoal Bay. Hideous or inspired, depending on your taste. Behind Maunday's Bay and at the headland linking it to Cove Bay are some white buildings of distinctively Arabesque architecture. The next serious large group of houses is in the area of Blowing Point. However, new buildings are appearing all the time.

The shoreline from Rendezvous Bay around Anguillita to Road Bay is fairly free of shoals, and you can sail just a couple of hundred yards off the coast. Offshore, you will see the large, flat 6-foot-high Blowing Rocks. You can sail either side of these, but do not approach too closely.

When passing the western tip of Anguilla, always go outside Anguillita; the water between Anguillita and Anguilla contains underwater rocks. Pass outside South Wager. This rock, which used to be 15 feet high and beautifully undercut into the shape of a head, was decapitated in a hurricane some years ago and is now barely awash. Between Sandy Island and Anguilla there is a mile of clear water to sail in, but avoid the 5-foot patch that lies a few hundred yards to the south of Sandy Island. This is normally easy to see as light green water.

Between Anguillita and Road Bay, anchoring is sometimes possible in Meads Bay and Barnes Bay. You must normally clear before visiting these bays, though captains using yacht agents, can come directly here and pretty much arrange anything.

Barnes Bay and Meads Bay

Barnes Bay and Meads Bay are two long strips of beautiful white sand, separated by a cliffy headland. There are hotels at the eastern ends of both bays. On suitable days, these bays make a great temporary anchoring spot for lunch or a swim. You can anchor in 20 to 30 feet of water quite close to shore, good holding in sand. There are no dinghy docks and trying to beach the dinghy could be hazardous in any kind of swell.

Meads Bay is somewhat more protected and has the advantage of the grand Mediterranean style Malliouhana Hotel. Put on your best beach shirt, land your dinghy, and wind your way along the path up the cliff. The restaurant has a panoramic view over the bay. Also in Meads Bay, Jacala is an excellent restaurant, so popular that booking even for lunch is essential. They serve the island's best lobster club sandwich. If you fail to reserve, go to Straw Hat, it has more seating room so you will get in and will not be disappointed in their fresh fish sandwich.

Viceroy, a large, fancy resort between Barnes and Meads bays, has the elegant and lovely Sunset Bar overlooking a pool and the sea. Visit for sushi and cocktails.

Road Bay

Road Bay

Road Bay is the main port of entry for yachts and one of the most pleasant anchorages in the northern Leewards. It is a long bay fringed by a perfect powdery beach. Along the beach is Sandy Ground Village with its collection of bars and restaurants, some of which are excellent. Behind the beach a large salt pond attracts a wonderful array of egrets, ducks, stilts, and other wading birds, especially early in the morning and at dusk.

Navigation

As you approach Road Bay, keep clear of the shoals along the southern shore. Otherwise, the bay is wide open. Avoid the northern tip of the bay, which is shoal. Anchor anywhere in the bay except in the main shipping passage. Road Bay is normally an excellent overnight anchorage, even in moderate northerly swells. The light on the northern headland often does not work. Bars come and go and some are louder than others. They usually quieten down not too late. If noise worries you, don't anchor too close to the beach.

Regulations

When you arrive in Road Bay, anchor. The holding is generally excellent, but do not pick up a mooring; they are all private.

Personal watercraft of all types, including Jet Skis, are strictly forbidden in Anguilla.

Superyachts must use a local agent (and smaller boats willing to pay may use them). This has advantages. They do most of the entry electronically; you can enter wherever you want in Anguilla (This enables you to go from St. Martin to Meads Bay for lunch and back without having to go to Road Bay). For short stops with no transfers, they will not normally need passports. The registered agents are Axa Yacht Services (Gabi Gumbs, 264-584-3826), LH Enterprises (Lesley Lloyd, 264-581-5683), BWA Yachting (Sue Ruan, 721-554-8918) and Simone Connor (264-476-6534/497-6534).

If you stay in Road Bay, Anguilla is one of the least expensive islands to visit, depending on your tonnage. They do not yet charge for overtime on weekends and all the staff are so wonderfully welcoming and friendly, clearing is a pleasure. If you visit other anchorages you need a cruising permit and that does cost extra.

Check in with customs and immigration behind the dinghy dock. Opening hours are daily 0830-1200 and 1300-1600. You can clear in and out at the same time and pay all the fees. However, you do have to

Chris Doyle

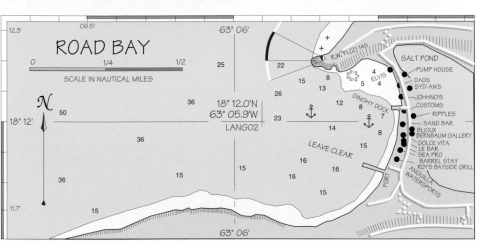

ROAD BAY

SCALE IN NAUTICAL MILES

0   1/4   1/2

12.3'   06.5'   63° 06'

N

18° 12'

18° 12.0'N
63° 05.9'W
LANGO2

11.7'

63° 06'

25   22   R.W.FL(2) 14S   SALT POND
                                        PUMP HOUSE
              15   8   4   ELVIS
26   13   5   4   DADS
                                        SYD-AN'S
36   23   12   8   DINGHY DOCK   JOHHNO'S
50   CUSTOMS
                                        RIPPLES
36   14   7   SAND BAR
                                        BIJOUX
                                        BERNBAUM GALLERY
36   15   LEAVE CLEAR   15   DOLCE VITA
                                        LE BAR
                                        SEA PRO
15   16   16   BARREL STAY
                                        ROY'S BAYSIDE GRILL
36   15   16   PORT   ANGUILLA
                                        WATERSPORTS
15   15

return within 24-hours before leaving to pick up the clearance. **Entry charges** into Road Bay in $EC are as follows:

Under 20 tons there is
Currently no charge.

20-50 tons	$ 60
50-100 tons	$110
100-250 tons	$215
250-500 tons	$290
500-1000 tons	$420
1000-2000 tons	$600
over 2000 tons	$960

(Divide by 2.67 for $US)

There is a **departure tax** of $5 US per passenger, and a security fee of $3 US per passenger.

Anguilla has several other attractive anchorages that you can sail to, many within the marine park, which closes at 1900. You may overnight in any suitable non-marine park anchorages which include: Crocus Bay, Barnes Bay, Meades Bay, Rendezvous Bay, and Cove Bay. To visit any anchorage outside Road Bay, you need a cruising permit, which you can get when you clear in. Those who have cruised here before will note that the mooring fees have been removed and it is all now in the single cruising fee which is simpler and better. However, a day ends at midnight so for overnighting you need to pay for two days.

The daily **cruising permit**, which applies to all yachts is as follows in $EC

	Up to 5 tons	5 -20 tons	over 20 tons
Day:	$75	$150	$355

For weekly rates multiply by 6. Monthly, quarterly, and yearly rates are available on request. A bonus to these charges is that they deter people, so the anchorages outside Road Bay are generally quiet and uncrowded. Anchorages you may visit outside the marine park are Cove Bay, Maunday's Bay, and Crocus Bay.

The marine park areas include Dog Island, Prickly Pear Cays, the whole of Seal Island Reef, Sandy Island, Little Bay, and, for shallow boats with local knowledge, Shoal Bay and Island Harbour. Anchoring in the park areas is restricted to demarcated areas (see our harbor sections). The park is only open 0600-1900. If moorings are available, you may use them. Yacht moorings are white and designed for yachts up to 55 feet. Note that when you pick up a mooring, you must put your own dock line through the end of the pickup line to allow more scope. If you want a bridle, use two ropes, one on each side. A single line bridle is likely to chafe through as the boat swings. Always snorkel on your mooring and check it is okay. Yachts of over 55 feet should anchor in sand or ask for instructions.

Dive moorings are red and are for local dive boats only. Do not tie your yacht or tender to them.

Those wanting to dive in the marine park must now go with a local authorized dive operator.

Communication, General Services

Roy, Johnno's, Sydan, Ripples, Elvis, Le Bar and most of the other hangouts offer free WiFi and you may be able to pick one of them up from your boat. Behind the dinghy dock are public toilets and free showers. Jerry jugging water is a possibility in an emergency, but keep in mind water is often in short supply here. A couple of people have private water lines on the dock. You would have to find one of them and negotiate. Ripples, Johnno's, and Sydan's sell ice. There is no laundry in Road Bay because water can be a problem. Laundries elsewhere include R & R Services (476-4388), and Tackling Laundry (498-4544). Any taxi driver should be able to arrange this for you and help you get your cooking gas bottles filled.

For pets needing medical attention, Pelican Pet Care has a mobile unit that will come to you (or at least to a nearby dock). You can call them at 264-583-0373.

Garbage bins are in the car park between customs and Johnno's.

The superyacht agents, listed under regulations, will handle anything you need, from customs clearance or technical support to full provisioning.

Chandlery, Technical Services

David Carty, at Rebel Marine, is a custom builder of power boats. His yard is shared with Anguilla Techni Sales who fit out the boats. Techni Sales keeps a fair stock of chandlery: all the things they install on their boats. They are agents for Volvo and Bombardier (Evinrude/Johnson) outboards and they can fabricate both stainless and aluminum and do installation work. They also sell medical and industrial gasses. You will find them at North Hill, not far from Sandy Bay. Ask to speak to Chris Carty.

For tools and general hardware, visit the big Ace Hardware at the top of the hill as you leave Road Bay.

A number of yachts cruising the Caribbean are registered in Anguilla, which is currently under the British Registry system. Non-British applicants need to find an Anguillan company to do this. Stott Marine can provide any of these services.

McCiver Peter does refrigeration. He is not specialized in marine units but may be able to help. (584-4153) or ask at Sydan's. Any of the taxi drivers (see below) can arrange anything else you need.

Transport

Stephen Taxi (772-5194), is most often

ROAD BAY

www.HeliPhotoCarib.com photo

Barrel Stay Restaurant

Modern French Cuisine on Sandy Ground Beach
A favorite choice of yachtsmen for over 24 years.
Freshly caught crayfish and lobster seafood.
Prime Black Angus steaks are our speciality.

WORLD FAMOUS FISH SOUP

RECIPE REQUESTED BY GOURMET AND FOOD AND WINE MAGAZINES

Sandy Ground Beach, Anguilla
Reservations: 497-2831   Cell: (264) 476-3044
www.barrelstay.com   Email: barrelstay@aol.com

around Sandy Ground, Maurice Taxi Service (Maurice and Sheroul) (476-0505, 235-2676) are sometimes there and they rent cars at a reasonable rate. Kitch (772-7742) also works with yachts. Bicycling is a great way to see Anguilla and bikes are available from Aslin (235-8931) who can bring them by.

Provisioning

An at Syd-An's has a food store with essentials, beer, soft drinks, and ice. If you need anything else from the bigger supermarkets, some fresh fruits or vegetables or a special can of something, give her a call and she will bring it in for you, saving you the taxi to town. If you are desperate for cash, Syd-An's has a credit card machine and may be able to help. An also has 14 rooms for rent at reasonable rates.

The nearest place when you need more is Syd and Pete's, a small supermarket on the right at the first traffic light on the road to town (farther than most will want to walk).

For provisioning, take a taxi or rent a car to visit one of the big good supermarkets. Proctor's in The Valley is modern and well laid out and open weekdays 0800-2000, Saturdays, 0800 to 2100. They have an excellent delicatessen, with good rotisserie chicken, and on Tuesdays and Saturdays they have tasty rotis from 0800, but go early or order as they don't last long.

Best Buy is farther, on Long Path Road, southeast of The Valley. They open every day except Christmas and Easter Sunday always from 0800-2100, earlier (0730)

on weekdays, and until later (2200) on Saturdays. Their food comes in by container on Wednesdays, so the best shopping is late Wednesday to Saturday.

Fun Shopping

Bijoux is a fine boutique on the road along the pond. They sell top quality causal wear, jewelry, watches, and accessories. They open at 0930 and stay open till 2200, Sundays 1130-1900.

Right opposite is Lynne Bernbaum's art gallery. Lynn is an excellent artist who experiments with many styles and themes. It will be hard not to find something you like. Her gallery opens Monday to Saturday 1600-2000, and she has both originals and prints.

Irie Life at Syd-An's, is a colorful clothing/beachwear/hat shop, along with sunglasses and some body decoration. She can top up your Lime mobile phone.

Restaurants

Most of Road Bay's casual waterfront restaurants have ideal beach-front locations where you can eat fresh seafood to the sound of lapping waves. All are within easy walking distance, so you can stroll down the beach and take your pick. A variety of nationalities and cuisines are available and the restaurants are fun, providing a good reason to sail to Road Bay. You can walk in to most places, but best make reservations for dinner at Barrel Stay, Veya, and Dolce Vita, as seating is quite limited.

Roy's Bayside Grill is next to the port and the only place open all day every day

Roy's Bayside Grill

A Casual Beach Front Restaurant
Located on the beach in Sandy Ground Road Bay, Anguilla
Family Owned & Operated for Over 30 Years

OPEN FOR BREAKFAST, LUNCH & DINNER DAILY
FULL BAR OPEN ALL DAY
FRIDAY HAPPY HOUR 5-7
FRESH LOCAL SEAFOOD & USDA PRIME STEAKS & CHOPS

WE SELL ICE
Free WiFi

CALL (264) 497-2470   email: info@roysbaysidegrill.com
VHF 16   WWW.ROYSBAYSIDEGRILL.COM
VISA MasterCard DISCOVER

DIVE CENTRE

SHOAL BAY SCUBA
ANGUILLA BWI

SCUBA SHACK
Roy's Bayside Grill
Sandy Ground

PADI
padi.com

Tel. (264) 235.1482
Fax. (212) 504.3045

www.anguilladiving.com
shoalbayscuba@gmail.com

from breakfast through to dinner. The dining area, perched on the beach and open to the sea is informal and everyone comes here: families, couples, expats, and there is even a place for big groups.

Roy, Mandy, and their daughter Claire and her husband Patrick, run this family restaurant where the food is perfection through simplicity. They use the best ingredients; the beef is Certified Prime Angus and the seafood is fresh and locally caught. The food is grilled the way you ask for it, adding just enough seasoning to bring out the natural flavors. For lunch every day they have an inexpensive daily special (currently $10 US), except Sunday, when they do a fabulous roast prime rib of beef and Yorkshire pudding lunch with all the trimmings. On Friday night they have a 1700-1900 happy hour with cheaper drinks and $15 entrée specials. Roy's offers free open WiFi.

The Barrel Stay (closed Wednesdays) opens only in the evening for dinner when you want something a little special. It is light and breezy, right on the beach, with

a high roof supported on mast-like poles and with open walls. Graham Belcher and Jill Shepherd own this restaurant and bring top-end cuisine to Sandy Ground. Graham is a world-class modern chef who has worked in Michelin-class restaurants, London's best hotels, and as executive chef for prestigious companies. Graham cooks as an art form, creating sophisticated gourmet food, including the decorative pasta and the dessert ice cream made in his kitchen from fresh ingredients. Graham and Jill do all this in an informal atmosphere where kids are welcome and especially catered to. The crème brûlée, which is served with a raspberry sorbet contained in a biscuit that rises like a half a moon and topped with decorative spun sugar, is positively celestial. If you love meat or fresh fish, you will find something to delight, including the Anguilla crayfish (lobster), in season.

If you walk back to the road and turn left, you will come to a lively restaurant and nightspot called The Pumphouse. This atmospheric bar is built in the old salt workhouse. You can still see all the

RENAISSANCE ISLANDS

machinery used for grinding up the salt prior to export. They open for dinner and the bar sometimes keeps going until the wee hours, quite often with live music. Food is available and varies from pizzas, salads, and burgers to a big steak meal. Outside they post both a music menu and a food menu, so you can check it out. Owner Laurie Gumbs is from Anguilla and his partner, Gabi, is from Germany. The atmosphere is informal and friendly. They open from 1800 and close on Mondays. Laurie has a lovely Carriacou sloop "Tradition" which is available for charter.

Sandbar (closed Sunday) is a smart and pleasing cocktail and tapas bar on the beach. Owners Alicia and Darren, originally from San Fransisco, and their staff welcome you warmly. The tapas are delicious, and while you can just come for a drink and a snack, most people want to try a few of the different flavors, by which time you won't need any more dinner. Don't miss the tuna poki with crispy wantons, the zucchini carpaccio and the spicy mahi fra diavoli. The Sandbar frozen rum cocktail makes a great accompaniment to the perfect view of the setting sun. They open at 1730 and it is popular, so it is best to book a table. The atmosphere around the bar is friendly and lively with conversation, rather than music. There are plenty of charming corners for a quiet tête-á-tête.

At the north end of the beach, Elvis has the best beach bar hangout. The bar, built out of an old Anguilla racing sloop in the middle of the beach, is irresistible. He opens every day except Tuesday, from 1600 until way late at night. Opening brings in a casual and friendly crowd, often with kids, to enjoy the on-the-beach feel and watch the sun go down to background music. By night, Elvis is the party place, with live music from Friday to Sunday, and a wild all-night party on the full moon. Elvis has a big screen for sports, so big you can pretty much see the action from halfway down the beach and he serves light food.

Ripples Bar and Restaurant is your friendly pub and eatery presided over by the owner, Jacquie, who is English. They serve fresh local seafood (fish, lobster, and conch), pub specials such as beef and Guinness or cottage pie, and also Indian food. Stella Artois is on draft. Ripples opens daily from 1200 to 0000 or later. It is easy to find: just walk back to the main road from the dinghy dock and turn right. Be there for Saturday's happy hour from 1700 to 1900, with a meat, fish, or vegetarian special for $12 US. You can also buy takeout pizza.

Le Bar is a new and pleasant restaurant right on the beach that was just about to open February 2015. It is owned and run by Didier and Veronique, who have owned many successful Anguilla restaurants. They will open for lunch 12 to 6 (except Wed.) during the season (November to June) and on some nights for dinner when they may also feature music. Their cuisine is French and will include good salads, fresh fish, and Anguillan crayfish (a small lobster).

Johnno's (closed Monday) is rough, ready, and right by the dinghy dock. Johnno makes great rum punches, tasty local seafood and chicken meals and snacks, and he usually has live jazz music on Sundays starting around noon.

Dad's is on the beach with big sitting areas shaded by a marquee. They have a skilled chef and you will get good food; peacefully at lunch, not necessarily so on the evenings when they sometimes have loud music, favored by the party crowd. If you ask, they should be able to turn it down.

Dolce Vita is an excellent Italian restaurant. It is owned and run by Abbi and Christopher and opens Monday to Friday 1200-1430 for lunch, when they also serve pizzas and sandwiches. For dinner, Monday to Saturday 1800-2130, there is a big main menu with seafood, meats, pasta, and more. Their pastas are top quality; the lobster pasta excellent.

The fanciest restaurant in Sandy Ground is Veya (open from Monday to Saturday for dinner only from 1830-2200). It is set back from the road leading to town, on the left before the hill gets steep. (A good appetite walk, but if you don't want to walk, call Veya. If they are not too busy, Jerry will come and collect you.) Veya is

• THE PUMPHOUSE •

Great Food • Live Music • Cocktails

Road Bay, Anguilla • pumphouse@anguillanet.com • 264-497-5154

in a Caribbean style building with a big open room leading onto the eating verandah and furnished with subtle elegance. Carrie Bogar, the chef, has had a passion for cooking since childhood. She studied at the Culinary Institute of America. Jerry, her husband, will welcome you. Everything from the bread to the ice cream is made on the premises and Carrie calls her food "cuisine of the sun" – worldwide flavors from warmer areas: African, Asia, Europe, and the Caribbean. Carrie has the master's touch of combining just the right flavors with a touch of contrast, and all is beautifully presented. This is a great choice for a special night out when you want a change from the beach.

Dale Carty's Tasty's Restaurant has an excellent reputation. It is on top of the hill and open for lunch and dinner. Farther along the hill is Darvin's tapas bar and night club, and way down is Unique's roadside shack grill. All have great views.

If you are driving around and would like something local and inexpensive, visit Mala's Cottage Roti Hut on the road to The Valley. The traditional building is cute and they serve rotis (curry wrapped in a tortilla-like skin) of chicken, conch, shrimp, goat, or vegetables. Local meals with vegetables and fresh juices are available.

Ashore

There are interesting short walks right in Road Bay to North Hill and South Hill on either side, which have great views of the bay. The track on the north side is overgrown and hard to spot. Pass Pumphouse and turn right up the pond. You will see two small block houses and a fancy house above them. Take the driveway towards the fancy house and walk just past the first block house. The trail leads off to the left, but you really have to look for it. On the south side, the easiest trail is found by heading up the main road. Turn right at the first little road, which ends and turns into a footpath. Another trail heads from behind a gravel pit in the public works area just beyond the road to the ship docks. When you reach the top, turn right on the road and take the small cliff road, with many view points. The South Hill views are more accessible than those on North Hill.

How about going inland? Any taxi will take you on a tour or you can rent a car or bike. Anguilla's many magnificent beaches and coves are its strong points and they are easily visited by land. North Shoal Bay is perhaps Anguilla's most picture-perfect beach, with a mile of powdery sand that dissolves into luminous green and turquoise water. Plenty of places are open for lunch.

By complete contrast, Junk's Hole and Savannah Bays are wild and wonderful, especially when Christmas winds are at their strongest. Line after line of breakers smash as they approach this rugged coast, filling the air with misty spindrift. Great for surfers – others can swim in the protected water close to the beach. Palm Grove, a

RENAISSANCE ISLANDS

White cheeked pintail, salt pond

Pond pelican in the salt pond

Stilt in the salt pond

beach shack bar, is fine for lunch.

Just about any road leading to the coast will reveal a delightful view. Make sure you include the picturesque fishing port, Island Harbour Village, where meals are available on Scilly Cay, in the middle of the bay.

Serious bird watchers might want to explore Caul's Pond, a saltwater pond that is a bird sanctuary. The best approach is down a small road close to a concrete plant in Deep Waters, north of the pond. It ends at a unused power plant where you can park.

You may also want to visit the main town, The Valley. It should be noted that The Valley is a long, but not unreasonable walk from Crocus Bay. In The Valley, the Anguillan Craft Shop, run by the National Council of Women, sells handicrafts that Anguillans make in their own homes. Stop by the Anguilla Drug Store, for English language newspapers, beachwear, souvenirs, and t-shirts.

Shopping in Anguilla is spread throughout the island and as you drive around you will come upon little shops in the most unexpected places. Drive slowly and be prepared to stop and look.

If you have transport, Geraud's Bakery is a great coffee or lunch spot with tasty pastries. You can pick up excellent bread, too. If golf is your thing, contact CuisinArt Golf Club, a professional, 18-hole, Greg Norman-designed golf course, with an elegant bar and shop.

Water Sports

Anguilla Watersports by Roy's offers paddleboard lessons, paddleboard yoga, and downwind tours, along with a kitesurfing school for beginners and up.

For messing about in the water and keeping your kids happy, Sea Pro is a watersports center and bar on the beach. Paddle boarding, wake and banana riding, water skiing, kayaking, boating, in-the-water trampoline - they have it all. Check their weekend specials for kids under 18.

Anguilla is surrounded by reefs and lies on white sand, so the diving is good. In addition, seven old ships have been sunk upright to make new dive sites. These attract huge schools of fish.

There are over 16 good dive sites. You must dive with one of the local authorized dive operators.

Matthew's Scuba Shack is part of Shoal Bay Scuba and is based at Roy's. Matthew is a first class professional who gets excellent ratings on Trip Advisor. It is a full PADI dive center where they teach you or take you diving. Drop down and talk to them about diving, or give them a call. For the large yachts they offer private dive trips, and they run excursions to the offshore islands.

Douglas Carty, of "Special D Diving," is often by Johnno's in Sandy Ground, where he has a locker. You can call him (235-8438). He has a good 30-foot dive boat with a bimini cover. Douglas is a great dive guide, good at spotting and pointing out fish and sea creatures that others miss, and no one knows the waters better. He also does boat trips.

Vigilant Divers, run by Rob and his wife Julie, provides personal diving for a select few; never more than four divers at a time, giving a ride out in his spacious 30-foot Boston Whaler with fresh fruit and bottled water. Bob trained in the army and is qualified both as an instructor and boat captain. He trained the Anguillan police to dive. Call him at 235-4096.

If you moor at Sandy Island, there are several dives. Sandy Island (30 to 70 feet) has a delightful profusion of sea fans and soft corals and is home to many small reef fish. Sandy Deep (15 to 60 feet) is inside the shoal patch to the south of Sandy Island. Dive down a small wall covered in hard corals with abundant fish. When you reach the sand bottom below, there is a good chance of seeing stingrays.

Prickly Pear dive is about a quarter of a mile north of Prickly Pear West and 30 to 70 feet deep. It is a beautiful underwater canyon amid a forest of elkhorn coral, where many ledges and caverns provide habitat for all kinds of fish. Nurse sharks are often seen resting on the sandy bottom.

The Little Bay dive is one of the easier ones to do from your yacht if you start off snorkeling along the cliff to the end where the water gets deeper. You have a chance of seeing eagle rays, manta rays, and turtles. It should be noted that most other dives, especially the wreck sites, are beyond the range of a dinghy and best visited with a dive shop. Frenchman's Reef (10 to 40 feet) lies a little farther southwest, down the coast from South Wager. Parts of the cliff have fallen into the sea, providing a beautiful garden of giant boulders. Here you will find soft corals and huge schools of brightly-colored reef fish. It makes an ideal first dive or refresher dive.

The wreck of the Ida Maria (60 feet) lies about one and a half miles northwest of Sandy Island. Deliberately sunk in 1985, this 110-foot freighter sits semi-intact on the bottom. Large groups of schooling fish make this an exciting dive. The Oosterdiep (75 to 80 feet) is a wrecked freighter which sits upright on the seabed about three quarters of a mile off Barnes Bay. It attracts large numbers of fish, including French angelfish. You can dive into the hold. There is a side trip to a reef about 100 yards away where you will find soft and hard corals and more angelfish. In the sand between the wreck and the reef are garden eels, rays, and conch. Paintcan Reef (80 feet) is about half a mile northwest of Oosterdiep. This reef covers several acres, with clear visibility and lush coral growth. As well as all the usual reef fish, large pelagic fish are sometimes seen.

The Maybel, originally a Second World War cargo ship called Hinda, was sunk in 1990, then lost in a hurricane. It has now been located and buoyed again. Ask Douglas Carty for details.

Grouper Bowl (25 to 50 feet) lies about halfway down Seal Island Reef. This wonderful elkhorn coral forest provides homes for a multitude of fish. Apart from the above, there are many more wreck sites, including the wrecks of the MV Sarah, MV Meppel, MV Lady Vie, and MV Commerce. These planned wrecks are excellent dive sites and have given Anguilla the reputation of being the wreck dive capital of the Leewards.

RENAISSANCE ISLANDS

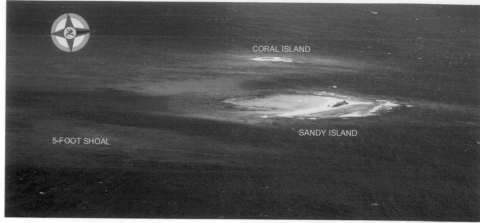

ANGUILLA'S OFFSHORE ANCHORAGES

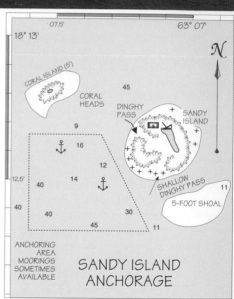

SANDY ISLAND ANCHORAGE

Anguilla's offshore reefs are protected by the fisheries department. Below we mention places that yachts may visit. Please note that anchoring anywhere else on the offshore reefs, including the whole of Seal Island Reef, is strictly forbidden. In all sensitive areas mooring buoys are in place, so there is no danger of anchors tearing up seagrass or reef structures. Note the correct mooring procedure: pick up the buoy, attach your own docking line through the eye splice on top of the buoy and leave plenty of scope. Do not attach the pick up line directly to your yacht. Moorings are only for yachts less than 55 feet long. Customs or the park authority will be able to give you the latest mooring information when you clear in.

Sandy Island

Sandy Island, one and half miles northwest of Road Bay, is a circle of sand with a few baby palm trees. There are both shoals and reefs here, so only approach in good light conditions. It is part of the park, so open 0600-1900.

A coral island, about 5 feet high, is clearly visible northwest of Sandy Island. The water around this island has many coral heads, especially in the direction of Sandy Island.

Give it wide clearance. There is a 5-foot shoal to the south of Sandy Island, which is clearly visible as turquoise water. Do not cross this, even in a shoal draft boat, as it generates large waves that sometimes break. There is a navigable passage some 30 feet deep between this shoal and Sandy Island. Sandy Island is surrounded by reef, which is quite visible; do not approach too closely.

Anchoring around Sandy Island is regulated because of possible damage to underwater reefs. The only permissible anchoring area suitable for yachts is shown on our sketch chart. Mooring buoys may be provided, but if not, you can anchor in the same area. Make sure you are anchored on an area of clear sand with no coral heads.

"Sandy Island... The Experience Lasts A Lifetime!"

For a relaxing and rejuvenating day on your very own little island paradise, join us on beautiful *Sandy Island*

Convenient boat clearance & yacht concierge services available at Sandy Island

Open daily 10am - 4pm, Nov 1 - August 31
Open by reservation only Sept 1 - October 31
Night hours available by request. Best location for New Years Eve private party.

Tel number: 1-264-476-6534 or 476-4104 or 235-4104
www.mysandyisland.com

There is a dinghy passage through the reef on the north side to get to the beach. You can beach your dinghy, or if it is too large for that, anchor in the clear sand directly to the west of Sandy Island. You can snorkel from the beach, but anchoring your dinghy on the reefs is forbidden.

It may turn out easier and cheaper to take the Sandy Island boat, $10 US per person round trip from Sandy Ground. Boats start at 1000 and the last boat returns at 1600. Call 476-4104/6534

Ashore

The island is sand, sculpted by wind and waves into ever changing shapes, so each time you visit you see something new. If you search close to the water's edge you can find small pretty shells. Explore the reefs around the island with a mask and snorkel.

Sandy Island Restaurant (476-4104/6534) offers you a wider choice of food than most other offshore restaurants. The menu includes fresh lobster and crayfish and a fine wine selection. Simone Connor (264-476-6534/497-6534), one of the owners is a yacht agent and can organize clearance for yachts who would prefer to come directly to Sandy Island. For the ultimate fête, you can rent the whole island for a private function.

RENAISSANCE ISLANDS

Sandy Island   Chris Doyle

PRICKLY PEAR BAR & RESTAURANT

Hang out with Allan, the self appointed BBQ KING, barman, mayor and postmaster of the island!

www.pricklypearanguilla.com
Cell: 264-235-5864
VHF Channel 16   Lunch Tuesday - Saturday

MasterCard   VISA

Prickly Pear Cays

These cays represent many a sailor's dream of paradise. Geologically, they are old reefs that have been uplifted to their present height of 60 feet. The sea has slowly eroded them to produce intricate rocky sculptures of fascinating design. There is a perfect creamy white beach that melts into the sea in translucent shades of pale green, turquoise, blue, and brown. The cliffs are picturesque, with many seabirds.

It is not worth venturing out here in unsettled conditions, in winds of more than 20 knots, or if there is a northerly swell. On the other hand, in settled light easterly or southeasterly winds, it makes a heavenly lunch stop. Overnighting is not currently allowed and could be a nightmare if the weather were to change.

Navigation

People normally approach Prickly Pear Cays from Road Bay. You can see them in the distance. Pass to the east of Sandy Island and head out, approaching along the southern side of the islands. The only permissible anchorage is in the lee of Prickly Pear East, where a headland provides a little protection. If possible, use the moorings provided. If not, there is a shelf of 25 to 35 feet, with sand and rock bottom, and good holding in places. There are many underwater rock ledges and it is easy get your anchor stuck in one of these. The best way to avoid this is to tie a trip line to the bottom end of your anchor and buoy it. If it does get caught you can pull it out backwards with the trip line.

Prickly Pear Cays   Chris Doylee

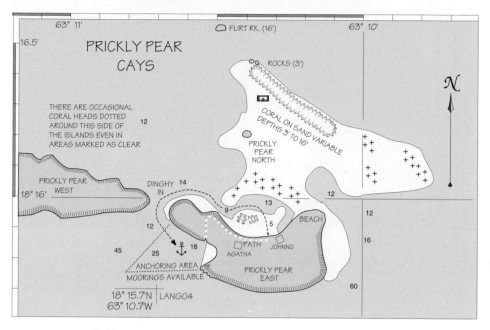

Ashore

Dinghy around to the relatively calm beach on the north side of the island. You can walk back across the island if you want to see your yacht from the rocks. The rocks ashore on the yacht anchorage side are sharp, but well worth exploring. There is a round rock pool fed by the sea. If you listen beside the pool, you can hear a rock sighing as the incoming water forces air down a tiny hole. There are more of these strange 'whistling' rocks and at low tide there are many tide pools. The underwater parts of these rocks are similarly strange and provide unusual snorkeling.

Day charter catamarans, laden with passengers from St. Martin, often visit the main beach in Prickly Pear. There are lounging seats and two lunchtime bar/restaurants. If you want a beach away from the herd, just keep walking – it goes on a long way.

PRICKLY PEAR CAYS

RENAISSANCE ISLANDS

ANCHORING AREA

DOG ISLAND

For lunch, check out the restaurants. Prickly Pear Bar and Restaurant [VHF: 16] is run by Allan who has taken over who is self-appointed barbecue king, barman and mayor of Sandy Island. It runs in the family, his mother Agatha did it for years before that. It has a big deck and thatch shelters by the water. They open Tuesday through Saturday, starting around 1000. You get a plate of great local food featuring local vegetables and their famous sautéed potatoes, with your choice of chicken, ribs, or fish. Lobster is available with advance notice. If you are low on cash, they accept Visa and Mastercard.

Johnno's will open for big groups and is most likely to be there on Wednesdays, Saturdays, and Sundays. It is easy to check with Johnno in Sandy Ground.

Water Sports

Hurricanes and swells have taken their toll on the snorkeling reefs, but if you have fair weather and dinghy around to all the little reefs and rocks north of Prickly Pear East, you will find it worthwhile. Since anchoring your dinghy on the coral is not allowed, drift with it, or designate a boatman to follow the snorkelers. You can dive here if you get permission from the park.

Dog Island

Dog Island is for the adventurous who want somewhere perfect and private and are willing to make an extra effort to get it. The beach at Great Bay will satisfy the fussiest aficionado. A perfect stretch of brilliant white sand merges into bright turquoise water. The best part is that there are no bars or regular day charter boats, and the odds are that you will get it to yourself. Ashore you can often find fine, small shells high up on the beach.

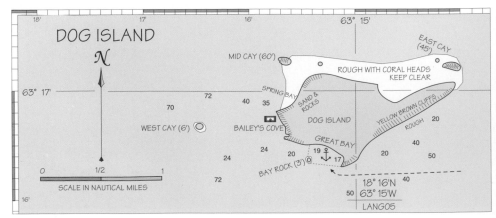

Navigation

Dog Island is 10 miles from Road Bay and you may not stay overnight. It is worth setting out early so you have plenty of time to explore, eat lunch, and beat back to Anguilla afterwards. The only permissible anchorage is Great Bay, which is usually rolly, but acceptable for lunch in moderate easterly and northeasterly winds (less than 20 knots). Don't bother going if heavy swells are running. If you are susceptible to a roll, prepare the picnic in advance.

You will usually be approaching from the east or southeast. It is easy to make out the conspicuous yellow-brown cliffs on the southeast coast. As you approach Great Bay, the 3-foot Bay Rock, which lies about 200 yards off the western end of the beach, stands out as a landmark. This is the only obstruction.

Anchor in the middle of the beach in about 18 feet of water. Make sure the anchor is well dug in and put out a second for added security. For the most part, the bottom is sand, but there are occasional slabs of white rock. Leave again by the south and keep well clear of Dog Island's rough and rocky northern coast.

Ashore

The surf is often heavy enough along the beach to make landing the dinghy risky. I would not try it with an outboard. If you do get the dinghy ashore, pull it up very high. Otherwise, put your lunch and shore things in a watertight container, anchor the dinghy just beyond the surf line and swim in. Not easy, but that is why you get such a lovely beach to yourself.

The island was owned by the late Jeremiah Gumbs, who was once going to develop it and built an airstrip. There were rumors of drug traffickers using it, so it was closed again. The family keeps livestock here and no one is permitted beyond the beach. (All Anguillan beaches are open to the public.)

Conditions permitting, you will find good snorkeling around Bay Rock and Bailey's Cove.

ANGUILLA'S NORTH COAST EAST OF ROAD BAY

To the east of Road Bay there is an attractive sweeping bay some two miles long. Crocus Bay is the most protected part of this and is an excellent overnight anchorage.

Crocus Bay

Navigation

If you are approaching along the coast from Road Bay, stay a few hundred yards offshore until you pass Katouche Bay, as shoals extend 60 yards or more offshore. If you are approaching from out to sea, Crocus Bay has a paved road that runs up the hill, and a big square apartment block sitting on top of the hill. At the north end of the beach is a large tin building that houses a water desalinization plant, and above that is a housing development. On the beach you can see da'Vida Restaurant. Anchor

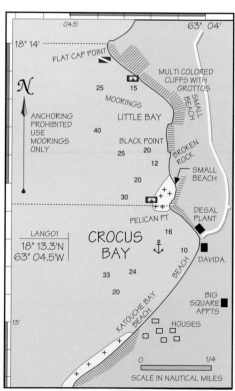

Ashore

da'Vida Restaurant is owned by Anguillan brother and sister team David and Vida who have created everything you could want to relax on the beach. By day, from 1000-1800, their casual Da' Vida Bayside is a great hangout with beach chairs, kayak rentals, a boutique and essentials shop, as well as a comfortable deck where you can get coffee, drinks, grilled lunch, or delicious sandwiches.

Come evening, da'Vida opens one of the best restaurants in Anguilla. You enter past a waterfall and into a big room with wooden beams, completely open to the beach view. Dress is casual elegant (not shorts and flip flops.) Their food is excellent; a fusion of Caribbean and Asian flavors they call Asio-Caribbean. They bring in fresh seafood every day and this is a great place for Caribbean lobster or its smaller cousin, the Anguilla crayfish.

anywhere off Crocus Bay beach south of Pelican Point. Anchor a fair way out as the wind can drop and a swell could carry your yacht toward the shore. Use plenty of scope. The attractions are good snorkeling, the beach, easy access to Little Bay, and The Valley is within walking distance for shopping. da'Vida (see below) started a substantial dinghy dock. Unfortunately, fisheries put a halt to the work, but it may get completed yet. In the meantime, you can pull your dinghy up the beach near the road, conditions permitting. Apart from Road Bay this is the only anchorage where you may stay overnight.

One end of the restaurant is a tapas bar, a great way to try some of the flavors. This opens 1700-2200, with a Thursday to Sunday happy hour from 1700-1800.

You can stroll up the hill and down the other side to The Valley. CeBlue is halfway up the hill, and they are open for breakfast so you can take a coffee break if you are heading up in the cool of the morning.

CE BLUE

DESAL PLANT

DA VIDA

CROCUS BAY

RESTAURANT & SPA

Celebrate Life.

Caribbean Asian Fusion

An Asio-Caribbean dining experience awaits you on a truly tranquil Anguillian beach. Situated in Crocus Bay, no door separates you from the beautiful Caribbean Sea. Our open dining room embraces, enlightens and pampers you with its Zen décor. A pure product of subdued taste, da'Vida entrance prepares you for their creative menu. The Asio-Caribbean fusion is great for the mind, body and spirit. 'Celebrate Life' or any occasion. Life's simply a pleasure at da'Vida.

MAIN RESTAURANT OPENING HOURS
Open: Tuesday to Sunday
Tapas 4pm – 9pm Dinner 6pm – 10pm
Live Entertainment: Wednesday and Saturday 8pm – Midnight

da'Vida Bayside

Bayside Bar & Grill: Open daily
10am – 5pm
Live Entertainment: Sundays 1pm – Close

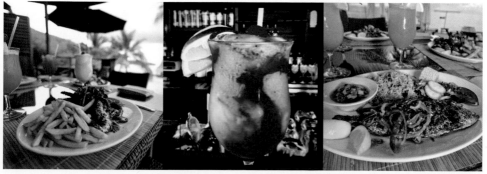

Crocus bay, Anguilla Tel(264) 498 5433/5434 Fax (264) 498 5435 info@davidaanguilla.com
www.davidaanguilla.com

They also open for lunch and dinner as a pizzeria/Italian restaurant.

Over the brow of the hill and down a little, you will come to Savannah, one of Anguilla's best art galleries. It is set in a lovely, authentic old building. The outside is small, but as you enter, it opens up in an almost Alice-in-Wonderland kind of way into a house of many rooms. Owner Frank Costin has spent several years creating this delightful collection of paintings, and he will happily tell you all about the artists, most of whom he knows personally. His range includes some fine Haitian sheet metal art, some unusually excellent marquetry, as well as paintings. Artists from Anguilla and many other islands are represented. Prints are for sale as well as originals.

Water Sports

When the visibility is good, the snorkeling off Pelican Point is excellent. You can visit Little Bay by dinghy or yacht.

Little Bay

For those addicted to undeveloped natural beauty, Little Bay is outstanding, even by Caribbean standards. Along the shore, 70-foot cliffs rise from turquoise water. They are multicolored, in reds, pinks, grays, and whites, textured by holes, caves, and grottos, which are home to tropicbirds, pelicans, and kingfishers. The pelicans spend much of the day dive-bombing schools of fish off the beach; the tropicbirds circle overhead and chatter; agile goats wander to the edge of the precipice. I can sit here for hours, just enjoying the view. (This is such an exceptional spot, that it is a shame that building has been allowed on the top.) You cannot anchor here, but you can pick up one of the moorings during the day. It is part of the park, so open only from 0600-1900. If all moorings are taken (rare), anchor in Crocus Bay and dinghy down.

Ashore, there are two small but delightfully secluded beaches. The only way to get to these by road is to climb down a cliff aided by a rope. Take a cooler and enjoy.

Water Sports

The snorkeling is excellent (except during and after northerly swells, when vis-

LITTLE BAY

ibility is poor). Along the cliffs all the way to the point are little caves, overhangs, and small walls with a variety of hard and soft corals and many small fish. About 20 yards out, you find a rather flat bottom with sand, weeds, and occasional stands of coral. Out here, there is a good chance of seeing turtles, spotted eagle rays, and barracudas. You can also do this as a dive.

East of Little Bay

The coast is fairly clear for almost 2 miles to the east of Little Bay. Then a large expanse of reefs and rocks extends up to a mile offshore. Embedded in the reef system are two small harbors, suited only to shoal draft boats. They are called Lower Shoal Bay and Island Harbour. It is possible to thread through a passage between the reefs, but once you are past Shoal Bay it can be rough and hazardous. To make it worse, you will be in the teeth of the wind head-

ing east, or dead down wind going west. The best thing to do with this coast is give it wide clearance.

If you are going east, you can take a good long tack out to sea – but don't hit Seal Island Reef. When you get to Scrub Island, you will see a wild and tempting beach on its western shore. There is no good anchorage here. The reef extends a long way from the beach, and the bay is shoal toward its northern end. There is one sand strip that runs into the beach. Should you happen by on a very calm day, you could try to anchor about one or two hundred yards off the beach in about 36 feet of water, but landing the dinghy is likely to be hazardous.

There is no problem in rounding the eastern tip of Anguilla between Windward Point and Scrub Island. Stay in the middle of the channel and do not go too close to the Anguillan shore.

ANGUILLA'S SOUTH COAST

There are lots of reefs along this coast all the way to Rendezvous Bay. While some bays are tucked in the reefs, none of them are well enough protected to be worth consideration for the passing cruiser. Give the coast a wide berth.

Rendezvous Bay

This is a large bay with over a mile of perfect white sand beach, and it is quite well protected. You can anchor here and as it is not part of the marine park you can also overnight here however, you must clear in first.

Cove Bay & Maunday's Bay

Cove Bay lies to the west of Rendezvous Bay. Although smaller than Rendezvous Bay. It too has a perfect beach and makes a fair anchorage in settled conditions. You need to tuck up in the eastern corner to get protection from the reef off its eastern point. A new dock, used mainly by the small fishing fleet that anchors here, makes this a convenient place to leave your dinghy. Things are changing as the surrounding land has now been taken over by Temenos, owners of the big adjacent golf course.

Maunday's Bay also has good protection in most conditions. The development behind is private, but there is another splendid beach here and all beaches are public. The Fisheries Department does not allow overnight stays in either of these bays.

Altamar Marina

A new and very fancy marina is planned just to the west of Maunday's Bay, at Altamar Resort. Currently stalled, it will be many years before this is finished.

COVE BAY

destination
ST. MAARTEN
the Marine Center of the Caribbean

www.yachtingstmaarten.com

Our little island wonderland is hands down the best place in the Caribbean to berth, provision, repair, and explore.

Just about everything is designed to make getting things done easier: a sheltered lagoon with several marinas and plenty of anchoring room; easy check-in procedures; duty-free status; large international airport with direct flight to the Americas & Europe; and a world-class marine service sector ready to cater to your every need.

Our selection of marine parts and supplies, hardware, food & beverages, household goods and consumer electronics is unparalleled anywhere in the Caribbean. With no import taxes or Customs red tape, prices are lower than anywhere in the neighborhood.

What is not stocked locally can be sourced and shipped in quickly by air, or economically by ocean freight.

Provisioning is a delight, with our melting-pot of cultures resulting in food from all corners of the world readily available.

Best of all – most of what you'll need is within reach of a dinghy dock. When hired help is needed, dozens of world-class professionals - shipwrights, mechanics, sailmakers, riggers, fabricators, electricians, electronics technicians, refrigeration specialists, painters and many others – are a service call away for a quick repair or a big job.

Our great air connections make it easy to get away for a quick trip home, or fly in friends, family or charter guests.

And, while getting your boat repaired in an exotic location, there's plenty to do: From numerous bars, restaurants, nightclubs and casinos to beaches, watersports, land activities, movies and music. Once the boat is ready to go, check out our relaxing anchorages and cruise our neighboring islands.

ST. MAARTEN
MARINE TRADES ASSOCIATION

Hiking among the butterflies

Chris Doyle

Sint Maarten & St. Martin

LTHOUGH THIS island is barely 7 miles in each direction, it is perhaps the best-known holiday destination in the Leewards. It is blessed with a multitude of superb white sand beaches, backed by pleasantly scenic hills. Its fame has come from the way it has embraced tourism wholeheartedly, with casinos, condominiums, and scores of hotels. The whole island is one duty-free shopping plaza. Shopping is not restricted to cruise ship passengers. Two of the Caribbean's biggest chandleries are based here: Budget Marine and Island Water World. With the help of their customers, they have generated enough buying power to be able to offer excellent prices to yachts. If you are buying a lot and set up an offshore account, you can often negotiate a discount.

St. Martin is divided across the middle. The northern part is French; the southern part Dutch. There is a charming story, completely unsupported by historical fact, that the French and Dutch were so civilized that, rather than fight over the island, they had a Frenchman armed with a bottle of wine walk in one direction and a Dutchman equipped with a flask of gin take the other. Where they met became the boundary, and the French ended up with a bit more because the gin was stronger than the wine.

In the early days, the island was important to the Dutch because of the salt ponds in the southern part, which is why they settled there. St. Martin was successful for a time as a producer of tobacco, and then of sugar. With the collapse of the sugar market, it started a long decline. In 1939 an attempt was made to halt this downward trend by making the island completely duty-free.

The strategy worked and St. Martin became the Caribbean's number one shopping mall. Today it thrives, hosting about a million visitors annually. Hotels are everywhere, cruise ships call daily,

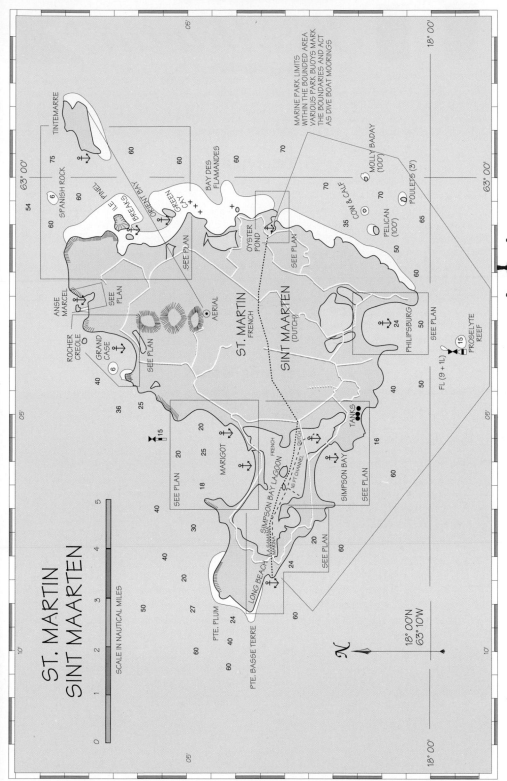

RENAISSANCE ISLANDS

ST. MARTIN
SINT MAARTEN

SCALE IN NAUTICAL MILES

0 1 2 3 4 5

18° 00'N
63° 10'W

TINTEMARRE

SPANISH ROCK

ILE PINEL

BREAKS

ORIENT BAY

GREEN CAY

BAY DES FLAMANDES

75

60

6

60

60

54

60

60

70

60

70

70

MOLLY BADAY (100')

POULETS (3')

COW & CALF

PELICAN (100')

35

65

70

50

60

OYSTER POND

SEE PLAN

SEE PLAN

ANSE MARCEL

SEE PLAN

ROCHER CREOLE

GRAND CASE

SEE PLAN

AERIAL

ST. MARTIN
FRENCH

SINT MAARTEN
(DUTCH)

PHILIPSBURG

SEE PLAN

24

50

15

PROSELYTE REEF

FL (9 + 1L)

6

40

36

25

15

20

MARIGOT

18

25

20

SEE PLAN

40

30

FRENCH

DUTCH

16 FT CHANNEL

SIMPSON BAY LAGOON

LA SAMANNA

MARINA

SIMPSON BAY

SEE PLAN

TANKS

16

60

50

40

50

40

40

20

20

SEE PLAN

60

24

60

LONG BEACH

PTE. PLUM

PTE. BASSE TERRE

27

24

40

60

50

60

MARINE PARK LIMITS
WITHIN THE BOUNDED AREA
VARIOUS PARK BUOYS MARK
THE BOUNDARIES AND ACT
AS DIVE BOAT MOORINGS

N

St. Martin

Regulations

You need to check with the port authority and immigration on arrival and departure, even when sailing from one side to the other. There are clearing posts in Philipsburg and Simpson Bay on the Dutch side, and in Marigot on the French side. Details of fees are given in the Simpson Bay, Philipsburg and Marigot sections. Once you are in either side, you are absolutely free to visit the other by dinghy, car, or on foot.

Telephones

The French side is treated as part of France; the Dutch side as part of the Netherlands. The two sides have different phone books and number systems.

All French St. Martin numbers now start with 0590 (regular) or 0690 (cellular). If you are dialing into St. Martin from a non-French territory, you have to dial the country code first, which is also 590, then leave off the first 0 of the number. Thus, if calling from the US, for regular numbers you will dial either + or 011, then 590-590, + 6 digits, for cell numbers + or 011 then 590-690 + 6 digits.

Dutch Sint Maarten is part of NANP Zone A, (like the US) with an area code of 721. To reach the Dutch side from the French, dial +1-721+ 6 digits

A cell phone is the easiest way to go. If you have your own GSM phone, you can buy a a local SIM and prepaid cards for UTS, Telcel (Dutch), or Carte Orange or Digicel (French). You can buy or rent a phone and buy sims from Mailbox and Business Point.

Shopping Hours

Normal shopping hours are 0800-1200 and 1500-1800, but many shops are open over lunch.

Transport

Flying in and out is easy as St. Martin has a large international airport serviced by many major airlines. The airport is close to Simpson Bay Lagoon, just across the road from the Aqua Restaurant dinghy dock, so it is practical to pick up and drop off passengers by dinghy. When you leave, the departure tax is currently $25 US.

Ferries run about once every 45 minutes between Marigot and Anguilla, and you catch them on the ferry dock. Some ferries go from Simpson Bay by the airport, but these are usually day-charter ferries. Taxi stand numbers are: Airport, 721-546-7759; Marigot, 0590-87 56 54, general Dutch side, 147

Typical taxi rates in $US are:

Philipsburg to Food Center	$8	Marigot to airport	$18
Simpson Bay to Philipsburg	$15	Philipsburg to airport	$18
Oyster Pond to airport	$30	Anse Marcel to airport	$30

There are extra charges for the number of people over 2, for extra bags over 1, between 2200 and 0600 and, in some cases, if you call them to come by phone.

St. Martin has an inexpensive regular bus system connecting the towns of Philipsburg, Marigot, and Grand Case.

Holidays

Holidays, both French and Dutch sides:
- Jan 1
- Good Friday and Easter Monday (Easter Sunday is March 27, 2016; April 16, 2017)
- May 1 (Labor Day)
- Ascension Day (May 5, 2016; May 25, 2017)
- Whit Monday, 50 days after Easter Sunday (May 16, 2016; June 5, 2017)
- All Saints (Nov 1)
- December 25

Holidays, French St. Martin only
- Jan 6 (Epiphany)
- Carnival Monday & Tuesday (Monday - Tuesday, 46 days before Easter: Feb. 8-9, 2016; Feb 27-28, 2017)
- May 8 (V.E. Day)
- July 14 (Bastille Day)
- July 21 (Victor Schoelcher Day)
- August 15 (Assumption of Virgin Mary)

Holidays, Dutch Sint Maarten only:
- April 30 (Queen's Birthday)
- May 5 (Liberation Day)
- July 1 (Emancipation Day)
- Last Monday in July and the following Tuesday - Carnival
- Nov 11 (Sint Maarten Day)
- December 15 (Kingdom Day)
- December 25-26

and there are hundreds of duty-free shops and restaurants, as well as over a dozen casinos. The current boom has created so much work that many cruisers have found temporary jobs here and there are excellent facilities for most kinds of yacht work.

The Dutch side has the Sint Maarten Yacht Club, which organizes many races, and which cruising sailors can join. The club is right next to the bridge, with a good dinghy dock. Wander upstairs and ask the manager for the racing and social program. They have a very active youth sailing program and, if you are staying a while, join the club. Your kids can enjoy the fun.

The Heineken Regatta is on the first full weekend in March, a world-famous international event that draws many famous yachts. The office is upstairs in the Yacht Club. The Course D'Alliance is a three-day cruiser's race from St. Martin to St. Barts, then onto Anguilla in November. There is sometimes the Offshore Regatta, which goes to Statia and Nevis in June. If you have a cat, you can join in the multihull regatta in March. There are many events, including informal races, year round. Their website is www.smyc.com.

Both sides have marine parks. Yachts can anchor or pick up a mooring in all their usual haunts. Fishing is not allowed near any of the popular dive sites, including most of the offshore islands and rocks. Moorings for divers and snorkelers are on many sites. The French marine park goes from Oyster Pond to Roche Creole, but excludes much of Orient Bay. Fishing, taking of anything, polluting, jet skiing, and water-skiing are all banned within this area.

St. Martin has good medical and dental facilities. A good clinic, easily accessible to yachts, is in the complex by Simpson Bay Marina. Check with Dr. Datema or Dr. Ubbo Tjaden. You will also find a modern dental clinic with dentists, hygienists, and an orthodontist.

Both the French and the Dutch have emergency lifeboats, from a rigid inflatable to an ocean-going rescue vessel. Call VHF: 16 or dial 911.

RENAISSANCE ISLANDS

Philipsburg   Chris Doyle

SOUTH COAST OF SINT MAARTEN

Apart from Proselyte Reef, the south coast of St. Maarten is free of shallows and a quarter of a mile offshore clears all shoals. Proselyte Reef lies about 1.5 miles south of Philipsburg. It is 15 feet deep, so it is only a problem for deep draft boats.

With the creation of the marine park, various buoys have been placed to mark dive sites and more have been placed on the park limits. Most are unlit, so keep a good lookout. Some are in open water, where they may be a hazard to an unaware navigator, though happily most are soft plastic.

When you are sailing from St. Barts to Philipsburg, short steep seas can build up around Pte. Blanche. If you are towing a dinghy, keep an eye on it.

Philipsburg

Philipsburg is the capital of Sint Maarten and lies at the head of Great Bay. It is built on a strip of land that separates the sea from Great Bay Salt Pond, which is sometimes rewarding for bird watching. Over the last few years the focus of yachting has switched more towards Simpson Bay. At the same time, the whole of Philipsburg has been vastly upgraded, with a long, broad walkway behind the beach and the rebuilding of Front Street with cobblestones, fancy new lamp posts and street décor, including fully-grown palms planted all the way along. While Front Street allows cars, priority has been given to pedestrians, making it a pleasant place to walk. It is a major cruise ship stop and there are always plenty of people about. It is an excellent place to shop, sit in a bar or café, watch life go by, and eat out.

Navigation

The best way to approach is to pass by the new cruise shop docks and then head in. Depths reduce suddenly from 30 feet to about 15 feet, then become rather bumpy, mainly between 9 and 12 feet, all the way in. Both marinas have been dredged, but

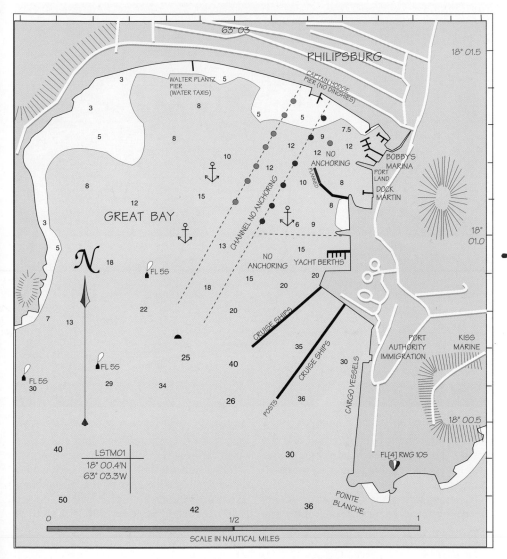

LOCAL RUMS GUAVABERRY

VINTAGE RUMS & LIQUEURS, SPICES
HOT SAUCES & HISTORY, ISLAND WIDE
OR VISIT ST MAARTEN'S WORLD
FAMOUS GUAVABERRY EMPORIUM

THE ORIGINAL WILD
GUAVABERRY
ISLAND FOLK LIQUEUR

AGED 5 YEARS IN OAK
REPUBLIC
RUM RON

read the rest of the story
in 5 languages at
GUAVABERRY.COM

PHILIPSBURG

Bobbys

Dock Martin

Beach & marina area

Cruise ship & superyacht berthing area

www.HeliPhotoCarib.com

then silt again. You will probably be fine with a 7-foot draft, but over that, ask the marina. The new Dock Martin breakwater gives some protection from the south to the marinas.

Passenger ferry traffic comes and goes via the well-buoyed channel. Anchor to the west or east of this channel, but if east, stay south of the Dock Martin breakwater.

Philipsburg is a good anchorage in most conditions, though it gets very rolly when the wind switches to the southeast, and during the day cruise ship tender wakes make it rolly, which can be uncomfortable for monohulls. A couple of times a year a strong southerly is likely to make it untenable. At such times, proceed down the coast to Simpson Bay Lagoon or to Marigot. Under no circumstances should you be in Philipsburg in a hurricane or seriously disturbed weather.

Regulations

In order to clear in or out of Dutch Sint Maarten, take your passports and ship's papers to the commercial port and check with immigration and the port authority. They are in the building on the right just before the barrier gate to the port. Office hours are Monday to Friday, 0900-1200 and 1300-1600; and Sundays, 0900-1200.

Anchorage fees per 3 days are as follows (in US$): up to 44 tons, $6; 45-99 tons, $9. Vessels over 99 tons pay $0.03 per ton. Departure fees (per week stayed): up to 24 meters, $10; 14-20 meters, $15; 20-28 meters, $25; 28-36 meters, $45; and over 36 meters, $85. There is also a clearance (CLE) fee, between $2-7.

Pilotage fees, when requested or compulsory, vary from $4 for a sailing vessel of less than 25 tons to $136 for vessels of 10,000 to 13,000 gross tons.

Communications

You will find phones by the Greenhouse. Cyber Surf on Front Street is one of several places that will get you online.

Great White Egret, Great Bay Salt Pond

Or take your computer to Chesterfields or Greenhouse, buy a coffee, and use the complementary WiFi. Or you can try one of the bay-wide WiFis.

General Yacht Services

Bobby's Marina (VHF: 16) has a good sized main dock and welcomes short-term visitors when space is available. The maximum size is about 150 feet though, a boat that big will not get in till they dredge.

They have a fuel dock, and are happy to have you use the dinghy dock under the bridge. They offer showers and toilets. You can haul your yacht here with their 80-ton travel lift. The yard is now small so only for those doing work. Do it yourself, or bring in a contractor, for which there is a fee.

Bobby's Marina group includes this marina as well as Bobby's Mega Yard and another haul out, both in Simpson Bay Lagoon (for details see *Simpson Bay Lagoon*). All Bobby's marinas are well managed by Jeff Howell, who has an excellent record of keeping boats upright in hurricanes. He removes and stores masts on monohulls as a matter of course, If you need laundry done, talk to one of Bobby's security guards and they will get a laundry service to pick it up.

The port authority has a good docking facility for about 4 large yachts up to 115 meters with full security inside the cruise ship area. They have water and fuel, but not electricity. They charge $5.50 per foot

up to 30 days and $5 per foot over 30 days.

Dock Martin is a small marina, usually full of day-charter yachts, with very occasional space for a transient. They have built most of a big breakwater, a first step in a planned expansion, including a bigger marina and a large shopping and restaurant area You are welcome to use their dinghy dock.

Chandlery

Island Water World in Bobby's Marina is an excellent chandlery. They keep a stock of paints, antifoulings, and all the resins and cloth you need to fix your boat before you paint it. You will find much general gear, including ladders, dinghies, outboards, solar panels, ropes, and fittings. This store is part of the larger Island Water World in Simpson Bay; so if you don't see what you need, ask.

Caribbean Auto, the Napa agent, has an excellent stock of filters, engine parts, spares, and accessories. Their shop is on A.T. Illedge Road, behind the salt pond.

Radio Shack is on Longwall Road. They are ideal for wire, switches, and fuses and miniature tools, or TVs and electronics for after the work is done. Many yachts buy short-wave radios and mobile phones here.

Technical Yacht Services

Two contractors based in Bobby's do most of the yard work. Mark's Paint Tech does glass and gel coat repairs, spray painting, and antifouling.

Iguana, Great Bay Salt Pond

RENAISSANCE ISLANDS

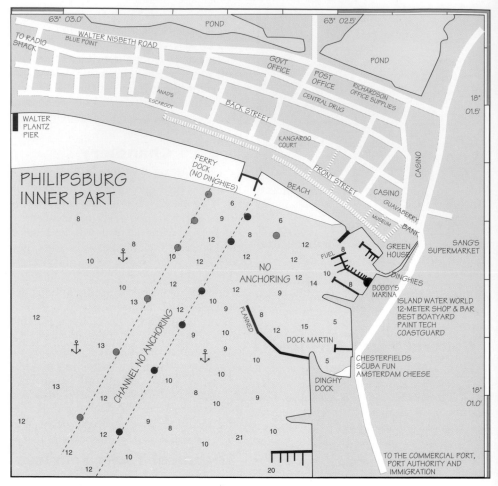

PHILIPSBURG
INNER PART

Best Boat Yard, run by Erik and Judith, does welding, machining, hydraulics, mechanics, plumbing, and antifouling.

Otherwise, Kiss Marine, run by Dave Dowling (an ex-cruising man himself) and Mark, is an excellent repair shop for all mechanical, electrical, and refrigeration problems, including generators. They do both commercial and yacht work and can overhaul a superyacht engine or come out in the bay and fix a put-put cruising diesel.

Transport

Avis car rental is outside Dock Martin. The main pier taxi stand number is 721-542-2359.

Provisioning

You should be able to pry some cash with your card at one of the ATM machines. One is in the car park, another near Greenhouse, or you can try the Windward Islands Bank, near the police station, which is the place to get cash from a Visa or Mastercard. The American Express agent is Maduro Travel.

Provisioning is easy. Sang's Supermarket, across the road from Bobby's, is a big modern supermarket that will have most things you need, and it includes a wholesale department. For moderate orders, you can borrow carts from Sang's to wheel your groceries back to the docks; wholesale orders will be delivered. Sang's has a deli section with lots of prepared foods and so is a great lunch place; .

Amsterdam Cheese & Liquor Store, is fancy, pleasant, and has many Dutch cheeses. They are in Dock Martin and knowledgeable about liquor.

To enjoy the fun of visiting a monster

Waterfront, Philipsburg

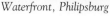

supermarket, take a cab or catch a bus (from Back Street near the police station) to Le Grande Marché, a state-of-the-art supermarket that is new, flashy, and huge, with produce from all over the world. They open daily 0800-2000, except Sundays; 0900-1400. You will find everything you need, and they will deliver it to any of the marinas for you. Almost opposite is St. Martin's first giant warehouse store, Cost-U-Less. This store has range of supermarket items, as well as housewares, office supplies, appliances, electronics, and health and beauty products. They open daily 0900-2100, except Sundays, when they close at 1500.

Up the road from Le Grande Marché are two hardware giants: Ace and Kooyman's.

Fun Shopping

Shopping in St. Martin is all duty-free and boutique lovers will be in seventh heaven. Philipsburg has two main streets: Front Street and Back Street. Front Street has the flashier, more expensive stores. Back Street is great for the bargain hunter, especially those looking for clothes. On Front Street you will find endless shops, selling everything from fine porcelain and jewelry to videos, cameras, and TVs.

Shipwreck Shop, also on Front Street, is the best place for art, handicrafts, magazines, local books, nautical clothing, and nice spray jackets. Philipsburg has the widest selection of electronics in St. Martin. The fashion-conscious can check out such stores as Benetton and Beach Stuff for trendy, chic, casual wear. Don't miss the big local craft market behind the courthouse for bags and "I was in St. Martin" t-shirts. The Central Drugstore, just across from the police station, fills prescriptions and has a wide range of vitamins, cosmetics, and health care products. Several good office supply stores are on the road running along the pond. Adolphus Richardson Office S upplies, has computers, can fix any software or hardware problem, and they are very helpful. Blue Point is a giant store with printer inks, tablets, computers TVs, just about everything. For other practical things, visit Cost-U-Less mentioned in *Provisioning*.

Philipsburg has a small museum in the Heritage Foundation, down an alley that goes back from the waterfront. The museum shop sells maps, prints, and books, including a hiking book. Gamblers will find two casinos very close by.

Restaurants

Many good restaurants are within an easy stroll of the marinas, several with happy hours patronized by yachtspeople. In changing times, I am happy to say Chesterfields stays the same and offers first-rate food from breakfast till night, right on the water. Happy hour is from 1700-1830, featuring lower priced drinks and snacks. It is popular with the quieter crowd out for a relaxing rendezvous. They have daily lunch specials and a good dinner menu. From time to time in season, they put on live background music. They have free WiFi.

The young active crowd gathers at The Greenhouse from 1630-1900 daily for the liveliest happy hour in St. Martin. Expect lots of bustle, invigorating music, two-for-one drinks, and half-priced appetizers. Things quiet down about 1900 when the dinner crowd arrives, livening up again about 2100 when the DJ begins. They have free WiFi.

In Bobby's, the 12-Meter Yacht Club is a pleasant waterfront bar, restaurant, and shop. They have a large variety of food, from burgers to fine fish.

Walk along the broad walkway or down Front Street and take your choice. Oualiche and Passanggrahan both have good reputations. L'Escargot on Front Street is set in a traditional old Antillian house. You will eat excellent seafood here, carefully prepared in the classical French style. They are open for both lunch and dinner.

L'Escargot is on a corner. If you walk down the side street at this corner, appetizing smells will greet you from Anand's, an East Indian and Créole restaurant serving great food for the cheap and cheerful crowd. It is open from 1200-1500 for lunch and 1800-2200 for dinner. You can choose whether you want your dishes mild, spicy, hot, or hot as hell.

The Kangaroo Court is in a pretty historic courtyard building on a side street by the courthouse. It has a delightful ambience if you visit on a non-cruise-ship day. They serve great salads, sandwiches, desserts, and coffee. It opens daily for lunch, coffee, and snacks.

Water Sports

Ready to go diving? Scuba Fun is a full scuba shop in Dock Martin. In the morning they take out certified divers, reserving their afternoons for resort courses and snorkeling. They do full certification courses, up to instructor. Scuba Fun rents gear to those on charter and sells a good assortment of diving and snorkeling gear, including tanks and BCs from the Scuba Shop, some below American list price.

Proselyte Reef is St. Martin's most popular dive. It lies south of Philipsburg, in depths of 20 to 70 feet. Plenty of soft and hard corals, lots of fish, and old cannons, anchors, and artifacts from the famous wreck of the HMS Proselyte, which went aground here in 1802. Another popular dive is the Amazing Maze, a series of rock formations that make you think you are in a fairyland. Abundant fish enhance the effect.

If the weather is calm, ask about the area's most dramatic dive, Moonhole. This open crater looks as though it was created by a meteor that punched a hole some 60 feet deep into the reef. The top almost breaks the surface, so the only approach is down a channel that leads into it. The walls are bare and moon-like; hence the name, but there are often sharks and rays, as well as many reef fish, inside. The reef outside is attractive.

Other dives within easy reach of Philipsburg include Hen and Chicks, where there is a forest of elkhorn coral from 20 to 70 feet with good visibility and lots of fish. Teigland is the wreck of a German freighter (60 feet deep) and the dive here has a reef with an old tugboat cable draped over it. The wreck is near a drop off. There is a good chance of seeing barracuda, turtles, and schools of pelagic fish.

Colin has assembled a fleet of 12-meter America's Cup contestants, including Stars and Stripes 55 and 56, Canada II, and True North 1 and 4. These magnificent machines race several times a day with three trained crew on each boat and the rest of the muscle power supplied by paying passengers, most often off the cruise ships, but if you hanker to sail one, go!

Changing lights on the causeway bridge

Chris Doyle

SIMPSON BAY AND SIMPSON BAY LAGOON

Simpson Bay is a large and pleasant bay surrounded by beaches. The eastern part makes a good sheltered anchorage. Simpson Bay Lagoon is about 12 square miles of completely protected, landlocked water. Access is by a channel and lifting bridge from Simpson Bay. Inside you are free from ocean swells. However, a new causeway running across the lagoon divides it in two. Access is by the causeway bridge. You can dinghy through either of the bridges anytime, but can only take your yacht through during opening times.

Bridge times. The swing bridge (Simpson Bay Bridge) is a conspicuous structure, currently painted blue. The entrance is down a small channel and is clearly visible. The center of the entrance channel has been dredged to 19 feet, though either side of center there are spots as shallow as 15 feet, so if you need all 19 feet, get your marina to pilot you in. The bridge is 56 feet wide. Year round bridge times are as follows: 0830 outbound, 0930 inbound; 1030 outbound, 1130 inbound; 1500 inbound, 1600, outbound, 1700 inbound. The bridge does not operate in extremely strong winds. It may have to close suddenly so always keep your radio on VHF 12 when transiting. You can call for information on 545-3183. Wait outside until the light turns green, as there is a current in the channel.

The Causeway Bridge is a swing bridge so yachts can go though both ways at once. It does not open automatically so if you don't call them to let them know you want to come through, they will not open. But if you do call (VHF: 12, "Causeway Bridge", they will open as follows: 0815, 0945, 1000, 1145, 1530, 1715).

The lagoon is large enough for a good dinghy sail and open to exploration for those who like something a bit different. Simpson Bay Lagoon is the yachting center of St. Martin. Many marinas and marine businesses surround the lagoon, on both the Dutch and French sides, and you can dinghy between the two. In recent years professional superyachts have become a large focus of the yachting scene, with several marinas built especially for them. However, the cruiser is still highly regarded, as many people involved in the boating industry are cruisers themselves who washed ashore here. Even by Caribbean standards, they are a friendly and pleasant group. You will find many happy hours in bars around the waterfront. A stop in Simpson Bay is likely to be happy and convivial.

Navigation

When approaching Simpson Bay from the east, swing out in an arc well outside Pelican Point and Pelican Cay. When you are past the island, you can anchor on either side of the channel. If you are staying some time, the calmest spot is close the beach in the southeast corner. Holding is good in sand, 9 to 12 feet deep. This is a good overnight anchorage that is not too bad even in southeasterly winds.

Dredging is fairly continuous in Simpson Bay Lagoon. Almost no room is deep enough for superyachts to swing at anchor, so they best go to one of the marinas. Contact a marina and be guided by their staff, who will send out a boat to bring you in through the bridge and to the marina, according to your draft. Yachts going into Palapa (which is the deepest) need to stay really close the mooring buoys as in some places it shoals fast outside.

For other yachts, the sketch chart gives the depths I found. Judging by the size of anchored yachts, these may be pessimistic – it could be that my echo sounder is picking up a foot or so of navigable suspended mud. Watch out for the unmarked shoals north of Isle de Sol. Leave a clear fairway into the channel and to the airport, with plenty of room for large yachts to maneuver into Palapa Marina. Anchor anywhere else except in the buoyed channels or off the end of the runway. (See our sketch charts, pages 85 & 90.) It is possible to get a dinghy under the bridge that goes to Snoopy Island. Take either side of the bridge, go slowly, and stay in the middle.

Our sketch chart shows the dredged channels into the marinas. Cruising through the rest of the lagoon looks interesting. We show the obvious shoal areas. The rest of it is navigable, with depths of 7 to 12 feet, though there are several shoals within 100 yards of the shore and there may be uncharted shoals farther out. Unmarked wrecks occasionally get left over from hurricanes, so navigate with caution. A 16-foot deep channel has been dredged to the inner part of the lagoon for Porto Cupecoy, a fancy new marina, and is well buoyed.

There is a dredged channel (about 6.5 feet deep) to the French side of the bay (see Marigot) and another bridge on that side. The easiest way to access it is to go round the west side of Grand Ilet. Unfortunately, only the first red marker was in place early in 2015. Every year people who grounded tell me this channel no longer exists. But I check it each time and so far it does. I suggest a careful dinghy check before you take your yacht and avoid days of strong winds.

Regulations

When you arrive, visit the immigration and lagoon authority station in their building on the north side of the entrance channel. They have a big dinghy dock and the office is open from 0800-1200 and 1330-1630 on weekdays and 0900-1200 on weekends. Start with immigration then check with the Simpson Bay Lagoon Authority, which is open at the same time. Take your ship's papers, passports, and your last clearance with you. The Simpson Bay Lagoon Authority will charge you whether you go in the lagoon or stay outside. On entry, tell them on which day you plan to leave and you then pay a fee. For a week (or portion thereof) it is as follows: (all US$) $20 for boats from 9 to 13 meters long; $40 for boats 13-18 meters long; $60 for boats 18-23 meters long; $90 for boats 23 to 28 meters long; $120 for boats 28-33 meters long; $150 for boats 33-38 meters long; $180 for boats 38-43 meters long; $210 for boats 43-50 meters long; $250 for boats 50-75 meters long; and $290 for boats over 75 meters. If you stay six weeks you only pay for four.

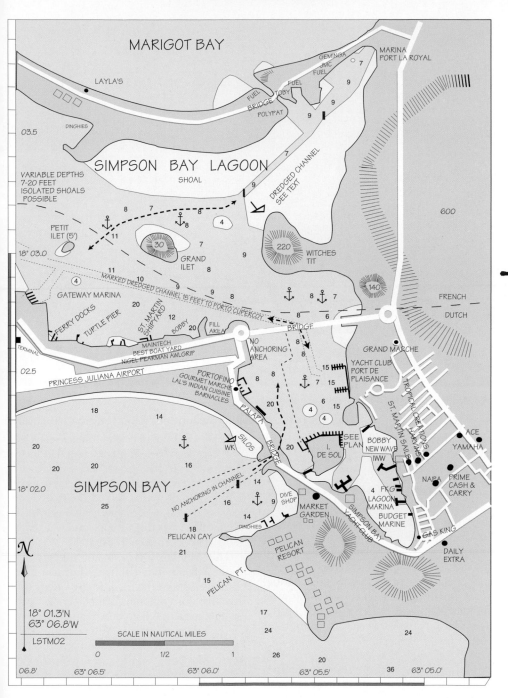

Everyone who passes inwards through the bridge during their normal opening pays fees as follows (all US$): $7 for boats from 9 to 12 meters long; $21 for boats 12-15 meters long; $42 for boats 15-18 meters long; $120 for boats 18 to 22 meters long; $200 for boats 22-28 meters long; $300 for boats 28-36 meters long; and $500 for those over 36 meters. Special bridge openings are available by request between 0600 and 1800 for $1,000.

You have to pay clearance fees when

Simpson Bay showing Dutch side lagoon and marinas

you clear out, which you may do 24 hours in advance. Fees (customs + port) are ($2+$5) up to 99 tons; ($5+$10) 99-499 tons; ($9+$20) 500 tons and up.

Communications

A Cruiser's Net run by Mike "Shrimpy" is on the air Monday to Saturday at 0730 on VHF: 10 . This gives a morning weather forecast, followed by helpful information on getting gas tanks filled, local entertainment, and coming events. Cruisers use channel 10 as a calling frequency, switching after contact. While in St. Martin, pick up the free Marine Trades Directory from most businesses.

WiFi at anchor is generally poor. You can buy a Telcel 3G USB system, or rent a dongle (3G cell phone modem for onboard use) from Business Point.

Business Point (VHF: 10), in Plaza Del Lago, is a friendly place. Hyacinth (Blondie) will offer you complimentary coffee while you check your email (on their computers or your own). She offers overseas phone, fax, (local and USA), mail, courier (official DHL point) and office services. You can Business Point as your address. Hyacinth can arrange airline tickets, car rentals, and tours, including The Edge ferry to Saba and St. Barts. You can browse their book swap and look at yachting magazines. Their office opening hours are weekdays 0800-1800, Saturdays 1230-1630.

The Mailbox office is on the ground floor behind La Palapa Marina. The entrance is from the road. Many yachts use this efficient communications center with phone, message, fax, broadband internet access, and mail services. It is an authorized Fedex dealer and you can send and receive here. Mailbox phone rates to the US are good, and you can rent prepaid cell phones and buy sims. They have lots of deals on email; ask for their plans. They run an express mail service to the US. The Mailbox can send packages worldwide, and you can use their US address. They provide secretarial and copy services and have a color copier. It is open weekdays 0800-

GATEWAY
ST MARTIN SHIPYARD
BOBBIES
CAUSEWAY
CAUSEWAY BRID
PALAPA
PORT DE PLAISANCE

1900; Saturdays, 0900-1700.

Greenhouse, Jimbo's, Lagoonies, and many bars offer free WiFi.

For mobile phones or internet via smart phone and computer link, Chippy has an office in the block next to the Megaplex Cinema. Telcel has an office on the left side of the road as you walk from Palapa Marina in the airport direction. Scarlet in the Simpson Bay Royal Village sells or rents special modems. This is good, but costly for the short term. If you are staying for months and willing to buy and register their modem for about $135, monthly rates are reasonable (two month minimum).

General Yacht Services

Bobby's Marina owns Bobby's Mega Yard, a new haul out facility next to Port de Plaisance. This is Bobby's biggest yard, with a 150-ton travel lift that can haul boats of up to 34-foot beam, 11 foot draft. (They also have a 75-ton hoist.) The yard has good security with a perimeter wall and living on board is not encouraged. This is an eco-friendly yard where all wash down water is treated, solids are removed, and clear, clean water is returned to the lagoon. Spray painting is not permitted unless you get the yard to build you a tent. As in all Bobby's yards, monohull masts are removed and stored during the hurricane season. The yard does all underwater work, but for other work you can bring in your own subcontractors. There is a 15% fee for this.

Bobby's has more of a live-aboard facility on the airport road, close to the Red Cross (VHF: 10). This yard has both 110- and 220-volt electricity, showers, toilets, and a laundry, and you can stay on the boat. Haul out is done with a 55-ton travel lift and they have room to store about 80 yachts. This may close due to a planned expansion of the airport.

In Bobby's is the Five Star Yacht Consultants, managed by ex-superyacht skipper Andy. They can help plan any project for yachts both large and small, and they do fuel polishing.

Lagoon Marina is small, with a

Relax or ready-up in an old fashioned friendly atmosphere.

LAGOON MARINA

By Land Or Sea
Bar & Café

Up to 10' Draft | 110/220 Electric | Water Shower/Toilets | Laundromat | Security | Storage Lockers

All within a stone's throw of the major Cole Bay marine suppliers and provisioners.
St. Maarten D.W.I.

FREE Internet Access
Reasonable Dock Rates
Full Compliment of Marine Services

+1-721 / 544 2611
www.lagoon-marina.com
info@lagoon-marina.com

comfortably wide modern dock and a big security gate; it is more reasonably priced than many. They have water, electricity (110/220-volt), and WiFi. In the building you will find a good laundry (0800-1700 Wednesdays, 0800-1900 other weekdays, 0800-1400 Saturdays), several technical services, showers, and toilets. Most other technical services are very close by. Lagoonies Bar and Restaurant is famous among cruisers (see *Restaurants*). The main channel in is marked: leave the red buoys to starboard to avoid the shallows. The dock has 10 feet at the outer end, shoaling to 5 feet or less close to the wall.

Simpson Bay Marina (VHF: 16 or 79A), is an Island Global Yachting (IGY) top quality marina, with generously wide, tile-decorated docks carrying electricity (110/220-volt, 60-cycle, 3-phase, and 100-volt single phase), water, telephone, and WiFi. Facilities include communications, showers, and toilets. The channel is dredged to 16 feet and they can accommodate about 130 boats and up to 30 superyachts of 180 feet. This marina also caters to

small yachts and they have many in the 40 to 50 foot range. Anyone unsure of the way in, and all superyachts, should call from outside the bridge and they will guide you into your slip. They have a fuel dock with ice and arrange high-speed fuel bunkering for superyachts. Anything their superyachts customers need, they will get, including repairs, boat care, provisioning, and laundry. It is usually necessary to book a place in advance. A Hertz car rental agent is inside the office.

Ashore is Plaza del Lago, a pleasant shopping and restaurant complex, which includes a bank and ATM machine. Some of the restaurants, shops, and businesses are covered in different sections of this chapter. The plaza contains a medical and dental clinic, a hair salon, a computer store, and there are casinos and a cinema nearby.

Harel Yacht Brokers is in Plaza del Largo, with another branch in Oyster Pond. They are full sales and service agents for Lagoon, Beneteau, and Outremer, and deal with all of their problems. They will give you good

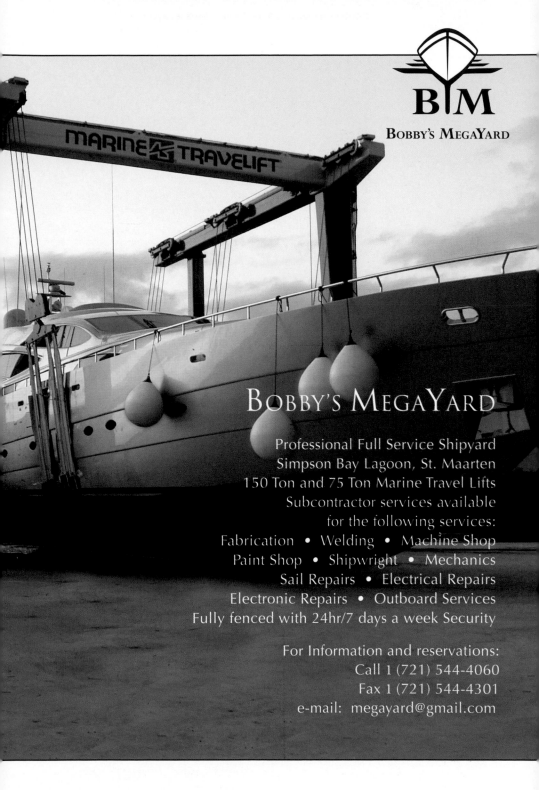

BOBBY'S MEGAYARD

Professional Full Service Shipyard
Simpson Bay Lagoon, St. Maarten
150 Ton and 75 Ton Marine Travel Lifts
Subcontractor services available
for the following services:
Fabrication • Welding • Machine Shop
Paint Shop • Shipwright • Mechanics
Sail Repairs • Electrical Repairs
Electronic Repairs • Outboard Services
Fully fenced with 24hr/7 days a week Security

For Information and reservations:
Call 1 (721) 544-4060
Fax 1 (721) 544-4301
e-mail: megayard@gmail.com

ANY JOB, BIG OR SMALL...

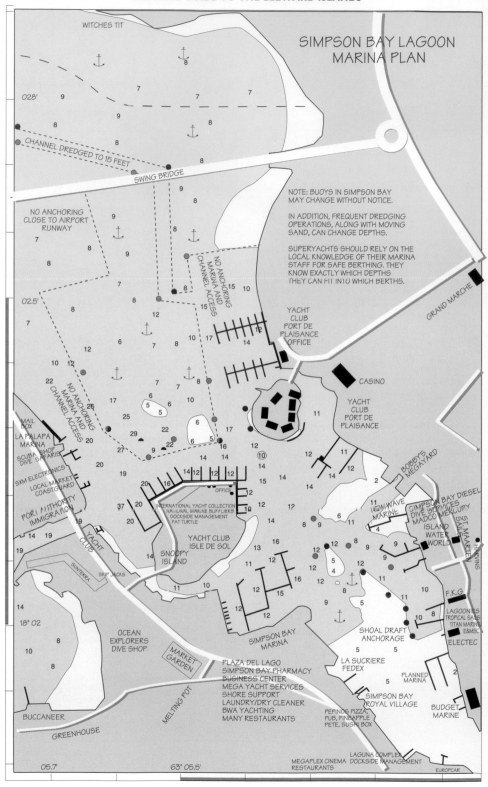

SIMPSON BAY LAGOON
MARINA PLAN

WITCHES TIT

028'

CHANNEL DREDGED TO 15 FEET

SWING BRIDGE

NO ANCHORING
CLOSE TO AIRPORT
RUNWAY

NO ANCHORING
AND
MARINA
CHANNEL ACCESS

02.5'

NOTE: BUOYS IN SIMPSON BAY
MAY CHANGE WITHOUT NOTICE.

IN ADDITION, FREQUENT DREDGING
OPERATIONS, ALONG WITH MOVING
SAND, CAN CHANGE DEPTHS.

SUPERYACHTS SHOULD RELY ON THE
LOCAL KNOWLEDGE OF THEIR MARINA
STAFF FOR SAFE BERTHING. THEY
KNOW EXACTLY WHICH DEPTHS
THEY CAN FIT INTO WHICH BERTHS.

GRAND MARCHE

YACHT
CLUB
PORT DE
PLAISANCE
OFFICE

CASINO

YACHT
CLUB
PORT DE
PLAISANCE

NO ANCHORING
AND
MARINA AND
CHANNEL ACCESS

MAIL
BOX
LA PALAPA
MARINA

SCUBA SHOP
DIVE SAFARIS

SXM ELECTRONICS
LOCAL MARKET
COASTGUARD

PORT AUTHORITY
IMMIGRATION

YACHT
CLUB

SUNTERRA

SKIP JACKS

BOBBY'S
MEGAYARD

NEW WAVE
MARINE

SIMPSON BAY DIESEL
DIVE SERVICES
MADCO MERCURY

ISLAND
WATER
WORLD

ST. MAARTEN
SAILS

HARKINS

OFFICE

INTERNATIONAL YACHT COLLECTION
NATIONAL MARINE SUPPLIERS
DOCKSIDE MANAGEMENT
FAT TURTLE

YACHT CLUB
ISLE DE SOL

SNOOPY
ISLAND

F.K.G
LAGOONIES
TROPICAL SAILS
TITAN MARINE
E&MSC

ELECTEC

SHOAL DRAFT
ANCHORAGE

PLANNED
MARINA

SIMPSON BAY
MARINA

OCEAN
EXPLORERS
DIVE SHOP

MARKET
GARDEN

PLAZA DEL LAGO
SIMPSON BAY PHARMACY
BUSINESS CENTER
MEGA YACHT SERVICES
SHORE SUPPORT
LAUNDRY/DRY CLEANER
BWA YACHTING
MANY RESTAURANTS

LA SUCRIERE
FEDEX

SIMPSON BAY
ROYAL VILLAGE

BUDGET
MARINE

18° 02

BUCCANEER

GREENHOUSE

MELTING POT

PEPINOS PIZZA
PUB, PINEAPPLE
PETE, SUSHI BOX

LAGUNA COMPLEX
DOCKSIDE MANAGEMENT

MEGAPLEX CINEMA
RESTAURANTS

EUROPCAR

05.7'

63° 05.5'

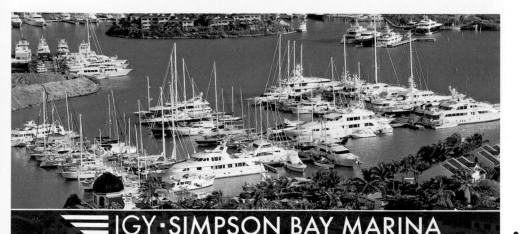

IGY·SIMPSON BAY MARINA
· ST. MAARTEN, DC ·

SERENE AND SECURE BERTHING. IGY HOSPITALITY.

- 120 slips for yachts up to 185ft with 13ft draft
- Pilotage in and out of marina
- Full-service fuel dock
- Concrete docks with 24-hour security
- On-site banking and pharmacy
- Bars, restaurants, shops, and chandlery

18°02′00.14″N | 63°05′26.00″W
t: +1 721 544 2309 f: +1 721 544 3378
Welfare Road #68, Cole Bay, St. Maarten
Dutch Caribbean

≡IGY MARINAS

igymarinas.com :: +1 855.362.5449
CONNECT WITH US 🟠 🔵 f ▶ in

RENAISSANCE ISLANDS

advice on any kind of repair or service you need, and will help if you wish to sell or buy a boat.

Bay Island Yachts, a big brokerage with worldwide connections, have links with the Business Point, so you can ask Blondie to put you in touch, or call Alain on his cell (0690-47-71-45).

Island Water World (VHF: 74) is a marina with room for about 55 boats, up to 65 feet. They cater to regular cruising boats, and can haul power boats up to about 30 feet with a forklift. (See *Technical Yacht Services*). They have a fuel dock, water, and electricity (110/220volt) on the docks and free WiFi (ask for the key). They do some amazing things for cruisers: they will lend you a courtesy bike if you ask, and even have a dinghy they may lend in emergencies (see *Chandlery*). The entrance channel has been dredged to 9 feet. You follow the main channel toward Simpson Bay Marina and turn to port into the well marked channel that heads towards FKG Rigging. When you get close to Island Water World's dock, swing hard to port,

following the outer dock. Once past that, it is deep into the rest of the facility.

St. Martin Shipyard, managed by Hank, is on the Airport Road. This friendly and helpful yard is in a slightly industrial area, with the inexpensive Boca Marina Bar and Restaurant built on piles over the water. They have docks for 25 yachts or more, from small cruisers on their own special dock, to 130-foot-long superyachts, tying stern-to in water 17-30 feet deep. They haul with a giant 70-ton Sea Lift trailer, that adjusts to your boat and cushions it and takes up to 16-foot draft. It is great for multihulls as it holds them from underneath and they rest on cushioning. They can take up to 40-foot beam. Little boats they haul by crane.

They have three onsite contractors, Maintech, Best Boat Yard, and Nigel Pierman, the quality Awlgrip paint specialist. You can get anything done here, and if the contractors in the yard cannot help, Hank will set you up with the right specialist.

Palapa Marina (VHF: 68) offers stern-to docking (any length) for about 25 boats. The water here is deep: if you can get through the bridge, you can get into Palapa. This has made them very popular with superyachts, and it is not unusual to see more than a dozen yachts here between 100 and 300 feet long. Water, electricity (110, 220, & 440-volt, 3-phase, 60-cycle), and WiFi are available on the dock. They have full communications, washrooms, showers, and a convenient laundry that is open to the general public. Several large charter yachts use Palapa Marina as a base. Their staff, headed by Valeska Luckert, attends to all the needs of their customers and offers crew placement and full provisioning.

Island Global Yachting, with marinas in several Caribbean islands, runs Yacht Club Isle de Sol (VHF: 78A/16), on Snoopy Island. It was built specifically for large yachts, with docks about 10 feet off the water. They have 220-, 380-, and 480-volt single or 3-phase electricity, WiFi, and full ISPS security. Water and fuel are delivered to all berths. Facilities include tennis courts, a swimming pool, a restaurant, provisioning, an air conditioned gym, and a chandlery. A lower dinghy dock can be found in the southeastern part of the marina. If there is no guard, the gate is probably unlocked. The staff will cater to all the needs of their customers. A car rental agency is in the office.

Yacht Club Port de Plaisance, (VHF: 16/67), part of which is built like a Mediterranean port, is a fancy yachting facility, with full ISPS security. The service is geared to superyachts and they send tenders to meet every customer to make sure they navigate the bridge and channel with no problem. They can take about 100 yachts, including the largest superyachts, in their new docks to the northwest. While Yacht Club Port de Plaisance is very much geared to superyachts, several berths in the prettier south harbor are suitable for cruising yachts.

The marina staff will take care of your fuel and water needs anywhere on their docks, and power (220, 380-volt single or 3-phase), and WiFi are provided. As you would expect from a marina of this caliber, they can supply just about anything. They adjoin the Princess Casino, its hotel and the new Princess Casino Country Club, whose swimming pools, health spa, gyms, lounging chairs, tennis courts, and other facilities reserved for resort guests are available to the crew and guests of boats on their dock. You will find a few restaurants (see *Restaurants*). Customers can rent hull cleaning rafts and electric baggage carts. You are as close here as you can get to the big Grande Marché Supermarket, which is by the entrance to the Princess Casino grounds. The best place to leave your dinghy is on the dinghy dock close to the port office.

Portofino Marina is to the north of La Palapa, just after the big fuel dock and gas station. Most of the space inside is taken up by small powerboats, with hoists to get them out of the water for storage between trips. There is also space for a few yachts on the outer wall. They have a dinghy dock at the northern end of the marina.

FKG Rigging also has some work berths. For details, see *Technical Yacht Services*.

The Gateway Marina, owned by Peyton Cromwell, is very close to the airport, in an ideal position to collect or leave anyone traveling by plane. There is a walkway so you don't have to brave the traffic. For superyachts they have a special dock for picking up guests by tender. They have a Magnum 60, skippered by Deon, that can deliver guests to your boat or to St. Barts or Anguilla. This is full-service, top-quality pick up and delivery. For cruisers they have a floating dock. You can pick people up here, or you can leave your dinghy for the day while you go visit Maho Bay. There will be reasonable charges (not decided yet), so you'll need to call to get the rates.

The marina part is currently undergoing change and most of their docks are taken long term. A channel at least 16 feet deep leads to the marina from the deep water at Port de Plaisance (see our sketch chart). When space is available they can take any size of boat.

Porto Cupecoy is way up in the western

A group at the yacht club watches a yacht squeeze through

Chris Doyle

end of Simpson Bay (see charts pages 85 and 110). The channel goes close by Port de Plaisance before heading west. It is well marked and dredged to 15 feet.

Porto Cupecoy is an elegant marina and residential development, with a Mediterranean feel, built by the same people who did La Samanna. They can take 10 superyachts and about 50 smaller yachts. The docks have WiFi, satellite TV, water and electricity, 110 volts on the small yacht docks and up to 408 volts for super-yachts. High speed fueling is available, as is laundry and WiFi. The marina opens onto a big courtyard whose downstairs is full of restaurants and shops. Opposite the car parking area is a very pleasant branch of the excellent Gourmet Market. A tennis court, large swimming pool, and gym should keep you healthy. They have an active marina team that will help you into your slip, look after your yacht while you are away, and arrange any repairs.

In strong winds, little waves tumble into parts of the marina; enough so that you should make sure you are well secured, but probably not enough to make you uncomfortable. In both Gateway and Porto Cupecoy you will need to go through the causeway bridge.

Garbage bins can be found in, or just outside, the immigration station and all major marinas. The government empties these and this is where part of your monthly fee goes.

The chandleries help out with the filling of cooking gas bottles. Take them before 0900 and collect them later in the day. The current schedule is Island Water World on Mondays and Budget Marine on Wednesdays. Gas King, on the road from Budget Marine to the main road, will fill gas tanks Monday to Friday; bring them in by 0900 get them back the same day. They also fix tank valves, and sell other gasses.

JC Constanzo and partners are building a fairly large marina between Electec and Budget Marine. It should be finished during the life of this guide.

If you need a vet, Dr. Gary Swanston has an excellent reputation and is just a short ride away (call 721-542-0111).

GATEWAY MARINA   www.HeliPhotoCarib.com photos

CUPERCOY MARINA

General Yacht Services, Boat/Carpet Cleaning

Shore Support in Plaza Del Lago have a fast and efficient carpet cleaning service.

Inter-Nett is part of an international yacht carpet and fabric cleaning service, they do fireproofing as well and have contracts with some yachts.

Tender Rental and Tours rents all kinds of tenders for yachts, and they provide full tender services: luggage and passenger collection or taking people to another island. It is a service well used by the big yachts.

Chandlery

Nowhere is better than duty-free St. Martin for chandleries and boat shopping. The two giant stores, Budget Marine and Island Water World, both have marine catalogs, stores in many islands, and have been essential to the cruising community. If you are planning considerable shopping, both stores have various discounts you can apply for if you open an account and the prices will be duty-free in St. Martin. It is worth watching their ads in local papers for extra special deals. Each store is different, and a trip to St. Martin would not be complete without visiting both to see what is new. Both stores sell engine oil and batteries, and will recycle your discards. If you need some item not on the shelves, either store will probably be able to special order it for you. I have had exceptionally good service from both stores. Island Water World helped me get warranty replacements for 10-year-old solar panels that were fading, and Budget once pulled apart a new windmill so I could get replacement blades. You are unlikely to get such good treatment in the US.

How can you not like a store that offers free courtesy bikes? Island Water World offers modern, single-speed, comfort bikes (you pay a $50 refundable deposit) so customers can cycle around.

Island Water World is not only a magnificent and well laid-out chandlery, but they became the Caribbean's first full online shop: www.islandwaterworld.com. Your account status is stored on the computer, so if you are a big buyer with a big discount you will see it online. The site shows real-time inventory, and when you purchase you will see the shipping options and costs, the main one being Fedex, on which they have a big discount. Their Advantage card is another innovation. Sign up for one and you will earn points (called miles) for each dollar spent. When you amass enough (the discount gets bigger the more you amass), you can spend it in any of their Caribbean stores or online. General manager, Birgit Rothel is very helpful.

IWW's large two story store has paints and resins, including Jotun, for which they are the Caribbean distributor for yachts, marine hardware, electrics and electronics, plumbing, charts and cruising guides, excellent fishing gear (with a serious fisherman to give advice), paddle boards, kayaks and fun stuff, ropes and ground tackle, safety gear, and back-saving seats. They always carry a big stock of inflatables and outboards. Most now have "ultralight" versions which for many of us makes sense. I find the Walker

Bay inflatables interesting as they have broad bows to maximize space and the ultralight ribs have an injected glass hull. The Highfield ribs with aluminum hulls look good, with a nice deep V entry and they offer a five year warranty on the hulls. They carry the full Caribe line and are sales and service agents for Evinrude and Nissan outboards.

IWW has branches in Philipsburg and Marigot in St. Martin and stores in St. Lucia, Grenada (two), and Curacao.

Budget Marine is in a huge building with its own dinghy dock. It is the original store in an island-wide chain, with branches now in 12 places, including Trinidad, Grenada, and Antigua. Budget Marine introduced the first Caribbean marine catalog, which is still the best. If you are in an island without a Budget Marine, you can call the St. Maarten office and they can arrange delivery anywhere in the Caribbean. They hope soon to be able to offer a single account that is valid in all the islands they serve.

They have a vast range of goodies and a large floor space, so you need to go and browse. They stock almost everything,

RENAISSANCE ISLANDS

from cutlass bearings and zincs, to cables, pumps, alternators, ply, and resins. They have a range of stoves and toilets, as well as a big new fishing department. They sell Tohatsu outboards and a full range of the well-known, fun-to-drive AB inflatables, including the ultra light models with plain aluminum hulls. They also stock some roll-up inflatables. For cruisers who want something more fun than an inflatable, they stock the Walker Bay plastic dinghies which, unlike inflatables, can be sailed and rowed. They make them even safer and more practical by offering an inflatable ring that makes them much more stable and kinder on your hull. They also sell kayaks and paddle boards, and a whole room of nautical clothing. Budget Marine is the agent for Raymarine and along with Atlantis Marine the installer, they won Raymarine's best dealer award. If you don't see what you want, ask customer service, for they have giant storerooms on several floors.

They have a good dinghy dock and are redoing their waterfront. Soon they hope to have a berth deep enough to come to take on major purchases, or pick up some water.

National Marine Suppliers is upstairs in Isle de Sol. They open only during the season, from November to May when the superyachts are here. They keep a fair stock of items that are always in demand, from cleaning materials to cruising guides, and specialize in bringing things in fast, aided by their larger company in Fort Lauderdale. For the truly desperate, they can put things on direct flights so they arrive on the next plane. Greg Bailey is the sales manager and Nancy Bush, also in the office, runs a crew placement as well.

Check out FKG Rigging. While not a full chandlery, they have ropes, hatches, and excellent rigging-related technical chandlery, as well as a good selection of aluminum stock. See Electec for electrics and tools (see *Technical yacht services*)

Ace, a giant hardware store, is also of interest. Turn right out of Island Water World, turn left at the corner on Wells Road and continue to the main road.

Technical Yacht Services
Sailmakers, Canvas, Cushions

St. Maarten Sails & Canvas is run by Rob Gilders who started this business 36 years ago. It has a terrific reputation for friendly and experienced staff who carry out professional repairs and alterations to all makes of sails, from superyacht to dinghy. They do all classes of work: biminis, canvas, cushions, and sails; from design and construction to modifications and repairs. Their canvas work is so popular, that many yachts wait till they are in St. Martin to get their work done. You will find them opposite Island Water World in a big loft with plenty of space and machines to match any job. This makes it easy to bring your sails in, but if there is a problem, ask about collection from all Simpson Bay Marinas. For new sails, St. Maarten Sails continues its association with Jannie Reuvers Sails in Cape Town during their transition to Ullman Sails. They can supply sails for all sizes of yachts, made to the highest international standards in construction and design at reasonable prices.

Ernst's Tropical Sail Loft has a huge working area in the new Lagoon Marina complex. To go with this, Ernst has probably the biggest industrial sewing machine I have yet seen. He is a North Sails agent and works with Andrew Dove in Antigua. You can get an instant quote for new North Sails. His loft is upstairs and he has a hoist and dolly to bring sails from your tender. During the season, much of his work is with superyachts (thus the monster machine). Ernst does all kinds of canvas work, including awnings, biminis, cockpit cushions, and specialty covers. He is helpful and knowledgeable and sells lots of fabrics and sailmaking supplies, including needles.

Tropical Creations Upholstery is a small local shop run by Joseph Hubert from the French side. Joseph can do cushions and canvas, but not sails. You will find him on the road to Ace, just after Harvins, behind the supermarket.

Technical Yacht Services
Rigging

FKG Rigging (VHF: 71) is run by Kevin, Gordon, and Shag. They have a dock and room for 10 boats in front of their yard, with water and electricity (110 and 220-volt, single and 3-phase), which they keep for boats having work done. The channel into their yard is dredged to 12 feet and clearly marked.

FKG Rigging is one serious rigging shop, with an endless stock of fittings of all sizes. They can repair or manufacture just about anything, from making new compression fittings on rod rigging, to setting you up with a complete new mast and rig. Swages and wire are available up to 28mm, with rod rigging up to 170. They have a pull tester to provide certificates when required. Their technical chandlery has lots of rope and rigging-related hardware, including winches, quick release shackles, circlips,

as well as rope and general hardware. Here you will find the best collection of aluminum or stainless stock in a variety of shapes.

They have a store dedicated to yacht hydraulics, including big boat hydraulics. This store includes a large retail shop, mainly Aeroquip equipment, and this is the place to come for any hydraulic work. They sell and service hardware, such as Antal and Lewmar, New England and Gleistein ropes, Recmann, Rondal, Furlex, and Profurl roller furling. In addition, they do SS tube work and lifelines. They have both a machine shop and all kinds of welding equipment, with a certified welder on the staff. They can do any kind of metal job and work on shafts up to 4 inches in diameter. They also build custom aluminum boats.

Technical Yacht Services
Electrics & Electronics

Electec (VHF: 10) is in a big building next to the Lagoon Marina, with its own dinghy dock. This company is owned and

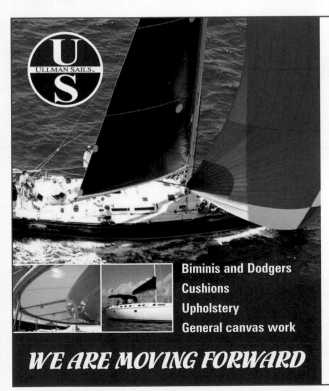

More technology.
More expertise.
More service.

The same
sailmaking team

St. Maarten Sails and Canvas N.V has teamed up with Ullman Sails

Biminis and Dodgers
Cushions
Upholstery
General canvas work

Opposite Island Water World
+1(721) 544-5231 /
+1(721) 520-6484

rgilders@ullmansails.com
admin@stmaartensails.com

WE ARE MOVING FORWARD

RENAISSANCE ISLANDS

FKG Services

- Rod Cold - Heading to - 170
- Wire Swaging to 1 1/8" - 28 MM
- Nicopress to 1/2" - 12 MM
- Hydraulic Services
- Pulling & Stepping Masts
- Refurbishing Masts & Booms
- Full Machine Shop

- Surveys & Evaluation of Masts & Rigging
- Tig & Mig Welding
- Bending, Tanks
- Pulpits, Pushpits
- Custom Hardware
- Full Stock of Stainles Steel, Aluminium & Delrin

- 12FT. of Water at our Service Dock
- Stern - To Dockage

Full Hydraulic Service & Installation
- Bowthrusters, Stabilizers
- Steering Systems, Power Packs
- Hydraulic Hoses to 2"

Pull Testing with Certificaion to 150,000lbs on site

Testing of Hydraulic Pumps Motors & Cylinders

37 WELLINGTON ROAD, COLE BAY, ST. MAARTEN

TEL: (599) or (1-721) 544-4733
FAX: (599) or (1-721) 544-2171

info@fkg-marine-rigging.com
www.fkg-marine-rigging.com

run by Leslie Struthers and Derek Little. It is an installation and service shop for electrics and instrumentation, and they repair all kinds of starter motors and alternators and some electronics. They are agents for Onan, Northern Lights, Fischer Panda, Master Volt, and F. G. Wilson generators, but will repair other makes as well. They are authorized sales and service agents for Interstate batteries and their prices are good. Electec sells and repairs Spectra, Village Marine, and Sea Recovery watermakers. Leslie Struthers or one of his team will come to your boat for installation and repair work. Their showroom has a wide range of electrical components, both for yachts and shore power. They sell and service Milwaukee and Makita power tools, and stock many useful tools, from extra long drill bits to a big variety of hole saws.

Atlantis Marine is an electronics shop in Lagoon Marina run by two really nice guys: Gui from Brazil (electronics) and Andy from UK (electrics). Gui will fix any kind of electronics and is certified for installation and service of Raymarine. He is good with computers, networks, WiFi, audio and theater thing, (including a fancy, big waterproof outside screen that shows where you are or movies, while your computer is dry below). Andy will take care of your generators, starter motors, and electrical problems. Their store has a good stock of electronics, especially the Raymarine line, but also CD players, elegant Lumitec LED lights and Phasor generators. They sell and service Sea Recovery watermakers. Their prices are competitive. They have a reputation for excellent work and service at a reasonable price and, together with Budget Marine, won the Raymarine dealer of the year award. Gui helps bring up and manage yachts from Brazil.

Andrew Rapley at Necol is an excellent choice for electronics. He specializes in fixing gyros and integrated navigation systems on super-yachts. He can install and deal with all the AIS integrated security systems. Necol is an agent for Furuno, KVH, Simrad, and B&G, among others. For racers, they like to set up complete integrated

Titan Marine Air provides sales, parts, installation, service and support for marine AC, refrigeration and water makers. Call for quotes and service for your boat, yacht or commercial vessel.

AIR by Dometic GROUP · CMAC SYSTEMS INC. · Dometic · Cruisair · FCI Watermakers · Vitrifrigo LLC AMERICA

Call: (US) +1 954-401-7997 or (SXM) +1 721-550-2853 · Email: info@titanmarineair.com

instrumentation. For cruisers and others: Rogue Wave WiFi systems, Max Sea charting systems, MacMurdo EPIRBs. They are ACR certified and can service all your electronic safety gear. Andrew works from home but he has a service tender that can reach everywhere in Simpson Bay and into Marigot Bay in just a few minutes, or he can get to Philipsburg on a motorbike. Andrew is a pilot with his own plane, so is able to make down-island visits for big yachts in dire straits.

Shai Talmi, "The Wired Sailor," has an upstairs office in Plaza del Lago but he is never there, so call. Shai is friendly and helpful. He specializes in computers, WiFi, marine information technology, and related systems.

Technical Yacht Services
Refrigeration

Titan Marine is in the Lagoon Marina complex and is run by Kobus and Ronel. They are friendly, good and happy to work on any size of yacht and they own a work boat to make boat visits. They sell Dometic, Aqua Air, Sub Zero, VF, and Eskimo Ice. They fix all brands of refrigeration and air-conditioning, and all watermakers and they sell FCI. Their shop stocks refrigeration spares and parts. They will happily design and sell you a new refrigeration system.

Permafrost was recently aquired by Mike and Sam who also bought Frostline, making them agents for most brands of refrigeration. This makes them well equipped for fixing all refrigeration and air-conditioning problems at their shop at La Palapa Marina. They have a vast stock of parts and pumps, they will work on any yacht, and have tenders to make yacht visits.

Rob of Rob Marine has a refrigeration and air conditioning shop at New Wave Marine Yard. He is an agent for Technicold and Headhunter and works on all brands. His Headhunter expertise and stock includes all their big yacht toilets and pumps. Rob is very happy to work on cruising yachts as well as the larger boats, but no longer makes dinghy visits – you have to be at a dock.

Mack at Macklon Marine Refrigeration repairs refrigerators and air conditioners, mainly on cruising and local boats. He has a container shop in New Wave.

Technical Yacht Services
Motor Mechanics

Simpson Bay Diesel Services, run by Armand Amato, has a fine, large workshop at New Wave Marine Yard, just north of Island Water World. Armand is the authorized factory service agent for Yanmar and Cummins and can give you really excellent prices on new Yanmars, which he orders specially. Bring your broken Yanmars and Cummins here to be fixed, as there is a good chance he will have the spares. Armand also works on other brands of diesel and is at home with the big GMs, MTUs, and Caterpillars from superyachts. Armand's workshop is well placed for removing engines for a rebuild. They have

RENAISSANCE ISLANDS

a machine shop.

Diesel Outfitters, owned and run by Ray Longbottom from Liverpool, is in a container in Bobby's airport yard. Ray is the Perkins dealer and his price on spares can be good. In addition, he can supply new Perkins engines. Ray works on all brands of cruising boat sized diesels, including Yanmar, Volvo, and John Deere. He also fixes gear boxes. He makes boat visits and can be a little hard to find. The easiest way is to use the phone: 721-556-4967.

SXM Power Center (ex Ocean Experts), the Yamaha agent, is right opposite Ace Hardware, set back but clearly visible. They are the only Yamaha agent on St. Martin and they work with all Yamaha products, including motorbikes, and are very big on personal watercraft. They offer sales, full service, and a big range of parts.

The Napa agent is just up Orange Grove Road. If you walk back from Budget to the main road and turn right, then immediately left, you should find yourself on it. They sell many useful filters, engine parts, and spares and accessories, such as water pumps, batteries, and oils. They can make up hydraulic hoses.

Check also: *Multiple and Other Services.*

Technical Yacht Services
Diving, Salvage, Towing

Deon's Aquatic Solutions is a salvage and underwater shop. Their equipment includes an underwater hydraulic hull cleaner and prop polisher, and they can clean hulls, weld, and cut. They have a 600 hp tug for serious towing, as well as some smaller launches, so when you need a tow into the lagoon, these are the people to call. They can raise sunken yachts and do all kinds of underwater work, including video surveys. They are ABS and Lloyds certified, can dredge in restricted areas anywhere in the Caribbean, and are experienced at lifting superyacht anchors.

Charlie's Atlantech Dive Services is based in Palapa. Charlie does underwater work, from repairs (including props and thrusters) and cleaning to surveys and lifting superyacht anchors. The good news for those cruisers who got stuck here a bit too long is that he will scrub hulls and props.

Technical Yacht Services
Multiple and Other Services

Island Water World can do in-the-water yacht repairs in their marina, including fiberglass repairs and outboard mechanical work and they can organize contractors for anything they cannot do themselves.

They have an excellent yard for working on dinghies and powerboats, including all yacht tenders, up to 30 feet. For inflatables they have a little lift, and can swing them up, pressure spray them, and give them back clean. They fix outboards and repair inflatables efficiently and well.

They haul solid yacht tenders and power boats to 30 feet with a big fork lift. They can do all manner of repairs and refurbishing on these and have an excellent reputation.

Should you suffer an engine breakdown, they can arrange to tow you into their marina, and they sometimes have an available dinghy if yours is stolen or they are working on it when you are out at anchor.

St. Martin Shipyard is not only a haul-out yard but can do any major hull repairs in steel and glass. They do sand blasting, spray painting (in sheds), and fuel polishing. They will help you find contractors for anything they do not do.

Budget Marine has their own one stop shop for your tender or dinghy at their outboard engine and inflatable shop. They sell and do warranty services for Tohatsu and will try to help out with most other makes of outboard. They repair all brands of inflatables.

Maintech, run by Roger, is a first class fiberglass and wood shop in the St. Martin Shipyard compound. They repair all kinds of glass, from large to small, and will do serious carbon fiber and kevlar work, as well as all the laminates. They are equally good at cabinetry and woodwork, and are the people to see when you need to rebuild hatches or do other lexan work. During the hurricane season, they often undertake complete refits on boats, contracting out any work that cannot be done in their yard.

Maritime School
of the
West Indies

International Yacht Training®

MCA® Recognized Courses
Master 200 ton Coastal
Master 200 ton Offshore
Master 200 ton Ocean
STCW'95, PWC (Wave Runners),
Mega Yacht Crew, RIB/Tender/VHF
course, GMDSS, Bareboat Captain,
ISPS, Stewardess course etc.
e-mail: info@MaritimeSchool.net
Free taxi boat service to all lagoon marinas!

Maritime School of the West Indies®
St.Martin French West Indies
St.Maarten Netherlands Antilles
Phone: +599 (1-721) 5231209 or +596 696 261612

Best Boat Yard has shops in St. Martin Shipyard and Bobby's in Philipsburg. It is owned by Judith Koning, and her husband Erik is her chief welder, helped by a team of seven others. They work in metal, on engines and on hydraulics. They weld and fabricate in stainless and aluminum and have a machine shop. They make davits, bimini frames and lots of custom parts. They repair all brands of inboard engines, along with their associated gear boxes. They have an excellent hydraulic technician and can handle most hydraulic repairs. They also apply antifouling.

Nigel Pearman is the Awlgrip specialist. He has many years of working with Awlgrip, including several in the Med. He hand paints to produce a finish that is better than most spray painters and more paint ends up on the boat instead of being carried away by the wind. It has the advantage of much less masking and no chance of overspray on your stainless and lexan. He has shops both in St. Martin Shipyard and over in Bobby's MegaYard. He does an excellent job and will normally build a

cover over the boat, (included in his price) which is very competitive with the regular spray job.

Over in Lagoonies, E & MSC is an excellent metal working shop for welding and machining all metals. Peter, the owner, specializes in high quality work for large yachts, and keeps them happy by doing things fast and well.

Madco, the big chandlery on the French side, owns New Wave Yard and has a branch here that just fixes Mercury outboards and inboards.

Haresh has a custom metal workshop called Havin's. It is a short walk on the road behind Island Water World, going toward Ace Hardware. This is one of the most advanced metalworking shops in St. Martin, shiny clean with state of the art equipment, including a computer-controlled lathe, and mill, allowing complex parts to be drawn on a computer to your specs and then made with a superb polished finish. They can fabricate in just about any metal, including aluminum, stainless, and titanium. They make spiffy T-tops (aluminum and canvas marine hoods). They design their own joining parts and hinges which are far better looking than the standard. In the summer they rely on the local market and resurface engine blocks and build custom tanks. They are usually fast, reasonably priced, and do excellent work.

Over in Palapa Marina, Chris runs Palapa Shipwright. He does marine woodwork, from replanking a hull to the finest joinery, and they repair and replace many teak decks.

Kenny Awlgrip is a mobile operation. Babo and his team will come to you by land or sea. They specialize in high quality Awlgrip spray or other finishes, both paint and varnish, spray or brush. They spray and repair gel coat, and redo nonskid. They design and apply yacht names.

Transport

When you need to get a plane ticket, Travel Planners is across the road from Palapa. To rent a car, you will find many agencies close by. Ask in Simpson Bay Yacht Club, Palapa Marina, or Isle de Sol. Paradise Rental is on Airport Boulevard between Palapa and Portofino. From time to time a water taxi service is available in the evenings. Ask around or scan the radio.

You can leave your dinghy at Gateway Marina (for a fee) for picking up and dropping off at the airport. For a really short-term dinghy pick-up it may be possible to use the two small ferry docks (for a tip).

Provisioning and Yacht Agents

Much of the provisioning is done by yacht agents who not only provision, but handle all the needs of their yachts, from fuel bunkering to concierge services.

These include Kass and Lila's Dockside Management, a well-run, professional yacht and ship agency. They offer a VIP service for fuel bunkering, finding marina berths, provisioning, arranging for air charters, scuba diving, and anything else. They do both yacht and airplane customs clearance and will work out visa problems. They have a Caribbean-wide network, so can take care of yachts throughout the islands. They have a big shipping department for moving anything from a needed part to a full container and they ship many tenders. Their most accessible office is in Yacht Club Isle de Sol, with the main office in the Laguna block.

Jane Harrison's Mega Yacht Services is close by Simpson Bay Marina, opposite Z-Best. She is a full superyacht agent who does everything from full provisioning and organizing flowers to arranging car rentals or airline tickets. Jane is happy to use her local knowledge to get you the best seat in a local restaurant. She does quite a lot of crew placement work, and represents the Little Ship Company in the UK.

BWA Yachting is in Simpson Bay Marina and run by Lucille Frye and her team. It is a professional agency, with a base in Anguilla

Simpson Bay Pharmacy

VOTED BEST PHARMACIES 9 YEARS IN A ROW

Widest variety of European and U.S. prescriptions and pharmacy items

Specialized in replenishing marine medical supplies
according to international regulations

Simpson Bay Pharmacy
Welfare Road 68, Simpson Bay
St. Maarten, N.A.
Tel: (1-721) 544 3653 Fax: (1-721) 544 3654
sbp.pharmacy@gmail.com

OPEN HOURS
Mon.- Fri. 8.15am - 7.30pm
Sat. 9am - 1pm Sun. 5pm - 7pm

www.sxmpharmacy.com

RENAISSANCE ISLANDS

run by Sue Luan, and one in Antigua run by James Benson. They have bases in the USVI and USA. They have a big provisioning department as well as an excellent crew placement service with a dedicated staff. They handle everything from customs to repairs.

In Shore Support, also in Simpson Bay Marina, you will find John Sinke and Simon Manley, who used to manage Sunsail. Simon has some of their old technical team with him. This makes them strong on technical problems, including project management if a job involves more than one contractor. They spend much of their time zooming out to customers in their tender, taking care of their problems. They are sales and service agents for Williams Tenders, have their own carpet cleaning company, and they handle everything the big yachts need, from provisioning and cleaning to customs clearance and visa problems.

Palapa Marina handles everything for their yachts and this includes a full provisioning and crew agency. They keep a lot of beer and liquor in stock and even cruising yachts will find this a convenient place to buy a case

or two. They offer full provisioning for the most demanding superyachts.

International Yacht Collection, a superyacht charter brokerage and crewfinder agency, has an office in Yacht Club Isle de Sol. They open during the season (December through April) to look after their yachts in a princely fashion. They have both a private plane and seaplane to help move guests around or help provision your yacht down-island. They offer free internet access for crews from their yachts.

While all superyacht agents provision, a couple are just dedicated provisioners. Alan Dutka is probably the largest of these, and is especially geared to the superyachts. His IDS Yacht Provisioning is in Isle de Sol. He can get everything so you never need suffer a miserable night for lack of the best Russian caviar or Cuban cigars.

Provisioning

You can go shopping for your own provisions and where you choose may depend to some extent on where you are anchored. For those in Simpson Bay, the Peli Deli over the Pelican Resort is a wonderful, small supermarket, open daily from 0730 to 1930, except Sundays and holidays when they open 0800-1800. To get there, walk upstairs through the resort to the next courtyard.

Inside the lagoon, Gourmet Marché is a very nice, medium-sized supermarket behind Portofino. They have excellent fresh foods, deli meat, and fish, as well as a good variety of cans and packaged foods. They open daily 0800-2000, except Sunday, when their hours are 0900-1400. This is the most pleasant of the waterside markets.

The biggest shop with easy dinghy access is Market Garden, across the road and just a few steps north of Plaza Del Lago. They open every day from 0600-2100. They have a big produce selection of variable quality, along with good frozen meat and seafood, and all the usual departments.

Daily Extra is another fairly big supermarket. Just go to the Budget Marine Dock and walk to the big main road (Welfare Road) and it is almost opposite. They have a good selection of everything, including fresh produce, and manager Wai Tin Chaong is happy to deliver orders you cannot carry back to the nearby docks. They open daily 0800-2000 except Sunday, which is from 0800-1300. Don't leave your dinghy at the Budget Marine dock after they close because they lock their docks and gate.

Sunterra Hotel has the Royal Deli, open every day, including all holidays.

In La Palapa, Connoisseur's Duty-Free is a comprehensive wine and liquor store. Special wines are brought in on request and they stock beer and cigars. Opposite Palapa and Plaza del Lago are small supermarkets.

Le Grande Marché is about a 15-minute walk from Island Water World, on Union Road, close by the entrance of the Princess Casino driveway. This is a fabulous, very large supermarket, always spotlessly clean, with a big selection. If you are buying a lot, they will deliver your groceries to the dock when they have transport.

La Sucriere is an excellent boulangerie/pâtisserie next to Fedex. They make everything themselves, from great bread to delicious cakes and pâtisseries. You can sit and have coffee or a sandwich on their big deck over the water. They open daily 0700-1900. There is a dock of sorts you could use to pick someone up, but it is not good for leaving a dinghy.

Prime Cash and Carry is on the same road as Napa, behind Budget Marine. They open weekdays 0800-1700, Saturday 0800-1600, Sunday 0900-1300.

Two drugstores offer everything from prescription drugs to gifts, including all the regular vitamins and health products. They are happy to give free advice and are especially helpful in topping up your yacht medical stores, including emergency dental kits. The Friendly Island Drugstore is at the Cole Bay Shopping Center, near Food Center, and Simpson Bay Pharmacy is at Simpson Bay Marina. The Simpson Bay Pharmacy is open every weekday 0830-1930, Saturdays 0900 -1300, and Sundays 1700-1900.

Fun Shopping

Plaza del Lago has good modern medical and dental facilities and Inter Coiffure, where you can get anything from a hair cut to a full body massage. On the other side of the road, next to the bridge, Sunterra Resort has several gift shops.

On airport road, near La Palapa, SXM Electronics has good non-marine computers, phones and cameras. They can sometimes unlock phones. At the Pelican Resort you will find sporty shops on the waterfront and more boutiques on the next level up.

Restaurants

Bars and restaurants abound. We will mention just a few. Outside the lagoon, dinghy to the Buccaneer Beach Bar, with its 80-foot dinghy dock. This is a boater-friendly place, great for meeting people who gather at the big, round, open bar. You will probably meet the owners, Jill and Bernard. Bernard was once a yacht delivery skipper and still keeps his boat out in the bay. Their barbecue opens 1130-2200 every day, offering simple, inexpensive fare such as Caesar salad with fresh tuna, steak sandwiches, and burgers. The chef stands behind the barbecue pit and cooks everything perfectly to your

RENAISSANCE ISLANDS

Going through the causeway bridge

Chris Doyle

specifications. They have daily selected shot drinks at a dollar, entertainment on Mondays, Wednesdays, Thursdays, and Saturdays. They serve pizza from 1700-2200. They also do occasional pig roasts.

Next door, The Greenhouse, a branch of the Philipsburg restaurant, has a very lively happy hour from 1630-1900. This is a good, reliable restaurant with a big menu to suit all tastes and budgets. They open from 1100. If you are anchored outside, this is the easiest place to bring your computer for free WiFi.

If you are missing all those Caribbean dishes, the Melting Pot is farther along, just before you get to the main road. It is run by a Trini and serves rotis, callaloo and crab, and more.

Back inside the lagoon, La Palapa's Soggy Dollar is a crew bar open all day and until late in the evening. It has a nightly happy hour from 1700-1900. In the same complex, you can eat well at Rancho Grill.

The Sint Maarten Yacht Club has an Antillean-style club house and dinghy dock on the southeast side of the entrance canal, with a deck that has a perfect close-up view of superyachts passing the bridge. It is a friendly place, but please do not abuse them by leaving and locking your dinghy where it says "no dinghies." The bar and restaurant has some great food. The kitchen opens daily at 0700 for breakfast, lunch, and dinner. The menu, which goes all through the day, has everything from seared tuna and ribs to hamburgers and sandwiches. Happy hour is 1600-1800 daily, with two-for-one on beers and mixed drinks. If the underwater lights are on, check out the tarpon in the canal.

A few steps from the Yacht Club is a pizzeria and from there on down to The Boathouse, seafood restaurants pack the waterfront; take your choice. One of these, Skip Jack's, is a big fish restaurant and market, open to the sea, and they have "choose your own" live lobster.

If you have kids, or just out of interest, visit Carousel, a big round ice cream, dessert and bake shop, with a real working carousel. Local families often come in here for dessert. Open 1400 to about 2230.

Two of the best inexpensive bars, which also serve good food, are in the Portofino Marina. Dinghy right in and tie up on the north dock. Barnacles Greek Bar and Restaurant is right in front of you. Owners Kallie and Alberto have Greek, Venezuelan, and American roots. They open from 1200 -2300. The seating is communal around a big round bar, with a few extra tables on the side and there are a few tables upstairs. The 1700-1900 happy hour includes $1.25 beers. Kallie is from Greece and they have a big Greek menu, but they also do burgers and bar snacks. Cruisers gather on Wednesday nights to meet and greet, enjoy the book swap, listen to live music, and enjoy cruiser food specials. A TV keeps you in touch with the big games or special music events. They have free WiFi.

Right next door, at the other end of the same dock, is Lal's Indian Cuisine. Lal's is one of St. Martin's great and friendly little bars. Lal, a local man of Indian extraction, presides over the tiny bar, writes down take-out orders (popular with charter boat cooks between charters), and spends his time chatting with customers who sit at high tables along the patio. Sit and enjoy a drink. When you get hungry, ask Lal for a menu, and he will serve you good traditional Indian food at a very reasonable price. Check out his southern India vegetarian specials.

Plaza del Lago is home not only to Simpson Bay Marina, but several eating spots. Danny and Tamela's Zee Best is an excellent café where you can get continental or a full American breakfast from 0700, plus French pastries, crêpes, fresh juices, and a great lunch.

Jimbo's is right in the center of a shopping complex, but it has been cleverly designed to create a delightful open garden atmosphere. It is arranged around a small pool and waterfall, so when the heat of the food gets to be too much, you can jump in and swim to the other side of the bar; kids love this. They serve Tex-Mex food to the accompaniment of rock and blues music. They have a mesquite grill and offer excellent salads, enchiladas, fajitas, chimichangas, sandwiches, and burgers.

Piece of Cake is a pâtisserie, delicatessen, and ice cream parlor in one, where you can

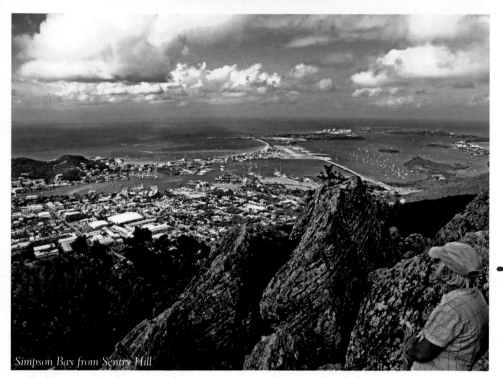

Simpson Bay from Sentry Hill

also get a good breakfast and reasonable daily specials for lunch or a light dinner, plus the best desserts and goodies. They are in Plaza del Lago, facing the road and open daily 0700-2300.

Top Carrot health food and vegetarian store has good fresh juices, sandwiches, and baked goodies, along with a new age boutique that should launch you into the twilight zone.

Head south along the shore from Simpson Bay Marina, and you will come to Simpson Bay Royal Village, with its own dinghy dock and a big collection of restaurants, ice cream parlors, and shops. Pineapple Pete's is a happening place with a cheerful staff. Domino's Pizza, which delivers to yachts in the marinas, is popular.

Over in Isle de Sol, Fat Turtle is a restaurant and hangout.

In Port de Plaisance, A Tasca is a good Portuguese restaurant open lunch and dinner except Sunday and Monday when they close. They have a happy hour from 1700-1900, and a very reasonable lunch special for about $10-12.

The Casino contains a couple of restaurants including Sushitto and Melange.

At the other end of the lagoon is Lagoonies, the favorite cruiser's hangout. Lagoonies is informal, inexpensive, and fun, and opens from 0800. The big bar is full of sailors and locals working in the yachting industry. It is a good place to meet other cruisers. They have a very popular happy hour every night from 1700-1800, except Sundays, when they close. Olivia runs the bar and restaurant which is French bistro style, reasonably priced offering a big variety for both lunch and dinner from burgers and salads up. They are music enthusiasts with local bands, currently on Tuesdays, Wednesday, Thursdays and Saturdays.

Two restaurants are in Gateway Marina, the Pink Iguana, afloat, yachtie-style and entertaining, opens about 1100, serves tapas and full meals and stays open late with entertainment a couple of times a week. The Crazy Cow onshore is, despite its name slightly more upmarket.

Ashore

Megaplex cinemas are part of a big mall with many cinemas, restaurants and more.

Port de Plaisance

Juan Pablo Piscione, an ex-sailor and a dedicated bike rider, runs Tri-Sport, where you can rent a range of bikes, from inexpensive models to high-tech mountain bikes. Upstairs in the same building is Mega Gym, the perfect place for your workout, whether you want to use their high-tech machines or take a class. Inexpensive daily rates work well for yacht crews.

Water Sports

Diving is good in this area. Dive sites include Explorers Reef in depths of 30 to 45 feet with plenty of soft corals, crinoids, and anemones. Large fish, including barracudas, rays, and groupers, are often sighted. The Maze, which varies in depth from 25 to 45 feet, has good elkhorn coral. You will likely see turtles, rays, nurse sharks, and large French angelfish. You can also visit Proselyte Reef and Cable Reef from here, described in our Philipsburg section.

The Scuba Shop, St. Martin's premier dive equipment retail, rental and service center, has their main branch in La Palapa Marina run by Kim (their other shop is in Oyster Pond). This is the best place to find snorkel and scuba equipment at great prices on the island. As authorized dealers for Scubapro, Sherwood, Mares, AquaLung and Suunto, they are a complete retail and service center with full international warranty. They are also sales and service agents for L & W and Bauer Compressors, an agency they partner with Shore Support, who can offer the same sales and service. For the adventurer and underwater photographer they carry the full SeaLife and GoPro brands along with all their accessories. They run a very professional dive equipment rental service to both charter and private boats and give their customers their own booklet to dive sites that you can visit from your yacht. Of special interest to yachts are tank adaptors for blowing up fenders or blasting bits and pieces to clean them, extra long hoses so you can leave your tank on board while you scrub the bottom, and mini tanks for cleaning and quick jobs. To make sure you are always entertained around the water, they also stock a full range of waterskis, wakeboards, paddle boards, kneeboards, towables and accessories from O'Brien Watersports. To compliment all the dive and water sports equipment, they sell some great yachting clothes, including fancy shorts and shirts from Columbia Sportswear and bathing suits, board shorts and clothing from O'Neill. As yachties themselves, the father and daughter team have made their reputation by offering excellent service and advice to the yachting community.

Dive Safaris work with Scuba Shop in the same complex (ask for their desk in Scuba Shop). Dive Safaris are the ones who will take you out diving and snorkeling. They offer full PADI certifications up to divemaster. They have full nitrox facilities, can do both hydro-testing and annual visual inspections on your tanks, and will fill tanks. They can also test many cooking gas tanks.

Luciana and Jeferson run Ocean Explorers, a good, informal combination dive shop and store on Simpson Bay Beach, outside the bridge. (If walking, it is on the beach opposite the road to Isle de Sol.) Ask for their map showing all the diving and snorkeling sites in the area. They have a well-stocked retail shop full of diving gear and accessories, plus t-shirts, and a big selection of underwater video camera housings, and some of the prices are great. The whole crew is into underwater photography and video, so if you are an enthusiast, this is the place to come. If you dive with them, they can make a video of your dive. They fill tanks

and frequently rent equipment to charter yachts. If the weather is calm, ask about One Step Beyond, their hidden bluewater dive. Depths vary from 45 to 90 feet over a large rambling reef where there are hundreds of fearless fish.

The Pelican Resort can arrange sports fishing, has a dive shop, and is the place to take the ferry Edge over to Saba.

FROM SIMPSON BAY TO POINTE BASSE TERRE

You can follow this coast quite closely, passing white sand beaches, and cliffs adorned with condominiums and hotels. Maho Bay is right at the beginning of the runway, anchoring here is both forbidden and unwise, and the "No Anchoring" area is buoyed. However, if you go by land there is a great beach bar where you can take a drink and where it feels like the wheels of incoming planes will part your hair.

In light settled weather, you can get temporary anchorage behind the dramatic white cliff at the eastern end of Anse Longue. The beach here is superb and it is the home of La Samanna, one of St. Maarten's most expensive and prestigious resorts. If you decide to visit, you may want to wear something more

RENAISSANCE ISLANDS

elegant than shorts, t-shirt, and flip-flops.

Porto Cupecoy, described under *Simpson Bay*, is inside the lagoon here.

NORTH COAST — WEST TO EAST

When approaching from the south, give both Pointe Basse Terre and Pointe Plum a few hundred yards clearance. Steep seas can build up off Pointe Basse Terre, and there is a shoal with a rock awash that extends out from Pointe Plum. The water is 18 to 25 feet deep up to a mile and a half off most of St. Martin's north coast. This makes for fine sailing in bright turquoise and green water. The coast from Pointe Plum to Marigot is fairly clear of rocks and a few hundred yards offshore clears all dangers. The coast from Marigot to Pointe Molly Smith is similarly clear of dangers. However, Pointe Molly Smith not only has rocks close to shore, but there is a reef with a small, 5-foot patch on

it that lies about 150 yards out to sea in a northeasterly direction. Either stay half a mile off this point or, if the light conditions are good, pass inside the reef. There is 19 feet of water inside it. To the north of Grand Case, you can see the 100-foot Rocher Créole off Bell Point. Pass outside this rock. In calm conditions with good light, you can explore the inside passage, where there is 8-12 feet. As you go north of Bell Point, pass outside Marcel Rock.

Marigot

Marigot is the capital of French St. Martin. It has the feeling of a picturesque and fashionable Riviera seaport, with an attractive waterfront market and handsome streets, bursting at the seams with boutiques and restaurants. Although the anchorage has lots of yachts, there is always room. The currency is the Euro, generally worth somewhat more than a dollar. Some shops and restaurants give equivalence, regardless of the rate, often a great bargain for those

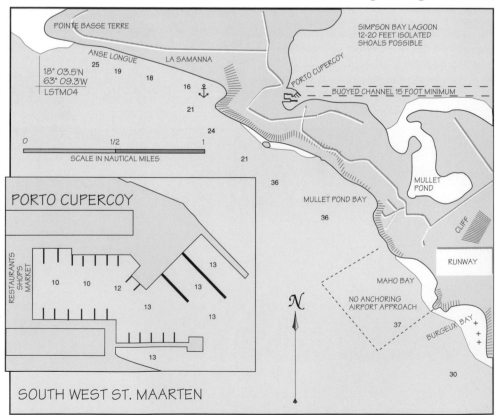

TOBY SARL TIME OUT BOATYARD & MARINA

Tél: (590)590520288

Follow Us On Facebook
www.facebook.com/timeoutboatyard

timeoutboat@hotmail.com

and Skype (tobysxm)

Stay with us in a good atmosphere on the yard or at our dock.
You will find all your needs.
Fair prices, well located near town and groceries.

SANDY GROUND BRIDGE - ST.MARTIN

with dollars. Marigot has its own share of Simpson Bay Lagoon and cruisers have favored the French side in recent years because if you check in with Marina Port La Royale, the fees are much lower than on the Dutch side. There are excellent technical services, whose pricing is geared more to the cruiser than the professional superyacht.

Navigation

The approach is wide open and free from dangers during the day. At night you need to miss some unlit steel buoys large enough to sit on after they have sunk your boat. One of these is a mooring buoy at 18° 04.88'N, 63° 06.35'W. On the other side of the bay, an unlit IALA buoy marks a 15-foot shoal at 18° 05.26'N, 63° 05.67'W.

The water starts shelving a long way offshore, but you can carry 8 or 9 feet right in close to town. Keep clear of the buoyed ferry channel. The wind can change here, so leave plenty of swinging room. During the winter months a swell or strong northeaster can occasionally make it uncomfortable to untenable. A green light flashes on the entrance to Marina Fort St. Louis, and a white light flashes on Port de Glaisbay. The fancy sector light to the north of the marina does not always work.

You can choose to go into Marina Fort Louis (VHF: 16), which has all-round protection and is out of any swells.

The entrance into the lagoon, is through Sandy Ground opening bridge, just west of the little cliff to the west of the town and hotels. The bridge opens Monday to Saturday at 0900, 1430 and 1730; on Sundays and holidays at 0900 and 1730. Marina Port La Royale, (VHF: 16, T: 0590 87 20 43) can give you updates on Sandy Ground Bridge. There is a large shoal area on the west side of the channel entrance. (See our Baie de Marigot sketch chart.) In northerly swells, steep waves build up outside this area, so you should approach the entrance from the east (town-side).

The channel has been dredged to 9 feet, and it should not silt much for the next few years. Outside the channel are lots of shoals and finding an anchoring spot takes good light and local knowledge. When you come in through the bridge, aim for a round aerial on the hills ahead. Keep going until you are lined up with the channel. Most buoys are currently missing but you tell when you are

Marigot Market

Chris Doyle

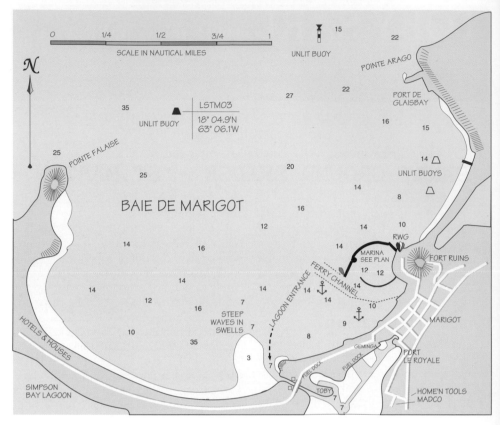

in the channel by the boats anchored on both sides.

To get into Chantier Naval, T.O.B.Y. (Time-Out) and the fuel dock, just follow the headland around, staying about 100 feet offshore. You have to go farther off just before the entrance, and then it is deep to go in. You need good enough light to be able to eyeball it.

Shoals separate the French and Dutch sides of the lagoon, but a channel takes you through. The channel's minimum depth in the center is about 6.5 feet. Leave the red buoys to port going to the Dutch side. Unfortunately, only the far end red buoy is left, so you need local help or a lot of dinghy work to do this without grounding.

Port de Glaisbay is a new commercial deepwater port in the northeast part of Baie de Marigot.

Regulations

Clearance is by do-it-yourself computer terminals. There is a $5 Eu clearance fee.

If you are going to be in the anchorage out in the bay, port authority like you to clear with them, as they charge port fees. If you are going into the lagoon or going elsewhere, clear in with Regine at the capitainerie in Port La Royale where port fees do not apply. Marina Port St. Louis clears their customers and can help others out of hours.

The port authority is in a small office in the ferry dock complex. They open weekdays from 0800-1200, and 1400-1600; Saturday, 0800-1200. While Marigot is the only port of entry, they do not really mind if you take a taxi to clear from one of the other French anchorages. If you are staying in Marigot Bay (this does not apply to inside the lagoon), you pay a fee depending on your boat length.

The initial administrative fee, including first day's anchoring charges, excluding clearance are:

8-13 meters, 20 Eu; 13-18 meters, 30 Eu; 18-23 meters, 40 Eu; 23-28 meters, 50 Eu; 28-33 meters, 60 Eu; 33-38 meters, 70 Eu; 38-43 meters, 100 Eu; 43-50 meters, 120 Eu;

"Voted one of the best laundries in the Caribbean"

Shrimpy's Laundry

E-mail: shrimpysxm@gmail.com
www.shrimpys-saintmartin.com
TEL: 0590 690 271 668
CELL: 1-721 580 0861

T.O. Stützpunkt für
St. Maarten

& Yacht Support

46 Rue Du Morne Rond, Sandyground 97150 Marigot, Saint Martin FWI

Shrimpy's T-shirt for sale

WiFi
Airport Shuttle
Book & DVD Sales
Cruisers Laundry
Second Hand
Marine Mart
Hull Cleaning

Now offering long and short term mini storage facilities and a limited number of crew quarters

"Cruisers Net Monday to Saturday on channel 10 at 7.30 am"

50-75 meters, 130 Eu; over 75 meters, 150 Eu. Thereafter, non-resident boats pay 0.25 Eu per meter per day up to day 3. From day 4 on, they pay 0.35 Eu per meter. Residents pay 0.13 Eu per meter per day.

One garbage depot is just outside the Marina Fort St. Louis and another just outside the Port La Royale Marina to the southwest.

Communications

The easiest thing is to take your computer down to Shrimpy's. He has a comfortable yachty hangout and WiFi at the best prices. The Morning Net on VHF: 10 is at 0730, and is run by Mike from Shrimpy's. While there, pick up one of his Lagoon charts, made with cruiser soundings. These are also available in many stores (for $1 for charity).

If you are out in the bay, you may be able to pick up Orange or Marina Fort Louis WiFi. Marina Fort Louis also has an email station, as does Marina Port La Royale. Inside the lagoon, Chantier Naval, T.O.B.Y. (Time-Out), Polypat, and Geminga have WiFi to cover their yards. Signals out in the lagoon seem poor. Many bars also offer WiFi.

General Yacht Services
Marinas and Haul out

Marina Fort Louis (VHF: 16) is run by Samagest and managed by Herve and all the staff speak good English. This marina has the advantage over Simpson Bay of being in the heart of an attractive town and having no bridge to bother with. The outer wall gives protection from seas all around. This marina has 185 berths with water, WiFi, and electricity (110-220-380-volts, single and 3-phase, 60 cycle). They also have showers, toilets, an email station, and communications, including courier. You will find a laundry and laundromat, a full provisioning service, and a fuel dock that sells ice. There is room for many small yachts and for about 17 super-yachts of up to about 200 feet. The controlling factor is usually depth, which the marina conservatively rates at 11 feet. Call

RENAISSANCE ISLANDS

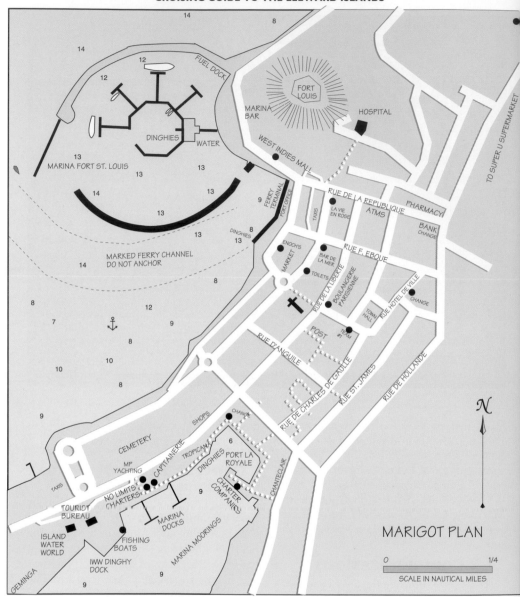

MARIGOT PLAN

0   1/4

SCALE IN NAUTICAL MILES

the marina as you arrive and they will come with a tender to help you tie your mooring line and get you into the dock. Access to the marina is by a magnetic card.

Those anchored out can get a card and use the marina facilities for 100 Eu a year, which includes a 30 Eu card deposit that is refunded when you return it. This enables you to leave your dinghy at their guarded dinghy dock, a big plus in a town where dinghies are stolen fairly frequently. You can use the marina facilities, although some

charges apply.

The marina helps organize Le Course d'Alliance, three days of racing in November, going from Marigot to St. Barts and Anguilla, before returning, and is home to Aquatic Adventure Diving. If you just want water, you can come in on the entrance dock outside the office.

Much of Marigot's waterfront is a long dock. The ferries and day charter boats use its northern end; dinghies should be left at the southern end. (Lock them well and do

Sailmakers

New sails
Repairs

26, Rue Lady Fish
Sandy Ground
St. Martin
Tél : 590-590 87.06.04

email: voilecaraibe.stmartin@orange.fr
www.voile-caraibe-incidences.fr

incidences

not leave them for long.) You can dinghy into the lagoon and park at the dinghy dock in Port La Royale. This is convenient for the tourist office, and IWW, which are a short walk west of the dinghy dock.

Chantier Naval, T.O.B.Y. (Time-Out), is in Sandy Ground, on the north side of the entrance channel, inside the lagoon. This slightly disorderly but cheerful and friendly place is owned by Englishman Michael Butterfield and managed by Keith Ellison. They have a stern-to (with moorings) docking facility on the north side, offering water and 220/380-volt 3-phase electricity. There is a large area for haul out and repair. They haul boats up to 18-tons, using a 65-ton crane. Hot showers, washing machines, toilets, email service, and storage lockers are available. Free WiFi covers the yard. You can do your own work or use contractors (no fees).

Chantier Naval, T.O.B.Y. (Time-Out), has a marine flea market on the first Saturday of each month, starting about 0830. If you have a lot of old gear to sell, you can get a stall for free, but you must book it in advance. Otherwise, come see what others have to sell. The market takes on a carnival atmosphere, with the addition of bars and roadside barbecues.

Jean Claude, the prior manager, is the coxswain and vice president for the French SNSM and the rescue boat is berthed at the marina. For rescue call MRCC in Martinique, (0596-17-92-92), VHF: 16.

Polypat Caraibes is a haul out yard on the south side of the bridge, run by Fred Wojcik, who, despite his name, is a Frenchman who speaks excellent English. They haul with a 60-ton crane, which makes removing masts

RENAISSANCE ISLANDS

MARIGOT BAY, MARINA FORT ST. LOUIS PHOTO

easy. Your crew can do the work themselves, or the yard can do it for you, but if you want to bring in outside contractors, you need to discuss it with Fred. Polypat is excellent at painting and fiberglass repairs. They are registered as a Gelshield agent for osmosis treatment. The yard has showers, toilets, 220-volt electricity, water to all the boats, WiFi, and 24-hour security. Polypat is an agent for Fontaine Pajot, Catana and Beneteau, and will take care of all their problems. They also agents for, and install, Flexiteak (decking).

Marina Port La Royale (VHF: 16) is well protected and welcomes visitors. You will usually find a place, but call Regine, the captain, to make arrangements. They take about 150 boats, including about 18 on the new outer dock and 50 bow and stern rental moorings. The maximum draft is 9 feet. They sell ice and water and have electricity on the docks (220-volt/60 cycles, with 110/220/280 3-phase, 60 cycle on the new dock). They offer showers and a laundry and are open Mondays, 0830-1300, 1430-1730; Tuesday to Friday 0830-1730; Saturday 0900-1200, 1500-1700. Marina Port La Royale is home to several charter companies and brokerage houses, most a few steps from the marina office. As part of a renovation, the port office is moving over next to No Limits Charters.

Geminga is a pleasant haul out yard just southwest of the Port La Royale Marina. They haul yachts with an 18-ton trailer (good for cats and monohulls) and can store about 200 boats. You can work yourself, bring in help, or they can find contractors to help you (no fee). They also have a 15-boat docking facility with water and electricity (220 volt).

JMC Marina and Boatyard is a little farther down the road. They haul boats with a 70-ton marine hoist that takes up to 23-foot beam, and they have a 135-ton crane in the yard. They insist that masts come out for storage, that yachts are insured, and in the summer they dig boats into the sand for security. They have a small docking facility. You can do your own work, or bring in contractors (no fee).

General Yacht Services
Fuel, Water, Gas

You can get drinking water at the DP fuel dock in the channel or in either marina. Cadisco sells non-drinking (well) water.

On the outside fuel is available from Yani's DP fuel dock in the canal (open every day 0700-1800, except Christmas, New Years Day and May 1), and Marina Fort St. Louis. On the inside, Cadisco has easy access and Boat Services' fuel dock is to the north of Toby and run by David and Virginie. They open daily 0700-1800 and have 9 feet of water at their dock.

L'Ile Marine takes gas bottles to be filled before 0900 on Wednesdays and IWW Marigot takes them on Fridays.

General Yacht Services
Brokers, Boat Care, Services

Mike and Sally's Shrimpy's is in a perfect spot on the north side of the canal, on the sea side of the French bridge. They have an excellent dinghy dock and this is the best place to leave your dinghy when you go to Simply Supermarket. Cruisers can hang out here, eat toasted sandwiches, drink coffee, beer, wine, and soft drinks. It is a friendly place. Mike does the Morning Net, knows most things about St. Martin, and is the Trans-Ocean rep, so he is the best person for advice. Bring in your dirty clothes for Sally's Laundry, which is a big operation with many machines. They have an inexpensive WiFi and a bring-and-buy shop for second-hand boat bits, as well as the famous Shrimpy t-shirts. Mike refurbishes and sells quite a few outboards and second-hand dinghies. During the season they open daily from 0730 till after the sun goes down.

Next to the Port La Royale Capitainerie, Anyway Marine Charter Company is a sales and service agent for Lagoon, Nautitech, Grand Soleil, and Teba. They can sell you one of these, or if you have one, they can sort out any problems. They have a charter fleet, mainly catamarans, both bareboat and with skipper. They sell new and second hand yachts – mainly the brands they represent. If

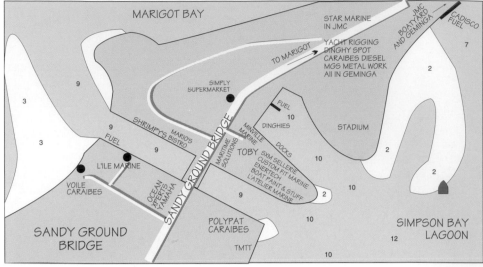

you buy a suitable new boat, they can charter it for you.

Pascal's Rêve Marine can rent you a little run-about; he has a good range on hand, some parked right in front of his office.

On the other side of the Marina, Emeric Monnier has a charter company, called MP Yachting, which charters power boats by the day. He is the sales and service agent for Jeanneau and will take care of all their problems.

Next door, No Limits Charters is run by Jan Roosens. Apart from charter, they offer yacht management, large yacht brokerage, and a maritime school where you can get an IYT Master's Certificate up to 200 tons. Lots of the superyacht crew train here. One of the instructors is a friend of mine from way back, Master Mariner Mel. Along with this is a crew placement service, handy once they have qualified you.

Jan also runs Yacht Assistance, a full superyacht support service that handles everything from customs clearance and technical support to provisioning. Jan is a photographer and does most yacht shots, from interior to aerial.

Marina Fort Louis, also offers yacht support.

Chandlery

Marigot has good chandleries. The new Island Water World chandlery is next to the tourist office in the lagoon. They have a small floating dinghy dock in the fishing complex in the lagoon behind the tourist office. For now you have to walk round the tourist office, but a more direct path is planned. The store is quite large, on two floors with lots of display space, and anything in the catalog can be quickly brought over. Managing director Valerie LeRoy is very helpful and she keeps a small sub office in Marina Fort Louis, and runs a back up communication service for those going on long passages.

Right at the entrance to the canal, with access to the water, is L'Ile Marine, a full chandlery shop, with a good little dinghy dock. They work with Budget Marine and can quickly bring in anything from the catalog. In addition to Budget Marine stock, they are agents for Maxsea software, Dessalator watermakers, Iridium Communications, and are agents for Yanmar sales and parts. They carry many brands of antifouling and all the French emergency equipment, including CE certified fire extinguishers.

Madco is big and heavily geared to fishing and sports boating, with yacht gear as well, and they are a major Mercury agent. Upstairs is a department geared to swimming pool and garden equipment. Madco is good for fishing gear up to a professional level, and you can find some kayaks and other crafts. They carry an excellent fastener section, all in 316 stainless, including new kinds of hinges and hex head fasteners, plus you will

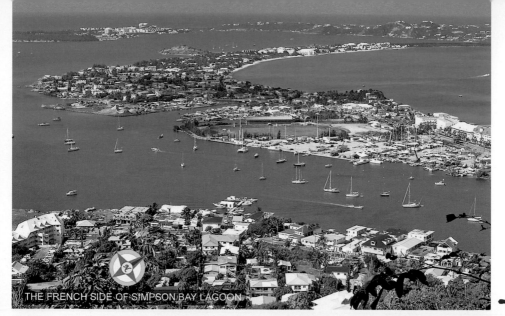

THE FRENCH SIDE OF SIMPSON BAY LAGOON

find general boating accessories and some yacht gear, including Plastimo. To get there, start at the Marina Port La Royale office and head away from the water to the road. Turn right, and when you come to a big shopping area, you will see it down a street to your right.

Close to Madco, but out on the main road, is Home 'n Tools, a large DIY, houseware, lumber, and hardware store, perfect for those with a project. They stock exterior grade ply, cut to any square size you need.

In Chantier Naval, T.O.B.Y. (Time-Out), Boat Paint and Stuff, is in a big building on the waterfront. They are PG Amercoat agents and they sell marine paints, antifoulings, resins and cloth, Nidacore, and Copper Coat, which you can do yourself. They carry sanding disks, all manner of painting tools, and even a few chandlery items.

Team Number One, opposite the Town Hall, is a water sports shop, with fishing, snorkeling, and diving gear.

Next to Chantier Naval, T.O.B.Y. (Time-Out), Tony Parrondo's Minville Marine sells commercial fishing gear and has a small dinghy dock by his office you can use for the supermarket. He runs a haul out yard for power boats for work and storage. It would be suitable for any size yacht tender.

Technical Yacht Services
Sailmakers, Canvas, Cushions

Voile Caraibe is a large, full-service sail loft that sells new sails of the Incidences brand. They are part of a Caribbean chain, with another store in Martinique and can tackle any kind of repair job or order you a new sail. They do canvas and cushion work, as well as make biminis or cushion covers. It is possible to order a sail in Martinique and

CARIBBEAN CHANDLERIES

L'ILE MARINE

BUDGET MARINE CARIBBEAN CHANDLERIES

Budget Marine's "French Connection"
Large selection of marine products. Visit store by land or by sea.
Ample customer parking and dinghy dock.
English and French spoken.

L'Ile Marine
Sandy Ground Bridge
Rue Lady Fish
Saint Martin

MARIGOT

BUDGET MARINE

Open: Monday - Friday
8am - 12pm & 2pm - 5pm
Saturday 8am - 12pm

T: (590) 05 90 29 08 60   www.budgetmarine.com
F: (590) 05 90 29 08 96   lile@budgetmarine.com

Marigot Canal

Chris Doyle

pick it up here, or the other way around. They are behind L'Ile Marine.

At SXM Sellerie in Chantier Naval, T.O.B.Y. (Time-Out), you will find Laurent who does canvas and interior upholstery work, as well as awnings and biminis.

Technical Yacht Services
Mechanics, Metalwork, Electronics

Sandy Ground is the main area for yacht services in Marigot. Most of them are near the opening bridge. It is easiest to visit by dinghy.

In Chantier Naval, T.O.B.Y. (Time-Out), Herve has the electronics shop Marine Elec. He is Raymarine certified and can fix all your boat electronic or electrical problems, along with the electrical side of your generator.

Nearby, Vincent at Electricien Marine is a good electrician who will work with all boat systems.

Cyberman (Tom) works mainly with cruisers and sorts out all their computer/smart phone problems, both hardware and software.

Technical Yacht Services
Mechanics, Metalwork,

In Geminga you will find an excellent diesel shop called Caraibes Diesel Services, owned by Erwan. They are full agents for sales, after sales service, and repair for Volvo and Caterpillar, and keep spares in stock, along with consumables like oil and filters. Erwan and his team will work on all sizes and brands of diesel and will soon get your engine purring again.

In T.O.B.Y. (Time-Out), FDM, run by Fabrice, is a good general mechanical shop that can fix both inboard and outboard motors.

SXM Marine Diesel Service is in Marina Port La Royale. This is a branch of a US shop and geared for the larger yachts as agents for MTU, Detroit Diesel, and Rolls Royce.

Just north, in part of the Polypat compound, sometimes amid piles of sand, is Frank's TMTT. This includes a first-rate metalworking shop run by Englishman Terry, who will fix anything metal you break or bend. He welds aluminum and stainless and has a machine shop. He does mast work and fixes many pushpits. If you need work onboard, he has access to a private dock where you can arrange with him to come alongside. TMTT also dredges and builds docks.

Technical Yacht Services
Refrigeration

Ener Tech is a refrigeration and air-conditioning business headed by Edward Kalna in Chantier Naval, T.O.B.Y. (Time-Out). Edward tells me he got his experience in the navy. He can pull apart and rebuild all makes of pump, including March/Scott and Calpeda.

Technical Yacht Services
Fiberglass and Painting

In Chantier Naval, T.O.B.Y. (Time-Out), Custom Fit Marine is run by Thomas, originally from South Africa, who spent some years in Trinidad building boats. He is on the canal side of the yard by Boat Paint and Stuff with a dock, very handy for onboard work. He can do all kinds of glass work, painting, gel coat repair, electrics, plumbing, custom carpentry, and he will reglaze and seal those crazed old hatches.

Star Marine, run by Yvon Mathieu, is in JMC boatyard. Yvon speaks English and does all manner of fiberglass repairs, including really large ones. He has a machine for osmosis and he sprays topside paints and antifouling. He also has several molds and builds runabout powerboats.

In Geminga, Pascal Register is the glass man and he does most of the structural repairs on boats in the yard.

Remi at SMB fixes glass and gelcoat, spray paints, varnishes, and puts on antifouling. They do a lot of work for the superyachts and work in all the marinas.

Technical Yacht Services
Rigging, Life Raft and Dinghy Repair, Carpentry

Life Rafts Etc. is a SOLAS compliant service station in St. Martin for several brands of life rafts, including Plastimo, Zodiac, RVD, Avon, Revere and Bombard. They are the first in the Caribbean to get certification inspecting Zodiac RIBO (the lifeboat ribs). They also sell and rent life rafts and service life jackets.

Owner Anke Roosens, a professional commercial captain, has a drop off point in Marigot (The Maritime School) and can arrange pick up in Anguilla, St. Barts, and most St. Martin anchorages. Their shop is in Cul de Sac in the north of St. Martin and they invite you to be present when they service your raft so you can check it out and ask questions. It is best to make an initial contact by e-mail: Info@LifeRaftsEtc.com, and Anke will get back to you within 24 hours. You can try calling Anke on her cell, 0690 74 43 30 or at 721-586-0060, but she is quite often out of range.

Patrick is the rigger. His shop, which is in Geminga, is called Yacht Rigging, and he has a very professional, custom-designed workshop. Patrick can ably handle all rigging problems. He is an agent for ACMO, Z-Spars, Facnor, Profurl and Arimar. He can swage rigging to 16mm.

In the same compound, you will find Patrick's Dinghy Spot. He repairs all inflatable craft and sells and is an agent for Sacs and Kardis. He can sell you a Yamaha outboard to power it.

Just outside Chantier Naval, T.O.B.Y. (Time-Out), on the left as you face the road, is a workshop called Maritime Solutions run by Lindsey James. Lindsey has collected a wealth of knowledge over his life and can work on any boat project, from carpentry, glass work, and painting to engine work and

Caraïbes Diesel Services

phone : (+590) 590 870 373
www.caraibesdiesel.com

Marine engineering / Parts and lubricants supply

Chantier Naval Géminga - Marigot
97150 Saint Martin FWI

Official dealer for Saint Martin-Sint Maarten

CATERPILLAR® **VOLVO PENTA**

plumbing. He is ideal for a major refit, tends to work on largish jobs, and he often gets booked up well in advance, so contact him early.

Away from the waterfront, down behind Super U Supermarket, Philippe Caamano has an excellent woodworking shop, called Caamano Marine. He has good machinery, a computerized design office, and a special dust-free varnishing and finishing room. He can do everything from interior design to beautiful cabinetry and veneer work. He specializes in marine work and can satisfy the most demanding superyacht customers. You do not have to drop by, he visits yachts all over Simpson Bay; just give him a call.

Provisioning

Yacht Assistance, run by Jan Roosens, offers a full provisioning service for the large yachts, as does Marina Fort St. Louis.

The market is always colorful, with numerous stalls selling local handicrafts. Wednesdays and Saturdays are the main food market days, when fruit and fish sellers arrive from Dominica, and the waterfront is crowded with shoppers looking for bargains.

Simply (an Auchan supermarket) is the easiest solution for a large shopping. Leave your dinghy at Shrimpy's or Minville marine. This is a large supermarket, good enough for a full provisioning for most yachts, with a big selection of duty-free liquors and tobacco, fresh produce, seafood, meat, delicatessen items, and ice, as well as all the staples and household things. They open 0730-2200, on Sunday 0800-2100. They have a café just outside.

Super U, on the outskirts of town heading toward Grand Case, is another, somewhat fancier, huge supermarket with everything for a major provisioning. It opens daily from 0900-2000, except Sunday when they close at 1300. It is within walking distance of the waterfront, but when you return loaded, you will want to ask the receptionist by the cash register to telephone for a taxi. In the same compound is a Cash and Carry for bulk buying.

Behind Minville Marine, Michael Minville has a fishing complex. For boats going out, he sells baitfish and ice, for those

www.GalleriesJeanJarreau.com

needing fish, he sells both fish and lobster and has some huge freezers.

On the opposite side of the lagoon, if you walk from Marina Royale a few steps towards Madco, West Indies Lobster sells lobster from Saba.

Fun Shopping

When quality counts, Marigot is St. Martin's premiere shopping area. You can buy anything here, from an inexpensive, brightly-colored t-shirt to chocolates that cost more than precious stones. The shops are cool and you are far from milling cruise ship passengers. If you start in the main harbor, your first stop should be the fancy West Indies Mall, with all its stores and restaurants. Stroll up Rue de La Republique, renown for its jewelry and precious ornaments. Next, wander down Rue Hotel de Ville and onto Rue Charles de Gaulle, where you can augment your wardrobe. Wander down and explore both sides of the marina, where there are many striking clothes shops. Inside the marina is an area where vendors set up stands selling souvenirs.

In the same area as Madco, @utodeal is a big computer store with lots of computers and accessories.

You will find plenty of ATMs on Rue de la Republique and many places all over to change money, though if you have US dollars, this is unnecessary, as everyone accepts the greenback.

Restaurants

If shopping hasn't given you an appetite, try walking up to Fort Louis. It is an attractive old ruin with a few cannons and a bird's-eye view of the marina, the bay, and Simpson Bay Lagoon. A pathway leads up just across the road from La Vie en Rose.

Eating out is a pleasure in Marigot, well known for its restaurants, which span the range from cheap and cheerful bistros to gourmet wallet busters. Walking and looking is part of the fun. I mention just a few.

In a corner overlooking the Marina Fort Louis, Yacht Club is a bar and restaurant open Monday to Saturday from about 1000 to 2200. It has a pleasant open ambience looking over the marina. They serve Italian food and in the evenings, as well as their regular menu, they serve sushi and fire up a pizza oven.

The market area includes a large building that houses many worker-style cafés and bars, offering a local Créole lunch very inexpensively. A particular favorite seems to be Enoch's, which faces the waterfront.

While on the cheap and cheerful, The Epi Center, near the post office, is a boulangerie/pâtisserie with shady pavement seating and a range of sandwiches and pastries. Visit for a breakfast of fresh coffee and croissants, and walk home with some excellent bread.

For a touch more style for breakfast or lunch (closed Sunday), La Carambole on Rue de Charles de Gaulle is an attractive new restaurant, moderately priced with daily specials.

For a special night out, with good French food, La Vie en Rose, looking out over the water has first-rate French cuisine and attentive service. It is a delightful place for coffee or lunch where you can sit outside and watch life go by in the best French manner.

Two interesting restaurants are in the canal at Sandy Ground (tie your dinghy outside). Andrea from Italy (ex-skipper) and Claudia from Dominica (a great hostess) run the Bad Monkey, a reasonably-priced, pleasant Italian restaurant which is closed Sunday but otherwise open lunch and dinner. On weekdays they offer a daily lunch special (food and drink) for 10 Eu. On Wednesday nights they have music.

Next door and way upmarket is Mario's Bistro. It opens at 1630, is fancy and excellent. They serve contemporary French cuisine. It is popular so you will absolutely need to make a reservation.

The West Indies Mall tends to have a couple of fancy and not too-expensive restaurants. The names are apt to change.

Port La Royale Marina is surrounded by restaurants that look out on the boats, and are open for lunch and dinner. The choice is vast and names do change a bit. Among those that are good value with very nice food and that have been around a while are Tropicana, Café de Paris, and La Belle Epoch. If you are going to be in Marigot for lunch, start with Tropicana. At the back, the Flibuste is the local hangout.

If you need some nights off the boat, you do not have to go ashore. La Case a l'Eau is a very comfortable, friendly floating guest house with three rooms. It is normally anchored by Witches Tit on the French side. It's owned by a cruising couple who lost their boat due to a failed park mooring in a storm in Ile Fourchue.

Water Sports

Aquatic Adventure Diving is in Marina Fort St. Louis. They will take you for a good dive, or fix your underwater problems.

Friars Bay

Friars Bay, just before Grand Case, is a popular day-time anchorage, with a fair beach and active beach bar. The approach is easy; just head in and anchor in about 16 feet of water. Avoid this place in northerly or northwesterly swells.

Grand Case

Baie Grand Case is a long sweeping beach-fronted bay, and the quiet town, built along the beach, is the gastronomic center of St. Martin, so be prepared to eat out. The anchorage is generally good for overnighting, though occasionally rolly. Grand Case is home to the French-side airport. For all its peaceful appearance, dinghies get stolen and boats robbed from time to time. So take precautions.

Navigation

At the southwestern end of the bay, about 150 yards northeast of Pointe Molly Smith, is a reef about 5 feet deep. Stay at least half of a mile off Pointe Molly Smith. Alternatively, in good light, you can go between the reef and the headland. There is 19 feet of water inside the reef, but note that there are rocks close to the headland.

The northern end of the bay gets some protection from Rocher Créole, a

GRAND CASE

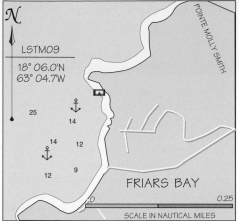

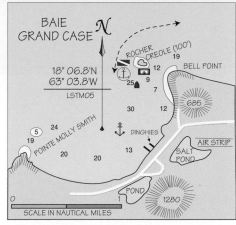

RENAISSANCE ISLANDS

conspicuous rock island some 100 feet high. There are underwater rocks close to the island. It is best to pass outside Rocher Créole, though you can find a passage some 12 feet deep between Rocher Créole and Bell Point, which is quite navigable except in bad swells. The bottom shelves to depths of 8 to 9 feet just before the passage on the Grand Case side, limiting the depth of boats that can use it. Anchor anywhere off the town docks in sand and weed.

For diving and snorkeling on Rocher Créole, use the marine park moorings. They have four yellow ones marked for 50 feet or 15 tons, and three white "dinghy only" buoys. The "diving only" buoys are for the dive shops.

Communications & Services

The dinghy dock is convenient, if dilapidated. Dinghy thefts and worse occasionally happen, so take the normal precautions. Glass-bottom boats sometimes use this dock and you need to tie up out of their way. This is not usually a problem in the evenings. The place to dump garbage is in the car park opposite Calmos Café. Calmos Café, along with many of the other restaurants, has free WiFi. You can top up on provisions or buy ice from any of the supermarkets.

Ashore

Grand Case has a long street of gaily-painted houses, most of them restaurants. Many are elegant and serve first-rate French cuisine; others are cute and inexpensive. All the restaurants have menus posted outside, and half the fun is to get up an appetite by reading them while walking along. Nighttime is warm and welcoming, people stroll around, shops are open.

Cheap and cheerful local bars look out over the sea between the two docks. Their barbecues go full time serving barbecued food

Local bars between the docks   Chris Doyle

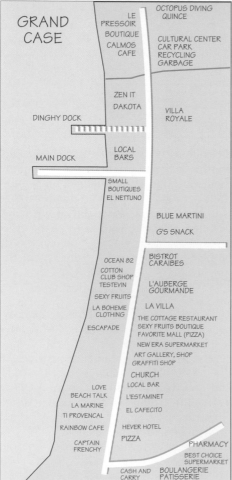

with plenty of beer to wash it down. They specialize in spare ribs, but also have fish, chicken, conch, and sometimes lobster. An excellent night to come is Tuesday for much of the season when they have "harmony nights." At around 1800 they close off the street, bring out the music, vendors line the streets, and the whole town becomes an informal party. This augments rather than detracts from the fine dining.

Since this is the area for fine food, you may choose to go up-market. If you stick with the restaurants that have been around a while, you will be happy – the reputation of the whole town depends on it. L'Auberge Gourmand, Testevin, and Ti Provencal, among others, or try one of the fancy new ones like Ocean 82.

The best beach hangout is the Calmos Café, run by Alex. It's open every day from 1000 until late and serves food from 1100 to 2230, with tables on the beach, facing the sea. They have free WiFi, which you might pick up out at anchor (you will have to ask for the password). Alex has beach chairs and shades, and prepares good salads, sandwiches, spare ribs, and local dishes. The barbecue runs most of the day to grill fresh fish and meat. It has a good atmosphere at night if you are going for the less expensive, simpler food, and, in season, he has live bands twice a week; currently Thursdays for Latin music, and Sundays reggae or jazz.

If you wake up the next morning with a terrible hangover, having spent all your money, you will be happy to hear that there is a large pharmacy in Grand Case that takes credit cards.

If one of your crew wakes up early in the morning, send him down to one of the boulangeries (south end of the street) to buy fresh croissants and pain au chocolat.

Shoppers will find a row of vendors close to the docks, and many fancy little stores all along the main street that specialize in art, elegant handicrafts, and clothing.

If you need a massage or some body work, Soothing Moments Spa is in Favorite Mall, and Hever Hotel has a spa.

Water Sports

Snorkeling and diving are good around Rocher Créole. In most conditions you can pick up a park mooring on the south side of Rocher Créole. Best treat this as a daytime spot only. If you start at the northwest point of Rocher Créole, there is good snorkeling and diving around its northern end. Rocher Créole tumbles down into the sea and gives way to a large area of boulders at 33 feet. These are covered with both hard and soft corals and there are many small reef fish, including a giant school of sergeant majors that live on bread handouts from glass-bottom boats. Jacks and larger fish are often seen close by. There is a dive shop at the northern end of Grand Case called Octopus. They can refill your tanks and, if you don't have your own gear, you can join them on a dive at 0900 or 1400.

Anse Marcel and Anse Marcel Marina

Anse Marcel is a small, well-indented bay with a beach, two big hotels, and the all-inclusive Riu Palace Resort. Riu owns Marina Anse Marcel. The outer bay anchorage is very pretty, with a white sand beach and turquoise water. Pelicans often dive together almost in formation and loud bird songs accompany dawn and dusk. Those who love to jet ski will find plenty of company here; those sensitive to their noise may be reduced to quivering wrecks

from about ten in the morning to four in the afternoon. The marina in the inner bay is small, peaceful, and very well maintained.

Navigation

You need to exercise caution when approaching from the direction of Marigot. After passing Bell Point, head way over toward Pointe des Froussards to go around Marcel Rock before turning into the bay. There is a small bay and beach before this rock, which sometimes causes confusion; Marcel Rock, about 15 feet high, has been mistaken for the 118-foot Roche Créole off Bell Point.

Anse Marcel is reasonably well protected, though a surge can enter, especially in the winter months. Anchoring is not always easy, as the bottom sand is covered in thick weed. In addition, the wind swings from all directions. If you anchor bow and stern, you can cut down on the roll. Keep well clear of the mooring buoy in the southwest of the bay, as it belongs to the giant day charter cat Scubi Two, which swings all over the place.

The entrance to the Anse Marcel Marina is by a clearly marked, narrow channel, about a quarter of a mile long, with only room for one yacht at a time, so sound your horn before going in. (There is a passing point half way down.) The channel is dredged to 9 feet. The marina is completely protected.

Regulations

You may clear in and out of the French side with Olivier, the port captain who has a customs computer.

Services

Docking, water, ice, toilets and showers are available at the 145-berth marina (VHF: 16, switch to 11). A fuel dock sells gasoline and diesel and is open daily 0800-1200, and 1400-1800. Olivier, the harbormaster, will drum up help, from a mechanic to an electronics expert, to work on your boat. They sometimes use Sun Maintenance, which is close by. It is run by a Dominican who speaks both English and French. Faxes may be sent. WiFi is available throughout the marina. Do your weekly wash in the big washing machine in the port office building. You can rent a car through Olivier. Those

RENAISSANCE ISLANDS

-

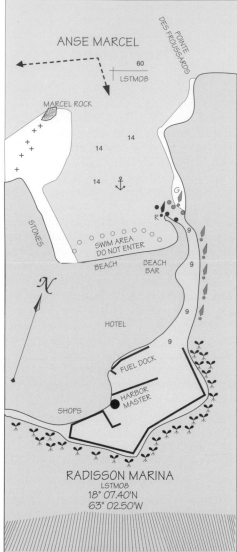

ANSE MARCEL

POINTE DES FROUSSARDS

60
LSTM08

MARCEL ROCK

14   14

14

14

STONES

G

R

SWIM AREA
DO NOT ENTER

BEACH   BEACH
BAR

9

9

9

HOTEL

9

FUEL DOCK

HARBOR
MASTER

SHOPS

RADISSON MARINA
LSTM08
18° 07.40'N
63° 02.50'W

outside but wishing to eat or shop in the marina will find a place to leave the dinghy. The marina is home to VPM Best Sail Charter Company.

Ashore

You can buy essentials at the Superette. Boutiques sell clothing, elegant household essentials, and beachwear.

Calypso, a good restaurant, is open from breakfast though dinner every day, with both a café area and a more formal dining room. They specialize in seafood and in the same block, you will find Da Tony, an Italian restaurant, open in the evenings.

Down by the beach is a cute little beach bar and La Table du Marché (dinner) both owned by the hotel Domaine de Lonvilliers.

You can buy a day pass bracelet to Riu Palace Resort which allows you a relaxing time at their beach and the Renova Spa.

Water Sports

Scuba Zen is the local dive shop run by Jean-Michel. They will take you diving, teach you, and sell you equipment.

When the weather allows, Scuba Zen visits one of the prime local sites, Spanish Rock. This underwater reef varies in depth from 7 to 45 feet and includes a wall. Being in the middle of nowhere, the water clarity is usually excellent. Lobsters are common and it is a feeding ground for doctor fish. There is also a chance of seeing rays, turtles, and nurse sharks.

The Circus at Tintamarre is another of their popular sites. The dive here goes to 55 feet and includes lots of small caves and hiding holes which house the huge profusion of reef fish that gave it its name.

Sports fishing trips can be arranged on large, comfortable fishing yachts. Ask at the marina.

FROM ANSE MARCEL TO TINTAMARRE

You can sail around the northern coast, staying a few hundred yards offshore. Spanish Rock is an offshore danger. It lies a good three-quarters of a mile off Pointe Nord, just north of a line joining the northernmost parts of St. Martin and

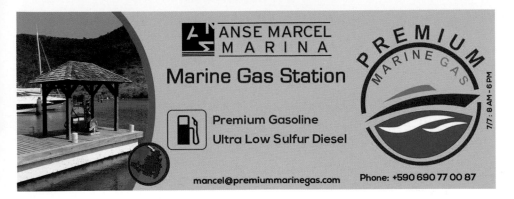

ANSE MARCEL MARINA

Marine Gas Station

Premium Gasoline
Ultra Low Sulfur Diesel

PREMIUM MARINE GAS

7/7: 8 AM - 6 PM

mancel@premiummarinegas.com   Phone: +590 690 77 00 87

Tintamarre. From Spanish Rock you can just see Rocher Créole, looking like it is part of the mainland. Spanish Rock is about 7 feet below the surface, which is too deep to see easily and too shallow to pass over. It breaks in heavy weather. If coming from the west, do not try to go outside it; it is so far off that you might hit it, thinking you had gone around it. Pass inside, sailing safely anywhere from a few hundred yards to half a mile off Pointe Nord. If you are coming from the Scrub Island Channel in Anguilla, head for Tintamarre Island and thus stay outside. Make sure the current does not set you down onto it.

Tintamarre

Tintamarre is a flatish island about 120 feet high and just over a mile long. There is a superb beach along its western shore which you will see very clearly if you are approaching from the west. The southwestern point of Tintamarre has a reef extending from it, which is easily identified by a small sand cay. The reef extends well beyond the sand cay, so give it wide clearance. A bank of sand and weed extends several hundred yards from the beach. Depths start at 24 feet and slowly shelve toward the shore. You should use one

ANSE MARCEL & RADISSON MARINA

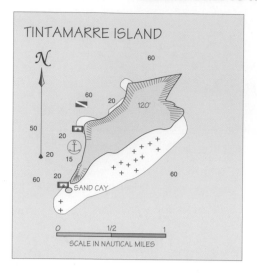

TINTAMARRE ISLAND

N

SAND CAY

SCALE IN NAUTICAL MILES

water is generally very clear. You can do a photogenic dive here in 37 to 50 feet. Farther out is a sunken tug encrusted with sea fans and other soft corals and there are lots of angelfish, sergeant majors, sennets, and snappers. To find the tug, take your dinghy around the northern end of the beach and head northeast. As you go, look behind you and line up the end of the rocky point north of the beach with the easternmost tip of St. Martin. The tugboat lies on this line. A buoy sometimes marks the site, but if it is missing, look for a large oval patch of turquoise water with a dark patch in the middle. Tie to the dive buoy.

ST. MARTIN'S EAST COAST

This windward coast can be rough and dangerous, but it does have several good anchorages. These should only be approached in moderate sea and wind conditions, and even then with caution.

There are reefs and rough water down most of the east coast, so give it a wide berth, unless you are entering a harbor. The offshore rocks at the south end of the east coast (Cow and Calf, Molly Beday, Pelikan, and Hen and Chicks) should be given good clearance. They can all be seen in normal conditions. Molly Beday and Pelikan are 100 feet high and make good landmarks.

of the 17 marine park moorings for boats up to 50 feet or 15 tons. Boats up to 33 feet may anchor in sand. No obvious provision is made for larger boats, they normally anchor further out. You can stay here for lunch and overnight in most conditions, though it can roll. In heavy swells you may want to give it a miss as landing the dinghy can be risky. The beach is fabulous and paths lead over to the southern shore where another long beach lies protected behind a barrier reef.

Water Sports

If you snorkel north of the beach, you will find lots of colorful reef fish and the

www.HeliPhotoCarib.com

TINTAMARRE

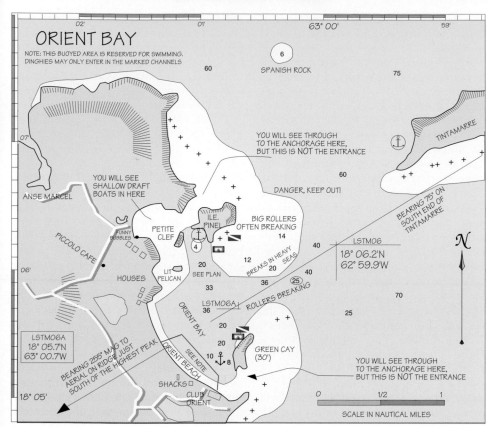

ORIENT BAY

NOTE: THIS BUOYED AREA IS RESERVED FOR SWIMMING. DINGHIES MAY ONLY ENTER IN THE MARKED CHANNELS

SPANISH ROCK

6

60

75

TINTAMARRE

YOU WILL SEE THROUGH TO THE ANCHORAGE HERE, BUT THIS IS NOT THE ENTRANCE

ANSE MARCEL

YOU WILL SEE SHALLOW DRAFT BOATS IN HERE

60

DANGER, KEEP OUT!

BEARING 75° ON SOUTH END OF TINTAMARRE

PICCOLO CAFE

FUNNY BUBBLES

PETITE CLEF

ILE. PINEL

4

BIG ROLLERS OFTEN BREAKING

14

40

LSTM06
18° 06.2'N
62° 59.9'W

N

HOUSES

LIT PELICAN

12

20

33

SEE PLAN

BREAKS IN HEAVY SEAS

20

36

25

40

ORIENT BAY

LSTM06A
36

ROLLERS BREAKING

70

25

LSTM06A
18° 05.7'N
63° 00.7'W

BEARING 255° MAG TO AERIAL ON RIDGE JUST SOUTH OF THE HIGHEST PEAK

SEE TEXT

ORIENT BEACH

20

20

10

8

GREEN CAY
(30')

YOU WILL SEE THROUGH TO THE ANCHORAGE HERE, BUT THIS IS NOT THE ENTRANCE

SHACKS

CLUB ORIENT

18° 05'

0   1/2   1

SCALE IN NAUTICAL MILES

RENAISSANCE ISLANDS

The others are low, but the mariner who keeps a good look out and is not sailing right into the sun should have no difficulty. For specific instructions for sailing to Orient Bay from any direction, see Orient Bay, below.

Orient Bay
Navigation

Orient Bay can be both dangerous and difficult. Read all parts of this navigation section and the sections on Green Cay and Ile Pinel before you approach. Orient Bay is a large bay open to the east, and subject to rolling onshore seas. However, there are reasonably protected anchorages in both the northern and southern ends, behind Ile Pinel and Green Cay (Caye Verte). As winds approach 20 knots, the waves are steep and consistently breaking in depths of 20 feet or less. It is unwise to enter in these conditions. Do not enter during the afternoon, when the sun is in your eyes. This is the area in which charter boats have the

most serious problems. About six were lost or badly damaged in one year alone, either trying to enter south of Green Cay, or being rolled in the big seas east of Pinel. (See our Orient Bay sketch chart.) Once inside, take care when going into Ile Pinel. Many charter yachts try to go around the wrong side of Petite Clef and run aground. If you follow the directions carefully and approach with a little apprehension, you should be fine. Keep the following things in mind: whether you come from north or south, you should have at least 25 feet of water all the way into Orient Bay and for much of the time the depths will be 30 to 60 feet. If you find yourself in less than 25 feet for more than a few moments, then turn around and head out again. The gap between the two islands is about a mile wide. If you approach an entrance that looks about a quarter of a mile wide, it is wrong. Turn around and go back out. If either of these things occur, or you are unsure of your position, sail over to Tintamarre and follow our approach directions from there. (See also "From Anse Marcel to Tintamarre," above, with instructions on how to avoid Spanish Rock.)

Approaching from the North. Between the north coast of St. Martin and Tintamarre, you will see the Ile Pinel anchorage through the gap between Ile Pinel and the mainland. Do not mistake this gap for the entrance.

If you look at our sketch chart of Orient Bay, you will see that there is a shoal bank, 12 to 20 feet deep, over the northern half of the bay that extends a long way offshore. This shoal, also clearly visible in our aerial photo, is missing from most other charts. Huge, dangerous, breaking seas build up here, so it must be avoided. If you follow our safe approach, you will be in 30 to 60 feet most of the way, with the occasional short bank of maybe 25 feet. If the depths are less than 25 feet, head back out again. The safest and easiest route is to sail right over to the beach at Tintamarre and start from there.

From the beach at Tintamarre, steer a course of 230° magnetic, which will take you in the direction of Green Cay. As an added aid, the entrance channel is on a line between the southern tip of Tintamarre and some aerials on a high ridge just to the south of the highest mountain you can see. The bearing is about 255° magnetic to the aerials going in and 75° magnetic to the south of Tintamarre coming out. As you approach the bay, you will see conspicuous developments onshore on your starboard bow.

As you get closer, you can identify Green Cay and you will see breaking water on the reef around it. Sail in around the north of this reef and Green Cay. If you like using waypoints, we give a couple on our sketch chart that might prove helpful.

Approaching from the South. The problem when sailing from the south is to correctly identify Green Cay. It is low lying (30 feet high) and merges perfectly into the background. The headland at the end of Orient Beach looks like an island, which adds to the confusion. It is important to read the following directions carefully.

After you leave Oyster Pond, keep a quarter to a half-mile offshore. The next landmark, just under a mile from Oyster Pond, is a group of large rocks that extend from the southern end of Baie des Flamandes. Sail for almost another mile past these rocks, passing Baie des Flamandes. Try to identify the false entrance to Green Cay as you sail by. You will see a big sweep of beach and probably some anchored yachts. At some point, you will see a big housing development. You will see what looks like a clear entrance about a quarter of a mile wide. Do not mistake this for the entrance! You cannot even approach it for a look without running into danger. The water shelves very suddenly and skippers who wrecked themselves here approached cautiously, keeping a good lookout, but found themselves aground before they spotted the shallows. You will get no warning from your echo sounder before you are aground. The island on the right-hand side of this false entrance is Green Cay, and you have to sail on another half mile or so to round it. You may see breakers extending for what seems like a very long way out from Green Cay. The reef does come out a long way here and you may well have to head farther offshore to stay outside it. (Stay in at least 35 feet of water.) As you pass Green Cay, you will see the beach and the yachts disappear behind it.

Once you have passed Green Cay and

AERIAL....255° M. JUST TO SOUTH OF HIGHEST PEAK

GREEN CAY

VIEW OF THE APPROACH INTO ORIENT BAY

Chris Doyle

132

Orient Bay   Chris Doyle

RENAISSANCE ISLANDS

the reef to its east, you can head on in. You will notice that when you are coming in the correct entrance, the bay is so wide (nearly a mile) that it doesn't have the feel of a channel at all. As you come in, you will start to see masts of the boats in and behind Ile Pinel, almost a mile to the north, and when you get farther inside, you will see the boats off Green Cay. Note the bearings on the radio mast and the south end of Tintamarre given on our sketch chart. Keep the following rule in mind: if you are coming from the south and you are not absolutely sure where you are, sail over to Tintamarre and approach from there instead (see above).

Approaching Orient Bay from St. Barts. Sail to the beach at Tintamarre and enter as from the north (above).

Ile Pinel Anchorage

The Ile Pinel anchorage is good for an overnight stop, though it does sometimes get rolly. Ile Pinel is a park and a perfect Robinson Crusoe island, with sandy beaches, waving palms, and a couple of hills, the highest one rising to about 100 feet. Closer to shore, Petite Clef is rocky, wild, and inaccessible. The anchorage is between these islands. It is a delightful spot, but there is not much room, and it often gets crowded. The Marine Park has 15 moorings for yachts up to 40 feet and 10 tons. They have not always been reliable. Anchoring is

allowed on sand, in theory only for boats to 33 feet. However, the park has been happily accepting fees from the charter companies for significantly larger boats. I would be guided by that.

Navigation

Approaching Ile Pinel from Green Cay. Many yachts have a problem here because the anchored yachts cause confusion. Besides the boats in Ile Pinel, you can see many more anchored well to the west of Ile Pinel, in an anchorage behind Petite Clef. This mainly shoal anchorage is reached through a twisty reef-strewn passage to the north of Ile Pinel. It is strictly for local boats with intimate knowledge of the reefs. However, the presence of these yachts leads many a navigator to try to enter this bay to the south of Petite Clef – and run hard aground.

Once inside Orient Bay, do not head into Ile Pinel until you are alongside Green Island and can see right up into the lee of Ile Pinel. Make sure you can distinguish boats anchored here from those inside Petite Clef, and make sure you have correctly identified Ile Pinel and Petite Clef. Do not attempt to go inside Petite Clef or Little Pelican from the south, as it is all shallow and dangerous. There is a 4-foot shoal right at the entrance to the Ile Pinel anchorage, marked with a small buoy. Leave it to starboard and you will arrive in the anchorage facing the wind, ready to drop sails.

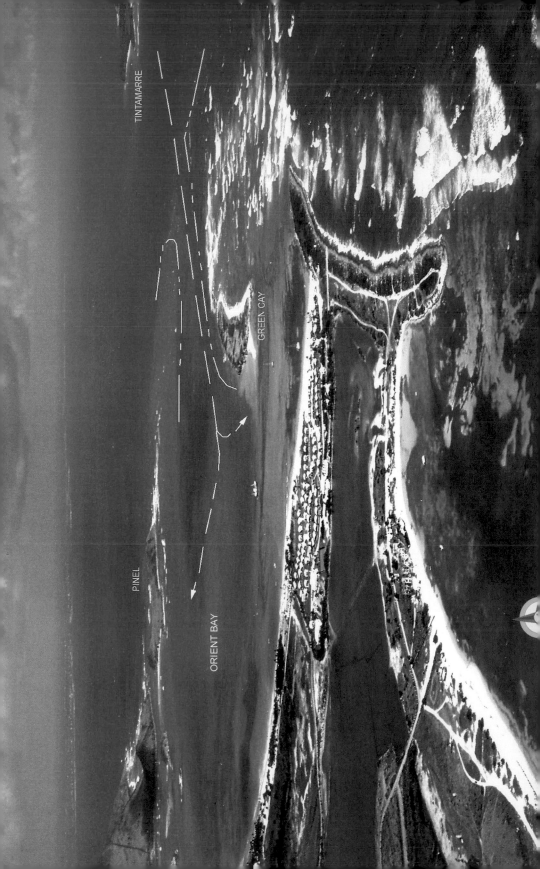

TINTAMARRE

GREEN CAY

PINEL

ORIENT BAY

Ashore

The island is great to explore, with little footpaths everywhere. There are several small beaches and the view from the hills is worth the easy climb (take shoes). On the shore are three attractive small restaurants (lunch only), with lots of beach umbrellas for day visitors, of which there can be many. They never venture far from the beach and are always gone by night. You might be able to leave your dinghy on the Karibuni dock across the spit, but ask first. If you take your dinghy past Petite Clef and back to the head of the big bay, you will find some small dinghy docks in very shallow water. If you walk back down the road, heading out as if to the main road, you will come to a few restaurants and shops.

Water Sports

For snorkelers and scuba divers, a reef follows the southern end of Ile Pinel. It is easily accessible from your yacht and only about 25 feet deep. Swim out inside the snorkeling zone marked by buoys and carry on around the reef. Much of the reef is an interesting skeleton, full of caverns and holes, which make hiding places for reef fish. It is decorated by lots of soft corals.

Green Cay Anchorage

Green Cay is a low-lying island with a sandy beach at one end. To its south is the long and lovely Orient Beach, the liveliest beach in St. Martin, and the eastern part is well known as the spot where holiday makers come to get a tan free of bikini marks. You can sail into the lee of Green Cay and anchor, or go on a bit farther and drop hook between Green Cay and Orient Beach. It shoals as you go in. This is not a particularly well protected spot, and you would not want to be here in a heavy northerly swell, but on a normal day it makes a good lunch time stop and you can anchor overnight in settled weather.

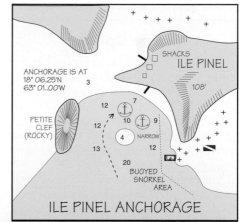

ANCHORAGE IS AT
18° 06.25'N
63° 01.00'W

PETITE CLEF (ROCKY)

SHACKS
ILE PINEL

108'

7
12
10
12
9
4 NARROW
13
12
20
BUOYED SNORKEL AREA

ILE PINEL ANCHORAGE

RENAISSANCE ISLANDS

ILE PINEL

DO NOT TRY TO ENTER HERE

PETITE CLEF

LITTLE PELICAN

A series of yellow buoys protects swimmers from jet skis, speedboats, and dinghies. Make sure you dinghy in through the marked channel at the eastern end of this area.

Ashore

The long beach here is cheerful and lively, packed with colorful beach brollies, bars, boutiques, and bodies; some more naked than others. A carefree holiday atmosphere abounds. You will find water sports facilities with catamarans, sailboards, parasailing, and jet skis. Any of the restaurants make a pleasant place to sit and watch the world go by. When you tire of the social scene, take a stroll down the road and visit the butterfly farm, where you can walk in a large screened garden amid hundreds of brightly-colored butterflies.

Water Sports

It is hard to imagine a better bay for dinghy sailing or sailboarding. At the eastern end you can rent sailboards and 15-foot fast beach cats from Orient Water Sports. They also sell ice. As you wander down the beach, there are many other stalls offering everything from parasailing to snorkeling trips around Green Cay.

The snorkeling around Green Cay is excellent, with many sea fans and other soft corals. The easiest place to start is along the north coast of the island. Wade around from the beach or anchor your dinghy nearby.

Scuba divers can also enjoy this site. It is only about 20 feet deep; a good beginner's dive.

Oyster Pond

Oyster Pond is a completely protected lagoon, surrounded by hills. Peaceful, pleasant, and small, it makes a great base for seeing St. Martin. You will quickly get to know the staff in all the bars and restaurants and be treated as one of the family. On the outside a superb beach is good for swimming and acceptable for snorkeling. It is an easy walk up Fife Hill, with its decorative cactuses and panoramic views. Inside, you can watch pelicans and terns diving, and when you tire of that, there is a good collection of restaurants. Captain Oliver's Marina (VHF: 67), The Moorings (VHF: 77), and Sunsail (VHF: 74) are all here. You can carry about 10 feet of water to the first docks.

Navigation

The approach into Oyster Pond can put hair on your chest. Sometimes you have to run downwind through steep seas onto a lee shore dotted with reefs. Occasionally, the seas get so bad that they break right across the entrance, and at such times it would be foolhardy to go in. At other times, the entrance is straightforward but, even at the best of times, this is no place to make a mistake, and you must be absolutely sure you have everything correctly placed before

GREEN CAY

Oyster Pond

you enter.

The entrance is marked by an outer red and white buoy and three red posts. These are privately maintained by Sunsail and Captain Oliver's Marina. The outer one was missing in 2015 and may not be replaced. In this case you can try to go to the GPS position we give for it, but use great caution.

From the north you will notice Fife Hill, with many buildings below. Keep well outside the reef off Fife Hill until you can identify the markers. (A charter yacht went a little too close in 2014 and was rolled over by the waves.) Go first to the outer waypoint (red and white buoy if it is there), then identify the red posts and head in. Once you are in the channel, stay within 30 feet of the red markers, leaving them to starboard.

From the south you can identify Oyster Pond from the row of prominent square-shaped buildings, one with a fancy glass atrium on the low land. This is the Oyster Pond Beach Hotel. This is the most built up part of the coast. If you are coming from the south, keep well out in deep water, as if you were going to sail right by Oyster Pond. Turn in when you can enter as if from the north. A quick glance at the sketch chart will show that cutting the corner toward the channel from the south would at best take you through the very rough 21-foot patch

with the 10-foot shoal in the middle, and at worst land you on the reef.

Keep in mind that this entrance is downwind and down sea. If you are towing a dinghy, take precautions. (The safest is to keep them so short they touch the stern protected by a fender.) If you plan to drop your sails before you enter, do it before you start your approach. Make sure you can release some jib in case of engine failure.

Once you are safely in the inner harbor, you can go into a marina or anchor, if you can find a space. There is a 2-foot shoal right in the middle of the harbor, but shoal draft yachts (3-5 feet) can feel their way in to find anchorage on its west side. Charter companies have placed moorings over most of the available anchoring space so anchoring room is very hard to find.

The band of deep water between Captain Oliver's outer dock and the shallows is so narrow that boats can only tie alongside this dock. If you are passing, stay very close to the boats on the dock.

When you leave Oyster Pond, you will be doing so against the wind into steep seas. You must power or motor-sail out. If you don't have a large auxiliary, then you will need the mainsail to help the engine. Have a plan of action should the motor fail on take off.

RENAISSANCE ISLANDS

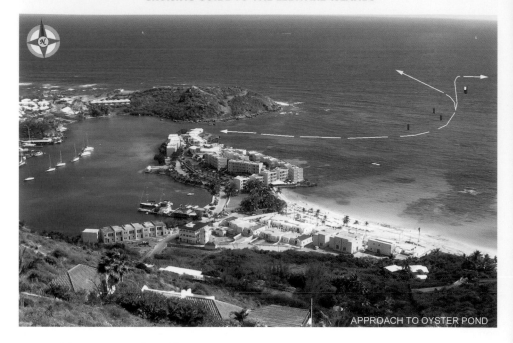

APPROACH TO OYSTER POND

Communications

In the marina, WiFi reaches those on the docks. Many bars have WiFi.

Services

Captain Oliver's (VHF: 67) 160-berth marina has water, ice, WiFi, laundry, dockage, telephones, and fax. There is a fuel dock, but it has not pumped fuel for some years. They plan to reopen it, in which case it will be open every day, 0815-1645. It also has garbage facilities for yachts staying in the marina. Car rentals are available. If you cannot raise them on the VHF, call their mobile (721-581-0790) or come into their fuel dock and talk to them. Avoid calling the charter companies unless you are a customer.

This is a good place to leave your yacht and a boat care program is available. The dockmaster will help in any way he can.

The charter companies Moorings (VHF: 77) and Sunsail (VHF: 74) are based here. They share a building and are knowledgeable about the area and are happy to give good advice. The Moorings sells boats coming out of charter. If you are chartering from here they will guide you out and in through the channel.

Harel Yacht Brokers in Captain Oliver's marina is a full sales and service agency for Lagoon, Beneteau, and Outremer, and deal with all of their problems. They will give you good advice on any kind of repair or service you need, and will help if you are looking to sell, buy or charter a boat.

Great House Marina has a good dock for about 14 yachts up to about 8.5-foot draft. They have toilets, water, and both 220- and 110-volt electricity. It is the home of PYC charter company. Great House Marina is part of Brokaar Marine Services. This company, run by John Brokaar, is a good place to come to for commercial diving and salvage.

Oyster Pond Beach Resort owns the 35-berth Oyster Pond Marina. They have geared it mainly to power boats, each with a lift.

Provisioning

Aux Pains d'Epices is a small supermarket open every day from 0700-2000. It is a short walk from Captain Olivers, but if you are provisioning they will deliver. Dirty Des Liquor Store is in the marina and open every day from 0830-1800.

Pier Grocery is a fancy market at Great House Marina and they open 0700-2200. They have a good stock of wines, a fair selection of food, gourmet ethnic sauces and spices, good coffee, ice, wonderful smelling baked goodies, and more. For cash, visit the

138

ATM in the lobby of the big Oyster Pond Hotel.

Restaurants

Captain Oliver's in Oyster Pond is a big marina and hotel with beautiful bedrooms, an exercise room, and restaurant. It is owned by Maggi, who has the sports bar on the waterfront. The main restaurant is perched on a platform on the lagoon, overlooking the sea to St. Barts. You can select your own lobster from the pool and, while you have a cocktail, admire the aquarium-like view of the glass-sided swimming pool, as well as view fish through the glass floor. The restaurant is open every day from breakfast to dinner and features nightly entertainment. During the season you can eat a full meal any time of the day.

The Iguana Bar at Oliver's features a pleasant platform looking out to sea and open to the breeze. They have a two-hour happy hour from 1700-1900, and in the evening long trousers are appreciated. Iguana Bar serves tapas. Between the Iguana Bar and the restaurant is an open fish pool with sharks.

The Dinghy Dock at Captain Oliver's, is run by Seth from the USA. Their two-hour happy hour is from 1700-1900, when you can mix your own drinks as strong as you like, making this a dangerous place in a safe harbor. They are open all day and you can select from the large menu posted on the wall, which has everything from seafood to burgers, and sandwiches. The daily specials are posted on a second board out front. They serve food till 2200.

Dirty Des Bar and Grill has a happy hour from 1700-1900 and they make theirs even more dangerous: mix your own in beer mugs. It is reasonably priced, with a big choice of

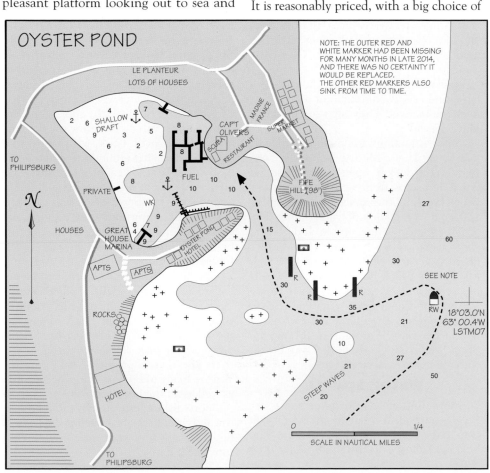

Oyster Pond approach during Christmas winds   Chris Doyle

food and open from 0730 till late, except Mondays, when they close.

Just past the Sunsail workshop is a good little French restaurant called Quai Ouest. They open for lunch and dinner, but do not hang about in between. They are closed all Sunday and for lunch on Monday.

Dephine's Madine-France, right outside the marina gates, serves breakfast from 0730, and stays open for lunch till about 1500. The food is French and very good. They close Sundays.

Le Planteur, farther down the road, is a fancy and very good restaurant with a view over the marina. They offer a reasonable lunch special.

Other attractions are on the south side, near Great House Marina. Stardocks Cafe, right on the dock, is open for breakfast and lunch. Just across from the dock, Mr. Busby's Beach Bar and other snack bars open about 1000 and serve both lunch and dinner. The beach location is unbeatable. Indeed, the gorgeous Dawn Beach is one of St. Martin's fairest. You can reach it by passing through Mr. Busby's Beach Bar, right behind Great House Marina. Next to the Great House Marina is the fancy new Oyster Pond Beach Hotel. Behind the lobby are two good restaurants. On the grounds is a Shipwreck Shop. Westin has a big hotel on Dawn Beach, with restaurants and beach bars.

Water Sports

Snorkeling at the entrance to Oyster Pond is not bad. You can dinghy out or walk over to the beach and swim from there. The best snorkeling is to the south, as far from the entrance to Oyster Pond as you can get. This also has the advantage that the current usually takes you north along the beach.

Divers setting out on a cruise should contact The Scuba Shop, run by Peter Frye. This excellent shop rents fishing rods and lures (a great way to catch your dinner) and both sells and rents all kinds of scuba gear, most of it priced well below US list. This is one of the better duty-free bargains in St. Martin. Scubapro, Mares, Shearwood, Suunto and Aqua Lung are all on sale. You can rent or buy SeaLife and GoPro cameras and accessories. Peter will fill tanks, and you can dinghy right up to the shop. Peter has put together both a snorkeling site flier and an excellent little book, with maps, that describes dive sites around the area that are easily accessible by yacht and dinghy. He gives these out at no charge. In addition to diving gear, The Scuba Shop sells yachting clothes, including some fancy shorts and shirts (Columbia brand). Peter has another branch in Simpson Bay, which is their gear-servicing center.

The dive sites near Oyster Pond are not easy to do from your yacht. Molly Bidet, the large rock you see right outside, is one of them. This dive is from 30 to 70 feet and has a large elkhorn garden on top. You go down a wall with dramatic overhangs and there are some impressive coral pinnacles. You are likely to see some large pelagic fish, as well as all the usual reef fish.

Sports fishing enthusiasts should ask at the activities desk about fishing charters. A big ferry called Voyager makes quite a few runs to St. Barts.

CAPTAIN OLIVER'S

SAINT MARTIN
SINT MAARTEN

MARINA | RESTAURANT | HOTEL ★★★★
OYSTER POND | 18°03'20"N 63°00'56"W

Enjoy long or short term dockage in this unique resort set astride the Dutch/French border. This friendly, professionally managed, tranquil marina offers all the usual facilities, including a full service fuel dock open 7 days a week, 24 hour security and a daily ferry service to St. Barths.

Discover the magical waterfront ambiance at Captain Oliver's Resort with a great choice of waterside bars and restaurants.

www.captainolivers.com

Contact Pascal Renold on
Phone | Fax (590) 590 87 33 47 | (590) 590 52 05 05 | (599) 581 0790
VHF 67 | email: captainolivers@domaccess.com

RENAISSANCE ISLANDS

PASSAGE BETWEEN ST. MARTIN AND ST. BARTS

St. Barts lies to the east-southeast of St. Martin. The sail from Philipsburg is usually a 12-mile romp to windward. The relatively shallow water, for the most part less than 100 feet deep, makes the sea a lustrous deep blue. A popular route is to pass between the Groupers and Table Rock, taking a lunch break at Ile Fourchue. If you plan your departure from the north end of St. Martin, rather than from Philipsburg, you can usually make the 15 odd miles in one exhilarating fast tack.

People usually give up sailing and motor after Anse du Colombier, as the winds get very fickle. The return trip is usually a run. If the wind gets dead behind, you can tack downwind to make for an easier sail.

Ile Fourchue

Gustavia   Chris Doyle

St. Barthelemy (St. Barts)

FOR THE SAILOR, ST. BARTS has the allure of a small island whose economy and well-being have always been intricately bound up with its picturesque port. The island itself had little to recommend it for settlement in the early days, as the rainfall is insufficient to support agriculture. However, St. Barts is strategically placed in the middle of the Lesser Antilles. Its fine small harbor and several sheltered bays made it important enough to be fought over by the British, French, and Spanish. It prospered under the French in the late 1600s when it was used as a base by pirates who came here to spend their quickly-gained fortunes. The most famous of these was Captain Montbars, a Frenchman who was so horrified by what the Spanish had done to the native populations that he decided to avenge them, doing well while he did good. He took on an indigenous crew who, no doubt, felt somewhat bitter, and did so well he became known with some terror as "Montbars the Exterminator." He finally disappeared in a hurricane and it is thought that his treasure

is still buried on the island, though it is more likely that it was spent on the island.

In 1784 the French gave St. Barts to the Swedes in exchange for free port rights in Gothenburg. The Swedes made it a free port, which it remains today. It had a second period of prosperity as a trading center during the American war of independence, when American rebels came here for supplies.

During the hundred years following 1852, its fortunes fell owing to changing trade patterns and several hurricanes. The Swedes sold St. Barts back to France in 1878 and today it is a commune of France, though an overseas one, which means it is free from many European laws. Over the last 30 years, this free port status has resulted in an astonishing economic recovery. At first, it was mainly inter-island trade. Small motorless sailing sloops would arrive here from down island and load themselves to the gunwales with alcohol and cigarettes to be smuggled back home. Although the customs officers in their home ports were properly taken care of, the return journey was nonetheless a long and hazardous sail to windward. The smugglers' biggest problem was to evade the customs men in St. Kitts and Nevis who would happily confiscate their cargo, no matter its destination. To keep out of their way, many would

St. Barts

Regulations

Clear in and out with the port captain's office in Gustavia (VHF: 12). Entry procedures and mooring fees given under Gustavia.

There is a 3-knot speed limit on all craft, including dinghies, and no water sports of any kind are permitte inside Gustavia port limits. A 5-knot speed limit is in effect within 300 meters of all coastlines, which precl waterskiing.

Large areas of St. Barts are in the St. Barthelemy Natural Marine Preserve, managed by Franciane Le Que These are marked by large yellow buoys that flash yellow at night, and we mark them on our sketch chart. B Ile Fourchue and Anse du Colombier are part of this park, as are Pain de Sucre and Les Gros Islets to the we Gustavia. The park office is on the waterfront a few steps from the port office. They open Monday to Saturd 0830-1230. In the park areas you may swim and snorkel. You can fish with a handline from the shore or a di ing dinghy. You may not use personal watercraft (jet skis), waterski, spearfish, hunt lobsters, or take anything from the seabed. You should never take coral or throw garbage in any coastal waters. All commercial operat including private yachts on charter, must visit the office and pay a fee ($2 Eu per person per visit). You may the yacht moorings in Ile Fourchue and Colombier when available. They are all yellow and all take boats up 60 feet/25 tons. They are large buoys with a line going right through them. Put your lines though the loop a end of the line and leave a minimum of 10 feet scope. Dive and check the mooring.

You may scuba dive in the marine park, but you need to visit the office They will give you a plan of 20 div sites, and you will pay a fee of $2 Eu per person per dive. There is no anchoring on the dive sites, but moori are provided for dinghies and tenders, which you may use for a maximum of 2.5 hours. Thirteen scuba diver the maximum allowed for one boat. No anchoring or fishing is allowed in Anse du Marigot. New user fees f are planned and will probably be collected by the port office when you clear.

Pass divers slowly, giving them at least 100 yards clearance. Do not chase or try to grab onto turtles!

Telephones

Carte Orange and Digicel are cell phone companies here. You can buy a SIM. You can also call from som businesses in town, as well as send email (see Communications).

All St. Barts numbers now start with 0590 (regular) or 0690 (mobile). You must dial this prefix, even on a local call. If you are dialing into St. Barts from a non-French territory, you have to dial the country code firs which is also 590, then leave off the first 0 of the number. Thus, if calling from the US, for regular numbers will dial: 011-590-590, then 6 digits.

Transport

Taxis are on the waterfront opposite Quicksilver.
Rental cars and scooters are available for hire. Use your own license and drive on the right.

Shopping Hours

Opening hours are from 0800-1200 and 1500-1800, but many shops stay open over lunch. Some shops open when the first day charter boat arrives (0900) and close when the last one leaves (1500).

Holidays

- Jan 1st
- Carnival Monday & Tuesday (46 days before Easter: Feb 8-9, 2016; Feb 27-28, 2017)
- Good Friday and Easter Monday (Easter Sunday is March 27, 2016; April 16, 2017)
- May 1 (Labor Day)
- May 8 (V.E. DAY)
- Ascension Day (39 days after Easter: May 5, 2016; May 25, 2017)
- Whit Monday (50 days after Easter Sunday, May 16, 2016; June 5, 2017)
- Corpus Christie (May 26, 2016; June 15, 2017)
- July 14 (Bastille Day)
- July 21 (Victor Schoelcher Day)
- August 15 (Assumption Day)
- Nov 1 (All Saints Day)
- Nov 11 (Remembrance Day)
- December 25 (Christmas)

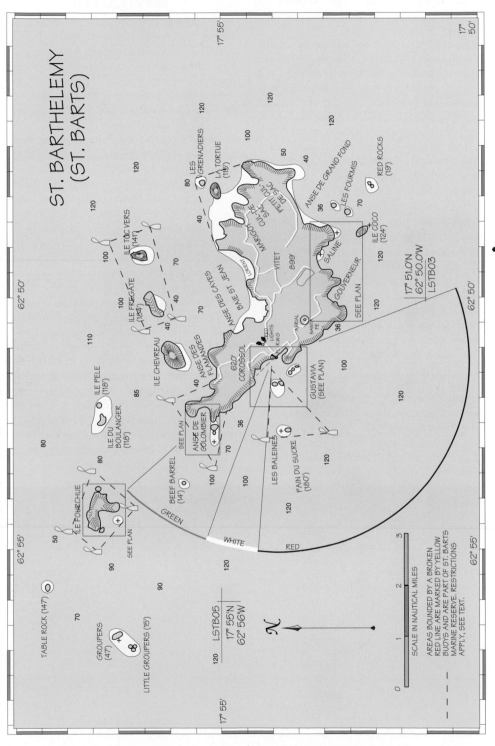

ST. BARTHELEMY
(ST. BARTS)

RENAISSANCE ISLANDS

sneak by night through The Narrows, the reef-filled passage between St. Kitts and Nevis.

Today St. Barts is in an unprecedented renaissance. With its sharply contoured rocky hills, a picturesque port, and gorgeous beaches, it has become a world-famous chic destination and the favored hot spot for the good looking, well-to-do "in" crowd, seasoned with a sprinkling of acting, singing, dancing, and sports stars, plus a Russian oligarch or two: the Riviera of the Caribbean. St. Barts has happily managed to keep some integrity of architectural style and is still quite charming.

Sociability reaches a crescendo around the New Year when a hundred or more superyachts arrive for festivities that include a spectacular fireworks display.

St. Barts has excellent cultural events, including a music festival (classical and jazz and sometimes ballet) in January, and many art shows, as well as carnival (visitors are welcome to join in). The day after carnival there is a mock funeral when effigies representing evil are paraded and burned.

The Caribbean Film Festival in April is excellent, the St. Barts Family Festival (music in certain restaurants) is in August, November has Swedish Week (music and dance), and Gourmet Week with visiting chefs. November 1 is All Saints, when everyone decorates the graves.

Navigation

St. Barts is surrounded by a host of small islands and rocks – some large and obvious, and others just awash. You can pick your own deepwater channels between these rocks, but study the charts well and keep a good look out. Do not try to go between groups of islands that lie together, such as Groupers and Petite Groupers, or Boulanger and Ile Pelé. The southeast coast can be very rough, so it makes sense to stay outside Red Rocks and Ile Coco.

A marine park is marked by yellow buoys. (See our chart of St. Barts, page 145.) These are large and a collision with one would probably ruin your day. Being yellow, they are easy to see by day; at night they have flashing yellow lights. However, the lights have been known to go out, and the buoys move. The locations shown on our sketch charts are approximate.

When using marine park moorings, use your own line through the loop and leave about 10 feet of scope. Never put a line from one side of your bow through the mooring and over to the other side or your boat will saw through the rope as it swings. Use two lines and return each to the same side. Always snorkel and check marine park moorings. They are well constructed and frequently inspected, but they do get abused. Check for cut or frayed rope.

ROCK AWASH

ILE FOURCHUE
www.HeliPhotoCarib.com

Greenery is returning to Ile Fourchue   Chris Doyle

Ile Fourchue

Ile Fourchue, a privately owned island, lies conveniently between St. Martin and St. Barts and makes a perfect stop. It is dry and rocky, with several steep hills and craggy peaks. Some of the hills are an attractive red color and their steep contours add interest to the view. For many years this island was left to the goats. Back in 2003 I wrote: "there is nothing here except goats who have devoured everything except prickles and, judging by the way some of them were coughing, they seem to have started on the prickles." Shortly after that they finished the prickles and the population crashed. The few survivors were removed. They left an island of bare rock with huge eroded gullies. It has been a pleasure to see the vegetation return, albeit slowly. Grass now covers much of the surface, there are thousands of small low plants and in the deepest gully trees now stand about 12 feet high.

Navigation

Ile Fourchue has a good-sized bay, protected from the north and east. A swell occasionally creeps in and makes it somewhat rolly. There is a rock awash off the southern headland and it is best to leave

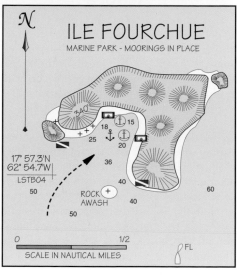

ILE FOURCHUE
MARINE PARK - MOORINGS IN PLACE

17° 57.3'N
62° 54.7'W
LSTB04

SCALE IN NAUTICAL MILES

this to starboard when you enter. Tie up to one of the yacht moorings. They can all take yachts up to 60 feet and 25 tons. Superyachts should anchor to the south of the moorings in deeper water. If there are no moorings left, anchor on sand, south of the moorings. Ile Fourchue is part of the St. Barts Marine Reserve and they maintain the moorings to protect the seabed: spearfishing, jet skiing, water skiing, speedboating, and damaging corals are strictly forbidden.

Ile Fourchue   Chris Doyle

Ashore

Scrambling around this island affords excellent views, but take cactus-proof shoes. Ile Fourchue is privately owned and must be treated with respect. Do not light fires or throw a major party, but you will probably be okay taking a quiet stroll.

Water Sports

Snorkeling and diving here can be interesting when small fish are massing, especially if pelicans and boobies dive right close to you. Snorkel along either side of the bay, close to the rocks. The best dive spot is around the island that forms the western corner of the harbor. Anchor your dinghy on sand in the bay between the island and Ile Fourchue and work your way out around the island and back. The depth starts at 25 feet and goes to 60 feet or more. You will have sand on one side, an intricate reef on the other, and a chance of seeing not only reef fish, but rays and turtles as well. If sea conditions make this dive unsuitable, try the other side of the harbor, along the eastern shore. It is a little shallower there, but still interesting, with plenty of fish. The rock awash, just off the southern point, is quite pretty, but too small to be worth a dive on its own. If you have a compass, you can dive there and swim back to Ile Fourchue underwater.

Anse du Colombier

This secluded bay lies at the bottom of a steep, craggy hill. The village of Colombier peeks down from way up at the top. The bay has a perfect beach, backed by a smattering of palms. There is no road access and the only way to get here is by boat or a mile-long trek over the hills. Anse du Colombier was originally owned by the Rockefellers, who built the house on the southern hill. Farther out on the headland is a conspicuous turquoise summerhouse that looks like it was lifted from the top of the Eiffel Tower. Anse du Colombier is part of the St. Barts Marine Reserve. Spearfishing, jet skiing, or water skiing, and damaging corals are strictly forbidden. In addition to yacht moorings, moorings for divers and snorkelers have been placed among the southern islands and rocks. Since the marine park took over and put down yacht moorings, the grass beds have returned, attracting many feeding turtles, which has become a great attraction.

Navigation

Anse du Colombier is a well-protected anchorage and a good overnight spot. During the winter months northerly swells occasionally find their way in. Ile Petit

148

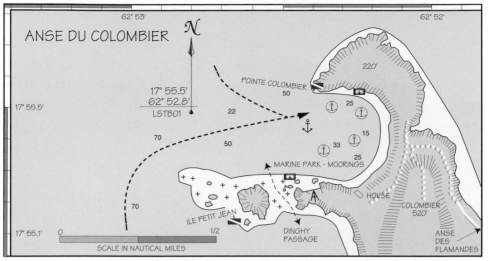

Jean lies just to the west of the southern headland and a series of rocks extends out beyond the island. Some of these are quite visible, others are awash, and some lie just beneath the surface, so pass well outside all the visible rocks when running between Anse du Colombier and Gustavia. Enter in the middle of the bay and pick up a park mooring. They all take yachts up to 60 feet and 25 tons. Superyachts, and other yachts that prefer to anchor, should do so in the middle of bay away from the moorings and grass beds.

Ashore

If you cross over the ridge by the steps at the north end of the beach, you will find a tiny trail leading to Anse des Flamandes. This takes you on an adventurous half-hour walk over hills with panoramic views of some of St. Barts' rocks and offshore islands. Sweet smelling spider lilies grow along parts of the path. You will pass hills of cactuses and hollowed out cliffs and see

RENAISSANCE ISLANDS

ANSE DE COLUMBIER

Anse du Colombier   Chris Doyle

butterflies and birds. The path ends at Anse des Flamandes, another appealing beach where there are some small stores.

An equally lovely hike goes from the beach to the village of Colombier: the collection of houses on top the hill that you can see from the anchorage. The path, which is surprisingly shady, starts above the beach at the beginning of the path to Anse des Flamandes. It follows the ridgeline much of the way up, with fabulous views in places.

Colombier boobies   John Douglas

Water Sports

The snorkeling in Anse du Colombier is good. For starters, there are turtles in the grass beds all around, and you can watch them feeding. However, do not molest them, chase them, or approach closer than 10 feet. Snorkeling is calmer on the northern shore, with lots of small fish but rather sterile rocks. The southern shore is a bit rougher but much more interesting, with more fish and colorful sponges.

Scuba divers have a choice of two sites, depending on conditions. You can dive on the western edge of Pointe Colombier in 25-50 feet. If you are anchored in the north part of the bay, start from your yacht and work your way out. There are many rock ledges and boulders. An even better site is on the south side of the small island, south of Ile Petit Jean. You will need to tie your dinghy to one of the small dive buoys put in by the marine park. You have a chance of seeing turtles and rays, as well the smaller reef fish.

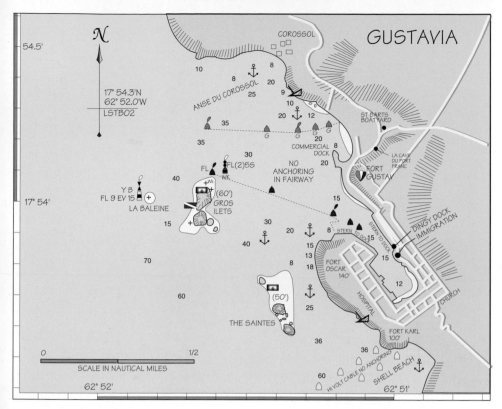

RENAISSANCE ISLANDS

Gustavia

Gustavia, St. Barts' main town, has the inherent charm of a small port. Red-roofed buildings are tucked around the protected harbor. Yachts are tied up along the shore and anchored outside the harbor, so a steady stream of dinghies and small boats treks in and out of the port. The waterfront has a pleasant walkway most of the way around, with flowers and plenty of places to sit and watch life out on the water.

The tourist office is next to the port office. Go there for a free copy of the latest tourist magazines and ask about evening live entertainment.

The port is a basin with hills all around, which you can climb for great harbor views. The lighthouse at Fort Gustav affords one of the best panoramas and is an easy walk. Fort Karl has steps going all the way up and gives a view, not only of the harbor, but also of Shell Beach, which is just a few steps from town.

Navigation

There are several offshore rocks and islands. If you are approaching from the north, the easiest thing is to come inside them. La Baleine is marked by a flashing buoy (9 flashes every 15 seconds). To be on the safe side, avoid going between this buoy and Gros Ilets. If you are approaching from the south, there is enough water to pass between The Saintes and the mainland, but shoal water extends to the east of The Saintes, so follow along the mainland shore. When you approach Gustavia, be prepared to thread your way through anchored boats, unless you come in the official buoyed channel. If you do come through the main channel, note that there is an isolated danger marker on the southern side of the channel by Gros Ilet. This marks the wreck of a freighter about 12 feet below the surface. Gustavia is so popular that anchoring can be a problem during the winter season. Moorings are laid in the

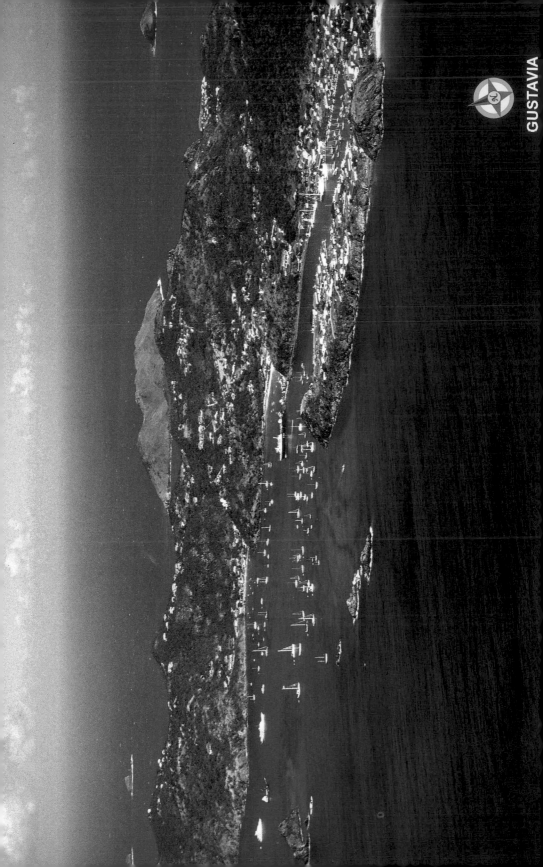

GUSTAVIA

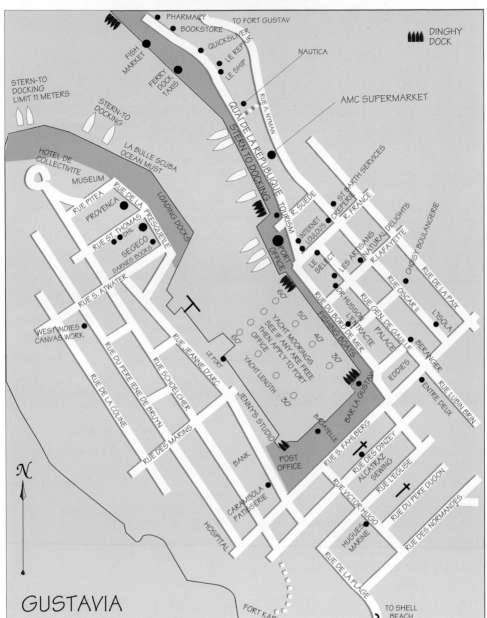

RENAISSANCE ISLANDS

GUSTAVIA

harbor in rows, according to boat length. (See our sketch chart). You need to call the Port of Gustavia to see if they have one available. Sometimes it helps if you check first, then dinghy in, and then tell them which ones you saw empty.

The next most popular spot is northwest of Fort Oscar. You must anchor seaward of the red channel buoys. The wind switches and yachts swing through 360 degrees. A few boats closest to the port are required to have stern anchors. Give these plenty of room, for if you anchor close you may swing onto them You need to dive on your anchor here, as the bottom is weedy. You can also anchor anywhere from here down to Shell Beach. Major cables come in just north of Shell Beach and are marked by yellow buoys. Do not anchor inside them.

Another anchorage is behind the

View from Fort Gustav

marked area between Anse Corossol and the fairway to the public dock. There is no problem being there, but it is a longer dinghy ride into port. All outside anchorages can be pretty rolly. Anchoring in the fairway is strictly forbidden.

A good option is to go stern-to one of the long new sections of dock built especially for visiting yachts. They now have these on both sides of the harbor. This requires considerable skill, as it has to be done in a crosswind. In the winter it is subject to swells, so you must tie your boat well clear of the dock. The secret is to set your anchor a very long way out, toward the far side. Add extra line if necessary. Plunking your anchor down in the middle of the channel is likely to result in an embarrassing drag.

Gustavia is a well-protected harbor under normal conditions, but winter swells creep in and it is often somewhat rolly. Gustavia is no hurricane hole, and you should evacuate at the first warning.

Regulations

Take your passports and ship's papers to the port office. (If you have pets, take their vaccination certificates.) The port office handles all yacht clearance and they will clear you if you are anchored in Colombier and come by dinghy. You can clear in and out in one step for stays of 24 hours; otherwise, clear in and return to clear out. A harbor boat patrols the yacht anchorage daily.

Clearance is by computer either in the port office or online: portdegustavia.fr. You will create and remember a password. At the end you must write down the small clearance number and take it in with you.

The Port du Gustavia stands by on (VHF: 12) and is open from 0700-1800. Get there half an hour before closing to clear. If you plan to come into the docks, call St. Barts Port Authority on VHF: 12, preferably an hour before arrival.

Yachts over 30 meters should dock or leave the dock between 0730 and 1530.

The maximum length for docking is 60 meters (sorry, Bill Gates).

You will be charged in Gustavia according to your location, and pay when you clear in. The charges are by the square meter (length times beam). Outside the inner harbor, charges are 0.2 Eu per square meter per day for private yachts and 0.25 for charter yachts. There is usually room to go stern-to, where in season charges are 0.8 Eu per square meter per day for private yachts, and 1 Eu for charter yachts. From June to November the rates are 0.3 Eu per square meter per day for private yachts, 0.5 for charter yachts. If you manage to get a mooring, charges are 0.5 Eu per square meter for private yachts and 0.7 Eu per square meter for charter yachts. You can ask about longer term rates.

The speed limit in the harbor is 3 knots, not only for yachts, but also for their tenders, and all water sports, including water skis, jet skis, windsurfers, fishing, swimming, and diving, are not allowed in the port zone. Barbecues are not allowed on the dock. Accidents can happen, and the port insists that yachts have liability insurance.

After you have cleared in, visit the Marine Park to get the most up-to-date information, and pay fees if applicable. The park office, closed Sunday, is otherwise open 0830-1230.

Communications

You can have mail or faxes sent to the Port Captain. It must have the name of your yacht and then: BP 695, Port du Gustavia, 97099 St. Barthelemy. Mail not clearly sent to a yacht is returned. Port de Gustavia has two bay-wide WiFis from the harbor and the commercial port. It is included in your port fees. Ask for a ticket when you check in.

Center Alizes, in an office upstairs next to Loulou's, offers complete communications, with phone, fax, and a large bank of computers for email and internet connection. (They have QWERTY keyboards.) This is an easy place to make an international call and for cheaper calls they

Shell Beach   *Chris Doyle*

offer special phone cards that are quite inexpensive, though you do have to punch in a lot of numbers. In addition, they offer business services, including photocopying and laminating, and they sell top ups for French cell phones. They take passport photos and print photos up to a large size. They open Monday to Saturday from 0830 to 1230, 1400-1830.

For a new phone, look for the two shops on Rue Oscar II. Several bars have free WiFi; Le Repaire has open WiFi.

General Yacht Services

Water is available on the yacht docks. Toilets and showers are available to all yachts (opposite the port office) from Monday to Saturday 0800-1700. You will find garbage bins. Please use the appropriate bins: glass, tin cans, used oil, and general garbage. There is stern-to docking and 60-cycle, 3-phase electricity, 220 and 380 volts, is available up to 20 amps right outside the port office with 220 volts farther along the quay. New berths have been added to the western side of the harbor; these have water and electricity. Those farthest away are limited to boats of less than 11 meters and used mainly by small, local open boats. The weather is posted daily at the port office.

The port also runs the commercial port, with full security. It is mostly used by cargo vessels, but they open it to big yachts over the New Year holiday. The commercial port has a fuel station, but call before you come if you plan to take on fuel, as it has often been out of service.

Getting US style propane tanks filled is not possible, though Loulou tells me that if you are desperate, Martin Greaux, in Anse de Cayes, may be able to help.

St. Barth Boatyard is set back from the water. They take yachts up to 20 tons with a crane, lifting them in the port and then trailing them back to their yard. They have storage for 40-60 boats on concrete standing with tie-down rings embedded every 12 feet. They have a large forklift for yacht tenders and powerboats up to 35 feet. Because of the road, they cannot store cats, but they can lift them for emergency work in the port. They also repair them (see *Technical Yacht Services*).

Wendy's Nautica FWI is a superyacht agent and a charter agency handling crewed yachts up to superyachts. They give full backup service to all their yachts. It is in the back of the Carré d'Or shopping mall, behind the Black Swan store.

Brice's St. Barth Services is a superyacht agent that supplies every kind of support service, from customs clearance and air charters to full provisioning and technical help.

Dr. Chantal Husson is a good G.P. just a few steps into town, and she usually sees patients without an appointment in the mornings. If you need a doctor out of hours, on a holiday, or weekend, we give the number in the directory of the "Dr. on call".

There are many specialists and dentists, the tourist office can give you a list. St. Barts has a well-equipped small hospital.

Ice is available from AMC supermarket. Any taxi will help you fill up your outboard gas tank. You can take laundry to the port office and they will help you call a service. Mom Blanc is one (0590-27-64-45) and my friend Loulou tells me "It is the best laundry for your money".

Chandlery

Le Ship, run by several brothers in the Magras family, is a great general and technical chandlery that stocks lots of product lines not available in St. Martin, and many of their prices are excellent. They sell and service Yamaha outboards, Highfield inflatables, and have a wonderful range of yacht gear, from dinghies and outboards through to hardware, stoves, and fridges, plus oil filters, pumps, electrical fittings, spare parts, and a fabulous collection of nuts, bolts, stainless fittings, and pipe fittings. They have an impressive range of lures and fishing gear, as well as diving gear. This is a good place for yachting shorts, fancy shoes, and replacing the hat that blew over the side. They represent Budget and can bring anything over from Sint Maarten.

Technical Yacht Services
Sailmakers, Canvas, Cushions

Moviegoers may wonder whether Alcatraz (O'Caraïbes) offers a hot line of striped crew uniforms. Not so. Alcatraz means "pelican" in Spanish and this workshop, owned by Evelyne Cajoule, does sail repairs, makes bimini frames and covers, keeps closed cell foam for cockpit cushions, and stocks a good selection of fabrics for covering berth cushions.

West Indies Sails also has a good shop. They do lots of kite sails and are agents for EH kites. They make cushions and do canvas work and can help with small sails or surf kites. If your job is too big, ask them about Jean-Luc who has a shop over in St. Jean.

Technical Yacht Services

Le Ship has a full rigging shop, and can handle all your rigging problems.

The St. Barth Boatyard is run by two Swedes, Per and Alf, along with more Swedish helpers. Come here when you are more interested in quality than cost and want an excellent job (They call themselves 2-Swedes Marine.) Apart from hauling and storage, they specialize in marine woodwork: anything from laying a teak deck to fitting fine cabinets. They do excellent glasswork, from patching minor blemishes to repairing major structural damage. They have done many factory repairs for Nautor Swan and can work in exotic materials like carbon fiber. They can handle rigging problems that don't involve swaging tools over 12mm, and they would be excellent people to use for a complete refit. They are good at respraying and have sheds to take boats up to 48 feet. They have a full welding and machine shop, and a mechanical shop for Vovlo Penta for whom they are agents for St. Barts, St. Martin, and Anguilla. They have a hydraulics shop and can service and repair hydraulic systems, or make new hoses. Call Natalie, the office manager, for information.

For other serious stainless welding jobs, see Regis at his company, Boatinox, in Lorient. Taxi your broken bits over to him, but call first to make sure he is there. He does a good job.

Ledee Beranger is the Yamaha agent, offering full sales and service. He helps with all mechanical problems and fixes any kind of outboard. His store is one of the best places to rent a car, scooter, or van. They handle phone calls, faxes, and ship provisions and they stock some marine hardware and fishing gear.

Hugues Marine is a big, first-rate mechanical shop on Rue Victor Hugo. Hughes and most of his eight assistants, including Bruno, speak excellent English. They repair and service inboard and outboard motors, as well as fixing electrical and mechanical electronic problems, and taking care of hydraulics and watermakers. They are agents for Sea Recovery watermakers, Kohler generators, and MRP sand FTP diesels. They have an excellent little machine shop in their facility, and a mechanical store selling parts and accessories, including stainless jerry jugs. They will happily come on board to check out your problem.

Navy Techniques is a full mechanical and electrical workshop for inboards, outboards, generators, and gearboxes. The owner, Christophe Domon, was an aircraft mechanic for many years before going into the marine sector in the Mediterranean. He then cruised over here and, after working for Hugues Marine, set up his own shop. He works out of his mobile shop and is a good mechanic.

JCG fixes electric tools, starter motors, and alternators. Call their mobile (0690-55-32-40).

Superyachts that need anchor untangling or lifting can arrange it through the port.

When we sailed to St. Barts way back when, Loulou's chandlery was one of the major stores. Loulou is still around, and can be helpful to long distance cruisers with general and marine information about St. Barts. You might find him down by Jenny's Studio, especially on a Sunday afternoon.

Transport

The taxi stand is right by the ferry dock, opposite Quicksilver. For hiking or driving tours, contact Helene Bernier (0690-63-46-09) (see *Ashore*).

Provisioning

The glitterati eat well and you won't lack for much at the AMC Supermarket, which is conveniently placed across the road from the yacht dock. This is a fine place to provision your yacht. It has super cool air conditioning and good fish, meat, and deli sections. They open 0700-2000, except Saturday, when they close at 1900, and are closed Sunday. You can phone or fax orders a day in advance and they will prepare them for you. They keep just about anything you may need for charter. Those with elaborate tastes should check their fine wine and liquor store directly across the road. They keep a few bottles open for

sampling. They do not offer bags; bring your own or take one of their old boxes.

La Cave Du Port Franc is just a few steps northwest of the commercial port and is run by the same family that runs the chandlery. They offer yachts good prices on wines and spirits.

Christian Greaux's Segeco is on the northwest side of the harbor, to starboard as you enter. They stock a wide range of wines, spirits, beers, and cigarettes, as well as non-alcoholic drinks, groceries, and food. It is a very convenient location for loading the dinghy.

Above AMC is Tom Foods, a big wholesale place. They will deliver to the docks. Access to their store is from the street behind.

When cost is no object, and what you need is nowhere else, try American Gourmet on Rue de Gaulle. It is a very fancy specialty food market with lots of beautiful jars and bottles.

For fresh fish, check the small fish market at the very end of the dock on the northeast corner, beyond the taxi stand.

Fun Shopping

Not since Montbars the Exterminator, has there been so much treasure loose in St. Barts. Gold, silver, fine jewels, and rich fabrics abound. You no longer have to risk losing your limbs to cannons while you pry it loose with a cutlass and blunderbuss. A small plastic card is quite sufficient. Yes, Gustavia is a major duty free shopping spot, with about two hundred shops, all packed in a few small streets. The emphasis is on exclusivity and quality rather than quantity. It is a place where the exotic is commonplace. Just the name "St. Barth" adds glamour and ups the price. Instead of boutiques, you find collections. Many have simple names, like Dior. Most are in the streets behind the waterfront on the northeast side of the harbor, behind the main docks, but others are scattered all the way round the port. All the famous names are here, including Little Switzerland, Cartier, Lacoste, La Perla, Hermes, and United Colors of Benetton. Indeed, it is de rigueur for high fashion shops to be able to include

St. Barth on their fancy shopping bags. Art galleries are also popular.

For the slightly more prosaic, there are very good hardware and household stores near the commercial port as you walk towards 2-Swedes. Feel I'm Home is a particularly lovely household and kitchen store, where you are bound to find something to improve the galley.

If you get tired of the fancy, check out Tom's Shop. It is packed with everything from t-shirts to kitchen things.

There are two bookshops, one on either side of the harbor with French and some English books, also paper, stationary, painting supplies, and more.

Jennifer May, who originally hailed from Cornwall in England, is a potter and artist who has an occasional School of Arts on the hill behind Fort Gustav. She knows all the local artists. Her gallery by the post office is occasionally open. If art interests you, give her a call at 0590-27-82-34.

Restaurants

Gustavia is a great place to eat out. About two dozen restaurants are dotted around the picturesque streets. They are always changing names and owners, so the best bet is to walk around and look.

Le Select is a popular, informal bar that is now the fashionable place to gather for an evening. There is always plenty of life here and you never know when Jimmy Buffet might pop in to give an impromptu rendition of "Cheeseburger in Paradise."

Eddie is a well known St. Barts restaurateur. His dad originally owned Le Select and Eddie ran it for a long time. His next venture was Eddie's Ghetto, and finally, he built Eddie's. It has an open courtyard, typical of the old Swedish houses, though it is reminiscent of the Far East, with a high, open, woven roof, attractive wooden furniture, and many plants. The stone walls date back over 100 years. Food is elegantly simple: perfectly prepared fish or meat with an appropriate sauce, and somewhat moderate prices.

Nearby, The Palace (formerly Eddie's Ghetto) offers a good French meal. Overlooking the harbor, Le Repaire, has open WiFi and is fair value.

Provenca, right at the end on the southwest side of the harbor, is a first class restaurant for both food and service. As the name suggests, their menu includes quite a few Provençal dishes. Midday is a good time to check it out as they offer a lunch plate special for about 12 Eu and a lunch menu for 18 Eu.

L'Entr'acte on the waterfront is inexpensive. They serve pizzas, sandwiches, and tasty Créole meals. They have free WiFi, and were undergoing a complete renovation when I passed by.

Restaurants have been built out over the waterfront along the end of the port – a prime location. Snack Bar La Gustav and Yosushimania are the latest incarnations of one of these spots with a great dinghy dock.

Farther along the same walkway, Bagatelle, opening evening only, is both good and popular.

For breakfast, coffee, pâtisseries, and lunchtime sandwiches. Carambole pâtisserie is very small but perfect. Choisy Boulangerie/pâtisserie, also very good, is larger and different in style. Both have outside seating.

Maya's (dinner only, closed Sunday) is a restaurant on the beach, behind the commercial dock. They are open to the beach, and, although the view is good, the real draw is the imaginative menu, with inspiration from the Orient as well as France and St. Barts. The menu changes daily.

If you need a little exercise to work up an appetite, hike up the road leading south out of town till you come to the big aerial on the hill. Santa Fe Restaurant is on the right. When visibility is good, the view is superb. This is a fine restaurant (closed Mondays) that feels miles away from the harbor. They serve a mixture of Caribbean, French, and Oriental dishes, all well prepared.

Ashore

Those who have been having a hard time finding shells can take the short walk over to Anse du Grand Galet, otherwise known as Shell Beach, and pick to their hearts' content. It is sign-posted from town.

RENAISSANCE ISLANDS

The beach hangout here is Do Brazil, with beach chairs, bar, and restaurant. This has the same owner as Yosushimania and Bar La Gustav in Gustavia. The food in Do Brazil is on the fancy side, with good seafood. They open for both lunch and dinner and have WiFi.

If you buy Jenny Stening's book on Gustavia, you can follow a walking tour of the town, which will introduce you to its early history and architecture. On the southwest side of the harbor, next to the fancy new Hotel de Collectivite (town hall), is the municipal museum of St. Barts, with an eclectic collection of pictures and artifacts showing St. Barts' history. There is a small entry fee. It is open until 1800 most days, mornings only on Saturday, and closed Sundays.

The interior of St. Barts is by far the prettiest of the Renaissance Islands and you can derive great pleasure from renting a moke (or a scooter if you dare) and driving around the countryside. The roads are often cut into the sides of the mountains. It takes some nerve, but feels like the closest thing you can get to flying on wheels. In one day, you can cover just about every road. Highlights include the southeast coast along Grand Fond, winding along the tiny mountain roads in Vitet,

and scrambling around the rocks at the end of the Colombier Road. Anse de Grande Saline makes a great stop for a walk and a swim. Two good restaurants here will make this a good lunch stop. One, Le Grain de Sel, is built right into the surrounding rock.

Baie St. Jean (including the airport) is a tourist hot spot, with lots of shops and restaurants, which often become crowded when cruise ships come in. You might like to visit Anse des Cayes. Part of the beach is good for bodyboard surfing.

If you prefer to be more active, call Helene Bernier (0690-63-46-09) and go hiking with her. She has transport and knows of tiny trails, mainly on private land, that take you up in the mountains to the highest peaks where you can sit on a rock with the island laid out below you. She has hikes at all levels and her difficult climbs involve some serious scrambling up rocks with precipitous drops close by. She does cultural and historical walks and full-day and half-day island tours by cab or by cab with hiking. For prices and more details check: stbartheasytime.com

Water Sports

Before you go diving, visit the marine park office at the port for a diving map and to pay the 2 Eu fee per dive. Use the moorings provided for diving; do not anchor. Diving on the rocks just outside Gustavia harbor is good, with plenty of hard and soft corals, sponges, and colorful reef fish, on such sites as Les Petit Saintes, Gros Ilet, La Baleine, and Pain de Sucre. In addition, between Gros Ilet and La Baleine (closer to La Baleine), lies the wreck of Non-Stop, a 210-foot power yacht that sank in 60 feet of water. La Baleine is one of the best sites.

Window shopping

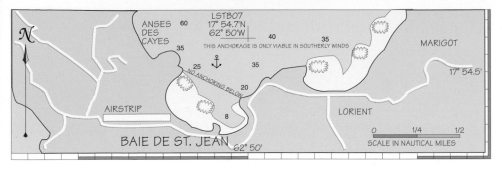

It is a small, rocky pinnacle that just breaks the surface. You can dive to 57 feet and will see giant barrel sponges, a variety of hard and soft corals, and plenty of fish.

There are several excellent dives farther off St. Barts. These are beyond the range of most yacht dinghies, so are best done with a dive shop. The Groupers includes two dives and they are considered among the best in the area. Little Groupers, the more southern group of rocks, make one dive, which is 20-70 feet around the southwest side. There are lots of rocks and gullies and there is a good chance of seeing turtles and barracudas. The larger rock and associated rocklets make another dive. If you go down on the small rock close by the large one, a tunnel goes right through and you can swim through it in calm weather. There are many walls and gullies, with lots of reef fish.

Table Rock is a dive for calm weather only. You can swim right around this island, which has a wall dropping to about 60 feet. Ile de Boulanger is another dive for calm weather only. Depths are between 30 and 60 feet, with lots of fish. Ile Coco has good diving for both novices and experienced divers. In one part, a wall drops to 60 feet with a sandy bottom littered with rocks, where you find stingrays, turtles, jacks, and nurse sharks. There is also an area with pretty caves in 20 feet of water where the colorful reef fish include parrotfish and trumpetfish.

La Bulle in Ocean Must Marina can help get you underwater. This is a small and friendly operation, and they are happy to fill your tanks or take you diving. It is run by David, Didier, and Johanna. Johanna is American and will make English-speakers

feel at home. They can handle any size of group, and are happy to do the custom dives most big yachts prefer.

The best sailboarding spot is in Baie St. Jean, where there is plenty of wind and some protection from the sea. For those who want waves, it is not far to the ocean. There are two rental agencies on the beach.

Baie St. Jean

Baie St. Jean is on the northern side of St. Barts, just at the end of the airport runway. When planes take off, they need to bank to the north and anchored yachts can be a real hazard. Therefore, the only permitted anchorage is outside the line between the headlands shown on our sketch chart. You will notice one or two small boats tucked up in the southeastern corner of the bay inside this limitation. These relatively small local boats with no live-aboards are allowed there.

The permitted anchorage is normally rolly and uncomfortable and not recommended. However, a few years back the winds were consistently from the south, and in these conditions it proved to be one of the better anchorages on the island. Those were somewhat exceptional conditions. People were also anchoring in Anse des Flamandes, which is normally really rough. In such conditions there is no problem anchoring in the area shown, and it is convenient for enjoying the popular beach ashore. However, do not anchor farther in the bay, as it will force the police to make a special, and possibly expensive, trip to ask you to move.

While here, check out the Sushi Bar and fancy Table de Jules in Lorient.

RENAISSANCE ISLANDS

ANSE DU GOUVERNEUR   ANSE DE GRANDE SALINE

ANSE DE GRANDE SALINE AND ANSE DU GOUVERNEUR

Anse de Grande Saline and Anse du Gouverneur are two fabulous secluded beaches, surrounded by scenic cliffs. They are not really anchorages and are untenable in strong winds or in any southeasterly wind. However, on a calm day with a light easterly or northeasterly breeze, it is possible to hang in here for lunch. Do not try to anchor unless it is calm and do not stay overnight, as conditions could change. Beaching the dinghy could be hazardous.

Anse de Grande Saline is the larger and more protected of the two. You can anchor off the rocks that lie in the northeastern corner. There is another small hidden bay a little farther toward the headland. Although small, this is perhaps the most protected spot, but take care, as the wind can swing around onto the shore. Walk back to the road for two good restaurants.

Anse du Gouverneur is acceptable as a lunch spot on calm days. Anchor off the western end of the beach. Do not attempt to get too close to shore, as the rollers get worse.

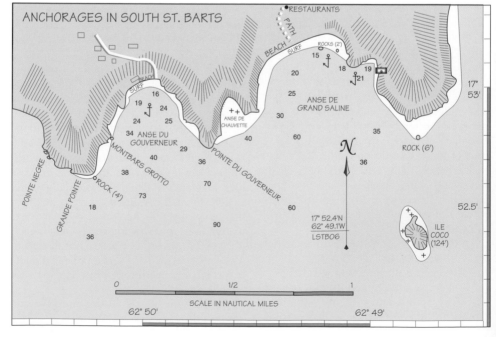

PASSAGES BETWEEN ST. MARTIN, ST. BARTS, SABA, STATIA, ST. KITTS, AND NEVIS

These islands are well placed for pleasant passages that are easily sailed in a day. Approximate distances and courses are given in our chart. If sailing directly from St. Barts to Nevis, it is usually faster to sail down the northeastern side of St. Kitts and then pass through The Narrows to Nevis. The reverse route is a good way to get back. Keep in mind that you will want to traverse The Narrows in good light. (Some charter companies do not allow this.) Passages between St. Martin or St. Barts and St. Kitts, in either direction, are usually good reaches, though when you are heading south you will have to beat 10 miles to windward along the south coast of St. Kitts. St. Martin is considerably farther from St. Kitts than St. Barts, so sailing from

St. Barts makes an easier passage. Passages between St. Martin or St. Barts and Statia in either direction are good sails that do not usually involve tacking. Although the sail from Statia to St. Kitts is generally hard on the wind, the sailing is pleasant and the distance across open water only about 10 miles, so it is very practical to visit Statia and then carry on to St. Kitts or Nevis. The passage from either St. Martin or St. Barts to Saba is easy, and if you are lucky, you will make it back to St. Martin in one tack. Normally, getting to St. Barts from Saba will involve beating to windward; so if you are not in a hurry, why not sail to St. Martin first?

RENAISSANCE ISLANDS

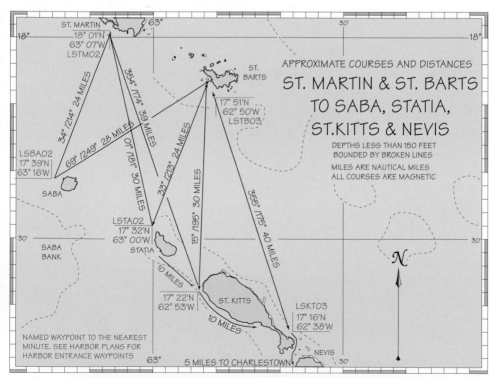

ST. MARTIN
18° 01'N
63° 07'W
LSTMO2

ST. BARTS
17° 51'N
62° 50'W
LSTBO3

APPROXIMATE COURSES AND DISTANCES
ST. MARTIN & ST. BARTS
TO SABA, STATIA,
ST.KITTS & NEVIS

DEPTHS LESS THAN 150 FEET
BOUNDED BY BROKEN LINES

MILES ARE NAUTICAL MILES
ALL COURSES ARE MAGNETIC

LSBAO2
17° 39'N
63° 16'W

SABA

354° / 174° 39 MILES
34° / 214° 24 MILES
69° / 249° 28 MILES
01° / 181° 30 MILES
33° / 213° 24 MILES
15° / 195° 30 MILES
355° / 175° 40 MILES

SABA BANK

LSTAO2
17° 32'N
63° 00'W

STATIA

10 MILES

17° 22'N
62° 53'W

ST. KITTS

10 MILES

LSKTO3
17° 16'N
62° 38'W

NEVIS

NAMED WAYPOINT TO THE NEAREST
MINUTE. SEE HARBOR PLANS FOR
HARBOR ENTRANCE WAYPOINTS

5 MILES TO CHARLESTOWN

N

anchorages of the islands that

BRUSH THE CLOUDS

saba • sint eustatius (statia) • st. christopher (st. kitts)

nevis • redonda • montserrat

Mt. Scenery, S

An old house, Saba

Chris Doyle

Anchorages Of
The Islands that Brush the Clouds

Saba, Statia, St. Kitts, Nevis, and Montserrat are small volcanic islands that rise steeply from the sea until their peaks touch the clouds. St. Kitts, the largest and tallest, is nearly 4000 feet high. Statia, the lowest, rises to nearly 2000 feet, although the island is only just 5 miles long. The high mountains trap passing moisture, which keeps them lush and green. For the most part these islands are surrounded by deep water, but to the southwest of Saba, the Saba Bank is about 600 square miles of sand and reef, 15 to 180 feet deep. It is fascinating to sail over this bank in gentle conditions, watching the reefs below. In heavy weather the shallow water can cause turbulent seas and is best avoided.

These five islands span some 90 miles and provide convenient stepping stones between Guadeloupe and St. Martin. The anchorages in the smaller islands can be rolly to untenable in northerly swells, and Basseterre, St. Kitts, was impossible in southeasterly winds until the marina was built. This lack of secure harbors has put them somewhat off the beaten track and kept them unspoiled. The passing sailor can be sure of a warm welcome.

While one or two of the anchorages are spectacularly beautiful, the main attraction of these islands is to explore on land. Ashore, they feel like five completely separate countries. Saba and Statia though quite different, are both parts of the Netherlands. St. Kitts and Nevis jointly form a single independent nation, and Montserrat, famous for its volcano, is a British colony. English is the accepted language throughout, though many people in Saba and Statia also speak Dutch.

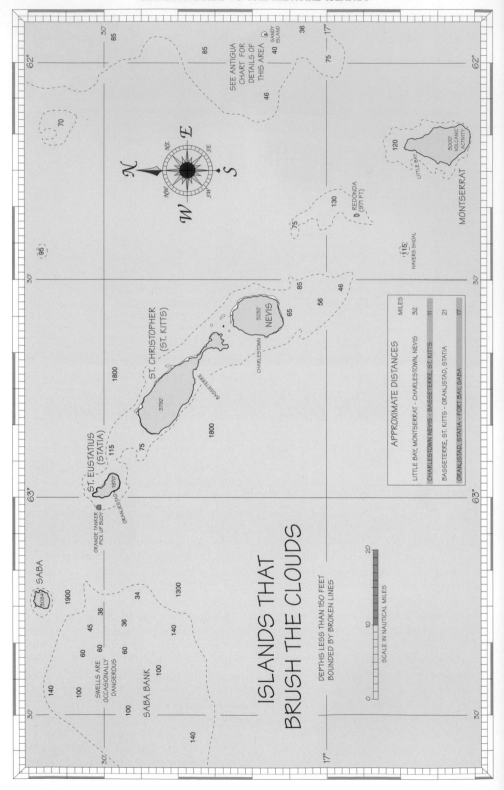

ISLANDS THAT
BRUSH THE CLOUDS

DEPTHS LESS THAN 150 FEET
BOUNDED BY BROKEN LINES

SCALE IN NAUTICAL MILES

SABA

SABA BANK

SWELLS ARE
OCCASIONALLY
DANGEROUS

ST. EUSTATIUS
(STATIA)

ORANGE TANKER
PICK UP BUOY

ORANJESTAD

ST. CHRISTOPHER
(ST. KITTS)

BASSETERRE

CHARLESTOWN

NEVIS

REDONDA
(971 FT)

HAVERS SHOAL

SEE ANTIGUA
CHART FOR
DETAILS OF
THIS AREA

SANDY
ISLAND

MONTSERRAT

LITTLE BAY

3000
VOLCANIC
ACTIVITY

APPROXIMATE DISTANCES

	MILES
LITTLE BAY, MONTSERRAT - CHARLESTOWN, NEVIS	32
CHARLESTOWN NEVIS - BASSETERRE, ST. KITTS	11
BASSETERRE, ST. KITTS - ORANJSTAD, STATIA	21
ORANJSTAD, STATIA - FORT BAY, SABA	17

Regulations

Tie to one of the four park moorings, or the quarantine buoy close off Fort Bay and go ashore to clear with the officials. If you have been here before, you can moor on the west coast, and dinghy in. Saba waters (including the Saba Bank) are part of a national marine park. Anchoring even a dinghy is prohibited, except in the anchoring zones shown on our charts. Littering or discharging foreign substances in the water is forbidden. When passing dive groups, stay 150 yards to seaward. (This includes dinghies.) You can download the entry forms at www.sabapark.org.

Ten overnight moorings for visiting yachts (up to 60 feet) with one for larger vessels (up to 150 tons) lie between Ladder Bay and Wells Bay, and four are off Fort Bay. (Servicing can sometimes reduce the number.) You are welcome to use these at no charge, other than the park fees. They are yellow or yellow with a blue stripe (see *Navigation*, below). The white buoys and the orange buoys are for diving only and you may not use dive buoys for your yacht. You may tie your dinghy to the buoy at Torrens Point for snorkeling. Call park manager Kai Wulf about mooring availability, sea conditions, and anything else: 599-416-3295/416-5750.

The park fees help pay for park maintenance. These are currently $3 US per person per week for those on board yachts less than 100 tons. Vessels greater than 100 tons pay $0.10 US per gross ton. Everyone pays $1 a day towards the land side of the park.

Port, customs, and immigration are all in a building on the dock by the security gate. Travis Johnson, in charge of ports, is very welcoming. There is a charge of $20 US (most regular yachts) up to $150 US (larger superyachts). Then check in with the marine park office. If there is no one there, you can fill in the form and drop money in the box. If you want to pay your port and park fees by credit card, the park has a credit card machine. In theory, officials are around from 0600-1800, but you will be lucky to find anyone around that early, or late, or during lunch, or if there is no other commercial traffic.

Spearfishing or taking coral is strictly forbidden. Anyone wishing to dive must do so with one of the dive shops. Gloves are not allowed for snorkeling or diving.

Telephones

You can make calls from the telephone office. Card phones are available. Dialing 00 gets you out of the country. Then dial the country code (1 for the USA, 44 for the UK). The country code is +599, cell coverage is like Sint Maarten, and when in Saba with a Sint Maarten cell, just dial the last 6-digits of the number.

Shopping Hours

Shopping hours depend on the proprietor, but try 0800-1200 and 1400-1600.

Transport

Saba is linked to St. Martin and Statia by several daily flights. Sit up front on the starboard side of the plane for the exciting landing on Saba, which resembles arriving on an aircraft carrier. The Edge ferry also comes several days a week.

You can rent a car or take a taxi. Garvis Hassell (599-416-6114) is happy to go on roads deemed too scary by other drivers. Taxi rates in $US are:

Sightseeing tour	$50.00
(up to 4, then $12.50 per head)	
Fort Bay to Windwardside	$15.00
Airport to Windwardside	$12.50
Fort Bay to Ecolodge	$17.00

Holidays

- Jan 1
- Good Friday and Easter Monday (Easter Sunday is March 27, 2016; April 16, 2017)
- April 30 (Queen's Birthday)
- May 1 (Labor Day)
- May 5 (Liberation Day)
- Ascension Day (39 days after Easter: May 5, 2016; May 25, 2017)
- Whit Monday (50 days after Easter Sunday, May 16, 2016; June 5, 2017)
- July 1 (Emancipation Day)
- Last Monday in July (and the next Tuesday) Carnival
- October 22 Antillean Day
- First Monday in December (Saba Day)
- December 25- 26

Travellers palm in flower, Eco Lodge   Chris Doyle

Saba

ABA RISES FROM THE sea like a fairytale picture of a forbidden land. A mere 5 square miles, it reaches a lofty 3,084 feet. Tall cliffs of red, pink, and brown rise almost vertically from the sea. Houses sit perched in seemingly impossible positions on the edges of precipices. Ashore, it lives up to its image, for, if there was ever a hidden Shangri-la in the Caribbean, it is Saba.

Until the early 1940s Saba was almost inaccessible. Everything had to come and go via Ladder Bay. This extraordinary landing on the leeward shore provides scant shelter from ocean swells. Some 800 steps are cut in the rock. The steepness of the steps and their elevation can be appreciated from the sea by looking at the old customs house, which is only half way up. Boats could only land when the sea was calm and even then men had to stand waist deep in water to handle the cargo. Everything from the outside had to be carried up, including, at different times, a piano and a bishop. The Sabans were able to prevent unwanted invasions by keeping piles of boulders stacked behind wooden supports that were cut down when attackers were half way up the hill. A road was built to Fort Bay in 1943, but with no port to shelter the bay, the island was still impossible to reach much of the time.

The 1500 inhabitants are descendants of hardy Dutch, Scottish, and English settlers, along with a few Africans who originally came as slaves. They have worked hard, side by side, to derive a decent living from this rugged land. They became great seafarers, fishermen, farmers, cobblers, boat builders, and, in more recent times, women have become skilled in lacework. Sabans take great pride in their work and are unimpressed by obstacles. The two main villages in Saba are named The Bottom and Windwardside.

Up until the 50s, the only way to get between the villages was to walk along a steep mountain track. Engineers came from Holland and said the steep terrain precluded the possibility of a road. So Joseph Hassel, born in 1906, took a correspondence course in road building and the Saban people hand-built their road. It took them several years and was finished in 1958. Dutch engineers were similarly disparaging about the idea of an airport. The Sabans called in Remy de Haenen, a pilot from St. Barts. He looked over their one flat-topped rock and figured landing might be possible. The Sabans flattened the area as much as they could by hand, removing big rocks and filling in holes. Remy landed, proving the feasibility of flying in.

Today Sabans have their airport (it's like landing on an aircraft carrier), a road to the sea, and a tiny harbor. Despite its lack of beaches, Saba attracts visitors. Some come to try the diving, rated among the Caribbean's best. Others come for a glimpse of this remote island, which developed

in isolation, away from the mainstream of Caribbean life. The first surprise is the beauty of the island. From the sea it looks like a rock, but up high in the hills the mountains and views are spectacular. The island is spotlessly clean, with villages of whitewashed, green-trimmed, red-roofed cottages that look like they were plucked from Europe sometime in the 19th century. There are cobblestone streets, low stonewalls, and small stone churches. The people are honest, straightforward, industrious, and cheerful. They have a strong sense of community and there is very little crime.

Saba is special, if you manage to visit it, you will never forget it. It is a nature island with many really lovely hikes, all generally are well maintained. Some years ago Saba became part of the Netherlands. From a cruising perspective the result has been the creation of a whole new bunch of bureaucrats. Once you get through this, you

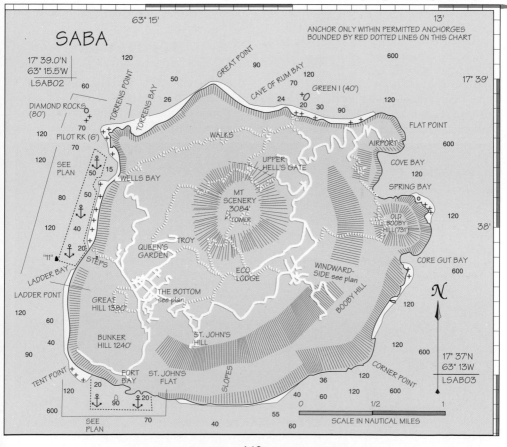

Dive the Sea Saba Difference

SEA SABA
ADVANCED DIVE CENTER
SABA • DUTCH CARIBBEAN

Unparalleled service:
-dive our relaxed schedule
-charter one of our 40' boats
-or hire our professional crew
Take advantage of our concierge-level service to arrange guided hikes, tours and more...
+599 416-2246 www.seasaba.com info@seasaba.com

will find Sabans among the most friendly and welcoming people in the Caribbean.

Industries include a small amount of tourism, the mining of gravel and sand from one of the hillsides near Fort Bay, and an international medical school whose students, when in residence, add about 30-50 percent to the population. This, plus the arrival of a few more visitors and the building of a few more hotels, has brought some changes: there are more shops and their stock is much more plentiful; restaurants are excellent and booming. There are even a couple of discos.

Saba is not the easiest of anchorages, though the addition of yacht moorings and a good dinghy dock in the port make it much easier than in days of old. A few bareboat charter companies make it off-limits for their guests. Those not allowed to visit by boat should consider going by air or ferry as a side trip. The least expensive way is the Edge ferry from Pelican Quay, Sint Maarten, usually on Wednesdays and Sundays, but they do change. If you want to stay a few days, the ferry Dawn runs over in the afternoon from Dock Martin in Philipsburg (599-416-2299, reservations@sabactransport.com). With Saba taxes, ferries comes to less than $100 return. Or Winair will fly you for about $150.

Navigation

Like all good hidden kingdoms, Saba doesn't come easily, and the cruising sailor who wishes to visit must be prepared to pay the price of possible frustration in the face of the elements. The trick is to listen to the

FORT BAY

Chris Doyle

weather reports and avoid visiting if heavy northerly swells or strong northeasterly winds are forecast.

Approaching is no problem, as the island is steep-to and a quarter of a mile offshore clears all dangers except for Diamond Rock and Green Island at the north end. A quick flashing white aero-beacon sits on top of Mt. Scenery, but even if working, it is usually obscured by clouds.

For much of the time, the west coast is reasonably calm. Ten yacht moorings are spaced along this stretch of coast. They are yellow with a blue stripe or plain yellow, (do not mistake the red or white dive moorings for yacht moorings) and are suitable for yachts up to 60 feet or 50 tons; the southernmost one is suitable for a yacht up to 150 tons. They are available on a first-come basis at no extra charge as a service of the Saba Marine Park. Each mooring has a tie up line attached to its top. This is easily recognized as it has a plastic-sheathed loop at the free end. Pass your own line through the loop and let out plenty of scope. It is best to make a bridle with two lines, fastening one to each side of your bow. (Do not use one continuous line for this, or it will chafe as the boat swings.) Superyachts wishing to anchor should do so outside the line of moorings in about 100 feet. If you call the park, they will direct you.

The swell here is often comfortably long and gentle, though if the tides are running

Iguana, Saba

strongly, you can lie beam to the swells for a few hours on the rising tide. While the coast is totally open to the north, the moorings are fairly deep, so unless a northerly swell is huge, you should be able to stay on the mooring. However, in a northerly swell it will roll. (Saba is better than Statia in northerly swells because of the depths.)

Four moorings off Fort Bay enable you to tie up close to the harbor. Fort Bay is usually much rougher then the west coast (except in northerly swells, when Fort Bay is better). You can tie to a Fort Bay mooring during the day where it is closer to get ashore, and move to the west coast for comfort at night.

If you arrive after 1400 when the dive boats finish, there is a chance you could tie up in the port and even stay the night (call Saba Port VHF: 16).

Cruising to Saba in earlier days could be frustrating because, having arrived, one

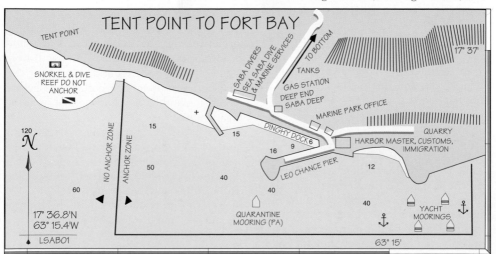

might sit for days waiting for conditions calm enough to land. Now you can take your dinghy inside the harbor and climb ashore dry. It is less than 2 miles from Well's Bay to Fort Bay so, even with a 2-horsepower outboard, you can make it in half an hour, though parts of the journey can be rough for a small tender, so do not overload it. The port has built a big new dinghy dock.

Sabans are intent on keeping their waters as pristine and beautiful as their land. Anchoring is restricted to sandy areas where coral will not be damaged. We show these on our sketch chart. Check in with the park office when you go to Fort Bay. (See also Page 167 and *Water Sports*).

Communications

Island Communications Services in Windwardside has internet, (use their computers or buy island wide WiFi cards) DVD rentals, US mailing, copying, and printing. They rent cars, send and receive DHL, and arrange airline tickets. They open weekdays 0900-1800, Saturdays 1000-1500.

Satel, the Saba telephone company, is in The Bottom. They can help you make a call or sell you a cell phone or a SIM (Telcell or Chippie). They offer island-wide WiFi, so if you bring your computer ashore or manage to get a connection from your boat, they can hook you to the internet with pre-paid cards for 1, 10, or 50 hours. These are available from the Satel office, and many stores.

It is hard to communicate from the anchorage. There has been talk for some years of either a VHF repeater or cell phone relay targeted at the anchorage. But it has not happened.

Services

You can get diesel and gasoline in jerry jugs from the gas station, open 0800-1500, Monday to Saturday. There are garbage bins on the dock. Ask the harbormaster about filling jerry jugs with water and, if that does not work, talk to Saba Deep.

The Marine Park is managed by Kai. He and his staff are extremely helpful. When

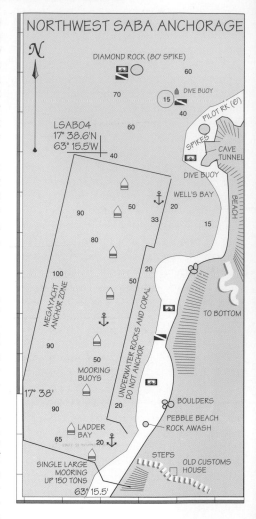

you check in, you can ask them everything about hiking and diving, as well as island information and weather. They will help you book meals, dives, and taxis. They can also tell you about sea conditions before you come and let you know about mooring availability.

Sea Saba has a yacht services department at their dive shop in Fort Bay. They can help out in emergencies and their mechanical shop includes light fabrication, TIG welding (all metals), and mechanical services.

You can drop laundry off at The Bottom Bean Cafe, and they call a woman who does laundry. If you are not too late, it is a same day service.

WELLS BAY

NORTHWEST SABA

MOORINGS

Fort Bay Anchorage

The Marine Park has four moorings and you may also anchor (see chart). It is usually uncomfortable and you would not want to be here in a southeast wind or large southerly swells, but this anchorage is okay in calm weather or when the wind is well to the north, and it is better to be here in northerly swells. You can come by day to go ashore, as the ride into the harbor is very short, then return to the northwest coast when you get back.

Ladder Bay Anchorage

This is the best mooring area in Saba. Use one of the 10 moorings or, if none are left, anchor out in 50 feet of water up to Well's Bay. Superyachts should anchor outside the moorings. The flattest bottom is towards the northern end. The southernmost mooring has heavy rope and is suitable for up to 150 tons. When you want to go ashore, do as any of today's Sabans would: use Fort Bay. Several yachtsmen have tried to follow in the footsteps of Sabans of old and use Ladder Bay. The high attrition rate when landing indicates that modern cruisers lack the skill and patience of old time Sabans. However, when ashore, a taxi can take you to the steps, which are maintained as a monument, and the walk down and up is delightful and gives you a feel for Saba's history.

Well's Bay Anchorage

This is a spectacular anchorage, below high cliffs with huge rocks embedded in them. Tropicbirds wheel and chatter above, and below you can find some of the Caribbean's best snorkeling. Use one of the moorings here. If they are not available and you need to anchor, do so in more than 33 feet of water to avoid possible reef damage.

During the summer months there is a beach here, but in the winter the sand washes away, leaving boulders. There is a road leading to The Bottom. The road from The Bottom to Windwardside is known as the "road that couldn't be built," and some taxi drivers think that the road to Well's Bay is the "road that shouldn't have been built," as it is so steep they cannot make it up with a full load. It is occasionally closed due to landslides.

If it's calm, you can land here to explore the beach. But if you head inland and swells arrive while you are gone, (quite likely) you may be marooned ashore for some days.

When leaving, most yachts can pass between the amazing Diamond Rock pinnacle and Torrens Point. Deep draft yachts should note the 15-foot-deep Man O' War Shoals in the middle, as well as

Jobean
GLASS ART

Unique Jewelry & Glass Art Classes

a touch of glass...

Jobean Forever Gallery now open in Windwardside!
Booby Hill - Saba - Dutch Caribbean - Tel: +599 416 2490 - jobeanglassart.com

underwater rocks extending from both sides, so do this in good light. The dinghy can be tied to the diving/snorkeling buoy at Torrens Point for snorkeling.

Provisioning

You can find a surprising variety of food on Saba, but don't expect the fancy supermarkets and provisioning available in St. Martin. The easiest place to provision is at My Store in The Bottom. This is an impressively large supermarket by Saban standards, but in keeping with the scale, rather than being a single big area, it flows through several small rooms. In The Bottom

you will also find the Saba Self-Service Supermarket, and there is also a Chinese store that stays open on Sundays.

Big Rock Market is in Windwardside, and this is a sizeable shop with a good range of groceries of all sorts. Unique is another supermarket at Windwardside, opposite the tourist office. It is a bit smaller than Big Rock, but has a good selection, including fresh produce. You will find ATM machines in both The Bottom and Windwardside.

Fun Shopping

Saban women are artistic. In the 1870s Gertrude Johnson learned to do a special

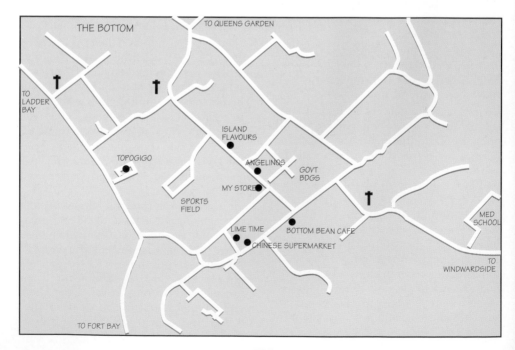

Mark Johnson
Custom Designs, Unusual Gems

The Jewel Cottage|Windwardside, Saba| Dutch Caribbean
www.thejewelcottage.com| info@thejewelcottage.com
(+599)416 6150

kind of embroidery from nuns in Venezuela. She brought this dying art back to Saba and the Saban women have been improving on it ever since. It is known as "drawing thread handwork" or "Spanish thread work." The largest selection is at the Hellsgate Community Cottage, though you may enjoy buying from a lace maker's home. There are elegant shirts, aprons, and household items.

Lace is not the only Saban art. You can find great local arts and crafts as well as casual clothing here. To look for these you will need to go to Windwardside.

The Jewel Cottage is owned by Saban Mark Johnson, artist, art historian and collector. He has created his own beautiful and unique space in his 150 year old Saban home where he artistically displays Jewelry. Some he makes himself, but he has also bought in a careful selection of works from some of his friends including Donna Cohen, Isabel Souccar, Patrick Auneau. and Allie. Each does outstanding work and has a distinctive style. A combination of a charming home, artistic displays and the

lovely jewelry make this a special place to put on your island itinerary. He is open in the winter daily from 1000-1800, outside those times call to see if he can open for you (599) 416 61 50.

You will find an interesting collection of charming shops in Lambee's Place. Everyt'ings is Saba's number one souvenir and general shop. It sells clothing, lots of handicrafts and t-shirts downstairs, and ornaments, decorations, candles, and art upstairs. The shop lives up to its name and anything you cannot find elsewhere is here; postcards, games, glasses and footwear. They also sell Saban lace and Saba spice liqueur. Much of the work is made on Saba, and they specialize in a large selection of excellent molas from the San Blas Islands.

The Sea Saba Shop has elegant t-shirts, casual wear, diving accessories, local books, souvenirs, and more.

Four Square Gallery shows the work of many talented local artists at very reasonable prices; also some pottery. One of the artists, Heleen, has a beautiful book

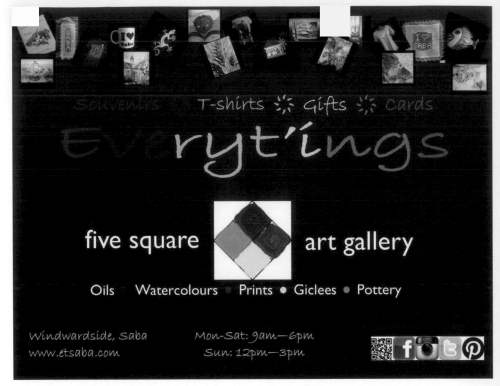

Souvenirs ❋ T-shirts ❋ Gifts ❋ Cards

Everyt'ings

five square **art gallery**

Oils ❖ Watercolours ● Prints ● Giclees ● Pottery

Windwardside, Saba   Mon-Sat: 9am—6pm
www.etsaba.com   Sun: 12pm—3pm

of her art called Saban Cottages, which is available here. If you want to see more of her work, call Heleen for a visit to her studio in Troy: 416-3348.

Across the road, the Trail Shop is part of the Saba Conservation Society (closed Mondays). You can buy maps, nature books, t-shirts, water, back packs, and eco-friendly souvenirs.

Also across the road is Flow. This delightful little store, sells lots of local crafts. You can get Saban lace here, some casual clothing, local products, and jewelry. You can taste and maybe buy the Saban liqueur called Saba Spice. It is made with lots of herbs and spices. The first sip reminds the uninitiated of cough medicine, but people manage to acquire a taste for it.

Take a pleasant short walk just out of town to Booby Hill, where you will find Jobean Glass Art, a wonderful working glass studio. Jo works with rods of glass to produce elegant jewelry, small glass sculptures of tree lizards, frogs, turtles, mermaids, and more. She also makes glass beads. These include imitations of (but you won't be able tell the difference) the famous slave beads once used in Statia, and Heineken beads made from the bottles. You can watch Jo at work creating handsome designs with different colored glass and she will even design something especially for you. Jo runs glass work classes on request.

Restaurants Fort Bay

Saba Deep operates an entertaining bar/ restaurant called The Deep End on the top half of their dive shop in Fort Bay. Sit and relax in cool bay breezes looking out over the bay. It is run by Cheri Waterfield, originally from Virginia. You can get burgers, sandwiches, wok specialties, and pasta dishes while trading underwater stories. The Deep End opens with the dive shop at 0830 and is a good place for breakfast or morning coffee and muffins and then lunch. They have free WiFi and may open in the evening for large groups by special request.

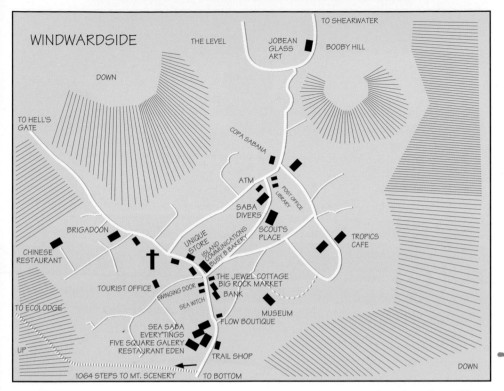

WINDWARDSIDE

TO SHEARWATER

JOBEAN
GLASS
ART

BOOBY HILL

THE LEVEL

DOWN

COPA SABANA

TO HELL'S
GATE

ATM

POST OFFICE

LIBRARY

SABA
DIVERS

SCOUT'S
PLACE

TROPICS
CAFE

BRIGADOON

UNIQUE
STORE

ISLAND
COMMUNICATIONS
BUSY B BAKERY

CHINESE
RESTAURANT

THE JEWEL COTTAGE
BIG ROCK MARKET

TOURIST OFFICE

SWINGING DOOR

BANK

SEA WITCH

MUSEUM

TO ECOLODGE

FLOW BOUTIQUE

UP

SEA SABA
EVERY'TINGS
FIVE SQUARE GALERY
RESTAURANT EDEN

TRAIL SHOP

DOWN

1064 STEPS TO MT. SCENERY

TO BOTTOM

Restaurants The Bottom

Eating out in Saba is a pleasure, with plenty of choice and restaurants in both The Bottom and Windwardside.

The Queens Garden Resort in Troy is within fairly easy walking distance of The Bottom, and is casually stylish. The courtyard is half-surrounded by a lush tropical garden that climbs the hill; other parts afford a panoramic view to The Bottom and the ocean far below. This is also a sizeable hotel and the managers, Hidde Verbeke and Claire Nuyens, keep an attentive staff. They serve excellent international and local food, and have a tank for live lobster.

In The Bottom, Paul Cizek has the wonderful Bottom Bean Cafe, where they make the best coffee, along with a ham, egg and cheese muffin for breakfast, baked treats at any time, or delectable sandwiches or salads for lunch, followed by gelato ice cream. He sells bottles of wine and liquor here, including ones you may not find in the supermarkets. He opens weekdays 0700-1700, Saturday, 0800-1500 and Sunday

1200-1500. You can drop laundry off here for Carmen who will bring it back the same day if you bring it in reasonably early.

Island Flavours was nearing completion when I visited. It was being built by Joani and her partner Steve. This will be one fine restaurant. Joani, who is probably the only Carib in Saba, originally hails from St. Vincent, and was chef for years at In Too Deep, and always dreamed of her own place. Check it out, it will be good.

Angelina's is a nice small restaurant where you can get good local food.

Topogigo is open all day every day and happy to serve you local food. It is a hot spot at night where people come to party, and popular with the young and not-so-young. When I was updating, I met a few with Topogigo hangovers.

Lime Time is an authentic Chinese Restaurant.

Restaurants Windwardside

Busy B is a wonderful little bakery and café in the Breadline Plaza, which they share with Island Communications,

Tropics Cafe   Chris Doyle

Eye Care Optical and the Verder pub. Artistically tiled courtyard and brick buildings, with umbrellas for shade make this a pleasant place to sit and watch life go by. Busy B is open from 0700-1600, with the best breads and baked goodies. They serve breakfast and lunch or just coffee and a snack. For lunch they have sandwiches and paninis and sometimes a smoked salmon sandwich special.

Verder has a pub-like atmosphere and serves food, usually a lunch special with a soda for $12.

Wolfgang and Barbara Tooten have Scout's Place, a guesthouse perched half way up a mountain in Windwardside. They have a good bar and restaurant, with local and international food. They bring in good chefs and often cook special food on Saturdays. This is a friendly place and the outer limit of their dining room is a tiny balcony with a spectacular view. Pop in for lunchtime specials or make reservations for dinner. They open for breakfast, and if you need a good place to stay ashore for a reasonable price, this is it.

Wim and Johanna's Tropics Café, closed Monday, is otherwise open for breakfast lunch, and dinner, and has a pool, a hot tub, and a great view over these to the hills and sea beyond. They serve excellent sandwiches, salads and grilled foods, including fresh local fish.

Sea Witch Bar & Grill has a pub-like atmosphere and serves good straightforward food, from hamburgers to local fresh fish.

The Swinging Door also has a pub-like atmosphere and serves world class hamburgers with ice-cold beer for both lunch and dinner (plus a Tuesday barbecue). Farther down the road, Brigadoon, with a view over the north side of the hill, is run by Michael Chamma and Trish. They open evenings only and close on Tuesdays. Michael varies his menu to use the fresh food that is available and has a Saturday sushi hour. He likes to cook seafood, steak, and rack of lamb. Trish tends bar and keeps you entertained. Guido's Pizza does good pizza and is often open when everyone else has gone to bed.

Restaurant Eden has pleasant dining

Windwardside   Chris Doyle

areas with the feel of a garden. The current owners, Norbert from Holland and Nina from Norway, are serious about their food, which is French in style, with some Italian and other European influence. The restaurant has just changed hands and I hope with the new owners you will eat as well here as before, whether it is a sashimi sandwich for lunch or a full evening meal. Currently they open every day for lunch (1200-1600) and dinner (1730-2130).

In the mountains above Windwardside (take a taxi) Eco Lodge is a special delight, hidden in the trees. This forest hideaway has cute little cottages for rent and a good restaurant. It has recently been taken over by Keith from Saba and Kelly from North Carolina. Keith is a top Saban chef trained in classical French cuisine who used to run the kitchen in Queens Garden. They are creating a big organic garden and their food is, as far as possible, local, including fresh fish from the harbor. Their cuisine is traditional Antillean with the emphasis on fresh flavors from top quality ingredients. It is right beside the Mount Scenery trail

(a very short shady walk from the top of the road), so ideal for a meal before or after climbing the mountain, but also a magical forest experience at night. Call them if possible at least an hour before you arrive because dinner is only prepared if you have made a reservation.

Ashore

The Bottom is built on a shelf, with steep slopes above and below. It is Saba's capital and administrative center, and is home to the medical school. The other village, Windwardside, is up the mountain. Both are charming and photogenic, and if you are just spending a day, a full taxi tour is the best way to see the island. This can be a very flexible arrangement. Whatever you want to do will be fit in. Time for shopping, photography, climbing the mountain, making a phone call, or having lunch can easily be arranged. The drivers are excellent guides. The roads are narrow and steep, facing many a sheer drop. Bring your camera. The tour rate is very reasonable and based on about a three hour ride. It can

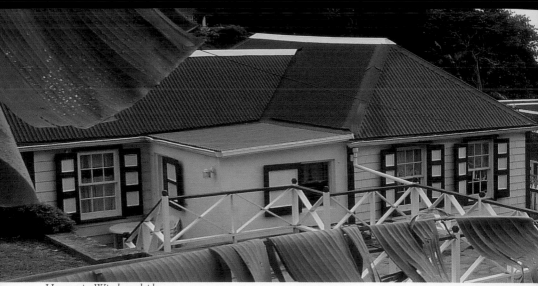

Houses in Windwardside

last much longer than that if you are being dropped off and picked up, so the driver does not have to be with you all day. But if you go way over what you would think reasonable for a short tour, you should pay some extra.

Hiking in Saba is excellent and trail maps are available at the marine park office, the tourist office and trail shop. There is some security in letting the trail shop know where you are hiking. Saba has many lovely hikes, which you can discuss with Kai in the Marine Park. Your first should probably be to the top of Mt. Scenery, which is about 3,084 feet high and is world class. The trail begins in Windwardside, but you can get a taxi to drop you off along a road that meets the trail higher up. Like everything else on Saba, the path is well maintained and it includes some 1,064 steps. The cloud forest vegetation of giant philodendrons, clusia, and tree ferns resembles a magnificent garden. Clouds passing below will sometimes give you a weird sensation of sitting on a cloud. If you are lucky enough to make it on a clear day, follow the path past the aerial to the end. You will be treated to one of the Caribbean's most spectacular and terrifyingly precipitous views, about 1,500 feet straight down to Windwardside. While at the top, you can take a trail that goes to the very highest point of the mountain, and for this some agility is required as you have to pull yourself on a rope that has been

placed on the trail. The views here can be amazing, but usually you will be in the mist. Allow 2 to 3 hours for the round trip hike, starting at the higher road. If you make it, the tourist office will issue you an award certificate. If you want a hiking guide, ask in the Trail Shop.

Water Sports

The snorkeling is fabulous and the diving stupendous. The self-supporting marine park was for many years the best in the Caribbean. Current laws forbidding independent diving have lost it this accolade in my opinion, but the diving is still great. Go to the marine park office next to the generating plant to get a brochure that describes all the dive and snorkel sites. The park maintains diving buoys on all the good sites, and will freely tell you anything you might want to know. Tom Van't Hof's book, *Guide to the Saba Marine Park*, describes all the dives. Saba has a recompression chamber for diving accidents.

The snorkeling at Well's Bay is first rate. Tie your dinghy to the dive buoy at the north end of the bay. There are two tunnels and a cave to explore, in waters packed with fish and turtles. The first tunnel is easily seen from the mooring and looks like a cave. You find the cave by going through the tunnel and turning right. The second tunnel is beyond the cave and is underwater.

Saba plunges down into the sea as rapidly as it rises. There are excellent dives

Chris Doyle

at all levels. Diving here is diving on the Caribbean's outer edge, and you might meet the unexpected anytime. Giant rays hammerhead and whale sharks have been sighted; turtles and stingrays are fairly common.

Any of the three dive shops will be happy to take you diving and meet you at your yacht. You can try to call them on the radio, but you have to call before you arrive in Saba or get one of the dive boats when it is going out or returning, as it is impossible to reach Fort Bay by radio from the anchorage, although some cell phones may work. Better still, make your dive arrangements when you clear in. If you have your own dive gear and tender, you can arrange with one of the dive shops to supply a dive guide. All dive shops now do nitrox.

Sea Saba (VHF: 16) has a shop in Windwardside and dive operation in Fort Bay. It is owned by John Magor and Lynn Costenaro, who have been on the island for over 25 years. John is an excellent underwater and land photographer. Sea Saba is a full PADI instruction facility. They have two 40-foot covered dive boats, and usually take a maximum of 10, with two crew. They can teach in French, German, Dutch, and English. Their workshop in Fort Bay helps out with marine problems.

Saba Divers have an office in Windwardside in Scout's Place and their dive operation is in Fort Bay. It is run by the owners, Vit Rosberg and Miroslav Hudecek.

They can teach in English, German, or Czechoslovakian. They have two large, solid, covered dive boats. They listen to VHF: 16, but even up in Windwardside are out of range of the anchorage. It should be easy to contact them on your sail over. They are a PADI operation and offer all the usual courses.

Saba Deep (VHF: 16) is the original dive shop and easy to find in Fort Bay. It is owned and run by Cheri Waterfield and is a PADI and NAUI facility. Cheri would eventually like to sell the shop, but in the meantime they dive in a low-key manner with very small groups and extra personal service.

Diving varies in Saba, from startlingly dramatic walls to serenely beautiful coral on white sand. Below are just a few of the 26 dives.

You can see Diamond Rock rising dramatically out of the sea from Well's Bay. It drops to a sandy The Bottom 80 feet below. The rock is covered with colorful sponges and many hard and soft corals; the fish life here is staggering. It seems that all the brightest colored reef fish have gathered and they are curious and unafraid of divers. Margates, snappers, sole eyes, durgons, and doctorfish are just a few of the species you will see. The dive site is not large, so swim slowly. As you swim around the rock, it seems that each new vista is more dramatically beautiful than the last. Occasionally there is a current.

ISLANDS THAT BRUSH THE CLOUDS

Bottom

Chris Doyle

Man O' War Shoals lies between Diamond Rock and Torren's Point. It consists of a large rock whose twin peaks come to within 15 feet of the surface. This is another dreamy dive that makes me feel I am swimming in an underwater painting. The rocks are well covered with a profusion of hard and soft corals and multi-colored sponges. This forms the perfect backdrop to a cast of thousands of fish that are completely unafraid. A few even stare in your mask, as if hoping to find some kind of intelligence. We saw a school of large and very tame jacks, a pair of tuna, and many margates, besides the usual reef fish. The area is small, but so beautiful it is easy to relax away an hour.

Torren's Point forms the northern point of Well's Bay and many spiked rocks stick up above the water. We have already mentioned the caves with reference to snorkeling, but this is also a shallow dive area, rarely getting deeper than 40 feet. Large boulders and rock formations rise from the sand, leaving sandy channels, gullies, and pools between them. The rocks have been well colonized by corals and sponges and there is a profusion of smaller reef fish.

There are several dives off Ladder Bay, starting at around 20 feet and dropping to about 90 feet. Here you will find many rocky ridges about 10 feet high, with sandy alleys between. There is an abundance of hard and soft corals, colorful reef fish, crabs, and shrimp.

Tent Point, just west of Fort Bay, is 30 to 80 feet deep, with pillar coral, colorful soft corals, and sponges, among which are lots of reef fish, some French angelfish, and the occasional turtle. Tent Reef Wall is a dramatic drop off, with purple and yellow tube sponges and black coral.

The next dives are perhaps Saba's most famous adventure dives: pinnacles that rise from 1,000 feet deep to within 90 feet of the surface. They lie together about half a mile offshore.

Third Encounter consists of a plateau about 100 feet deep with a deep drop off on most sides. Coral mounds rise above the plateau. The climax of this dive is the Eye

of the Needle. As you swim into the blue unknown, an amazing slender pinnacle appears before you, rising from great depths to 90 feet below the surface. It is so pretty you may want to hold your breath – but keep breathing! There is a painting of it on the backside of the Marine Park brochure.

Twilight Zone is in the same general area. A series of rocky outcrops rise to 80 or so feet below the surface from a ledge that in some places drops away as far as you can see. There are many deepwater gorgonians and sponges and many tame fish, including groupers and jacks.

Outer Limits is the third dive in this area: a long narrow ridge at 90 to 100 feet and over the edge of it, a dramatic drop off to nowhere – and another dramatic profusion of fearless fish.

The Old Gin House   Chris Doyle

St. Eustatius (Statia)

STATIA IS A SMALL ISLAND with a large history. From the anchorage you can see a long cliff just behind a sandy beach. At the base of the cliff a few buildings are nestled between old stone ruins, which tumble into the sea. On top of the cliff the present small town peeks out through trees. To the east a perfect volcanic cone rises to 1,800 feet. Ashore, a donkey grazes peacefully; little movement breaks the tranquility.

Imagine now, the Golden Era during the mid to late 1700s, when Statia was the trade capital of the Indies, and one of the world's busiest harbors. Up to three hundred sailing ships lie at anchor. All along the shore a sea wall protects a long street of shops and warehouses. Goods are available here from all over the world: fine fabrics, silver, gold, household supplies, slaves, guns, sugar, tobacco, and cotton. Thousands of tons of commodities are traded daily in a colorful, noisy, bustling town, with hundreds of small boats going from ships to shore. During

these years, the European powers were fighting each other; in addition, England was unsuccessfully trying to put down the upstart American rebels. The major powers wrapped their colonies in a mass of red tape and taxes, stifling trade. The Dutch, who owned Statia, remained neutral and opened Statia as a free port. It became possible to buy or sell anything here, along with the appropriate papers. Countries not allowed to deal with each other could deal with Statia, so Statian papers were attached to many things produced elsewhere. For example, in 1770 Statia produced about 600,000 pounds of sugar, but exported 20 million pounds. It was officially approved smuggling, and the inhabitants, some 8,000 mixed Dutch, English, and Jewish merchants, got very rich. Statia became known as the Golden Rock, but the prosperity was not to last.

In 1776 the Andrew Doria, an American vessel, came into harbor and gave a salute. Governor de Graff, not sure what to do, decided to fire a return salute, but two guns less. He didn't realize that, although Andrew Doria was a merchant ship, she was under the command of an American rebel navy

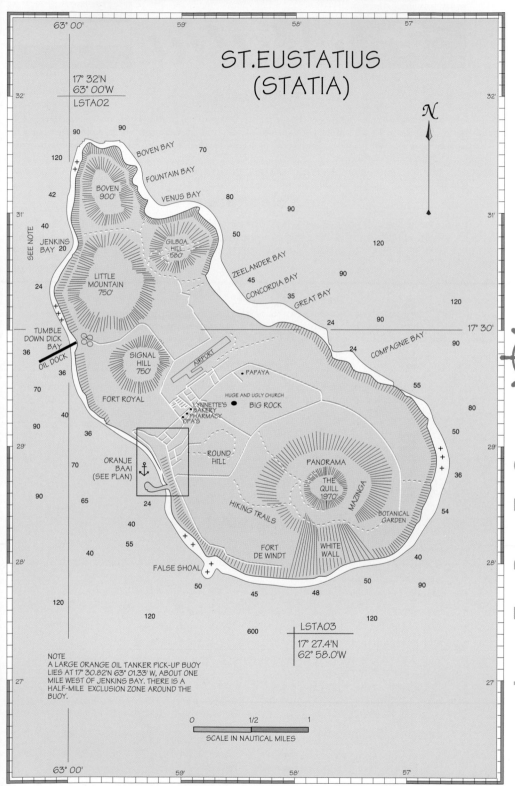

ST. EUSTATIUS
(STATIA)

63° 00' 59' 58' 57'

17° 32'N
63° 00'W
LSTA02

32' 32'

90 90
120 BOVEN BAY 70
42 FOUNTAIN BAY BOVEN 900'
SEE NOTE 40 VENUS BAY 80
31' GILBOA HILL 580' 90 31'
JENKINS BAY 20 50
24 LITTLE MOUNTAIN 750' ZEELANDER BAY 45 120
  CONCORDIA BAY 90
  35 GREAT BAY 120
TUMBLE DOWN DICK BAY 90 24 90 17° 30'
36 OIL DOCK 24 COMPAGNIE BAY 90
36
70 SIGNAL HILL 750' AIRPORT PAPAYA 55
40 FORT ROYAL HUGE AND UGLY CHURCH 80
90 LYNNETTE'S BAKERY BIG ROCK 50
36 PHARMACY OPA'S
29' ROUND HILL PANORAMA +++ 29'
70 ORANJE BAAI (SEE PLAN) 36
90 65 THE QUILL 1970 MAZINGA 54
24 HIKING TRAILS BOTANICAL GARDEN
40 FORT DE WINDT WHITE WALL 40
55
28' 40 FALSE SHOAL 50 48 90 28'
50 45

120 120
120
600 LSTA03
17° 27.4'N
62° 58.0'W

NOTE
A LARGE ORANGE OIL TANKER PICK-UP BUOY
LIES AT 17° 30.82'N 63° 01.33' W, ABOUT ONE
MILE WEST OF JENKINS BAY. THERE IS A
HALF-MILE EXCLUSION ZONE AROUND THE
BUOY.

27' 27'

0 1/2 1
SCALE IN NAUTICAL MILES

63° 00' 59' 58' 57'

ISLANDS THAT BRUSH THE CLOUDS

Regulations

See *Regulations* in the main text for clearance procedures. Statia is part of the Netherlands. All Statia coastal waters are part of the National Park, and they charge $10 US per night (or $30 US per week), a fee that includes the use of their moorings. If you go hiking, you should also pay the $6 US per person annual fee.

Scuba diving is only allowed through the local dive shop or guide.

Telephones

Chippie or Telcel cell phones work here. You just dial the last 7-digits even if your phone is a 721 phone. Eutel in town has a bank of phones, and they can put money on Telcel and Chippie phones. Dial 00 to get out of Statia, then the country code (1 for the USA; 44 for the UK).

Shopping Hours

Shopping hours depend to some extent on the proclivity of the proprietor; try 0800-1200 and 1400-1800. Some food stores are owned by Seventh-day Adventists, and they close Saturday until after sunset, and then open to 2100. On Sundays some supermarkets open 0900-1300.

Transport

Statia is linked to Saba, St. Martin, and St. Kitts by several daily flights. For transport within the island, both car rentals and taxis are available. Typical taxi rates in $US are:

Sightseeing tour	$20.00 per person
Airport to Town	$8.00 per person
Harbor to Quill	$12.00 per person
Short ride	$5 per person

The National Park office will arrange a cab for you.

Holidays

- January 1
- Good Friday and Easter Monday (Easter Sunday is March 27, 2016; April 16, 2017)
- April 30 (Queen's Birthday)
- May 1 (Labor Day)
- Ascension Day (39 days after Easter: May 5, 2016, May 25, 2017)
- Whit Monday (50 days after Easter Sunday, May 16, 2016; June 5, 2017)
- July 1 (Emancipation Day)
- Carnival takes place over the last two weeks in July; only the last Monday of this time is an official holiday.
- October 21 (Antillean Day)
- November 16 (Statia/America Day)
- December 15 (Kingdom Day)
- December 25- 26

ORANJE BAAI

www.HeliPhotoCarib.com

captain. Thus Statia became the first nation to salute an American naval vessel. British officials didn't think much of this, and even less of the fact that an American ship later captured a British ship near Statia and took it back to the States. This, plus the fact that Statia sold weapons to the rebels, led to war between England and Holland.

Admiral Rodney arrived and Governor de Graff, who did not know what to do about the salute, knew exactly what to do about Rodney: he surrendered. Rodney confiscated all the ships and warehouses, but found less cash and valuables than he expected. Rodney noticed that for a small population the merchants were having a lot of funerals. He ordered one to be stopped and looked in the coffin. It was full of coins and jewelry and a little digging in the graveyard revealed much more. He rounded up a hundred Jewish men for deportation. When his men searched them and ripped open the lining of their clothes, they found another 8,000 pounds sterling. Rodney stole this, too, before sending them to St. Kitts. He then held a giant auction that netted him and his crew a fortune. This was not too popular with British subjects who lost property. He was sued and questions were asked in parliament. Luckily for Rodney, he won the crucial "Battle of the Saintes" just in time and all was forgiven.

By the late 1700s Statia was again Dutch and trade was flourishing, but in the early 19th century the changing political and economic climate in the Caribbean ended Statia's role as the Caribbean's first shopping mall, and there followed a long decline and massive emigration. The sea wall, which had been built on sand, slowly sank and subsequent hurricanes destroyed most of the lower town. The last ruins can still be seen, and the old Gin House and two old warehouses have now been beautifully renovated.

Statia looks decorative and orderly. The historical society, with funding from Holland, has done an excellent job of restoring many of the ruins and old buildings. It is also getting busier; traffic is now noticeable. The economy depends on the huge oil storage depot in the north of the island. Statia is currently part of Holland but the process by which this was decided was not entirely legal, so Statians may get to choose again.

Many of the 3,400 inhabitants were born in Statia, but immigrants from all over the

ISLANDS THAT BRUSH THE CLOUDS

Dutch Reform Church   Chris Doyle

world have filtered in recently so Statia is quite a wealth of people and languages. They welcome visitors with genuine warmth. Statia is so far off the beaten track that the very few visitors you meet are likely to be interesting. To put icing on the cake, the scuba diving is impressive and there is a selection of enjoyable restaurants.

Navigation

Statia is steep to. A quarter of a mile offshore clears all natural underwater dangers, but several rocks and reefs are within 100 feet of shore and some extend considerably farther. In particular, False Shoal rises to within 2 feet of the surface, 300 yards offshore.

White Wall is conspicuous from the south. It is a massive limestone slab that has been thrust up from under the sea.

A long fuel loading dock lies about a mile and a half north of Oranjestad, the main town. Northwest of this, about 1 mile off Jenkins Bay, is a large orange oil tanker terminal buoy, which flashes at night. Numerous tugs and barges are anchored and moored around the dock, and often floating fuel lines go from them to shore, so you must pass outside the terminal buoy and give it a half-mile clearance. Many tug mooring

buoys have several hundred feet of floating mooring line trailing downwind.

Statia National Marine Park has put in many unlit dive moorings and one lit one.

Oranje Baai is the only real anchorage. Most of the time it is acceptably calm, but it is no place to be in a hurricane or other disturbed weather system, including a really bad northerly swell. Regular easterly swells normally bend round the island to arrive in Oranje Baai from the south. If it is enough to make your boat roll, try a stern anchor to keep the stern to any swell. The green buoy off the breakwater should be red to fit in with IALA B. However, they seem to have forgotten they are not in Holland. To be safe, go outside it, not between the buoy and the wall. Occasionally, large container ships need significant room to anchor. Anchor north or east of the no anchoring zone shown (currently not buoyed).

The Statia Marine Park charges $10 US a night (or $30 a week) for being in the park. They maintain 11 moorings you can use, white with a blue stripe and a floating pick up rope, which will take up to 30 tons. Use of the moorings is included in the fee but you are welcome to anchor if you prefer. If you use rope, snorkel to make sure it cannot catch and chafe through on one of the many

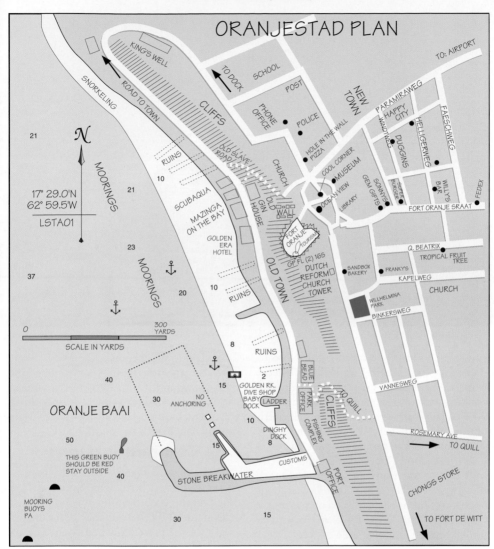

ORANJESTAD PLAN

abandoned mooring posts. If mooring, pick up the floating line and put your dock lines though the eye at the end, and give it at least 20 feet of scope. It is best to use two separate lines, one to each side of the bow. Never moor with a single line from one side of the bow, through the mooring to the other side of the bow. Your boat's motion will saw through the line. In case of a surge, you can keep your boat a lot calmer by attaching to the mooring and then taking out a second anchor well to the east. Use this second anchor to bring your stern to the swells. Those on cats will not have to worry about any of this.

If you use a mooring, snorkel on it and check the condition; the water is very clear. Early in 2015 mine looked good, but I have had recent letters about moorings breaking free and boats going adrift. Consider putting down an anchor as a back up.

The Statia National Marine Park office covers both the marine park and the land park. Check in after you clear in. They open weekdays 0700-1700.

The Statia Port Authority sometimes stands by on VHF: 16/14; Statia Marine Park on VHF: 16/17. The port offers no protection from the occasional northerly swells. Moderate northerly swells are not

ISLANDS THAT BRUSH THE CLOUDS

Mazinga on the Bay Chris Doyle

bad, especially if you are not too close to shore. In exceptionally bad swells, you don't want to be here. The port has a dinghy docking area on the south side of the baby dock or you can tie your dinghy to the north of the baby dock.

A light on the fort sometimes flashes 3 every 16 seconds. Several red lights on the hills just to the north of Oranjestad mark the airport, and a red light that flashes about once a second has been placed on top of the Quill. The port sees a lot of activity from tanker tenders bringing crew ashore.

Regulations

Since becoming part of the Netherlands, entry procedures have tripled, but the process is easy enough. On arrival, check with the harbormaster at the head of the town dock. Normal office hours are 0800-1600 weekdays, 0900-1100 weekends and holidays. Charges are according to size and the number of passengers, and typical rates are $30 US for a small yacht up to a tonnage charge for a big superyacht. There is also a $1 per passenger fee, which is good for three days; renewal costs $5. Now check with customs and immigration in the container office. Their hours are Monday to Friday: 0800-1600, Weekends 0900-1100. Some officials come from Holland or Bonaire, and change frequently so the treatment you get varies. In general, things go more smoothly if you are lucky enough to deal with a Statian. Finally check with the marine park.

Communications

Eutel has a hotspot, you will have to go up and pay a little. The National Park office on the waterfront has a good internet station and WiFi that you may get at anchor so ask for the password when you check in. They sell postcards and stamps and will mail letters for you.

King's Well has open WiFi for their customers, and you might get it from your boat. You will also find a telephone office and a post office.

The local library has a bank of internet computers.

Services

Sun Rain Laundry will collect and deliver from the dock - call 318-1644 or 1647, or ask the marine park to do it for you.

The Marine Park office has toilets and showers ($2 a shower), they give out tourist information, have an internet station and

We do what you want!

While on Statia we will be happy to help you with Island info, temporary repairs, and **Of course some of the best diving to be had in this part of the world!!!**

PADI "GOLD PALM"RESORT...NITROX AVAILABLE

V.H.F. ch. 11 or 16 • Phone/Fax 599-318-2964
e-mail: grdivers@gmail.com

We are the island representative for:

**Sun Sail
The Moorings**

tell you how to get ice. They are open 0700-1700 Monday to Thursday, 0700-1600 Fridays, closed weekends and public holidays. They also run the land park, and can sell you a yearly $6 US hiking badge, along with trail maps. It is run by managers Hannah, Violet, and Jessica.

You can arrange with the port office to come alongside the dock to take on diesel. The minimum is 100 gallons. For smaller quantities or gasoline, you will have to take a taxi and jerry jug it from the gas station.

Golden Rock Dive Center (VHF: 16/11) acts as the local representative for Sunsail and Moorings. In an emergency, Golden Rock Dive Center can supply water via a long hose if you go bow-to the baby dock. This is labor intensive for them, so there is a $45 US charge. For any yachting problems, call them on the radio or try their office by the baby dock. They will either sort you out themselves or find someone who can.

A tap has been placed on the new dinghy dock but after two years it is still not hooked up. Maybe it will happen just now.

Energetic people can walk over most of the island; others can take a taxi or rent a car or ATV. You will find garbage bins inside the port, outside the dinghy dock, outside the fisheries complex, and farther along the road towards the Golden Era Hotel.

Shopping

Statia is no longer duty free, but the prices still seem reasonable. If you are low on cash, take your credit card to the ATM machine opposite Mazinga Gift Shop, or the one by the airport.

If bread is on your shopping list, it is well worth the 10-15 minute walk toward the airport to visit Lynnett's Bakery. They bake many kinds of bread and all are excellent, along with donuts, pain au chocolat, and other goodies. They have tables, and serve sandwiches and coffee in a basic manner.

Sandbox Tree Bakery is closer to the dock, and though the choice is not nearly as large, you can get very acceptable fresh, hot local bread, at 1600.

Statia has some good supermarkets. Duggins is the best, complete with fresh produce, frozen meats, and delicatessen items. They open 0800-2000, except they close Friday at sunset, opening again Saturday sunset to 2200, and Sunday, 0800-1800. Upstairs is their department store, a fascinating collection of everything from stationary to sheets. This closes over lunch and by 1600.

The Chinese-run Happy City is a smaller market close by, open Saturday mornings when Duggins is closed. GRP Pharmacy is over by the airport.

Gem Gift Shop sells good chocolates, souvenirs, some stationary, and toys.

Mazinga on the Bay is near the Old Gin House. It is in one of the ancient warehouses, which the owners have lovingly restored to beautiful condition. It is a shop, bar, and sells ice creams, which you can enjoy out on the balcony overlooking the water or on the street side to watch life go by. You can buy cases of beer, bottles of wine, liquor, cheeses, and specialty foods, as well as gifts, and things for the beach. But don't go early, they open Wednesday to Sunday from 1300-1800.

The dive shops also have small boutiques.

ISLANDS THAT BRUSH THE CLOUDS

Oranjestad from the fort

Restaurants

The first restaurant you will see is the Blue Bead, which is cheerful and open to the view over the water. It is not cheap, but the food is good. Across the road and a little farther down, the modern Golden Era Hotel has a convenient bar and dining room that almost hangs out over the bay. It is cheerful, and offers both local and international dishes. Rooms are available.

The Old Gin House is set in a beautifully restored elegant historic stone and brick building. With lounging areas and the main reception inside, it is Statia's fanciest small hotel, popular with Dutch workers on government contracts. Their restaurant, across the road looking over the bay, is more modern in design, and a good choice for an upmarket meal. They always offer a variety of both fresh seafood and meat dishes. Lunch is simpler than dinner. They open daily for breakfast, every day except Thursday for dinner, and every day except Tuesday and Wednesday for lunch. Happy hour is 1600-1700.

On top of the hill on the north end of the bay is Laura and Win's King's Well, in a big spread out building. This is a great place, a home-away-from-home, rather than a formal restaurant. Different enough, it would make a good subject for a novel and, come to think of it, I have met a novelist hanging out there. Laura has an Irish background, and Win comes from northern Germany and the back end of their restaurant has a wonderful cliff-hanging view down to the bay. Win owns a Kelsall cat, and he loves yachting people.

Laura loves animals and keeps a flock of macaws, countless iguanas, dogs the size of ponies, (watch they don't step on your toes), and other interesting creatures. The macaws have taken over town. You will hear them from the anchorage and they look resplendent flying through the trees.

King's Well is a hotel and has rooms (if the anchorage gets too rolly they will find you one). They open for hotel guests, friends, family, and anyone on a yacht,

Chris Doyle

especially in you mention this guide (but not the general public) in the evening from 1800-2000, but as you pour your own drinks at the bar on the honor system, it is okay if you arrive early for sunset. Laura bakes beautifully and Win produces excellent German cuisine. His smoked barbecued ribs are famous, as are his steaks, schnitzels, rostbraten, and fresh fish. Plenty of cold beer is on hand. You eat very well here, and they will be delighted to tell you all about the island.

You do need to book in advance. Give them a call 599-318-2538 or walk up and make a booking.

In town, ask the tourist office about the current hot spot for local food. Ocean View Terrace, right opposite the Fort, is quiet and relaxed, reasonably priced with good straightforward food. They open Monday to Friday 0830-1330, 1830-2100, and Saturday from 1830. It is a good choice, but call and book to make sure they will be open.

In the heat of the day, the air conditioning at Super Burger will cool you while you enjoy good burgers, milk shakes, or ice cream. They have a giant screen for sports events. Frankey's (closed Wednesdays) often has live entertainment on Sundays and at any other excuse. Another local restaurant is Willy's, and you can get Chinese food at the Cool Corner, and Sonny's (under renovation). Hole-in-the-Wall Pizza sells good takeout in the evenings. The airport is about a 10-25 minute walk once you are in town. Close by Lynnette's Bakery, past the pharmacy, is Russel and Patricia's Opa's Snack bar. They open every day for lunch and dinner and as a bar. Russel will make sure you feel at home and this is one of the cheaper places to eat in Statia, with burgers, fishburgers, sandwiches, and pizzas. A good time to visit is lunch when they cook a daily special - could be fish, chicken, curry, who knows? Take a chance and enjoy.

Ashore

Statia has a quiet charm, which quickly grows on you. The walk to Oranjestad is a

One of Laura's Macaws

good introduction. Climb up the old cobbled Slave Road. Above, flowers are as colorful as the picturesque gingerbread houses, many beautifully restored. Day-old chicks forage safely along the edge of the road. You can visit the main attractions in the first hour. Fort Oranje has been beautifully restored and is the site of the tourist office where you will often find Charles Lindo, the director. The nearby museum is in the house in which Admiral Rodney lived during his stay and you can get a sense of how pleasantly cool living in it must have been. Different rooms show ancient history, recent events, and part has been furnished as it might have been long ago. The museum sells a historical walking tour map and sells an illustrated book to go with it. The tower of the Dutch Reform Church has been rebuilt, and the surrounding ruins attractive. You can walk here on a path from the back of the fort, which is open when the gates are closed. An interesting old Jewish cemetery lies at the end of Princesweg Street. For maps and information, check the Marine Park office, the tourist office, or the museum.

Hiking is tranquil and easy on Statia. The trails have been well laid out and posted. Visit the National Park office, which is also the Statia Marine Park office. A $6 US yearly pass has been instituted for their upkeep, and they give you hiking maps. Guides are also available for $40 US for one or two, plus $15 for each extra (based on 3 hour hikes), but they do need two days' notice (email: info@statiapark.org). You can go with or without a guide and set your own pace. One of the most rewarding hikes is up The Quill volcano. The quickest way is to follow the path that starts between the marine park office and the Blue Bead, which brings you to a road. Turn right on this road then take the next left. Walk to the top of that road then follow the signs. It takes about one and half hours to reach the rim of the volcano from the port. There is a rock with a good crater view a few yards to the right. From the rim you can go down into the crater, or up to the panoramic view. Either will take about half an hour.

The path into the crater may be a bit tough in wet conditions, because it can be muddy and slippery. Allow half an hour or so each way. You will see massive silk cotton trees here, with buttress roots 6 or 7 feet high. The base of the crater is home to many strangler figs. These trees originate when one of their sticky seeds germinates high in the branches of another tree. The seedling roots grow to the ground and then fatten, strangling the host and producing incredibly convoluted wooden sculptures. Other things to look for include black and yellow striped heliconid butterflies, purple-clawed hermit crabs, and harmless red-bellied racer snakes (*Alsophis rufiventris*), which are only found here and in Saba. Doves abound in The Quill. Look for the red-necked pigeon (dark blue with a red neck) and the bridled quail dove (light brown belly and white stripe under the eye). There are many feral chickens, and since hikers have fed them, they have become very tame.

Turn hard left at the rim for the panorama trail. It is a scramble and you will have to use your hands to pull yourself up the steeper parts and it can be slippery. You need somewhat of a head for heights, as the final view is precipitous and spectacular, straight down over town and the northwestern part of the island. Morning light is best and don't forget your camera. Allow 20-30 minutes each way.

More trails to explore in this area include the Mazinga Trail, a path around the mountain, and a trail to White Wall and the new Botanical Garden.

Other hikes are in the northern part of the island. Gilboa Hill is a much longer hike, especially if you walk to the trail head. You walk in semi-open dry scrub and hike to great views and will see endless old stone wall ruins, including primitive fort ruins and a distillery.

Signal Hill is a really nice hike, not too long, but it includes oil company land so you must have a guide. You will see an old fort and get a view of the anchorage (afternoon light is the best).

Ever fancied being on an archeological dig? Call Reese Cook, the director of archeological research (318-5670). He can always use extra hands for a day or more.

Water Sports

The water is usually clear. You can snorkel in the anchorage along a ledge close to shore, and on the ruins of the old walls under the water. Some old cannons are still off Golden Rock Dive Center. Snorkeling here is passable, and occasionally exceptional, as on the day I set my anchor and saw a stingray, several jacks, a baby angelfish, and a stone crab, all within a few minutes.

Divers will not want to miss Statia, as there are exceptional reefs and hundreds of fish of all types, from the smallest wrasses to large black-tipped sharks. Dive moorings have been placed on the dive sites. Since the advent of the Marine Park, a study has shown a tenfold increase in fish diversity. The Statia National Marine Park controls diving and snorkeling around the entire island to a depth of 100 feet. There is a fee

Dive Glide   Chris Doyle

of $6 per dive or $30 for a year of diving. All diving must be done with a dive shop, If you want to dive with just your own boat group, either dive shop can supply a guide.

The Golden Rock Dive Center (VHF: 16/11) has its office at the head of the baby dock. Glenn and Michele Faires and their crew have been at this over 18 years and have a relaxed, easy manner. Their shop is a five star PADI resort center, they do nitrox, and they have a 30-foot dive boat with a big swim platform, plus a custom catamaran dive boat with a cover. Glenn has invented and developed "Dive Glide" an underwater glider which you control by buoyancy using its built-in tanks. It makes free diving exciting, and with care could also be used with scuba.

They are happy to pick up people from yachts, and they take people snorkeling as well as diving. Glen will arrange island tours and fill jerry jugs with water. Golden Rock Dive Center also does high-action catch and release fishing trips and has a small boutique.

Scubaqua Dive Statia is a CMAS/PADI shop owned by Ingrid and Menno, set in one of the old warehouses, which they have beautifully restored. They run a professional shop and speak French, German, English, and Dutch and are welcoming and friendly in all of them. They have two good boats, one for 12 and one for 20, and plenty of staff who like working with yachts and, if you want to dive from your tender, can usually afford a diver as a yacht guide. They offer

ISLANDS THAT BRUSH THE CLOUDS

SCUBAQUA
Dive Center St. Eustatius

Unspoiled Caribbean diving - small groups
nitrox for free – channel 16 - dive@scubaqua.com

nitrox diving at no extra charge, will help repair diving equipment, and have a bar and a boutique that sells snorkeling gear. They rent kayaks and plan to sell Aqualung equipment which they use.

The Marine Park includes 34 dive sites and snorkel sites. Some are close to the big drop-off and start at 80 feet, with a wall that seems to go down forever. Rock ridges form others with sand valleys between. In the north of the island, there are reefs and rocks on a sand bottom, with many rays, turtles, and sharks. It has been estimated that a turtle is seen for every 55 minutes of diving.

Statia has two dramatic new wreck dives. The Charlie Brown is a 300-foot- long cable-layer. It lies on its side to the southwest of the island in about 100 feet of water; the top is at about 48 feet.

It is still whole and in good condition, and for the experienced penetration dives are no problem. The Chien Tong is a Taiwanese fishing vessel about 200 feet long. This one is sunk upright in about 75 feet of water at the edge of the anchorage. It has already attracted lots of fish.

Stenapa Reef is unusual: a man-made reef of old wrecks, including a cut-up World War II victory ship, a tugboat, and a large barge. This site attracts lots of fish, including large jacks, grunts, stingrays, flying gurnards, and snake eels. Turtles are sometimes seen and garden eels live in the surrounding sand. Interesting animals are found on the wrecks themselves, including tunicates, a variety of corals and sponges, and frogfish.

The Cliffs are near the southern end of the island. This site starts in a coral garden at 65 feet, and then falls away in a wall. You can go down as far as you feel comfortable, but you won't make the bottom as it drops to 1,200 feet. The wall is encrusted with coral and sponges and is home to black-tipped sharks, turtles, groupers, and angelfish.

Hangover Reef is also toward the south of the island. This reef is 40-60 feet deep and well decorated by sea fans and anemones. There are lots of cracks and crevices where you see elegant spotted drums and high hats and, on lucky days, seahorses and frogfish.

Double Wreck has the remains of two boats that sank in 60 feet of water. For some reason, this site attracts an unusually large number of fish. Hundreds of grunts use this as their daily resting place. Big barracudas patrol the waters above. Moray eels, southern stingrays, and flying gurnards hang out on the bottom.

Grand Canyon (70-130 feet) is Statia's most dramatic dive. A series of volcanic fissures separates this large sloping wall into many smaller walls. Superb visibility and a variety of large animals, combined with the Grand Canyon backdrop, make this dive unforgettable.

Marina Telca, Brimstone Hill behind — Chris Doyle

St. Christopher (St. Kitts)

ST. KITTS IS GREEN AND pleasant, with a dramatically steep central mountain range rising to 3,750 feet. Much of it is covered in rainforest, which is often shrouded in passing clouds. At these heights live many thousands of African green vervet monkeys, descendants of a few originally brought here as pets by planters. The land between the mountains and the sea is gently sloping and fertile, relatively flat, and easy to drive on. For many generations this was planted in sugar cane, which was abandoned some years ago and now the cane fields are slowly reverting to woodland.

The Caribs called St. Kitts "Liamuiga," which means "fertile isle." Columbus renamed it after his patron saint, and nowadays it is known either as St. Christopher or by the abbreviated St. Kitts. Sir Thomas Warner landed here with a group of settlers in 1623, making it the first British Caribbean colony. A French group joined them, and the two nations teamed up to massacre the 2,000 Carib inhabitants before they fell out between themselves. After 150 years of fighting and uncertainty, St. Kitts, with its sister isle, Nevis, became British under the treaty of Versailles in 1783. Today they are a fully independent, twin-island state with a British tradition and about 50,000 inhabitants. In graciousness and outstanding visual beauty, these islands have not changed too much from the old plantation days. Most of the large estates have been converted to small luxury hotels and restaurants. The economy is based mainly on tourism.

A railway, built for collecting the sugar cane, once ran right round the island, passing through perfectly scenic countryside. St. Kitts Scenic Railway renovated part of this so you can take a luxury train ride, which offers spectacular views. You need to book well in advance (465-7263).

In the north, St. Kitts Marine Works haul out with its Telca Marina under Brimstone Hill is working and practical. In the south,

197

St. Kitts

Regulations

St. Kitts and Nevis are one country, though both have considerable autonomy. Basseterre, Telca Marina, and Christophe Harbour are St. Kitts ports of entry. Fees are given under Basseterre.

Visiting yachts may not use any jetskis or similar craft. Importation of such vehicles is banned. Scuba diving may only be undertaken with a local dive shop.

Telephones

Get a Digicel or Lime SIM for your phone, Chippie also works. To call the USA and Canada, dial 1 + the number. For other countries, dial 011, then the country code (44 for the UK).

Shopping Hours

Weekdays 0800-1600. Many shops close Saturday afternoon. Supermarkets have much longer hours.

Transport

St. Kitts has a large international airport with daily flights to San Juan and Miami and weekly flights to New York, Toronto, Atlanta and Charlotte. LIAT and Winair fly interisland.

Taxis are plentiful and many of them stand by on VHF: 16. The following rates are what you might expect to pay for up to four people during the day (night fees are higher) in $US:

Tour of Brimstone Hill	$50
Island tour from Basseterre (3 hours)	$80
over 3 hours +$30 per hour	
Island tour from White House Bay	$130
Basseterre to White House Bay	$26
Basseterre to Deepwater Port	$10
Basseterre to Frigate Bay	$12
Basseterre to the airport	$10
Basseterre to Carombola	$16
Basseterre to Palm Court	$08
Dinner return Spratt Net/Ottley Hall	$44
Dinner return Nirvana at Fairview	$30

Rental cars are available. You will need to get a local license that costs $24 US and is also good for Nevis. This fee is sometimes built into the rental rates. Drive on the left.

Buses run up the west coast to Dieppe and the east coast to Sadlers. They run about once an hour and the last bus returns at about 2200. In the mornings they leave from the waterfront (see our town map). Fares are very reasonable (no more than about $8 EC, $3 US).

Airport departure tax normally included in the ticket is $22 US
- Jan 1
- Jan 2 Carnival
- First Monday in May (May Day)
- Good Friday and Easter Monday (Easter Sunday is March 27, 2016; April 16, 2017)
- Whit Monday (50 days after Easter Sunday, May 16, 2016; June 5, 2017)
- Second Sunday in June, Queen's Birthday
- First Monday in August
- Sept. 19 (Independence Day)
- December 25-26

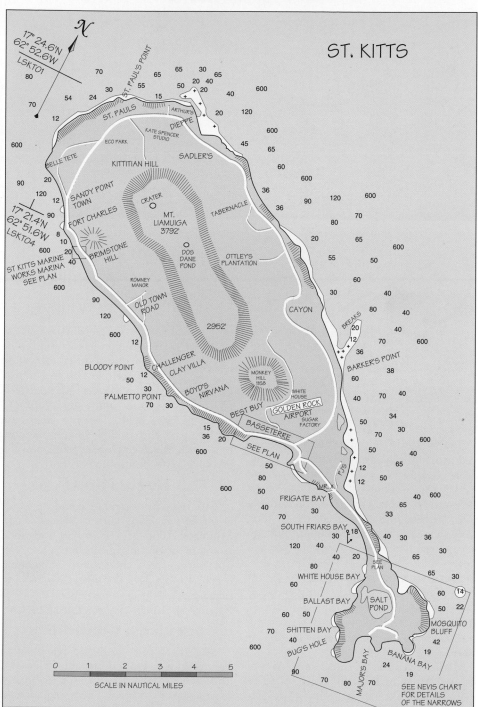

St. Kitts

Christophe Harbour is upmarket and fancy, and will grow huge in the end. Both these are expanding and changing the whole yachting scene in St. Kitts and Nevis,

opening more opportunities.

The big local regatta is the 3-day Booby Island Regatta which includes such races as Chase the Monkey and round Nevis race called "Round the Rock".

ISLANDS THAT BRUSH THE CLOUDS

St. Kitts Marine Works and Telca Marina

Chris Doyle

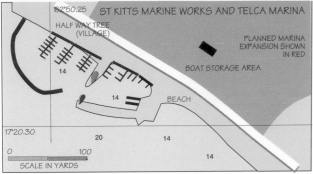

62°50.25 ST KITTS MARINE WORKS AND TELCA MARINA

HALF WAY TREE
(VILLAGE)

PLANNED MARINA
EXPANSION SHOWN
IN RED

BOAT STORAGE AREA

14

14   BEACH

17°20.30

20   14

0   100   14

SCALE IN YARDS

Navigation

The leeward (southwest) coast is fairly steep-to, and a quarter of a mile offshore clears all dangers. Give the northeast coast good clearance because of the reef off Dieppe Bay in the north and the shoals off Barker's Point farther south. Stay inside the 14-foot shoal to the northeast of Mosquito Bluff, as waves break here in heavy weather. See the Nevis section for details of The Narrows that separates St. Kitts from Nevis. Dieppe Bay has a small reef-protected fishing harbour. You need local knowledge to get in and holding is poor (sand over shale). Customs recently refused a cruiser permission to go there.

Marina Telca and St. Kitts Marine Works are in Half Way Tree Village. This is an official port of clearance.

Brimstone Hill and Halfway Tree Village

St. Kitts Marine Works haul out and Telca Marina lie under the southeastern flank of Brimstone Hill in Halfway Tree Village. The setting is scenic, amid old chimneys and sugar cane fields. This is a great base for seeing St. Kitts; all day long buses zoom by to town, which costs about $3 EC and you can hike up to Brimstone Hill Fort.

Regulations

This is a port of clearance and the office is in the yard. The current officer is Mr. Mitchum (766-5567). However, they tend to rotate. If you call Telca Marina they can tell them you are coming. Until immigration sets up their half of the office, you have to take a bus (or the customs may take you) to Sandy Point Village. For rates, see *Basseterre*.

Services, Chandlery

St. Kitts Marine Works and Telca Marina belong to Reg Francis, an able, pleasant, and straightforward Kittitian with lots of experience in salvage and heavy equipment. If you ever have a problem, Reg is an excellent person to contact.

The marina is shown on our sketch chart. Currently it has four berths on the dock, and room for one or two on the travel lift

Kittitian Hill   Chris Doyle

dock, with extra possible places by tying up to the barge which usually sits just inside the entrance. Reg is planning to expand this about the time this guide comes out to an 80-berth marina. The planned extension is shown in our sketch chart in red. When the new outer wall goes in, the current north wall will be removed leaving room for a dock that can take two big boats (up to 150 feet). Most of the berths are geared for yachts up to 50 feet or so. The controlling depth is 12 feet, though much of it is deeper. The marina is very protected and they will try to squeeze you in until the expansion, after which there will be plenty of room. Do call in advance.

The travelift is 150 tons, extended to take a beam of 35 feet. There are two forklifts, including a 42-ton one that has slings and can lift yachts of about 10 tons. There is about 14 feet of water to the slip. Digging keel holes, tying down cats and securing yachts against hurricanes are easily arranged. Reg has a crane for removing masts. He has expanded his haul-out yard to cover 25 acres, so he always has room. This is not a manicured yard; it is adequate but basic, field storage. There is security with cameras, toilets, and showers. If you are living on board, stock up on bug spray. His prices are reasonable and he doesn't charge extra for cats.

Reg himself has a metalworking team and they can weld and repair all yacht materials and pressure wash, antifoul, and do minor glass repairs. St. Kitts Marine Works is an agent for Budget Marine and can order any parts you want from them.

David at Indigo Yachts has a base here and does most of the major work. He is good and very experienced. Whatever your problem, he can fix it (see *Basseterre*). He can also help with some parts.

Joe's Taxi Service (668-5393) is run by Joe, who lives in Dieppe Bay and does not mind coming up north to take people around.

I met Schemeda Hazel up at Kittitian Hill where she was organizing tours and activities. If you need help organizing trips or general services, such as laundry, Schemeda is willing to help (869-766-2039/465-2415, schemedahazel@gmail.com).

Ashore

This is a very quiet area. To provision, take a bus to Basseterre; they run every few minutes. Or for a couple of items catch a bus the other way to Sandy Point Town, a mile and half to the north, which has a couple of smaller markets.

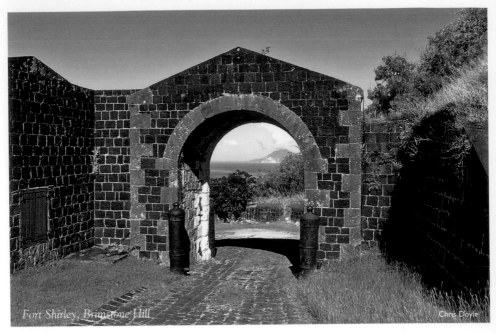

Fort Shirley, Brimstone Hill   Chris Doyle

Brimstone Hill Fortress is a wonderful, strategically-placed historic fort. You can walk from Telca Marina. It is a 20-minute hike up the hill if you cut off the first half mile by taking a bus to the road leading uphill. It is lovely and cool at around 0800. The fort does not open till 0930, but we went in and enjoyed it before the crowds came and paid on the way out. They seemed to think that was okay.

The fort is a lasting monument to the old enmity between the British and the French. British-built, it was captured by the French in a siege during which 1,000 British soldiers held out for some months against 8,000 French. Eventually, they arranged surrender with full honor. The fort is being painstakingly restored. You may be lucky and spot a troop of the monkeys that live here; they are a little less nervous than their mountain brethren. The Western Place of Arms offers an outstanding view. On a clear day you can see six islands, from Montserrat to St. Martin. The Fort twice suffered unprovoked attacks from above by lightning that blew up the powder room and did considerable damage. Several small museum rooms depict life in the old days and illustrate the Battle of St. Christopher, in which Hood gave DeGrasse such a thumping

that he had to retire to Martinique for a couple of months. This gave Admiral Rodney sufficient time to come out and join Hood for the decisive "Battle of the Saintes." At that time France and Spain were poised to drive Britain from the Caribbean, but this victory gave England undisputed mastery of the sea. D.L. Matheson's informative booklet on the fortress is available in the souvenir shop.

Kittitian Hill is a 400-acre fancy development under the slopes of Mt. Liamuiga, with lovely views over the north coast to Statia, Saba, St. Martin, St. Barts, and occasionally Anguilla. The first stage is the 80-room Belmont Farm Hotel (rooms are for sale to investors) with its lovely Kitchen Restaurant. An 18-hole golf course, spa, and The Table restaurant for gourmet food are coming soon. The fancy Kitchen Restaurant looks to the north coast on one side and the mountains on the other. Chef Marc, from St. Lucia, fed us royally. The courses are small and delicious but the minimum, even for lunch, is four so you don't leave hungry. They will soon be opening a beach bar with food in Dieppe Bay.

While you are in the north, ask about the Kate Design Gallery, a great place to look at Kate Spencer's original art. It is just below Kittitian Hill. She has originals and

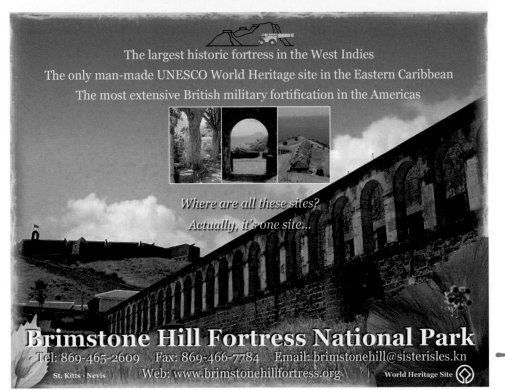

The largest historic fortress in the West Indies

The only man-made UNESCO World Heritage site in the Eastern Caribbean

The most extensive British military fortification in the Americas

Where are all these sites?

Actually, it's one site...

Brimstone Hill Fortress National Park

Tel: 869-465-2609   Fax: 869-466-7784   Email: brimstonehill@sisterisles.kn

Web: www.brimstonehillfortress.org

St. Kitts · Nevis   World Heritage Site

prints on sale, and even if you are not in the market for art, you should come by to check out her placemats, note cards, and silks, all beautifully designed. Kate is the widow of Philip Walwyn, legendary St. Kitts ' boatbuilder and sailor who has built and sailed many boats from Spronk cats to Kate, a beautiful replica of an historic gaff rigged 12-meter. As Philip died recently, Kate's plans for the studio may have changed.

Old Road Town lies about halfway to Basseterre from Telca Marina, and buses run all the time. Sprat Net is a good beachfront dinner restaurant on the main road, open Wednesday to Saturday for dinner only. It is owned by fishermen who decided they could do better by selling their fish as meals. It has become very popular and they tend to have live music some days.

In the same town, Romney Manor is set in a beautiful old 10-acre estate garden dominated by a giant saman tree, which covers nearly an acre. Ask for the road that leads to it and walk up. Romney Manor is the headquarters for Caribelle Batik. Originally, there was a beautiful estate house, but it burned down, and three new workshops and display rooms have been built on the old foundations. Here you can watch as white sea-island cotton, as soft as silk, gets covered in a riot of lively colors. Spend some time in the workshops and enjoy the magnificent manor grounds. Try to visit on a day when there are no cruise ships.

Up in the hills above Romney Manor, Sky Safaris have set up a series of ziplines so you can fly (or fly and walk) through the rainforest above the Wingfield River. This is an adventurous and exciting experience you will long remember.

St. Kitts' 3,700-foot mountain range is a completely different world of cool, dark rainforest, elfin woodlands, volcanic craters, and lakes. You might want to opt to make it to the top of Mount Liamuiga (Mt. Misery), where you look down on the neighboring mountainous island of Statia before descending into a 1,000-foot crater that puffs steam from several vents. The trail runs right by Kittitian Hill. You can try to find a guide locally or guides from Basseterre could pick you up on their way.

ISLANDS THAT BRUSH THE CLOUDS

BASSETERRE

Another roadside attraction in this area is the St. Kitts eco-park. I have not been but it has a mix of plants from Taiwan and St. Kitts, both in and out of a giant greenhouse and some buildings are powered by solar panels.

Basseterre

Basseterre, the capital, is the site of the original French settlement in St. Kitts. It is a delightful old town, built on the waterfront with architecture that varies from solid British to fancy French. It was largely rebuilt after a fire in 1876 and The Circus is modeled after Piccadilly in London. The Circus area and surrounding blocks contain handsome old buildings with decoratively painted shutters that make this one of the Caribbean's more attractive capitals.

The lovely old treasury building is the nation's museum, with several artifacts and great old photos showing how it was long ago. The St. Christopher Heritage Society has an office here. You can visit them and check out their selection of books and maps for sale. This is the place to come for serious research.

Port Zante extends the town's waterfront by some 25 acres and includes a marina and cruise ship dock. The whole area is one bustling shopping mall. With many businesses from St. Martin, it feels a bit like

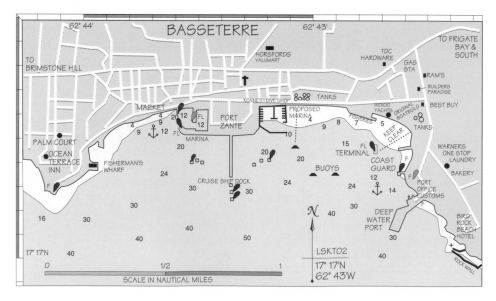

an outpost of Philipsburg.

Navigation

Be cautious when approaching Port Zante at night, as there are quite a few cruise ship berthing posts, some of which are lit.

Basseterre is open and faces south. If the wind has any north in it, or is east and light, the whole bay is calm and pleasant, and the most convenient anchorage is just outside the new marina. As the wind becomes east and strong, and especially if it goes a hair south, then small seas build up in the fetch from the coast around White House Bay. At this point, the anchorage outside the marina is tenable (the holding is good), but rolly and choppy enough to make you feel you are at sea. People do anchor here in these conditions for the convenience of being close to town. However, for comfort, anchor close to the deep water harbor on the east side of the bay. It is a long dinghy ride to the marina and, while not easy, it is possible to get ashore in the deep water harbor, where you can clear customs.

When the wind switches far enough south, the swells curve around Nevis from the open sea, roll up the southern peninsula, and end up in Basseterre. At these times, it is not unusual to have short steep seas over 3 feet high rolling in. In this case, head down to White House Bay. If you really have to be here, the only place to anchor is close

to the deepwater harbor, just in front of the coast guard dock. It will be uncomfortable, but nothing like being farther out. If there is any chance of a southerly swell, keep in water at least 14 feet deep. For comfort in these conditions, it is best to anchor bow and stern, facing into the swells. But it is much better not to anchor anywhere in Basseterre in these conditions.

A marina is a wonderful asset, and the protected new Port Zante Marina is an excellent place to stay and from which to view and tour St. Kitts. The outer wall has been extended, and it completely cuts out the swells, allowing for secure, calm berthing inside.

You should also cruise down to the south coast bays. A good road connects Basseterre to the south end of the island, so it is possible to organize your sightseeing from there. All the bays have good road access.

Regulations

Basseterre is the main port of entry in St. Kitts. Customs are both at the cruise ship dock near the marina and at the deep water harbor, and they stand by on VHF: 16. The customs regulations have been updated. You should be able to get permission to visit all the places you want between St. Kitts and Nevis and then check out wherever you are when you want to leave. Even better, if your stay is a week or less, you may be able to

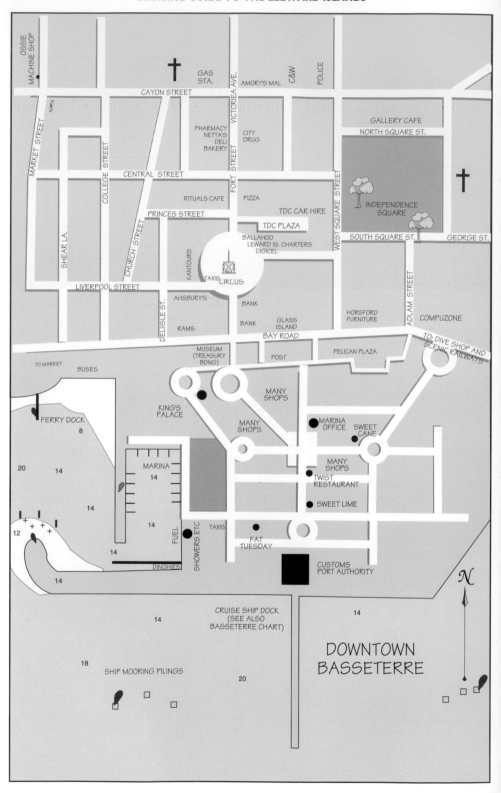

OSSIE MACHINE SHOP

MARKET STREET

NAPA

GAS STA.

CAYON STREET

VICTOREA AVE.

AMORY'S MAL

C&W

POLICE

COLLEGE STREET

PHARMACY NETTA'S DELI BAKERY

CITY DRUG

FORT STREET

GALLERY CAFE

NORTH SQUARE ST.

CENTRAL STREET

RITUALS CAFE

PIZZA

WEST SQUARE STREET

INDEPENDENCE SQUARE

PRINCES STREET

CHURCH STREET

SHEAR LA.

TDC CAR HIRE

TDC PLAZA

BALLAHOO
LEWARD IS. CHARTERS
DIGICEL

SOUTH SQUARE ST.

GEORGE ST.

KANTOURS

TAXIS CIRCUS

LIVERPOOL STREET

AHSBURY'S

BANK

DELISLE ST.

RAMS

BANK

GLASS ISLAND

HORSFORD FURNITURE

ADLAM STREET

COMPUZONE

BAY ROAD

TO MARKET

BUSES

MUSEUM (TREASURY BDNG)

POST

PELICAN PLAZA

TO: DIVE SHOP AND SCENIC RAILWAYS

FERRY DOCK

8

KING'S PALACE

MANY SHOPS

MANY SHOPS

MARINA OFFICE

SWEET CANE

20

14

MARINA

14

MANY SHOPS

TWIST RESTAURANT

14

FUEL

SHOWERS ETC

TAXIS

SWEET LIME

14

12

14

14

DINGHIES

FAT TUESDAY

CUSTOMS PORT AUTHORITY

14

14

CRUISE SHIP DOCK
(SEE ALSO
BASSETERRE CHART)

14

N

18

SHIP MOORING PILINGS

20

DOWNTOWN
BASSETERRE

Welcome To St. Kitts

St. Kitts, an unspoilt beauty that still radiates with an authentic Caribbean charm and warmth is favoured by many visitors for its lush tropical conditions, friendly people and historic sites. On this fairly unknown island awaits an adventure that will stay with you your whole life.

While in St. Kitts make sure to visit Port Zante, a shopper's paradise offering beautiful promenades surrounded by elegant shops boasting an eclectic blend of designer goods, jewellery, premium cigars, and spirits, fine linen and souvenirs at duty free prices. Also offered is an amazing multicultural dining experience with selections from Chinese, East Indian, American and Kittitian local cuisines.

For those who enjoy water sports, the Port Zante Marina is home to the island's best catamarans and scuba tour providers. This 37 berth marina offers berthing for vessels up to 150 + ft in length with a draft of 14 + ft on the western bulkhead.

Continuous growth and development has transformed Port Zante into the ideal cruise facility and in turn has created superb conditions for economic growth in St. Kitts-Nevis.

Tel: (869) 466-5021/6988

Fax: (869) 466 5020

Port Zante
ST. Kitts   West Indies

The facilities of Port Zante have now made St. Kitts a must-see on all yachtsman's itineraries.

Email: portzantemarina@gmail.com

Website: www.portzantemarina.com

get inward and outward clearance at the same time.

Customs hours are 0600-1900 daily. Usually there is a customs officer in the cruise ship complex (a few steps from the marina) from 0800-1545. Outside those hours, you may have to go to the deep water port, though you may not find anyone there on weekends. The boarding officers who do the clearance stand by on VHF: 16. Weekend clearance involves overtime charges (normally $10 EC). Customs collects a $10 EC customs charge ($50 if you are over 100 tons) and a $20 EC yacht charge. In addition, port dues are collected in the port office, across the hall from customs. For yachts: $10 EC up to 20 tons, $15 EC for 21-30 tons, $20 EC for 31-50 tons, $35 EC for 51-100 tons, $60 EC for 101-150 tons, over that size you start getting into pilotage and other charges, but the fees are fairly reasonable. Port fees are not collected again in Nevis, and St. Kitts port charges are less expensive. Passengers are charged $5 US per head. Normally, there is an immigration officer in the cruise ship complex, otherwise you can visit immigration at the police station in town. When the police station is closed, you can find immigration at the airport, but make sure a jumbo jet has not just arrived.

There are several agents for large yachts (see *General Yacht Services*).

Communications

Port Zante has WiFi in the marina and several commercial stations are available outside. Ballahoo Bistrot and many bars offer WiFi. If you need a computer, try Compuzone, opposite the Pelican Mall. For cell phones, Lime is near the police station, and Digicel is in the Circus. With their SIMs you can access the internet via your smart phone or other device.

Chandlery

David, at Indigo Yachts, is a good place to start for chandlery items. He has a large stock on hand for his boatyard and can sell to the occasional visitor. He is an agent for Island Water World and brings in a weekly shipment by sea, or if you need it

ISLANDS THAT BRUSH THE CLOUDS

The Circus   Chris Doyle

faster, by quick pack. He can also source, clear, and deliver parts duty free, including both cruising boat and specialty superyacht gear. He has proven successful at finding the scarcest spares. They are agents for and stock Sea Hawk antifouling paints and can guarantee the paint job.

Reggie at St. Kitts Marine Works is agent for Budget Marine (see *Brimstone Hill and Halfway Tree Village*).

Giant hardware stores like Horsfords and Builder's Paradise sell housewares, tools, paints, fillers, plumbing parts, lumber, electronics, and occasionally some rope and stainless fasteners.

General Yacht Services

The marina basin is dredged to 14 feet. It takes about 37 boats, but 26 of these are permanent locals. Advance booking is advisable, especially if you have a multihull. Call dockmaster Trucky (662-0135). Port Zante plans to add another marina on the east side of the property.

Large boats (up to 120 feet) can arrange to lie outside the western wall, though take care coming in as a big shoal extends about halfway down the wall. This is not a fancy marina with lots of services, but it is quite functional and is run by the Port Zante management team, the people who developed this area. Arriving yachts should call Port Zante on VHF: 68. If you need fuel,

they can arrange to deliver it to your boat by truck (100-gal minimum) or will take and fill your cans for a small amount. (They can refill your outboard gas that way.) Water and electricity are available on most docks: 30 amps on many; 60 amps on some, and 100 amps 3-phase on one. There is a garbage disposal. The marina has a toilet and shower block. The overall manager is Keith Phillip and Indira manages the office. The staff is friendly and helpful and will help with car rentals or other services. This is the best and calmest berth for your visit to Basseterre.

If you are anchored outside the marina, you can leave your dinghy in the marina - definitely the best place to leave it. They charge $5 US per day. The dinghy dock is way up inside the long dock used by charter boats.

Superyachts that cannot get in can take on water and fuel by arrangement with the marina on the outside dock or by arrangement with the Port Authority on the cruise ship dock (when available). Overnight stays on the cruise ship dock are possible with water, fuel, electricity, and phone. Prop polishing can be arranged. There is security both on the cruise ship dock and in the marina.

Four agents in St. Kitts will be happy to give any help to yachts, from VIP clearance to full provisioning or technical assistance. They can pre-clear you so you can go right

Indigo Yachts
Where Innovative Design Meets Skilled Craft

CONTACT US:

Tel: (+869) 466 1753

info@indigoyachts.com

www.indigoyachts.com

The premier boat yard in St. Kitts since 2001!

Parts supply

Bottom & top side painting

Mechanical & electrical installations

Design & new builds

Minor repairs & major overhauls

~

Agents for many reputable brands including Yanmar,
Perkins, PYI, Pacer Marine and Sea Hawk!

If you are in Port Zante Marina and need to find us in a hurry,
you can call Percy Taxi VHF 16 or tel. (869) 663 9153

to White House Bay if you want.

St. Kitts Yacht Services is run by Anthony Abourizk; Serviz by Ricky Brown, and at Delisle Walwyn, a big ship agent, big yachts are handled by Mr. Alexander or Ms. Ried. Nevis Yacht Services works in both St. Kitts and Nevis, and they are described under Nevis.

Ras is a cool guy who used to help out with boat jobs in the marina. He is now on a long job, but in the meantime his mother Loretta lives close to the marina and does boat laundry. Give her a call 669-1618.

You can get also get your laundry done by Warner's One Stop. They will collect and deliver from your yacht in the marina or the docks at the deep water port. They will do their best to meet your needs, but they are busy, so getting things done on time can be a problem. It may work out faster if you deliver the laundry and collect it yourself. Give them a call in advance, if possible.

Trinity Inn guesthouse in town has washing machines. They also do horse riding, have rooms and a restaurant. This keeps them busy so, again, time can be a problem. They are a 7-minute walk at the western end of Central Street where it ends. I would call them first to see what you can arrange. Speak to Wilfred Walters.

Unfortunately, for those anchored out, the deep water port is not yacht-friendly. The agile can find a place to tie a dinghy, and scramble up the rocks. If you have non-agile crew, drop them off at the roll-on dock. It is probably better and easier to dinghy to the marina and leave your dinghy there. The garbage bins on the docks in the deep water harbor are not really for yachts, but they do not mind you using them if you bag the garbage well. Sol EC can fill your cooking gas cylinders.

Leeward Island Charters (VHF: 16) runs the day-charter cats Eagle, Caona, and Spirit of St. Kitts. Most of the charter cats of St. Kitts were designed and built here by Dougie Brooks. They sail brilliantly and the crew love to sail them. The Leeward Island Charters office is in the Ballahoo Bistrot. Jessica, in the office, will answer any questions you may have

ISLANDS THAT BRUSH THE CLOUDS

Gallery Cafe   Chris Doyle

and give you the latest weather. This is the unofficial base of The St. Kitts-Nevis Boating Club, so ask if there are any upcoming events or check online: skyachtclub.com. They sometimes sell local charts. In addition, they sell t-shirts, and a few accessories, and if you want to see how it feels to sail at 16-26 knots, these are the people to talk to.

Technical Yacht Services

Indigo Yachts is an excellent place to go with boat problems. It is on the waterfront near the deep water harbor, and run by David, who has worked in the design office of Camper and Nicholson. He has his own yard in Basseterre, with full design and building capabilities. He has built many yachts and boats and understands all kinds of yacht systems, up to superyacht. He works with a team of up to 18 employees, both here and at St. Kitts Marine Works. This large yard has excellent vacuum-bagging tables, as well as a carpentry shop, and they can do any kind of technical construction. They keep marine ply, glass, cores, and lots of hardware in stock. David can do a surprising amount here on St. Kitts, and if a problem is out of range, he will have the right contacts to bring someone in. They can help you source and import parts, however hard to

find. Indigo Yachts is agent for Yanmar diesel and Balmar electrical products, and they can fix all Edson steering problems.

Densil and Mike own Original Boatbuilders. They are Kittitians who have built boats for many years and worked on such beauties as the Spirit of St. Kitts, Eagle, and Caona. They have a carpentry shop and can help with any woodworking job you may have.

TDC is an agent for Yamaha outboards, with full sales and service, and they can help out with other brands. Call them on VHF: 18.

See also *St. Kitts Marine Works* above.

Transport

Most taxi drivers have VHF radios and the taxi channel is VHF: 13. Several of them have made yachts an important part of their business and also listen on VHF: 16. Call "any taxi" on one of those channels and you are likely to receive a reply. The phone numbers of some good ones are in the directory.

A big taxi stand in The Circus is just a short walk from the marina, and taxis hang out in Port Zante on cruise ship days. Taxi drivers will be happy to collect you from South Friars Bay, White House Bay, or, when

Port Zante   Chris Doyle

it comes on line, Christophe Harbour.

TDC has car rental agencies in both St. Kitts and Nevis (Thrifty Rentals). If you wish to see both islands, they'll give you a free swap when you go from one to the other. This makes it particularly easy if you intend to spend most of your time in one island and just hop over to the other for a day. You can take any rental car on the Sea Bridge ferry.

TDC Travel (VHF: 18), right next to TDC Plaza, is agent for UPS and Quick Pack. As travel agents, they handle all airlines except American, and can arrange all kinds of island tours. Kantours is the local American Express agency.

Provisioning

Ram's and C & C are close by the marina and acceptable for buying a few things. For a big provisioning, take the short taxi ride to the big supermarkets outside town: Horsfords Value Mart, Ram's, and Best Buy are all good, and each will have a few things missing in the other.

Horsfords is large and modern, on the edge of Basseterre in a big mall. You can walk there, but probably not back with the shopping. It is vast, with a deli and bakery. They are open on Sunday mornings.

Ram's is the closest to the deep water port and has just about anything you could want

at reasonable prices. They open 0830-1900 Monday through Saturday.

Best Buy has a store near the deep water port and another about a mile west of town. It is a big store with a deli and big produce section and they open later than the others.

Fun Shopping

Port Zante is a giant shopping mall geared to cruise ship passengers. This, and the architecture, remind me of Philipsburg. Stores here sell jewelry, fine watches, liquor, t-shirts, and trinkets.

The style changes as you walk among the old buildings in the main part of Basseterre, with more traditional Caribbean architecture and many more shops.

The Circus is picturesque and well worth looking at for a moment or two. From here you can go up Fort Street.

Pelican Plaza stands between the old town and Port Zante It is a lower-rent area, where you can look for bargains in more local shops.

Right opposite Pelican Plaza is a lovely little store called Glass Island, which carries the glass work of Leonie Carey. She learned from Italians how to create beautiful jewelry, ornaments, and dishes, using a kiln to melt the glass.

The Gallery Café, see *Restaurants*, has

BALLAHOO
BISTROT

BREAKFAST, LUNCH, COFFEES, FRESH JUICES, WINES & COCKTAILS SERVED ALL DAY
MONDAY TO FRIDAY 8 TO 5 / SATURDAY 8 TO 4
TEL. +1 869 465 4197 FREE WIFI

a lovely collection of art, much of it by Spencer and Cameron, but also other local artists.

Restaurants

Eating out in St. Kitts is a pleasure. There are good restaurants in town as well as a few really interesting ones out of town, if you are willing to take a short taxi ride. But let us start with a café. Gallery Café is an art gallery with wonderful paintings and a café in the back that opens onto a garden with seats and tables. The coffee is good and nicely served, but visit for the home-made pastries and baked goodies, which are absolutely delicious.

The Ballahoo Bistrot (VHF: 16) is an airy upstairs restaurant with tables on a long balcony overlooking The Circus, and it is a wonderful place to sit and watch the world go by and perfect for breakfast or lunch. Food and drinks are available from 0800 to closing time at 1700. The French owners give a French and French Créole accent to the food, which varies from quite elaborate French dishes to lobster sandwiches, tasty burgers, and salads. There is usually an inexpensive daily special, making it the best lunch spot in town.

Sweet Cane Restaurant and Bar is the hot new restaurant on the east side of Port Zante. The food is fantastic, with delicious wraps, burgers, salads, fish and chips, crab stuffed shrimp, and spinach/crab stuffed grouper. The wait staff is very friendly. Davi and her husband (the chef) own the restaurant. It is so popular that a lot of times there's lines to be seated, and a continuous stream of people pop in and out to collect their takeaway.

Circus Grill has an equally attractive spot on another corner of The Circus. This is a very pleasant restaurant that serves not only grilled seafood, steak, and lamb, but Créole and Indonesian dishes. They have a big Caribbean buffet at lunch on Fridays. Rituals Café is good for coffee, snacks, and lunch.

The Ocean Terrace Inn (OTI) is a large hotel that cascades down the hill to the waterfront, with many pools and bars and different levels. It was closed early 2015 for extensive renovations but was expected to

I ❤ Sweet Cane
RESTAURANT

POSITIVELY
The Best Burgers, Wraps, Fritters, Crab Stuffed Shrimps, Crab & Spinach Stuffed Grouper

Check Our
Daily Specials

Mon - Sat 11-8
PORT ZANTE
869-465-4345 | 869-665-7628

reopen long before this guide comes out. The OTI is part of the TDC group, so you can call TDC on VHF: 18 for reservations. OTI offers special room rates for yachts when available, and their restaurants (Fisherman's Wharf and the Verandah) offer occasional entertainment.

You can get to their restaurants by taking your dinghy to Fisherman's Wharf, their waterfront restaurant. It has dinghy docking, but it is small and you may have to beach the dinghy. The Fisherman's Wharf (dinner only) is a pleasant fish restaurant that comes complete with water lapping at the edge and nautical decor. The menu is large enough for all tastes and pockets, with everything from their famous clam chowder to fresh lobster and swordfish. Up the hill, you can get a more traditional breakfast lunch and dinner at OTI's Verandah Restaurant where they have a Sunday brunch and a Friday West Indian buffet. For lunch try the Fantasy Bar & Grill, located by the Fantasy Pool, where you can enjoy a wide range of sandwiches, salads, and cool drinks from 1100 until 1700.

Next door to OTI, Serendipity is a gourmet restaurant where Chef Alex will cook you excellent food, which you eat looking out over the harbor. Perfect for a special night out.

King's Palace is an authentic Chinese restaurant upstairs in Port Zante: inexpensive, clean, and air-conditioned, with lots of dishes using local seafood.

Twist, also in Port Zante, serves Chinese, Indian, Thai, Mexican and European food. I tried the Indian, which was excellent and hot. The service was friendly and good, the music mind-scramblingly techno. Try also Sweet Lime.

There are a couple of restaurants not too far out of town that make wonderful dinner destinations because of their ambience as old plantation houses set in luxurious gardens. Ottley's Plantation Inn, a 20-minute drive from town on the windward side of St. Kitts, is excellent. It is a lovely old family-run estate, with fancy lawns full of royal palms. Behind the hotel is a pleasant, shady walk in an area that was once cultivated and has been allowed to return to forest. Meal guests are welcome to relax in the garden and they

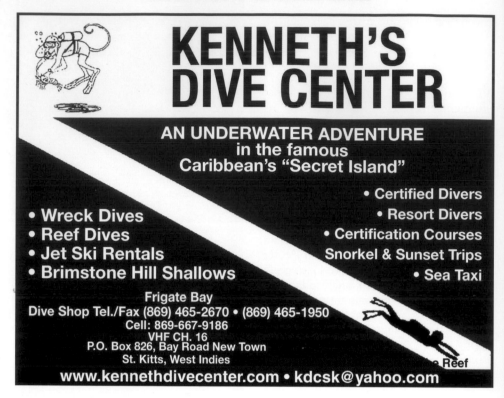

KENNETH'S DIVE CENTER

AN UNDERWATER ADVENTURE
in the famous
Caribbean's "Secret Island"

- Wreck Dives
- Reef Dives
- Jet Ski Rentals
- Brimstone Hill Shallows

- Certified Divers
- Resort Divers
- Certification Courses
- Snorkel & Sunset Trips
- Sea Taxi

Frigate Bay
Dive Shop Tel./Fax (869) 465-2670 • (869) 465-1950
Cell: 869-667-9186
VHF CH. 16
P.O. Box 826, Bay Road New Town
St. Kitts, West Indies

www.kennethdivecenter.com • kdcsk@yahoo.com

have a pool. They offer light lunches except on Sundays, when they do a big champagne brunch from 1100-1400. Dinners are fancy gourmet food.

Nirvana Restaurant at Fairview Estate is about 10 minutes out of town on the main road to Brimstone Hill. It is not quite as grand as Ottley, but has lovely gardens, a swimming pool, and a part of the old house is a museum with period furniture (Ottley has something similar). The dining room is pleasant and the food very good, with a Thai accent. Whichever one you visit, go early and enjoy the grounds. Reservations are advisable for dinner in either one.

Larkland Richards Bird Rock Beach Hotel has its own dinghy dock, a short ride east of the deep water port. The Bird Rocks are near the entrance, so I would advise going in by day before you try it at night. This place has changed recently with the addition of a long sea pool and adjoining captive dolphin enclosure, run by Dolphin Discovery. The new Waterfront restaurant overlooks this. They also have a restaurant for the gourmet.

Ashore

St. Kitts is a rewarding island for those who like to explore ashore. It has an unmapped network of small farm roads that crisscross the cane fields and wander into the hills and up to the edge of the forest. These are great for mountain biking and hiking.

Near at hand, Palm Court is about 10 minutes walk from the marina, next to OTI. Palm Court is a perfect place to spend some hours away from the boat. They have a beautiful garden, a spectacular pool overlooking the marina, lots of comfortable chairs, recliners, and hammocks, plus a bar, lunch restaurant, and boutique specializing in shell work. There is a kid's corner and an old Rolls Royce. You can visit for a couple of dollars, have lunch, or treat it as your home all day for $10 US. If you like it quiet and beautiful, avoid big cruise ship days. Elvis from Gibraltar Tours told me about this place and will be happy to take you if you prefer to ride.

The Royal St. Kitts Golf Course, owned by Marriott, has 18 holes and all equipment is available for rent. Advance booking is essential during the winter season.

If it is time to take in a movie, Caribbean Cinemas is a modern multi-theater facility just west of Basseterre, next to Best Buy.

Water Sports

Divers will want to explore St. Kitts' extensive reefs, which start at around 40 feet deep and slope down as far as you can go – the fish getting bigger as you descend. Local laws insist that all diving be done with a local dive shop. There are several to choose from. Kenneth Samuel, a Kittitian PADI dive master, is the most experienced and knowledgeable, starting with his fishing days when he would free-dive down to 120 feet for lobster. His love of diving turned him to sports diving, and he has now been teaching and taking groups diving for over 35 years. He runs several purpose-built catamaran dive boats.

He can take any size group and collects people from yachts and hotels. He hires several Padi instructors and specializes in private groups from yachts who want to go on their own and he has a 34-foot speedboat. Kenneth is happy to act as a dive guide for big yachts with large tenders who want to use their own equipment. For large yachts, he will come down to South Friars Bay or Christophe Harbour. Kenneth helps anyone with special needs who would like to dive, and he has a four-person diver's apartment for rent. Call Kenneth's Dive Center on VHF: 16 before 0800, between 1300-1400, or in the evening after 1700 to arrange a pickup, or phone anytime: 465-2670, 664-6809 or 667-9186. Kenneth will fill tanks if you need to work on your boat.

Austen MacLeod's Pro Divers is based at the OTI. Two PADI instructors are available and full-certification courses can be taken. They stand by on VHF: 16. Bird Rock Beach Hotel has Dive St. Kitts. They have a good dive boat and sometimes listen to VHF: 16.

Among the many dive sites is Sandy Point Bay, which lies at the north end of St. Kitts. This is a superb dive. The reef starts at 40 feet, and the coral formations are beautiful, with both hard and soft corals and giant sponges. The reef teems with fish. The MV Talata was wrecked in 1985 and lies off the west coast of St. Kitts on a reef with depths of 30 to 60 feet. The River Taw was a 144-foot vessel that now lies on sand in about 50 feet of water. This is a good dive site for novice divers. Coconut Tree Reef, not far from Basseterre, is a lovely reef that starts at 40 feet and plunges to depths of more than 300 feet, with plenty of reef fish. See also Monkey Reef and Nag's Head, described in the Nevis section.

SOUTH ST. KITTS

The southern part of St. Kitts is connected to the main island by a long, narrow peninsula. The formation is both attractive and unusual. Hills of yellow, brown, and green surround several large salt ponds. It is dry, with cactuses, century plants, and flocks of sandpipers that feed in the shallow ponds. It is the easiest place to see monkeys. A road runs right down to the end. This area has the most and best protected anchorages in St. Kitts. It is also home of the huge new Christophe Harbour development.

Frigate Bay

Frigate Bay lies at the gateway to the southern Peninsular. For years forbidden to yachts, it is now open again. This is the main tourist area in St. Kitts, with beach bars, restaurants, and water sports. The water is shallow a fair way out, so it is easy to anchor in 15 or 20 feet; try to find a sandy spot for your hook. In southerly winds and swells it can be rolly, though not quite as badly as Basseterre. In these conditions you can move on down the coast till it is calm. At the eastern end of the beach is a stone breakwater and somewhat serviceable dinghy dock.

Ashore

Frigate Bay is a holiday area, with nice beaches, a golf course, a casino, and many bars and restaurants all open to visitors. You can find all the activities you might want here from Mr. X Watersports, who has everything from lounge chairs to Hobie cats, including windsurfers. He takes people waterskiing, snorkeling, and on boat trips, and is helpful with local information. Mr. X serves food in the evenings at Frigate Bay

ISLANDS THAT BRUSH THE CLOUDS

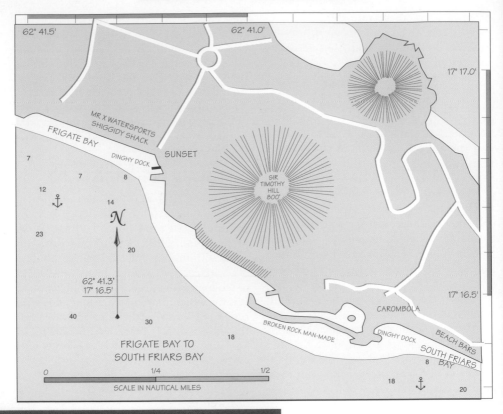

FRIGATE BAY TO
SOUTH FRIARS BAY

SCALE IN NAUTICAL MILES

Salt Plage

out of his little food caravan, Shiggidy Shak, where you can eat barbecued lobster and chicken. Sunset Café is part of the Timothy Beach Resort and their Dock Bar is a popular gathering place with a sunset view.

When you want a really good restaurant, grab a cab to Marshall's in Horizons Villa Resort. It is within walking distance so you can walk back, which is more downhill.

South Friars Bay

South Friars Bay is generally a good anchorage. It is open and is easy to approach. With the building of the Carombola Restaurant, which has a good dinghy dock, it has become possible to use this as a base for exploring the island, as well as enjoying the beach. (See our chart of *South St. Kitts*)

Frigate Bay

South Friars Bay, showing the Carombola dinghy dock

Chris Doyle

Ashore

The Carombola is a huge and lovely restaurant with a good dinghy dock, which you are welcome to use when eating there, and they generally don't mind you using it at other times. This is an excellent place to come from Wednesday to Sunday for fine dining in a perfectly romantic beachfront atmosphere, and they have a fine wine cellar. (They also wholesale wines.) They are open for lunch when cruise ships are in the harbor. Lunch on these days is quite casual. General manager Chris Evelyn is welcoming and very helpful.

From Carombola south is a lively beach with many small beach bars, restaurants and water sports. One of the best is the Shipwreck Bar, way down at the south end. There is some reef off here, so you have to dinghy in at the south end between all the buoys. Shipwreck is open every day from noon to 1830. On weekends they serve breakfast and there is live music on Sundays from 1600-1800. Raman, often the man in charge, doles out peanuts to the wild monkeys, so this is an excellent place to see them.

White House Bay

White House Bay and Ballast Bay are both well protected and both part of the Christophe Harbour development. The only navigational hazard is a long reef between them that sticks out from Guana Point, privately marked by Christophe Harbour with a white buoy that flashes at night. Give it good clearance. White House Bay is much smaller, but it has easy road access.

A reef and rocks on the south side of the bay come out several hundred feet from shore. To avoid these, anchor north of the new Salt Plage Beach Bar. The reef used to have a wreck on it, but only scraps are left. This wreck had a huge colony of blue, painted tunicates. Happily, a few of these seem to have found suitable substrate on nearby rocks.

Anchor in the middle of the bay in 15 to 25 feet of water. It is sandy close to shore.

Ashore

If you look southeast from the bay, you will see a building overlooking the salt pond. This is the office of Christophe Harbour land sales and they have open WiFi that you might be able to pick up.

THE SMALLEST THINGS LEAVE THE GREATEST IMPRESSION.

A superyacht marina is your driveway. A white sandy beach is your backyard.
Discover The Marina at Christophe Harbour. Approved for Citizenship by Investment.

+1 869.465.9755 | ChristopheHarbour.com/marina

CHRISTOPHE
HARBOUR
ST. KITTS

Obtain the Property Report required by Federal law and read it before signing anything. No Federal agency has judged the merits or value, if any, of this property. This i intended to be a solicitation or offer for purchase in states and/or jurisdictions where registration is required. Prices, plans, products, and availability are subject to change wit notice. Illustrations are artist's renderings only and may differ from completed product. Use of recreational facilities and amenities may be subject to separate club membe requirements, payment of fees, and/or other restrictions.

In the bay you will see the Salt Plage Beach Bar, with its big lounging dock. You may use this to access the bar when it is open (evenings only from 1500), but it is not a general use dinghy dock (see Christophe Harbour). There is a public road to the beach a little north of Salt Plage and you can beach your dinghy there.

On a clear night Salt Plage has a lovely atmosphere with palms and rusty galvanized sheeting to bring back the atmosphere of the old salt works on which it is built. The big deck has lots of seats and some nets where you can lie out over the water. It is open, so if rain threatens, grab a seat at the bar, the only dry place. They serve finger food, and three dishes between two seems fine for a meal. They open every day from 1700.

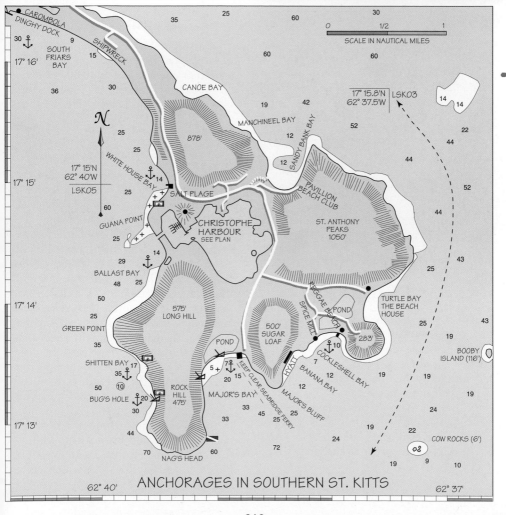

ANCHORAGES IN SOUTHERN ST. KITTS

ISLANDS THAT BRUSH THE CLOUDS

BALLAST BAY

CHRISTOPHE HARBOUR

WHITE HOUSE BAY

Chris Doyle

White House Bay and Christophe Harbour

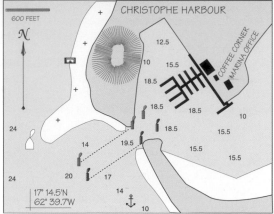

Christophe Harbour and Ballast Bay

Ballast Bay, right next door to White House Bay, is much larger with a long, stony beach. Once you are clear of the reef off Guana Point, anchor anywhere south of the channel. The entrance to the marina is in this bay just south of the reef, and is marked.

With the arrival of Christophe Harbour, this southern part of the peninsular is developing rapidly. They own nearly all the land, with the exception of the corner from Banana Bay to Turtle Bay.

Regulations

Christophe Harbour is an official port of clearance. Early in 2015 no customs station or officers were on hand, however clearance was possible here (or anywhere else in St. Kitts and Nevis) if you use an agent. A customs post is planned, probably during the life of this guide.

Services

Christophe Harbour is open, with the first stage completed. When finished it will be one of the largest private navigable harbors in the Eastern Caribbean. The first 22 berths for yachts of 100 feet or more is completed (they have sold 9 of these berths), as is the entrance, which is dredged to 20 feet. There is room for three larger yachts up to 300 feet stern-to. A long dock currently used for tenders and maybe short term stays for smaller yachts is in place. Yachts at anchor in White House and Ballast Bays may use this dock for shore access. By the time this book comes out the fuel station should be open and you will be able to come in for diesel, gasoline and water. Large yachts in the marina can fuel up on any of the docks. Tenders and small yachts will use the tender dock. At this stage they should have garbage facilities (for which there will be a charge). The marina number

Christophe Harbour nearing completion

Chris Doyle

(the first number to call) is 466-8738. If you cannot get through, try Aeneas Hollins, the man in charge (762-1785), or Linda Pearson, the dockmaster (763-1168), or the marina guest services manager, Melanie Dupre (762-2522).

Ashore

The Christophe Harbour development plan is forging ahead. The Pavilion Beach Club at Sandy Bay, which includes a restaurant, beach bar, and fitness center has been completed. It is private by day but open to the public for dinner Tuesday to Saturday, 24 hours advance booking is necessary. Salt Plage is open (see White House Bay).

A Park Hyatt is well under construction in Banana Bay, and by the time that is finished, an 18-hole Tom Fazio golf course will be open on the north face of Long Hill. You are welcome to use a network of hiking trails, but ask in the marina for details. They have permission for up to 2,000 private residences (some are already built). The area around the marina office will eventually have shops, cafes, restaurants, and marine services.

The work done so far is top quality, with excellent landscaping. A sales office with all the plans is in a building on a little knoll overlooking White House and Ballast Bays.

See the section on *Cockleshell Bay* for more nearby restaurants.

Shitten Bay and Bugs Hole

Shitten Bay and Bugs Hole are two bays whose rather unappetizing names belie their quiet beauty. Both are backed by cliffs and are deep except for the occasional rock close to shore. They make fair lunchtime anchorages and there is excellent snorkeling.

Major's Bay

Major's Bay, on the south side of St. Kitts, is deep, and you can carry 14 feet close on the eastern side. The northwestern part is 5-7 feet deep, with two wrecks ashore. A giant concrete block, an old mooring, is about 4.5 feet deep. I mark it as a rock. The Sea Bridge Ferry runs to Nevis from here, and you have to leave a clear channel into the dock. However there is room to anchor fairly close to shore between the channel and a conspicuous beached barge.

If you land your dinghy on the beach you are within dinghy range of Banana Bay and Cockleshell Bay. The seabed is mainly sand, covered in weeds. If you can find a patch of sand between the weeds, holding is good. It can be a little rolly in here if the wind is from the south, but this the best-protected bay for northerly winds and the best choice should a cold front threaten.

ISLANDS THAT BRUSH THE CLOUDS

MAJORS BAY

Banana and Cockleshell Bay

If you come in close to Cockleshell Bay's eastern headland, you find calm enough anchorage for a day stop, and can often overnight here. It is good in easterly and northeasterly winds, but not so good if the winds come from the southeast. How far you can come in will depend on your draft, but you can usually find a calmish spot in 11 feet right off Reggae Beach.

Ashore

Reggae Beach is a popular local hangout owned by Gary Pereira and managed by Sonia Dyer. It is open seven days a week from 1000-1800, with a dining room right on the beach. They have WiFi, showers, and toilets, and sell ice.

This is a popular place to spend beach time. Ocean kayaks and deep-sea fishing trips are available, and they can arrange a fast ferry service to Oualie Beach in Nevis. (You can of course, also use the regular ferry, the Sea Bridge.) On cruise ship days, it is very much the happening place with lots of action; other days are quiet and relaxed. At Reggae Beach they serve everything from hamburgers to seafood. The food is good and service attentive. You can visit the boutique. They have a landing/dinghy dock, but you will need a stern anchor.

Roger Brisbane's Spice Mill is farther down the beach and a bit more upmarket, with finer food and a handsome building of sun-bleached wood. They have a beach bar, boutique, loungers, and kids' floating toys anchored out. They open 0900-1700 daily for lunch and Tuesday to Saturday from 1800 for dinner. The food is very good, and the service a bit slow, which should not be a problem in the relaxed and pleasant ambience. If you give them a day's notice, they can arrange to pick you up from White House Bay for lunch, but not dinner.

Lion Rock Bar, a Rasta beach shack is right next door and makes a good hangout. They offer reasonably priced drinks and good local food.

The big new Park Hyatt will come on line during the life of this guide and offer more restaurants.

Cockleshell Bay, Banana Bay to left

Chris Doyle

Botanical Gardens   Chris Doyle

Nevis

FROM SOME ANGLES Nevis looks like a sombrero, peaked in the center and low around the edges. Clouds usually cap Nevis Peak, which is over 3,000 feet high. On occasion, they cling to the summit and fall down the sides, looking just like snow. Some say this is why Columbus named it "Nuestra Senora del las Nieves" (Our Lady of the Snows), after one of his favorite churches. Early attempts were made to settle the island from St. Kitts in 1628. The first town, called Jamestown, was built near Fort Ashby, but it sank into the sea after an earthquake and tidal wave in 1680. Various battles between the British and the French hampered development until 1783, when Nevis became British for an extended time. It flourished as a plantocracy and there are many old plantations and sugar mills on the island. The old mills are crumbling, but the plantations have been converted into hotels where visitors can relive those gracious old days without the evils of slavery upon which they were built. Two historical figures associated with Nevis are Alexander Hamilton, who was born here, and Horatio Nelson, who married Nevisian widow Fanny Nisbet.

Nevis, with a population of around 12,000, is quiet and peaceful, with lovely views, picturesque houses, and delightful people. Exploring the island is highly recommended. Nevisians have been careful to preserve their architectural heritage and many traditional Caribbean-style buildings survive.

The mountain is clad in dense forest and with a suitable guide you can make it all the way to the peak. The less energetic can visit the Golden Rock Estate, buy a trail map, and take a stroll or hike. Going at 1530 will give the best chance of seeing wild greenback monkeys. Return for tea in the majestic garden setting of the estate.

Several people lead historical, plantation, and forest tours. Information

Nevis

Regulations

Nevis, together with St. Kitts, is one country (though every few years Nevis talks of secession). Visiting yachts may not use jet-skis or similar craft. Scuba diving may only be undertaken with a local dive shop. The best port of entry for yachts in Nevis is Charlestown. Customs procedures are given under Charlestown.

Telephones

Lime and Digicel cell phones work here. Both have offices in Charlestown. To call the USA, dial 1 + the number. For other countries, dial 011+ the country code (UK is 44). The country code for St. Kitts and Nevis is 869.

Shopping Hours

Weekdays 0800-1200 & 1300-1600. Some shops are open on Saturday morning and some supermarkets open on Sundays. Bank hours: weekdays 0800-1300. On Fridays they also open from 1500-1700.

Transport

Taxis are plentiful and available at the head of the dock in Charlestown. Add 50% to the following rates between 2200-0600. They are for up to 4 people in EC:

Charlestown to Golden Rock	$45
Charlestown to Gingerland	$40
Charlestown to Botanical Gardens	$40
Charlestown to Oualie	$40
Airport to Oualie	$27
Charlestown to Airport	$53
Charlestown to Newcastle	$59
Island tour (3 hours)*	$200

*(For more than 4 people, add $50 per person)
Rates from 2200 to 0600 are plus 50%, $3 per bag over two bags.

There is an inexpensive and infrequent bus system. We give points of departure on our Charlestown map.

There are plenty of rental cars available. You will need to get a local license, which costs $24 US. It is also good for St. Kitts. Drive on the left.

The Sea Bridge car ferry goes from Tamarind Bay to Majors Bay and frequent ferries link Charlestown and Basseterre.

Superyacht owners with private planes will love the new Nevis Airport, with its fine modern facilities.

Airport departure tax is $22 US, usually in the ticket price.

Holidays

All the same holidays as St. Kitts (see St. Kitts), in addition, the first Tuesday in August is Culturama holiday.

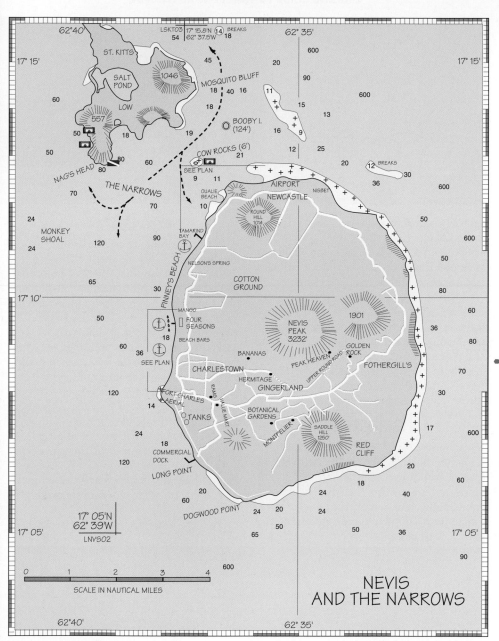

NEVIS
AND THE NARROWS

ISLANDS THAT BRUSH THE CLOUDS

on these, bird books, and trail maps are all available at the Museum of Nevis in Hamilton House.

Navigation

Nevis's west coast is relatively free of dangers and a quarter of a mile offshore keeps you in deep water. A long commercial L-shaped dock extends from the shore off Long Point, a couple of miles south of Charlestown. Streetlights line the dock. There is a navigation light that looks like a flashing red and white sector light at its outermost point. Unlit barges and buoys are often anchored close to shore, between the port and Charlestown.

Stay well off the east and south coasts from which reefs extend almost half a mile. The north coast is separated from St. Kitts by The Narrows, which are 15 to 20 feet

COMMERCIAL DOCK OFF LONG POINT

deep. Two visible rocks are Booby Island, some 125 feet high, and Cow Rocks, which are only 6 feet high. A mile and half east of Booby Island there is a large shoal with patches of coral that reach the surface.

While it is easier to stay on the western side of both islands, it is not hard to traverse The Narrows. If coming from the north, round Mosquito Bluff on St. Kitts and pass midway between St. Kitts and the islands in the middle (Booby and Cow). Reverse the procedure for leaving. See also the St. Kitts navigation section.

Charlestown

Charlestown, Nevis' only town, is a picturesque country town with many historic buildings of stone and wood. The renovated waterfront area has a pleasant open liming area facing the dinghy dock. Great little shops abound and there is a choice of restaurants.

Navigation

If approaching from the south, stay a few hundred yards off Fort Charles, as it is shallow some way out. Yachts of less than 90 feet are supposed to pick up one of many moorings that have been laid in varying groups from town to Tamarind Bay. The moorings have enabled grass beds to grow back. The main visitor moorings are white with NPA on them. Each has a pick-up line with an eye. Put your lines through the eye. Never run a line from one side of your boat through the eye to the other – the boat movement will abrade the line. You pay a mooring charge whether you use them or not. Larger yachts may anchor in deeper water. The moorings have been poorly maintained and yachts have drifted away, so snorkel on your mooring to make sure it is okay.

The favorite mooring area is north of

MAJORS BAY

COW ROCKS

BOOBY ISLAND

OUALIE BEACH

THE NARROWS

CHARLESTOWN & PINNEY'S BEACH

town, just off Pinney's Beach. Pinney's Beach is miles long, backed by beach vegetation, with Mount Nevis ascending into the clouds behind. Gliding pelicans fold their wings and crash boldly in the sea. St. Kitts, lying to the north, appears to be part of Nevis in a sweeping panorama.

Years ago it was even more beautiful, when the beach was backed by miles of palm trees, whose slender trunks and lacy leaves caught the sunlight. Unfortunately, when Four Seasons Hotel was built, a disease was introduced that first sickened all the palm trees around the hotel. These have now been treated and look fine, but nearly all the other palm trees on the beach have died. Other beach trees are taking over from the palms.

The Four Seasons Hotel on Pinney's Beach makes a conspicuous landmark. Four Seasons built four stone breakwaters in front of their hotel, about 100 yards from the beach. They maintain red and green entrance lights for their own tenders, and all the breakwaters were originally marked with flashing orange lights. These no longer seem to be there. The breakwaters make for interesting snorkeling and seabirds roost on them.

Regulations

Charlestown Customs opens weekdays 0800-1600; weekends and holidays 0900-1300. The customs, immigration, and port offices are together upstairs in the Cotton Ginnery, just behind the dock. New customs regulations are yacht-friendly, though you do need to tell them which anchorages you plan to visit when you check in. You can check into Nevis and out of St. Kitts. You can check into Nevis, visit St. Kitts then check out of Nevis. If you are staying a week or less in both islands you can usually get inward and outward clearance at the same time, allowing you to visit both islands. After checking in with customs, check with port and immigration. In my experience, most Nevis customs officers are among the best.

At customs you pay a yacht entry fee of $20 EC, a customs charge of $10 EC, ($50 if you are over 100 tons).

Port fees as follows: up to 100 tons $50 EC plus $12 EC per night, boats of 100-500 tons pay $100 plus $25 EC a night along with $218 EC for navigation lights.

Everyone pays a $4 EC per person per day environmental levy (I wonder which part of the environment gets that?). Fare paying passengers are charged $5 US per

ISLANDS THAT BRUSH THE CLOUDS

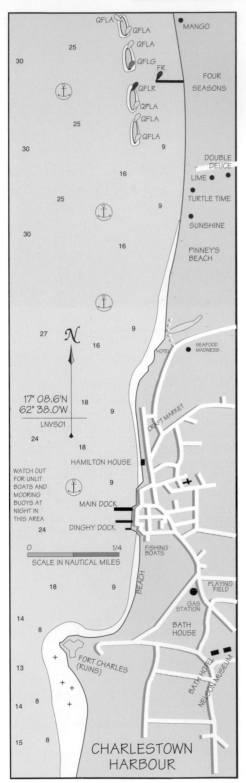

head. In addition, you pay moorings fees (moorings are compulsory) as follows:

Up to 35 ft $40 EC for up to two days; $54 EC for 3-7 days

36 - 60 ft $54 EC for up to two days; $67 EC for 3-7 days

61 - 90 ft $67 EC for up to two days; $81 EC for 3-7 days

Port fees are not collected again if you visit St. Kitts.

Communications

If you pick up a mooring near the beach bars, you might be able to connect through Sunshine's or the Lime Bar WiFi.

Nearly every bar and restaurant on the island has open WiFi, so you can connect just about anywhere.

If you have a smart phone or SIM internet device, Lime or Digicel can sell you a data package and you'll have good reception in the anchorages.

Services

Nevis Yacht Services can take care of all your needs while in St. Kitts & Nevis, and are happy to offer advice on what to see, do and where's best to eat. They can help with clearance, maintenance and repairs, source parts for your yacht, help with shopping, laundry, and ice. Their team ashore has lots of experience on yachts and life on Nevis. Contact Brett, Miles or Jonni on VHF 68 or call 469 6545/ 667 7466/ 664 9171.

The St. Kitts superyacht agents also have representatives in Nevis.

Water and fuel are available on the dock. Fuel comes by truck, so there is a minimum. Smaller amounts can be carried in jerry jugs. Water in EC costs $25 for 50 gallons, $35 for 75, $50 for 100, $75 for 120 and over that, $100.

Call Nevis Port on VHF: 16 for permission to come alongside. Keep in mind that it is a dusty ferry dock, not designed for yachts. Inexpensive blocks of ice are occasionally available from the fish part of the market.

CCC, owned by Mark Theron is a good, fully professional canvas and sail repair shop near the waterfront. Mark and his team can fix your sails or build you a complex awning or bimini, and they weld

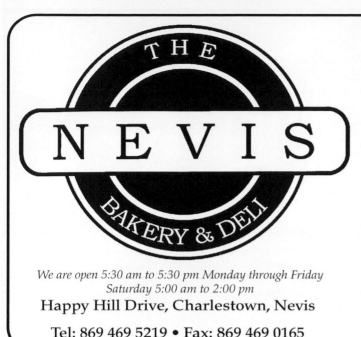

Shop at our modern bakery for a variety of fresh and delicious bakery goods — *baked from scratch.* Try our French bread, croissants or puffed pastries. Also our Danish, cinnamon rolls and coconut tarts and the best roti and focaccia. Shop our deli for other tasty treats.

We are open 5:30 am to 5:30 pm Monday through Friday
Saturday 5:00 am to 2:00 pm

Happy Hill Drive, Charlestown, Nevis

Tel: 869 469 5219 • Fax: 869 469 0165

in aluminum and stainless, so they can build frames, or fix most anything else you have broken.

Garbage bins are just off the dock. You can fill most cooking gas bottles; ask any taxi.

Sunshine's Beach Bar may help with ice and can send your laundry out – or you can take it yourself to the laundry, which is by Rams. However, be aware that laundry here is about the most expensive in the Eastern Caribbean.

Greg, who owns Yachtsman Grill, is an agent for Evinrude outboards and he both sells and services them.

FedEx has an office in Solomon Plaza in Memorial Square. Kustom Airbrush and Signs can create any kind of boat name, from computer transfer to airbrush.

If you have any questions about the island, ask at the Nevis Tourism Bureau opposite the D.R. Walwyn Plaza. They love yachting visitors, wish to encourage yachts, and are very helpful. Ask for a copy of the latest map that includes hiking and biking trails.

If you need a doctor, the first stop should probably be Dr. Rawlins (Government Road) or Dr. Jacobs (on the Solomon Plaza). Call to find when they will be in their offices.

Provisioning

The fresh food market has a good variety of produce, especially on Saturdays. You can occasionally find fish in the market, fresh when the boats come in, otherwise frozen, and block ice is sometimes available.

Nevis Bakery on Happy Hill Drive will supply you with fresh bread, Danish, pastries, and other great baked goodies, in small or charter-sized quantities. Or just pop in and pick up a snack. You will do better here than in most supermarkets where they often bring in frozen bread, then unfreeze it for sale.

Three supermarkets in town have many things, but there may well be items you cannot find. (This is also true of the bigger supermarkets out of town, though they are much bigger.)

Best Buy probably has the most in terms of vegetables and fruits and a big selection of cans and cleaners.

Superfoods has a big wine and liquor section and a big frozen section. Fresh

ISLANDS THAT BRUSH THE CLOUDS

Main Street, Charlestown

stuff is limited, but you will find cans and packages. Superfoods is open weekdays from 0800-2000, Saturdays from 0800-2100, and on Sundays and most holidays they open 0900-1200. If you are buying a fair quantity, they will deliver it for you to the dock.

Main Street Supermarket is in by far the prettiest building and has a good selection of cans and dry goods.

If you need more shopping than that, take a cab or catch a bus to Ram's Mall and Value Mart, two big supermarkets opposite each other south of town. (It is a longish walk.)

Rams opens Monday to Friday 0830-1900 and Saturdays 0830-2000, and they have a good fruit and vegetable selection. On the opposite side of the road, Horsford's Value Mart is modern, very clean and spacious with some produce, frozen foods and dry goods, as well as a small deli. They open 0800-2000, 0800-2100 on Friday and Saturdays, and from 0800-1700 on Sundays.

A big Best Buy much farther down the road near Golden Rock is the best for deli and meat.

TDC and Horsford's Nevis Center are both excellent large hardware stores just out of town that stock everything from housewares to rope.

Fun Shopping

The Cotton Ginnery is right opposite the dinghy dock. This is a plaza with some small boutiques, including one selling Nevisian handicrafts.

Mildred Williams at Caribco has managed to gather an interesting collection of t-shirts, souvenirs, and ornaments, all with a Caribbean flavor. Pemberton's, a duty-free shop, sells perfumes, jewelry, and baubles with a tropical flavor.

Nevis Handicrafts Cooperative (occasionally open) sells crafts, honey, jams, and chutney made on Nevis. You will find more crafts at Crafthouse, a mile or so out of town on the road behind Pinney's Beach.

Restaurants
Charlestown

Café des Arts is a tiny building in a lovely garden setting close to Hamilton House. Elizabeth Smith, the owner, opens Monday to Friday at 0800-1400. She has lots of different coffees, and serves cakes and muffins, as well as sandwiches, salads, and quiche for lunch. It is open on Tuesday nights for burgers (including veggie burgers) and chili. Elizabeth will happily give you local information.

For a local lunch, walk down the road towards the police station and visit Wilma's Diner, which is set in a cute old house. Wilma used to work as one of the chefs at Montpelier, though here she does good old Caribbean-style lunch plates.

The Cotton Ginnery has two little inexpensive food shacks.

The Patio (closed Sunday) is run by the

The Cafe des arts

A tranquil oasis in Charlestown in the gardens of Hamilton House Museum.

**Serving all day breakfasts, sandwiches, salads & homemade quiche, smoothies & local drinks.
Burger Night Tuesday 6 PM until**

Open 8 AM til 2-ish·Monday through Friday·869-667-8768

same people who have Superfoods and is in the same square. It opens mainly for special events. They have a lovely big patio so that you can sit outside – great when there is cricket playing at Grove Park, because it's right next door.

Across the road from Pinney's Beach, Seafood Madness, owned by Freddy and Andy, serves a wide variety of seafood on a large screened porch. About four Chinese restaurants are dotted around town, including Young's Chinese Restaurant, Gold Coast, with a balcony view of the street, and Excellent Fast Food Chinese.

Pinney's Beach Hotel has a restaurant.

There is an excellent restaurant a short taxi ride out of town straight up into the hills in Hamilton. Set in a typical Caribbean house with a lovely garden, including many fruit trees, Banana's offers elegant eating in a peaceful country atmosphere. You sit on a big balcony overlooking the garden. Gillian, the owner, has an upmarket, inventive cuisine. She has lots of fresh local fish and occasionally has fresh mussels and salmon flown in. It opens every day for lunch and dinner except Sunday, when it closed for lunch. Lunch is lighter than

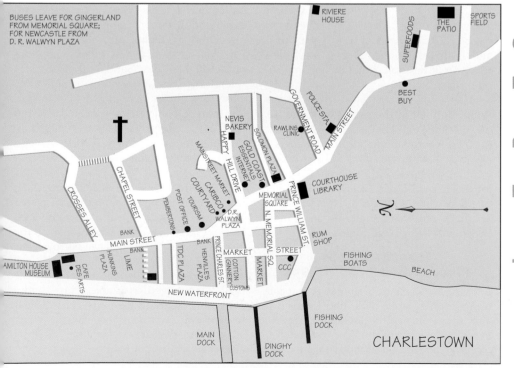

ISLANDS THAT BRUSH THE CLOUDS

Charlestown, with Mt. Nevis behind   Chris Doyle

dinner, with salads, open faced sandwiches, lobster linguini, or catch of the day.

Banana's is also an art gallery, with paintings both on the walls and in a separate gallery, which sells jewelry and a few artistic handicrafts. If you want to visit, there is usually someone around from 1000 onwards. If you come for the art, also check out Patricia Art (imaginative mosaics), Carolity Cantrell (paintings), and Iziah (sculpture). They are all close by. Reservations for dinner at Banana's are essential.

Also a bit out of town, (you go past Rams, turn left at the roundabout and it is on your left), Old House Café is a pleasant, inexpensive restaurant on the patio of a traditional old house. The food is good and local, as are most of the clients. It is open for lunch and dinner except Mondays and Tuesdays when it closers at 1600.

Check out the restaurants at Pinney's Beach and Gingerland (below).

Restaurants
Pinney's Beach, South End

Pinney's Beach is so gorgeous you may want to laze away days here, and it is also the main yacht anchorage. Several excellent beach bars are open for lunch or dinner. They are all grouped together just south of Four Seasons.

Double Deuce is just behind the beach. This is a big building with a generous balcony and a pool on the deck. This is a happening restaurant run by Lyndeta, who is a great local chef, and Mark, who was the executive chef for Montpelier. The atmosphere is pleasant, relaxing, quiet, and kid friendly, with a trampoline and slide. On Thursday nights they get lively with karaoke, as they do on other occasional music nights. On Sunday they cook a splendid roast lunch after which they close and usually stay closed all Monday. Otherwise Double Deuce is open daily from 0900 until... However, from winter 2015 on they plan to open Monday, Wednesdays and Saturdays for a buffet breakfast from 0700-0900. Lyndeta and Mark produce perfectly grilled fresh local seafood, including tuna, wahoo, and whole red snapper; or, organic beef-burgers, chicken, ribs, and steak with local vegetables. They serve some of the best seafood in Nevis. You can borrow a few board games, browse their book swap, and use the freshwater shower, or jump in the pool. They have darts, table tennis, and a pool table. Walk in for lunch, but dinner reservations are advisable. Mark, being a yachting person, looks after yachting customers well.

Home of the changing "chalkboard" menu... accommodating the freshest catch of the hour! Even the famous Double Deuce fresh hand made burgers are occasionally erased.

Enjoy lunch, dinner, relaxing by the pool, or surfing the web with free Wi-Fi.

Beach Restaurant & Bar Double Deuce

Lyndeta & Mark

Daily events, music, dancing, and entertainment often erupt... karaoke on Thursday evening.

Reservations (or to check the food and entertainment menu): **869.469.2222** or **869.667.0356**

10am until late • www.DoubleDeuceNevis.com • Pinney's Beach, Charlestown, Nevis

Sunshine's is world famous and has been here forever. You cannot leave Nevis without visiting for a rum punch or "killer bee." It attracts escapees from the Four Seasons Hotel, locals, and yachtspeople who eat under the colorful shelters. It is run by Sunshine, whose cheerful manner keeps people coming back and makes it an entertaining hangout. Sunshine's is right on the beach and recognizable by its big sign and bright colors. Pull your dinghy up right outside. One of Sunshine's killer bee drinks will get your mood up and make you ready for his daily barbecue of fresh fish, lobster, and chicken, cooked as you like it. Pull in for a swim and lunch, or come for a sunset drink and stay for dinner. Sunshine delivers yacht laundry to the laundry, sells fresh fruit and vegetables, and will help dispose of yacht garbage. He has WiFi, which you may be able to use if you pick up a mooring close by.

Next to Double Deuce is Randy's Lime. It has some big spaces, with places to hang out and relax. They have free WiFi, and will supply customers with a few jugs of

Sunshine's Beach Bar & Grill

No trip to Nevis is complete without meeting the internationally renowned "Sunshine." Sample his world-famous rum drink, the "Killer Bee," and his acclaimed grilled lobster — the finest in the Caribbean. Open for lunch and dinner, Sunshine and his nephews will treat you to fresh grilled seafood, chicken and ribs while you listen to reggae, blues and jazz from Sunshine's unique CD collection. Yacht services available: cubed ice in a bag, fresh fruit and vegetables, laundry services. Catering available for group events. Email inquiries to address below.

(869) 469 5817 • Pinney's Beach
VHF Channel 68 • email: renita_36@hotmail.com
Visit our website at www.sunshinesbeachbar.com

ISLANDS THAT BRUSH THE CLOUDS

233

not only the **coolest place** to hang on the beach but a **paradise for yachtsmen. free:** ice, wifi, garbage disposal and a **rum punch!** laundry at a small cost as well as **great fresh food** for lunch and dinner. call: **869 469 1147 or 869 662 9620 vhf channel 12**

chill out. the upper deck has the best **sunset,** exclusive **cocktails** and daily **live entertainment** from 6.30pm

Lime BEACH BAR & TOURS NEVIS W.I.

water or some ice. Lime is fun, friendly, hip, and child-friendly with always fresh and delicious food, including fresh fish and lobster. Open for lunch and dinner, they have a live band and DJ every Friday night for dancing on the beach. An upper deck bar has been added offering a more intimate space a specialty drink called a Booby Trap. Sushi coming in the near future.

Next door, Turtle Time is an Asian fusion restaurant on the beach run by the same people who have Indian Summer (see *Anchorages north of Charlestown*) and managed by Hiren (Rain), so the service is excellent. They have something for everyone, wok dishes, egg rolls, wraps (including lobster wrap) and fresh grilled fish. The bang bang shrimp is excellent as are their dragon tails and lollipop chicken and fish. Try their signature drink the Tipsy Turtle, but avoid racing with hares

afterwards.

Anyone having problems with Caribbean culture shock will feel at home at the fancy Four Seasons Hotel on Pinney's Beach, a large beautifully landscaped American establishment with a gentle touch of Nevis. They have two restaurants (the Grill and the Coral Grill), plus the Cabana Beach Bar for lunch, and a large boutique. These, as well as their 18-hole golf course and tennis courts, are open to visitors when they aren't full (not usually around Christmas and the new year). However, their hospitality toward yachtspeople does not extend to tying up at their dock, which they reserve strictly for their own boats. They don't even like yachts to land their guests on the dock.

Four Seasons runs a separate beach bar called Mango, just north of their boundary. The view north from here is the prettiest on the island: pulled-up fishing boats forming

Come For
A Turtlely
Awesome
Time!

TURTLE TIME

BEACH BAR & GRILL

Opening Hours
Are From
12PM to 10PM
Closed Wednesday
Bar open till late
on Fridays and
Saturdays.

Pinney's Beach, Nevis, West Indies   869-469-9911

the foreground for a perfect view of Pinney's Beach, with St. Kitts behind. Mango opens daily for lunch and dinner and serves mainly Caribbean food, spicy for those who like it that way. It can on occasion be full of people from Four Seasons, so dinner reservations are advisable.

(See also the sections on *Anchorages north of Charlestown* and *Gingerland*.)

Transport

Ferries run about once an hour between Nevis and St. Kitts from the ferry dock. In addition, St. Kitts' Sea Bridge runs a car ferry from Cades Bay to Major's Bay. It leaves Nevis on the odd hours starting at 0700 and leaves St. Kitts on the even hours. This makes it quite practical to take a rented car over for a day.

You can take a taxi, walk, or rent a car. Taxi tours are reasonably priced. Keep this in mind if you want to do something specific, as making it part of a tour might be the answer. For example, the rate to Long Point Port (for out-of-hours clearance) and back is pretty outrageous, but you could make it part of a tour and get to see the whole island for just twice that fare. I cannot fathom why taxis charge $3 US more to visit the Botanical Gardens than the adjoining property of Montpelier.

Fitzroy Williams, otherwise known as "Teach," because of his earlier profession as a schoolteacher, runs an excellent taxi, tour, and car rental agency called Teach Tours. He is friendly and informative and is happy to show you the island by car or organize hiking, rainforest, and other tours. Call Teach on his cell: 662-9022. He also has a couple of cars for rent.

Mountain bikes are another good way to see the island and rentals are available from Winston's Bike Nevis at Oualie Beach.

HERE'S WHERE TO DINE WHEN YOU DROP THE HOOK IN NEVIS

A gracious, colonial dining porch wraps around the oldest wooden house in the Caribbean. Local dishes are the core cuisine and are brought to their peak of perfection and variety every Wednesday night at the Caribbean pig roast. It's one of the most popular events on the island. The bar is an island favourite that creates cozy atmosphere where local characters and island visitors mingle while enjoying the best rum punch Nevis has to offer. It's here that tall tales about mountain climbs and the high seas are exchanged. Call 869.469.3477 or visit www.hermitagenevis.com.

Cars are few enough that you can still feel comfortable on the roads. In addition, newly opened trails such as the Upper Round Road are a natural for mountain bikes. Try renting one, taking a taxi up to Golden Rock, and coasting all the way back down (after you have dragged it along a few trails).

Three other places you can rent cars from are Strikers Car, TDC, and Noel's Garage. They all give good service, and these days with the new ferry going over to St. Kitts, you can use the same car for both islands. However, if you are moving your boat from one island to the other, talk to TDC as they might have you return your Nevis car and pick up one in St. Kitts.

A reader highly recommended Abba's Guided Tours.

For mobility with a little fun, call Yachtsman Grill and rent one of their open Polaris 4-wheel drive vehicles. They come in a variety of sizes to suit your group. They also rent Vespa scooters and do guided tours by land and sea.

Ashore

The Nelson Museum puts Britain's famous hero into the natural and cultural context of Nevis as it was in his day. Americans who have never heard of Nelson can find out who he was. For those of us who remember him as a dry lesson in history, the museum brings him to life. It opens weekdays 0900-1600, but ask in Hamilton House to make sure it has not moved.

The Hamilton Museum, director Evelyn Henville, is in the house where Alexander Hamilton was born. Both the museum and the garden are charming and open weekdays 0800-1600 and Saturdays 0900-1200. The museum has a library devoted to history and natural history, including the island's archives. They have a big building and garden next door for special exhibits. Ask about horse riding, as active member John Guilbert owns the Nevis Equestrian Center. You can also ask about guides, eco-tours, and trails.

Mark Theron knows a lot about rum.

Three Services

one company

City Drug Store Limited

TDC Thrifty Car Rentals

TDC Home and Building Depot

#NOPLACELIKETDC

TDC (Nevis) Limited, Main Street, Charlestown, Nevis, West Indies | T: (869) 469 5430 | F: (869) 469 1329 | E: tdcnevis@sisterisles.kn | W: www.tdclimited.com

He visits various hotels and gets invited on superyachts to do a rum presentation, which involves learning about rum and tasting six different rums. If interested give him a call (662-4114).

Gingerland

The choice land in the old days was "Gingerland," just south of the mountain. Here, on fertile soil, one is elevated enough to be both cool and graced with a pleasant view. It is here that most of the large old plantations were built and a few have been converted to small luxurious hotels with exceptionally fine dining rooms. These are grand old places, oozing with class, and absolutely perfect for sampling the fine style of the island. You can dress up as much as you want. Ties are not essential, but shorts and flip-flops do not go down too well in the evening. Dinner at $50-$100 US, makes them excellent value for elegant dining, and they all have much less expensive lighter lunches, including salads,

and sandwiches. I can think of no other island where I would prefer to have that special night ashore. You can walk in for lunch, but dinner reservations are essential.

Richard and Maureen Lupinacci rebuilt the derelict old Hermitage building back in the 1960s as a small guest house in the days when there was little tourism. They created the current Hermitage Hotel one small step at a time and the family has always run it.

The Hermitage is charming. Built in the 1640s, it predates the other estates and the original building, where you dine, is all built of wood. The main frames go way down into the earth to hold the building in storms, and as it was built of Lignum vitae, one of the world's heaviest and oiliest woods, the wood is still in good shape, even where it has been buried for centuries.

The dining area is part of this charming old building and is on a big balcony, which has been artfully added so it looks original. It is lovely and feels quite grand.

When they expanded into a hotel, they

GOLDEN ROCK INN

NEVIS, WEST INDIES
WWW.GOLDENROCKNEVIS.COM
869-469-3346
HOTEL AND RESTAURANT, OPEN DAILY

GOLDENROCK INN NEVIS

did so by adding many small, authentic wooden houses from Nevis, each one beautifully restored and painted. Many of these were bought from owners who were upgrading, and rebuilt on site. Hermitage is quite open, with the mountain in the background. You will probably see their Belgian cart-horse and a donkey walking around. Before-dinner drinks are served in a friendly old living room. The meal (à la carte) is served on a patio overlooking the garden courtyard. Food and service are excellent. On Wednesday nights they roast a suckling pig and because this is a very popular event, advance booking is essential.

The Lupinaccis are sailing folks and have Brasic, a sailing boat, which their son Richie enjoys, as well as Intermezzo, a 34-foot power boat, which they charter as a water taxi to St. Kitts or for fishing charters.

Golden Rock Inn is approached by a long drive lined with old stone walls. Handsome historic buildings are set among bright flowers. This magnificent estate covers some 96 acres on the edge of the rain forest. The estate goes back to 1801 when it was owned by Edward Huggins.

Always lovely, Golden Rock evolved into the spectacular when Brice and Helen (Harrington) Marden, artists from New York, became the main owners. Their aims are artistic rather than commercial and the emphasis has been on enhancing the original and new architecture so the whole has become a work of art. The new dining area, with water gardens and a distant view, merges into the lush main garden, and is just lovely and perfectly complements the original structure.

Luckily, they have not become too formal, and during the day people wander around in shorts. Yachtspeople are always made very welcome. If you get up early enough, it is a spectacular breakfast spot and dinners are excellent value.

The beautiful gardens also make Golden Rock a delightful choice for lunch (sandwiches, including a wonderful lobster sandwich, salads, and grilled foods) or tea. Monkeys are often in evidence and during

Spectacular colorful display of flora
from all over the world

Garden Hours: Mon-Sat 9am-4pm
Call for Sunday openings (869) 469-3509

Galleria Gift Shop: Open 9am-4pm (869) 469-2673

Oasis Restaurant: Lunch served Mon-Sat
Call for Dinner openings
(869) 469-2875 or 469-3509

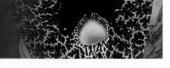

Phone: 869.469.3509
Email: info@botanicalgardennevis.com
www.botanicalgardennevis.com

THE BOTANICAL GARDENS
OF NEVIS, WEST INDIES

lunch you can feed crumbs to the birds and lizards in the front garden. If you want to hike into the rainforest to the water source (a 4-hour round trip), this is the place to start. Consider coming here for lunch and walking back to town by the Upper Round Road. This newly finished trail is along both old and new roads that follow the route of the early agricultural roads. It only takes a few hours to walk back to town with beautiful views along the way. The trail continues all the way to Nisbet Plantation.

Another attraction in Gingerland is the Botanical Gardens of Nevis, owned and run by the local Douglas family. The centerpiece of the gardens is a restaurant and the artful Galleria boutique, set in a gorgeous building that faithfully resembles an old estate house.

There is no charge for visiting the restaurant and boutique, though there is a fee for wandering through the various beautiful gardens. The six acres of plants are from all over the world, and include orchids, cactuses, over 100 species of palms, flowering trees and vines, as well as rivers

Golden Rock   Chris Doyle

ISLANDS THAT BRUSH THE CLOUDS

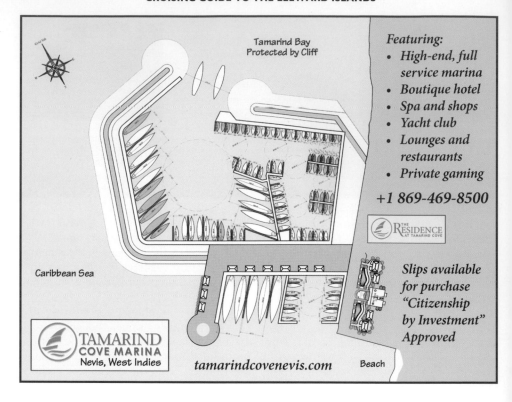

Tamarind Bay
Protected by Cliff

Featuring:
- *High-end, full service marina*
- *Boutique hotel*
- *Spa and shops*
- *Yacht club*
- *Lounges and restaurants*
- *Private gaming*

+1 869-469-8500

THE RESIDENCE AT TAMARIND COVE

Caribbean Sea

Slips available for purchase "Citizenship by Investment" Approved

TAMARIND COVE MARINA
Nevis, West Indies

tamarindcovenevis.com

Beach

and fountains. You will see hummingbirds, frogs, parrots, and tropical fish. They have a shaded rainforest conservatory, with Amazonian type attractions and many plants, including cocoa and coffee. They open Monday to Saturday, 0900-1600.

Their restaurant, Oasis in the Gardens serves delicious, authentic Thai and Asian fusion cuisine with excellent service. It is on the second floor balcony with lovely views of the formal lawn-circle garden, Mount Nevis, and the sea with St. Kitts in the distance. They are open for lunch Monday to Saturday and on some evenings. Call and ask about dinner nights.

Montpelier has a grand entrance gate and heavy stone walls. It is owned by the Hoffman family from the US, and Tim Hoffman is general manager. Drinks are served in an impressive living room; you repair onto the balcony with a great view over the lights of Charlestown for a grand fixed-menu dinner (served 1830-2100, closed Mondays). Benjamin Voisin is the chef and the cuisine is a

blend of European and Caribbean flavors. Everything, including the bread, is made on the premises. Indigo, their pool bar, is open Monday to Thursday night with an à la carte menu. It is also open for lunch. People come here to relax, chat, and sometimes take in a board game as they sample the food.

For the grandest meal, ask to eat in the Mill. This is an exclusive setting with just a few tables inside an historic old stone mill. Here they offer a very elegant four-course champagne dinner.

While here, you can check out their small boutique. Reservations are essential for dinner.

Water Sports

Nevis has pleasant diving, with big fish and good visibility. Local laws stipulate that divers must go with a dive shop. Dives include Thermal Vents Reef, from 35 feet to 95 feet, with lots of black coral. Overhangs and small canyons provide good hiding places for spotted drums, highhats,

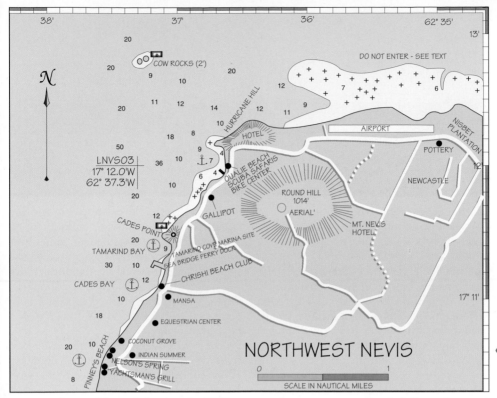

Map labels:
38' 37' 36' 62° 35' 13'
20
COW ROCKS (2')
20 9 10 20
N
20 11 12 14 12 12 9
50 18 8 10
LNVS03
17° 12.0'W
62° 37.3'W 36 10 9
20 6 4
10
12 20
CADES POINT
TAMARIND BAY 9
30 10
CADES BAY 12
MANSA
18
EQUESTRIAN CENTER
20 10 COCONUT GROVE
INDIAN SUMMER
NELSON'S SPRING
YACHTSMAN'S GRILL
8
PINNEY'S BEACH
HURRICANE HILL
HOTEL
OUALIE BEACH
SCUBA SAFARIS
BIKE CENTER
GALLIPOT
TAMARIND COVE MARINA SITE
SEA BRIDGE FERRY DOCK
CHRISHI BEACH CLUB
DO NOT ENTER - SEE TEXT
AIRPORT
NISBET PLANTATION
POTTERY
NEWCASTLE
ROUND HILL
1014'
AERIAL'
MT. NEVIS
HOTEL
NORTHWEST NEVIS
17° 11'
0 1
SCALE IN NAUTICAL MILES

arrow crabs, and large lobsters. At 90 feet you can see the vent where hot water fizzes upwards.

Coral Gardens begins at 50 feet and has lots of tube sponges, sea fans, and anemones. Packed with hard and soft corals, this area seems to continue forever. It is home to schools of Atlantic spadefish and large schools of horse-eyed jacks.

Monkey Shoals is a 2-square-mile reef, 5 miles offshore. The depth varies from 40 feet to 100 feet. Visibility here is usually over 100 feet. This is home to French and gray angelfish, nurse sharks, black-tipped sharks, glassy-eyed sweepers, and yellow-tailed snappers. You will see majestic stands of pillar coral, large brain coral, and elkhorn coral.

Nags Head plummets to 75 feet. Here the large boulders are stacked on top of each other, making great hiding places for crustaceans, crinoids, and parrotfish. Eagle rays cruise past divers in formation.

Booby Island Dive is in The Narrows. This almost circular reef is packed with lobster, French grunts, horse-eyed jacks,

southern stingrays, hawksbill turtles, and large nurse sharks.

Those wishing to dive should contact Scuba Safaris' Ellis Chaderton, a NAUI and PADI trained instructor, who comes from the island and knows his waters well. Scuba Safaris has nitrox, a big cat, or a small boat for those wanting personal dives. Based at Oualie Beach, Ellis will pick up divers from yachts in any of the Nevis anchorages and he stands by on VHF: 16. (See also *Water Sports* under Oualie Beach.)

ANCHORAGES NORTH OF CHARLESTOWN
Northern Pinney's Beach to Oualie Beach

After you leave the first cluster of moorings off Four Seasons and head north, a second cluster starts at Cotton Ground and Nelson's Spring, with the large modern buildings ashore. Moorings continue up to Tamarind Bay, and you can anchor in

ISLANDS THAT BRUSH THE CLOUDS

OUALIE BEACH

TAMARIND BAY

Oualie Beach. The whole northern area is often calmer than Charlestown, though much of it is susceptible to northwesterly swells. The very calmest spot is tucked up in Oualie Beach. I often use Oualie Beach as my base as it is relatively calm, has a dinghy dock, and is close by good restaurants. In times of northerly swells, Oaulie Beach is always good for landing as they have a dock. On calm days you can beach anywhere, but in northerly swells the next best beach landing is close up to the south side of the Sea Bridge ferry dock.

This whole area covers about two miles, so it is within dinghy and energetic walking range. Some excellent restaurants and bars make it a good place to hang out and enjoy Nevis.

A new development is under construction north of the Sea Bridge ferry dock, and the buildings are now nearing completion. The plan is to build a marina right in front of the residences, which will include a fancy private yacht club and spa. This is the work of Tamarind Cove Marina with its Residence at Tamarind Cove. When it is finished, it could be a good option for island-style living with a boat in front.

The Nevis Yacht Club is in Oualie Bay, right next to the hotel. They make a big effort to train youngsters in Nevis with boats they manage to cobble together, which right now is about 6 Optis, a couple of Sunfish, and a couple of Lasers. The parent association for both this and the St. Kitts Yacht Club is the St. Kitts Nevis Sailing Association. On the first Sunday of every month they gather either here or at the St. Kitts Yacht Club, which is next to

Yachtsman Grill

Chris Doyle

242

Chrishi Beach Club   Chris Doyle

Spice Mill in Cockleshell Bay, for racing, socializing and food. It is a good time to get to know some local sailing people. The current commodore is Mark Theron from CCC in Charlestown and you can call him to find out what is going on at 662 4114.

Navigation

If coming from Charlestown, follow Pinney's Beach north, staying about 900 feet offshore. Moorings start at Nelson's Spring and continue up to Cades Point. At the northern limit of Cades Bay is a dock used for the Sea Bridge car ferry. There is a gap in the moorings to allow for the ferries and then more moorings are at Tamarind Bay. As you go north from Tamarind Bay to Oualie Beach, you have to give a couple of hundred yards clearance as it is shoal closer to the shore. There are depths of about 7 feet outside the shoals, which can be rough and break in large swells. If you make a sweep well outside the bay and come in close to Hurricane Hill, there is about 9 feet of water close to the hill. There are three moorings in Oualie Beach, but they are permanently taken by local boats, so if you want to be here, you will have to anchor. It is the most sheltered spot, but

holding is poor on thick sea grass. The only way to hold is to find the odd spot of sand. This is impossible in big northerly swells when all the water becomes murky and unreadable.

Services and Communications

Oualie Beach Club has an excellent dock, lit at night, which you are welcome to use for your dinghy. Make sure you tie up clear of the end part that is used by the dive and fishing boats, and a stern anchor is necessary. Oualie Beach Club will help out with water in jerry jugs or shallow draft boats can come alongside the dock (probably 3.5 feet for comfort, but you may get in with another foot if you work the tides). This is an excellent service for powerboats and cats. The Oualie Beach Club sells ice and the staff helps dispose of garbage and organizes car rentals and arranges anything you need. There is an internet station in the reception area. The dock here is the most protected and the best in Nevis.

Yachtsman Grill, at Hamilton in Cotton Ground, rents Polaris 4x4 vehicles

ISLANDS THAT BRUSH THE CLOUDS

in varying sizes, as well as Vespa scooters for touring the island even on the smallest trails. They are agents for Evinrude and BRP, and they sell and service personal watercraft. They have WiFi, which you will get from your yacht on a close mooring. They sell cases of cold beer and can help with shopping.

A dinghy dock is badly needed in this area, especially during northerly swells. The sane and obvious place to put it is in the lee of the Sea Bridge ferry dock where there is plenty of room. If the government is serious about supporting yachting, this would be a great place to start.

Shopping

Mansa is a good local grocery with fresh local and imported produce, as well as some cans and bottles. In addition, they have a big seating area and sell excellent homemade local juices by the bottle. They have a restaurant which sometimes serves food, beginning at 0700 and continuing till well after dark.

Restaurants

The Yachtsman Grill is a restaurant at Hamilton, the big resort just north of the house built almost on the beach supported by a pile of rocks. It is owned by Greg and Evelyn, yachting people who welcome those on yachts. The restaurant is bright, airy, on the beach on one side and a pool on the other. It has a nautical theme, including the upside-down boat entrance and a large collection of perfectly restored antique outboard motors.

Their executive chef serves excellent and elegant food, including the best seafood and steaks. Or you can get sandwiches, wraps, salads, and snacks from noon until closing around 2200. They keep a wood-fired pizza oven going and whip out the best thin-crust Italian style pizzas anytime. The big TVs behind the bar tune into major sports events, when they often offer specials.

They want it to be a hangout for yachts, so they offer WiFi, showers, help with groceries, or whatever else you need. Come, take a beach lounger, and relax. (See also *Services.*)

The Coconut Grove is a very fancy beach restaurant built of poles supporting a giant thatched roof. Gary Colt, the owner, was a professional wine specialist, so they have an international cellar with over 400 carefully selected wines. On the food side, you will get an excellent meal, beautifully served. Stephen Smitt, the chef, trained at the CIA. The basic cuisine is French, infused with Caribbean flavors, using local fresh ingredients, especially fish. The restaurant was awarded the top new table in the world in 2006 by Condé-Naste, as well as an award of excellence by Wine Spectator for 2009/2010/2014. They open every day for dinner upstairs in a big open building. It is closed for lunch unless a big group makes a special arrangement. This is a choice place to come for a special night out.

Almost opposite Coconut Grove, on the other side of the road, is Indian Summer, a good authentic Indian restaurant. They are warmly welcoming. They have a tandoori oven and their signature dish is tandoori dauai, a dish that includes a series of tapas-sized barbecued meat dishes. They offer a good and inexpensive daily lunch special. They open Tuesday to Sunday for lunch, 1200-1430, and dinner, 1700 - 2200. Dishes can be mild, medium, or spicy.

Chrishi Beach Club is owned by Christian and Hedda from Norway and they open noon until 1700. This is a great (and popular) lunch place. The food is light, but really delicious, with salads, pastas, sandwiches, seared sesame tuna, and delicious brownies or sorbet for dessert. They open for dinner during the season on Tuesdays and Saturdays. It is kid-friendly with swings and things to keep the little ones entertained.

If you are interested in property, they are building villas on the waterfront (one is completed). You can find a calm spot to pull up your dinghy in the lee of the ferry bridge dock. They plan to put in a dock sometime.

The Oualie Beach Club, owned by John and Alistair Yearwood, is a little waterfront hotel with a restaurant and bar. Both the

TEL:-(869) 664 2843

E-mail:-
bikenevis@gmail.com

location and service are good and they open daily for breakfast, lunch, and dinner, and have a good dinghy dock. The menu is wide-ranging, but always includes local fresh fish, perfectly cooked, and everything is artistically served under the direction of a top chef. During the season they have musical entertainment on Tuesdays and Fridays.

In the same complex, you can find Alistair Yearwood at Oualie Realty. He is a goldmine of information and well worth talking to should you be interested in property.

(See also North of *Oualie Beach*)

Ashore

Nevis is quiet enough to cycle around in reasonable safety. Most of the roads are around the coastal plain and are relatively flat, which makes a bicycle a very pleasant way to get to know the island. You can do the whole island loop road in a morning or afternoon (the good guys can do it in an hour and half), or take a day and really relax. There are many dedicated and slightly more difficult (up and down) trails in the area. In Oualie Beach Club, Bike Nevis (Wheel World Cycle Shop) rents all kinds of bikes, road, mountain, tandem and more. They rent by the day or week, and if you are in Charlestown, they will deliver, though you might be better off anchored at Oualie Beach, where they are located, as shore access is easy, the prettiest rides are close by, and town is not a very long ride away. Bike Nevis is owned by Winston, who was born in Birmingham of Nevisian parents and has returned to his roots. He has a great sense of humor and was once

the Caribbean mountain bike downhill champion. He does an excellent job as founder and organizer of the Nevis Olympic Triathlon and the Nevis to St. Kitts Cross Channel Swim (both in March), among many others. As you can imagine, this is a good place to meet other enthusiasts or discuss the next Caribbean Cup. Winston also does kayaking and biking tours

For those who like to ride horses, the Equestrian Center is not far from Nelson's Spring.

Water Sports

Nevis Water Sports is owned and operated by Ian Gonzalez. His water sports operation includes by far the best sports fishing trips on the island. You can sit in the bar and watch them haul the catch ashore. He operates a water taxi between St. Kitts and Nevis, which can be very handy if you have guests arriving or leaving and you don't want to take the yacht over. Rentals include fishing gear, snorkel gear, and sunfish. This is the base of the Nevis Yacht Club Sports Fishing Competition, a major sports fishing event that takes place sometime in October. Call them on VHF: 16.

Oualie Beach is the home of Scuba Safaris, which we have written up under Charlestown water sports.

North of Oualie Beach

Newcastle, on the north coast of Nevis, used to be an important harbor. There is an almost impossible entrance amid breaking seas through a channel in the reefs. The

ISLANDS THAT BRUSH THE CLOUDS

reef, known as Carpenter Reef, is reputed to work equally well on fiberglass. The harbor is now shoal, windy, and totally unsuitable for yachts. There is a plan for a marina here, but it is just a plan.

Down on the beach, Pizza Beach, operated by the Mount Nevis Hotel, serves pizzas and other snacks, mainly on weekends and holidays. Prices in both are reasonable. The new airport is close by.

Newcastle has several other restaurants that can easily be visited by land from the other anchorages. The Mount Nevis Hotel serves top-notch food on a comfortable balcony overlooking The Narrows.

The Nisbet Plantation Hotel is a lovely historic house set in a coconut grove leading to the beach. You can relax with a drink on the massive veranda that has both a lounging area and a separate dining area.

There is a beach restaurant for lunch. Thursdays is the most popular day, weather permitting. The manager holds his rum punch party at the beach restaurant, followed by dinner with a calypso band for entertainment.

They bring in fresh seafood for this event and serve it as a buffet. Dress is somewhat formal. If you come by day, you can visit their boutique.

There is good clay in Nevis and the Newcastle Pottery is a cooperative of five local potters who make attractive and inexpensive unglazed earthenware.

REDONDA

Redonda lies between Montserrat and Nevis. It is a handsome rock, one mile long and almost 1,000 feet high. There is no proper anchorage, and climbing on the island is in any case difficult and dangerous.

Redonda has a strange history: phosphates were discovered here in 1865 and mining began. In 1872 the British decided they had better take over Redonda before the Americans did and they annexed it as part of Antigua.

Phosphate production grew, 100 people worked on the island, and personnel and equipment were pulled up and down on a two-bucket cable car designed so that the weight of the up-going load was balanced by seawater, which was first pumped into a reservoir at the top, then used to fill the descending bucket. In those days there were houses on the top and a wharf.

In 1914 the phosphate production stopped and the mining lease was finally given up in 1930. In 1978, Antigua, now independent and keen to confirm ownership of the rock, set up a post office and issued a series of stamps to commemorate 100 years of phosphate mining. There was talk of reopening the mine. The post office was abandoned a year later and subsequent landslides and hurricanes have destroyed it.

There is also the story of the Kingdom of Redonda. In 1865 Matthew Dowdy Shiell, an Irish-Montserrat merchant, had a long-

Redonda Rock

Chris Doyle

awaited son after eight daughters. Being a sexist, he wanted a kingdom for his son (the daughters could go marry) and, as no one had yet claimed Redonda, he did. In 1880, when Shiell's son, M.P., was 15, they took a day trip over to the rock with the Bishop of Antigua and other friends and Shiell had the bishop crown his son King Filipe I of Redonda. They had a good time and consumed much alcohol.

M.P. Shiel (he dropped the second "L" on his name) moved to England and became a brilliant writer of Gothic romance and science fiction. Although never hugely popular among the general public, he was held in the highest esteem by literary figures of his day, including H.G. Wells. He maintained his title and held court in London, creating several literary duchies to the realm. In his later years, M.P. Shiel spent some time barraging the British government to get recognition of his title as King of Redonda. First they ignored him and then, to keep him quiet, gave him a pension for his contributions to literature.

Shiel died in 1947, but not before passing his crown to fellow writer John Galsworth (King Juan I). Juan I ended up taking to drink, bestowed titles in exchange for beer, and tried unsuccessfully to sell the kingdom on several occasions.

Before he died in 1970, he passed the title on to Jon Wynne-Tyson (King Juan II). In 1979, a group of Shiel enthusiasts, including King Juan II, paid a visit to the island and planted an ecological flag on top.

King Juan II, tiring of his royal role, abdicated on April 1st 1998, and Robert Williamson, a writer and artist who lives in Antigua, announced it had been passed to him. (He claimed he had to be on the short list as he was only 5 feet 2 inches tall.) King Robert (Bob the Bald) kept a flamboyantly colorful royal yacht (used in Pirates of the Caribbean). He mounted an expedition to Redonda with 16 loyal subjects, and appointed many nobles to the realm. Since no country recognizes the king, anyone can claim it, and Bob was the best and most entertaining pretender to the throne.

However, the king, according to the Antigua and Barbuda Museum, and as

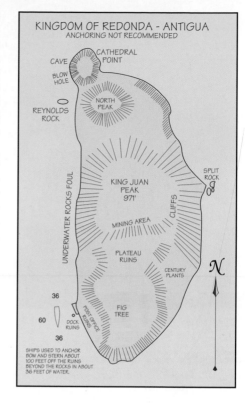

directed in a letter written by Jon Wynne-Tyson, is Javier Marius, the Spanish novelist. Javier may, at a literary level, be more deserving, but Bob was around and fun and made the whole thing more local.

Interestingly, Bob had and Javier has a Redonda Literary award. Bob's was geared specifically to the Caribbean, and awarded by Caribbean Compass in 2000. The winner was Mary Geo Quinn from Antigua. Javier's started in 2001 and is still going as far as I know. Winners include Umberto Eco, Eric Rohmer, Alice Munro and Ray Bradbury.

In the meantime, Redonda is left to its own devices. A tantalizing vision on the horizon, it is very much for the birds and, if you sail close by you will see them wheeling high over the peaks. A few boobies may accompany you for a short while.

You get a magnificent view of the cliffs and can see the remains of habitation. There are just a couple of trees and lots of cactuses and succulents.

ISLANDS THAT BRUSH THE CLOUDS

Drinking from Runaway Ghaut. Legend says anyone who does this will return.

Chris Doyle

Montserrat

ONTSERRAT'S first European settlers were Irish who arrived from St. Kitts in 1630, having experienced problems with the Kittitian Protestants. A second wave of Irish settlers arrived in 1649, after Cromwell conquered Ireland. They began as small farmers growing mixed crops, but the economy of the island slowly changed. Sugar became the main crop, slaves were introduced, and over the years the smaller farms became uneconomical. Many of the Irish returned to their homeland. They left behind smiling eyes, Irish names such as O'Brian, Dublin, and Ryan, and an Irish stew called "goat water." Today, Montserrat is known as the other Emerald Isle.

Today, as you sail past Montserrat, it is like two different lands. The southern half is starkly beautiful, a harsh terrain dominated by the awesome Soufriere Hills volcano, barren and smoking against the skyline. The remains of the ruined capital, Plymouth, are a humbling reminder of nature's power over years of human endeavor. On the southeastern coast, you can see historic windmill towers and buildings buried to their roofs in volcanic ash, and boulders the size of large houses spewed out by the volcano, lying miles below the summit. By contrast, the island's north is lush and green, with verdant mountains and handsome modern houses perched on the hills.

What you cannot gauge from the sea is the extent and beauty of the northern part of Montserrat. Most of the habitations follow the road that runs from Little Bay in the north, along the west coast to Salem in the south. This area is protected from the volcano by the Center Hills mountain range, and what you see is an island of almost picture book perfection. On one side, lush dark green mountains are steep and convoluted. On the other, the land falls away to the coast, offering a perfect panorama of the Caribbean Sea, with views of the islands of Redonda and Nevis to the

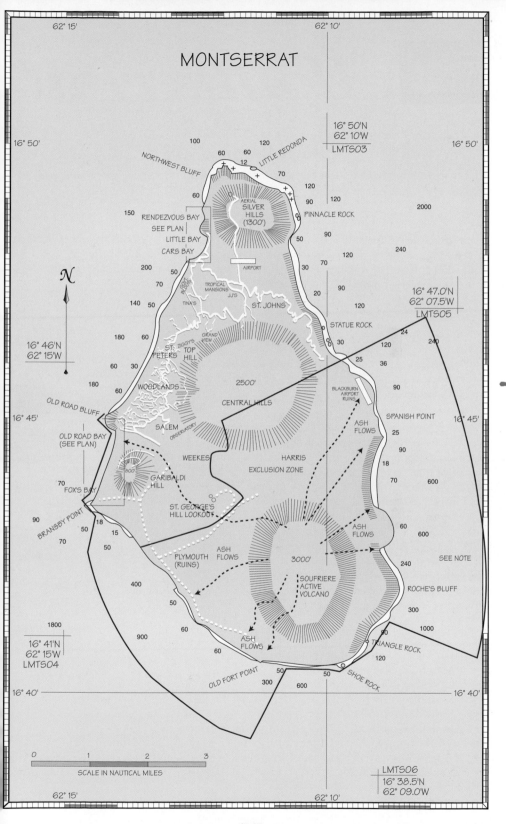

MONTSERRAT

Regulations

Yachts should proceed to Little Bay, the port of entry for clearance. For details, see Little Bay.

Telephones

A Lime mobile is your best bet. You can also use Digicel, but this only works if you have a 4G phone and 4G SIM to go with it 2G will not work. To dial to the USA or Canada, dial 1, then the number. For other countries use 011, plus the country code (UK is 44), then the number. For reverse charge and card calls dial 1-800-CALL USA.

Shopping Hours

Weekdays (except Wednesday) 0800-1600; Wednesday and Saturday, 0800-1300. The Royal Bank of Canada and the Bank of Montserrat open Monday to Thursday 0800-1400, Friday 0800-1500.

Transport

Montserrat has an airport with an 1,800 foot runway and is linked to neighboring islands by Winair. Low clouds and windy and rainy weather can close the airport.

A ferry between Antigua and Montserrat runs Thursday to Saturday, more often from before Christmas to the new year.

Taxis are available. Typical rates in $US for up to four people are:

Little Bay to airport	$13
Little Bay to Ram's and return	$50
Half-day island tour	$100-150

Over four people is usually a per person charge.

Rental cars are available. You need to get a local license, which costs about $50EC. Drive on the left. Departure tax is $55EC.

Holidays

- Jan 1st, New Year's Day (note Dec 31 is also a holiday)
- March 17, St. Patrick's Day
- Good Friday and Easter Monday
  (Easter Sunday is March 27, 2016; April 16, 2017)
- First Monday in May (Labor Day)
- June (around the 10th), Queen's birthday celebrations
- Whit Monday (50 days after Easter Sunday, May 16, 2016; June 5, 2017)
- August Monday (First Monday in August)
- December 25 and 26
- December 31 (Festival Day)

Carrs Bay and Little Bay

Chris Doyle

west. At nearly every turn, coconut palms or brightly colored flowers provide the perfect frame for a photograph. Houses are typically modern-day Caribbean, which means they can be small, brightly painted wooden houses shaded by dark green breadfruit trees, whitewashed bungalows, or fancy modern mansions.

In 1995, the population was around 11,000 people who farmed, fished, and were employed in the tourist industry. Many Americans and Canadians bought homes here to escape the northern winters. The Soufriere Hills volcano first erupted in 1995, and major eruptions in 1997 led to the evacuation and eventual destruction of the capital, Plymouth. Living and business conditions became very harsh, with volcanic dust polluting the air nearly every day. There followed an exodus of nearly two thirds of the population, and those who did not have homes in the north had to resettle in the safe zone. The current population is around 5,000.

In the summer of 2003 the huge volcanic dome collapsed and the volcano showed every sign of going to sleep. This led to the reopening of many areas. The government removed the ash (some of it several feet thick) from many roads. People started repairing their damaged houses. You could go very close to Plymouth and up the hills behind it for dramatic views of the path of destruction and the ruined town. Then, early in 2006, there was another spurt of dome growth, lots of activity, and several major eruptions, including one of the biggest ever on February 11, 2010. The exclusion zone was moved back up from Bransby Point to Old Road Bluff. The Vue Point Hotel, having been completely renovated and booked solid for the season, was evacuated. It is not easy living with a volcano. The volcano is still smoking after all these years, but it has been quieter and you can now go all the way to Richmond hill for an excellent view of the buried city.

The tone of the island is quiet and rural. There are hills with cows and goats and few enough cars that you don't feel threatened as you walk along the roads. The mood is generally upbeat and very friendly. Most

Montserratians living on the island today are delighted to be there and not in some tenement in London. The outlook is to the future: to bring in more tourists, to bring back Montserratians who fled, to create more jobs.

Just as the volcano in the south testifies to the power of nature, the northern end testifies to humans' ability to adapt and thrive in the face of adversity.

Navigation

Radio Montserrat (88.3 or 95.5 FM), gives volcano updates about once a week. Call the Montserrat Volcano Observatory at 664-491-5647, or see the volcano links on www.doyleguides.com. Both land and maritime exclusion zones remain in effect; I mark these approximately on the sketch chart. If you want up-to-date details, go to doyleguides.com advisories and look for the Montserrat volcano link. If dust starts falling, your yacht may be subject to falling ash, which is messy.

If you sail around the east side of the island, you can see an extra square kilometer of land that was formed by volcanic activity towards the southern end of the east coast. It is marked on our chart. Considerable shoaling has taken place in the Old Road Bay area, where the beach has now grown to amazing proportions. Even without further volcanic activity, shoaling will continue for many years as effluent washes down. There has been considerable shoaling in the Plymouth area, where a significant part of the deepwater pier seems to have walked up the beach, though since a 2-km maritime exclusion zone operates here, this shoaling is not likely to affect those sailing by.

Montserrat is steep-to. A quarter of a mile offshore clears all shoals. A northwesterly current hits the windward shore, divides in the middle, and sweeps round both the north and south coasts at 1 to 2 knots. There is usually less than half a knot on the lee coast. Montserrat has no well-protected harbors and it is no place to be in a hurricane.

The port of clearance and main anchorage is Little Bay. Little Bay is far from the volcano and considered safe. In regular strong northeasterly trades, Little Bay is often rolly

as the swell comes round the corner. It is best avoided in bad northerly or northwesterly swells, when the anchorage can be horrible and getting ashore is impossible. You can radio the Montserrat Port Authority on VHF: 16 (or phone 664-491-2791) as you approach and ask for a report on the harbor conditions.

Little Bay and Carrs Bay

Little Bay is the main port in Montserrat. It is set in beautiful country, which you can explore, given suitable anchoring conditions. There is now a grand scheme to build a town in Little Bay, expand the port, and build a marina and fishing port. So far the community center, the museum, the basketball court and the market building, are finished. The community center, which you can see from the anchorage, is multi-purpose with a great theater. The money for the building was organized by Sir George Martin, who used to have a recording studio here, and many of the groups who had recorded in it put on a benefit concert. Check out the "helping hands" on the wall.

The market building has not worked out as a market and instead has small offices and shops. You can get National Trust info from the museum, which is open Monday to Friday 1000-1400.

The dinghy can be left at the extreme inside (beach side) of the dock. It may be easier to pull it up on the landing ramp. Little Bay is within walking distance of some restaurants and shops.

Navigation

Little Bay and Carrs Bay provide excellent anchorage when the wind is southeast or easterly at 10-20 knots, conditions that normally prevail from March to October. However, it is rolly when the wind is from the northeast, or from the east and very strong (25 knots), or during northerly swells, conditions you find most often from December to February. Having said that, if you want to visit, can stand a little discomfort and there are no really bad swells you will make it. Carrs Bay and Little Bay both lie south of Rendezvous Bluff and are divided by Potato Hill. The

Montserrat

A SHORT HOP FROM ANTIGUA BY AIR OR FERRY

**For Day Tours & Overnight Trips
contact your Hotel Tour Desk or Travel Agent
For further information call 664 491 2230 / 8730**

www.visitmontserrat.com

LITTLE BAY

best anchorage is in Little Bay. You can go to the north of the fishing boat moorings, or right up close to the beach. It is sometimes calmer farther out in 40 feet of water, close to the fishing boats. Leave clear access for the ships as shown, and make sure you have a good anchor light. The remains of a reef up to 30 feet deep in the area are shown on our sketch chart. Avoid anchoring in this area, because your anchor might get caught in a ledge.

Regulations

Little Bay is the only port of entry. Montserrat Port Authority monitors VHF: 16. They use the Sailclear.com system.

There is a port authority fee of $35 EC (most yachts), up to $210 for some of the really big shiny ones (over about 200 tons). Passengers (not crew) pay a fee of $13.50 EC per head. Customs hours are Monday through Friday, 0800-1600. You will find customs officers out of hours at a cost of $100 (up to 8 on board) and $120 (over 8) weekdays, and $120 (up to 8) and $150 (over 8) on weekends. Customs will give you an in-and-out clearance valid for 72 hours, so you can stay and enjoy. After you have cleared customs, you have to visit port authority, immigration, and sometimes port security. All the offices are right by the port entrance.

Communications

In 2015 we got an open Lime WiFi signal on board, but it may not be permanent.

Services

Raphael White and Oswald West are good guys who have been trying to provide moorings as Shamrock Moorings (VHF: 16/86). They have had some legal and technical problems and when I visited there were still none, but they hope to be back in operation one day. They are useful to know as they can do underwater work and Raphael is happy to help with customs clearance and organize anything else you might want. Not too many superyachts visit, but he is the best bet as an agent. (Raphael, 495-4868/6, Oswald, 492-9177, shamrock.moorings.plus@gmail.com)

Provisioning

The closest supermarket is Victors, on the road to St. John's from Carrs Bay. The largest supermarket is Ram's in Salem, and you will definitely need a taxi for this one. Ram's has a good selection of fresh produce, as well as dry goods, cans, and frozen foods. There is also Ashok's and Angelo's, near Tina's Restaurant, and Norman's, farther down the road.

Local vendors set up on the roadside in various places, mainly near Salem. The

Royal Bank of Canada has an ATM.

For shoppers, the renowned silky sea-island cotton is still available on the island at Luv's Cotton store in Salem.

Ashore

A taxi tour of the island should be a priority. You'll see excellent views of the volcano and the remains of Plymouth, which it destroyed. Usually you can do this from Richmond Hill these days as the threat level is low.

Joe Phillip is a fearless and knowledgeable tour guide and taxi driver who seems to know everyone on the island and interacts with them all. He carries an iPad crammed with information, from hour-by-hour weather in Montserrat (you can call him for information) to photos of what the island looked like before the volcano.

He keeps a radio in his van, so you can call him on VHF: 08, call sign "Avalon". It is best to phone him on his cell: 664-492-1565 before you arrive. Another good driver is St. Clair Lee, 664-1990.

The volcanic ash is rich and fertile except in riverbeds where it gets washed. You do not realize how much ash is there, as it is quickly covered in vegetation. In the rivers, where the soil gets washed away, the remaining sand and gravel are now being sifted and exported. This is Monsterrat's biggest and perhaps only export. The observatory makes a great stop. It has an overview of the area affected by the volcano and they have a vivid 20-minute movie, which they show at 15 minutes past the hour on Mondays to Thursdays, starting at 1015 and finishing at 1515 ($10 EC per head). (Joe can arrange a private viewing at other times with one of the volcano staff, which is really interesting, but be prepared to make a contribution as he has to come in specially.)

The Central Hills, apart from protecting northern Montserrat from the volcano, are a deeply wooded area with lots of wildlife, including the Montserrat galliwasp (*Diploglossus montiserrati*) a critically endangered snake-like lizard found only on Montserrat. People have sighted over a hundred species of birds, as well as bats,

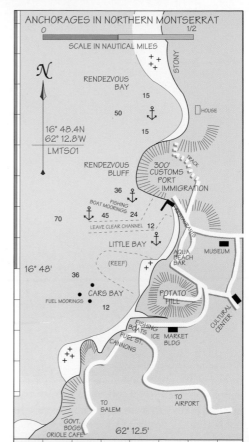

ANCHORAGES IN NORTHERN MONTSERRAT

Little Bay Restaurant terrace

255

Looking at Soufrière Hills volcano over Old Road Bluff and Isles Bay

agoutis, feral pigs, and more. You can arrange hikes with one of the three excellent guides. James Scriber-Daley (Scriber comes from his old calypsonian name "the Mighty Describer"), who is one of the foresters (496-1325), or Mappie (known as "Pie"), (496- 1732), or Gambi (493-1292). These guys are very enthusiastic and willing to hike at night with headlamps. If you prefer to go on your own, buy a trail map from National Trust or the tourist office.

Restaurants

The waterfront by the port has been resculptured behind the beach and houses a collection of nicely built local restaurants. These include Time Out, Bitter End Beach Bar, Race Track, and Soca Cabana. They may not be all open at once, but you can usually get a good local lunch or dinner. You may find the music over-amped at night.

At the south end of the beach, Aqua Montserrat has a beach bar and grill (in the old Green Monkey building). It is run by Veta who was born in Montserrat but went to the UK to finish her education when the volcano blew. Now she is back running freediving, unusual hiking, lionfish hunting and other tours (see *Water Sports*). The official opening hours are at the moment Saturday and Sunday, 1000-2000. They operate on the principle "we catch what we eat", but call them up and make a booking and they will open at pretty much any other time also.

Oriole Café is within walking distance of Little Bay for the moderately energetic. It is at the entrance to the government offices and is open from Monday to Saturday for breakfast, lunch, and dinner. You get good local food at reasonable prices – dinners are a little more elaborate and expensive, especially if you choose lobster.

Tina's is high on the hill on the road leading from Little Bay to Salem. You need a little more energy to hike to this one or it is worth the taxi ride. They serve good-sized portions of local food at very reasonable prices and are open for both lunch and dinner.

Ziggy's has been in operation from way

before the volcano, offering gourmet food, though they have moved from their original location in Plymouth to the west coast.

Cheerful and cheap local restaurants include JJ's. Go up the road to the airport, but bear right at the Y junction. It is just beyond the conspicuous radio tower. People's Place is on the road, quite a long way past Oriole.

The action bar is Yvett's Lyme. It opens daily from about 1100 and serves a local lunch. In the evening it is a bar that serves burgers, chicken, and fries. They have a big TV for sports and usually have entertainment on the weekend. It could be anything: a show, live music, bingo, crab racing or karaoke.

Olveston House near Salem is a special restaurant. It is the private residence of Sir George Martin, with a pool, tennis court,

Isles Bay Beach Bar

Chris Doyle

257

RENDEZVOUS BLUFF

RENDEZVOUS BAY

and pretty grounds offering a glimpse of the volcano. It is now managed as a guest house and restaurant by Carol Osborne and Margaret Wilson. They usually open Tuesday to Saturday for lunch and dinner, and Sunday for lunch only. Friday nights tend to be informal, very popular, and they serve fast pub food. Other nights you can eat more elegantly. Reservations are essential, except maybe for Friday night.

The Isles Bay Beach Bar is built on the newly formed beach deposited by the volcano. It is a big building, open to the breeze and views with wide decks, is the home of the Montserrat Yacht Club, and opens Thursday to Sunday from 1230. It is a hang-out and meeting point for expats coming by for a meal (the food is often 1600-2000, but they serve food all day on Sundays).

Theresa Silcott's Grand View Guest House is high in the hills. They have a nice restaurant, but I would call in advance to make sure it is open. This would be a great spot for a morning hike then return for lunch. (The hike starts close by their restaurant.)

Water Sports

Montserrat has many good dives. One of these is called the Dome. It is an old volcanic dome covered with corals and sponges, with lots of big and small fish. Another dive is Lime Kiln Beach. This can be done from a boat or from the shore. It is an easy dive to about 50 feet, following various ledges with plenty of fish and coral.

Andrew and Emmy, who own Scuba Montserrat, can also take you diving or kayaking to Rendezvous. They have a shop just as you exit the port gates.

There is also Aqua Montserrat who have a freediving club (see also Aqua under *Restaurants*). It is run by Veta who is a scuba diver but prefers snorkeling and freediving. She offers snorkeling tours, lionfish hunts and even some hiking tours. Give her a call (664-393-4227) to find out more.

Rendezvous Bay

The half-hour walk along the track from Little Bay to Rendezvous Bay over the 300-foot Rendezvous Bluff is very pleasant. It starts in a quarry, on the left side. The path leads up a hill, along a fence, and then swings to the right. It is a bit of a scramble in places.

You can anchor in Rendezvous Bay to the north of Rendezvous Bluff. It is marginally more protected than Little Bay in some swell conditions. A reef extends a fair way out from the northern stony part of the beach, so eyeball your way in and anchor off the sand. Rendezvous Bay is Montserrat's only white sand beach. It is approachable only by path or boat. There is a house behind the beach. You will need

OLD ROAD BAY
SHOWING THE PROGRESSIVE EXPANSION OF THE LAND.
INSET BELOW THE BAY AS IT WAS,
A JOE PHILLIP PHOTO

SHORELINE 2007
SHORELINE 2001
SHORELINE PRE VOLCANO

to clear in at Little Bay and get permission to visit Rendezvous Bay before you go. Snorkelers can dinghy round in suitable conditions.

Old Road Bay

Old Road Bay is about 3 miles south of Little Bay. The changes are interesting. Before the volcano erupted, this was an area of pretty houses and hotels, with a golf course in the valley. Since the volcano, rains have washed down enough volcanic sand and rocks to cover the golf course with up to 30 feet of sand and rocks and encroach upon the sea, expanding the beach so far that it comes out to the edge of the headland, so now the bay is no longer a bay, but an open roadstead. Our sketch charts and photos show some of the changes in the coastline. We have taken no depths but it probably shelves gradually.

When the volcano is active, this area is very much in the danger zone. You will not get permission to anchor here as the volcano still shows signs of activity, although the exclusion zone has moved right in close to shore. However, having cleared in, some people have anchored here to visit the Isles Bay Beach Bar or hang out in this area. So far no one has bothered them.

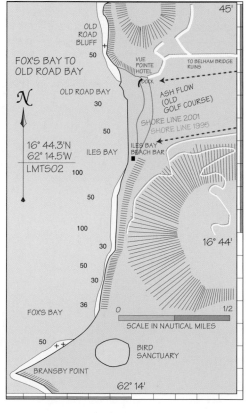

FOX'S BAY TO
OLD ROAD BAY

N

16° 44.3'N
62° 14.5'W
LMTS02

OLD ROAD BLUFF

OLD ROAD BAY

ILES BAY

FOX'S BAY

BRANSBY POINT

VUE POINTE HOTEL

TO BELHAM BRIDGE RUINS

DOCK

ASH FLOW (OLD GOLF COURSE)

SHORE LINE 2001
SHORE LINE 1995

ILES BAY BEACH BAR

45'

50
30
50
100
50
100
30
50
30
36
50

16° 44'

0   1/2
SCALE IN NAUTICAL MILES

BIRD SANCTUARY

62° 14'

259

Ashore

In 2005, it was wonderful to see the Vue Point Hotel fully open again and looking great, with the gardens carefully tended. To achieve this the owners, Carol and Cecil Osborne, had over 2,500 truckloads of volcanic ash removed. This included excavating the swimming pool, which had become a sandpit. I had hoped this was the final victory at the end of a long battle they waged to keep this hotel open in some form, whenever they were allowed in the area. However, in 2007 it was back in the exclusion zone and has stayed there.

Plymouth

Plymouth was once one of the most charming small Caribbean capitals, on a very human scale with lovely old buildings, fronted by the sea and backed by hills. They had just completed a brand new dock when the whole town was destroyed by the volcano. An exclusion zone is in effect around the town. However, when the volcano is reasonably quiet, as it has been lately, you can get a cab driver to take close by to see all the buildings buried by the volcanic ash.

A few Plymouth remains with the main pier

Chris Doyle

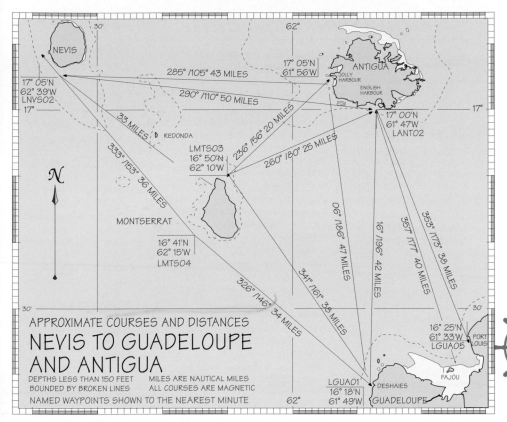

17° 05'N
61° 56'W

17° 05'N
62° 39'W
LNVS02
17°

285° /105° 43 MILES

290° /110° 50 MILES

33 MILES D REDONDA

333° /153° 36 MILES

236° /56 20 MILES

260° 180° 25 MILES

NEVIS

ANTIGUA
JOLLY HARBOUR
ENGLISH HARBOUR

17° 00'N
61° 47'W
LANT02

17°

N

LMTS03
16° 50'N
62° 10'W

MONTSERRAT

16° 41'N
62° 15'W
LMTS04

06° /186° 47 MILES

16° /196° 42 MILES

357 /177 40 MILES

353° /173° 38 MILES

326° /146° 34 MILES

341° /161° 38 MILES

30'

APPROXIMATE COURSES AND DISTANCES
NEVIS TO GUADELOUPE
AND ANTIGUA
DEPTHS LESS THAN 150 FEET   MILES ARE NAUTICAL MILES
BOUNDED BY BROKEN LINES   ALL COURSES ARE MAGNETIC
NAMED WAYPOINTS SHOWN TO THE NEAREST MINUTE

62°

LGUA01
16° 18'N
61° 49'W

DESHAIES

GUADELOUPE

16° 25'N
61° 33'W   PORT LOUIS
LGUA05

FAJOU

30'

Passages Between Nevis, Montserrat, Antigua and Guadeloupe

Montserrat lies to the west of both Antigua and Guadeloupe, making for easy downwind passages to Montserrat and tougher sails in the other direction. Montserrat and Antigua are only 20 miles apart at their closest point, so with a weatherly boat one can easily slog over there in a day. You can sometimes make it into the lee of Antigua in one tack but when the wind is north of east, it is a tough beat.

A northeasterly wind gives a pleasant sail from Montserrat to Guadeloupe. It is more of a struggle when the wind shifts south of east, but it is not too hard to get into the lee of Guadeloupe and motor sail to the anchorage of your choice. From Nevis directly to Antigua is about 50 miles with the wind on the nose. (It is about 44 miles if you leave from Oualie Beach and go through the reefs to the windward side.) Although it is about 70 miles from Nevis to Guadeloupe, I have occasionally found it more pleasant to sail to Guadeloupe, stop for the night and then sail to Antigua the next day in strong northeasterlies.

As long as the volcano remains active, it makes sense to pass around the north side of Montserrat, so you don't get your boat covered in ash. When sailing from Guadeloupe around the north end of Montserrat, make sure you stay a good 2 miles off the southeast coast.

The Cruising Guide Directory

This directory is arranged by island in alphabetical order. The following abbreviations have been used:
F = Fax, VHF = VHF radio channel.

With restaurants we also give an approximate price guide in $US which is what you would expect to pay for dinner including a drink. (Lunches are usually less.) **$A** = over $60, **$B** = $30-60, **$C** = $15-30, **$D** = under $15

ANGUILLA

Anguilla phone numbers are NANP with an area code of 264, From USA or other NANP area dial 1 plus the number, within Anguilla just dial the last 7-digits. From overseas dial + 1 plus the number.

ANGUILLA SERVICES
EMERGENCY/OFFICIAL
General, 911
Hospital, 264-497-2551/2
Dr Hughes, 264-497-3053
Dr. B. Clyde, 264-497-0765
Police, 264-497-2333
Road Bay Customs,
264-497-5461, VHF: 16
AIRLINES
Air Anguilla, 264-497-3643/2643
American Eagle, 264-497-3501
Anguilla Travel Services,
264-497-3613
Barnes Travel, 264-497-2788
LIAT, 264-497-5000
CHANDLERY - FISHING GEAR
Anguilla Techni Sales,
264-497-2419
COMMUNICATIONS
Roy's Bayside Grill,
264-497-2470, info@roysbayside-grill.com
Sydan's, 264-497-3180/235-7740/729-1738
sydans@hotmail.com
GENERAL YACHT SERVICES
Axa Yacht Services, (Gabi Gumbs)
264-584-3826, gabi@axayachtser-vices.com
LH Enterprises, (Lesley Lloyd, yacht agent) 264-581-5683, 011 599 553 3994 info@lh-enterprises.com
Simone Connor, (yacht agent)
264-476-6534, mysandyisland@hotmail.com,
Stott & Co., 264-497-2744,
F: 264-497-3350, yacht registration

MISCELLANEOUS
Anguilla Watersports, 264-584-1204/1201
Marine Park, 264-497-2871
Golf Course 264-498-5602
Tourist Board, 264-497-2759, atbtour@anguillanet.com
Sea Pro, 264-4998-0073/584-0074
TRANSPORT
Curtis Taxi Service, 264-772-5194
Fedex, 264-497-3575
Maurice Taxi & Car Rental,
264-476-0505/235-2676, VHF: 16, mauricetaxiservices@gmail.com
Stephen's Taxi, 264-772-5194, VHF: 16
TECHNICAL YACHT SERVICES
Anguilla Techni Sales,
264-497-2419, welding, installa-tion, Volvo/ Bombardier

ANGUILLA SHOPPING
FUN SHOPPING
Bijoux,, 264-4583-0323
Irie Life, 264-498-6526
Savannah Gallery,
264-497-2263/476-2263, savannah@anguillanet.com
PROVISIONING
Best Buy, 264-498-5555/4444, dugginsenterprises@yahoo.com
Proctors, 264-497-2445/2446, jwproctors@anguillanet.com
Sydan's, 264-497-3180/235-7740/729-1738
sydans@hotmail.com

ANGUILLA HOTELS & RESTAURANTS
Barrel Stay, 264-497-2831/476-3044, Jill@barrelstay.com, $A-B
CeBlue, 264-462-1000, $B
Dad's, 264-581-dads, $B
da' Vida, 264-498-5433, info@davidaanguilla.com, $A
Dolce Vita, 264-497-8668, dolcevita@anguilla.net, $B
Elvis Beach Bar, 264-772-0101/498-0101, $D
Jacquie's Ripples, 264-497-3380, ruan@anguillanet.com, $B-C

Johnno's, 264-497-2728,, johnnosanguilla@yahoo.com, $C-D
Le Bar, 264-497-2728, 772-3229, lebar.anguilla@gmail.com, $C
Mala's Roti Hut, 264-497-5030, $D
Nico's, 264-497-2844, $D
Prickly Pear Bar & Restaurant,
264-235-5864, pricklypearanguilla@yahoo.com, $D
Pumphouse, 264-584-3826, Pumphouse@anguillanet.com, $B-C
Sandy Island, 264-476-4104/6534 mysandyisland@hotmail.com, $D
Roy's Bayside Grill, VHF: 16
264-497-2470, 264-498-0154, info@roysbaysidegrill.com, $A-B
SandBar, 264-498-0171, sandba-raxa@gmail.com, $C-D
Veya, 264-498-8392, $A

ANGUILLA DIVING
Special D diving (Douglas Carty),
264-497-4567/235-8438, specialdiving@gmail.com Dive shop
Scuba Shack, 264-235-1482, shoalbayscuba@gmail.com
Vigilant Divers, 264-235-4096, robscubainstructor@hotmail.com

MONTSERRAT

Montserrat phone numbers are NANP with an area code of 664, From USA or other NANP area dial 1 plus the number, within Montserrat just dial the last 7-digits. From over-seas dial + 1 plus the number.

MONTSERRAT SERVICES
EMERGENCY/OFFICIAL
Customs, 664-491-2456
Port Authority, 664-491-2791/2
Montserrat Volcano Observatory, 664-491-5647
Hospital, 664-491-2836, emergency: 664-491-2802
Police, 664-491-2555

AIRLINES

Montserrat Airways Ltd, 664-491-3434, info@flymontserrat.com

MISCELLANEOUS

Aqua Montserrat, 664-393-4227

Montserrat National Trust, 664-491-3086, mnatrustandw.ms

Tourist Office, 664-491-2230/8370, F: 664-491-7430, info@montserrattourism.ms

TRANSPORT

Avalon's Taxi and Tours, 664-492-1565, VHF: 08 "Avalon", joephillip@live.com

Be-Peeps, 664-491-3787, car rentals

Neville Bradshaw Agencies, 664-491-5270/5235, car rentals (Many other taxis and car rental firms can be accessed through the tourist office)

St. Claire Lee, 664-492-1990

MONTSERRAT SHOPPING

BANKING

Bank of Montserrat, 664-491-3843

Royal Bank of Canada, 664-491-2426

FUN SHOPPING

Carol's Corner, 664-491-5210

Luv's Cotton Store, 664-491-3906

PROVISIONING

Ram's Emdee, 664-491-2289/5847, F: 664-491-2568

HOTELS AND RESTAURANTS

Grand View, 664-491-2284, $C

Isles Bay Beach Bar, 664-415-3787, $C-D

JJ's Cuisine, 664-491-9024, $B-D,

Olveston House 664-491-5210, $A-C

Oriole Restaurant, 664-491-7144, $C-D

Soca Cabana, 664-493-1820, $C

The Lyme, 664-491-5559, $D

Tina's Restaurant, 664-491-3538, $D

Tropical Mansions, 664-491-8767, F: 664-491-8275, hotel@candw.ms, $B

Ziggy's, 664-491-8282,

F: 664-491-8282, $A-B, Ziggys@candw.ms

MONTSERRAT SCUBA DIVING

Scuba Montserrat, 664 496-7807; VOIP U.S. number: (804) 335-1492 scubamontserrat@gmail.com

NEVIS

St. Kitts/Nevis phone numbers are NANP with an area code of 869, From USA or other NANP area dial 1 plus the number, within St. Kitts/Nevis just dial the last 7-digits. From overseas dial + 1 plus the number.

NEVIS SERVICES

EMERGENCY/OFFICIAL

General Emergency, 911

Nevis Customs, 869-469-5521/5419 (for Charlestown ext 2183)

Nevis Port Authority, 869-469-0788/0651, Charlestown, 469 0393, Ken's cell: 663-7424, VHF: 16, nevports@sisterisles.kn

Alexandra Hospital, 869-469-5473

Evelyn's Drug Store, 869-469-5278

AIRLINES

Evelyn's Travel, 869-469-7447, travel agent

Nevis Express, 869-469-9756, F: 869-469-9751

COMMUNICATIONS

Essentials Internet Café, 869-663-0390/8972

Federal Express, Main Street, 869-469-5351, courier

GENERAL YACHT SERVICES

Tamarind Cove Marina Dev. Ltd., 869-469-8500, 869-662-8074, info@tamarindcovenevis.com, Coming Soon

Nevis Yacht Services, VHF: 16, 869-469-6564/667-7466/664-9171

TECHNICAL YACHT SERVICES

CCCL Nevis, 1-869-469-1166/764-2000, mark@cccl.kn or mark@ccclsystems.com, sail, canvas, and stainless work

Kustom Airbrush, 1-869-663-8358, airbrushskn@yahoo.com

MISCELLANEOUS

Botanical Gardens of Nevis, 869-469-3509/2673

Equestrian Center, 869-469-8118/3106, guilbert@Caribsurf.com, horse riding

Hermitage Plantation, 869-469-3477, horse riding

Nevis Water Sports, Oualie Beach Club, Nevis, 869-469-9060, F: 869-469-9690, VHF: 16, seabrat@sisterisles.kn, deep sea fishing

Nevis Historical Society, 869-469-5786, F: 869-469-0274, nhcs@sisterisles.kn

Nevis Gases, 869-469-5409, fill cooking gas

Nevis Tourism Authority, 869-469-7550, F: 869-469-7551, dliburd@nevisisland.com

Oualie Realty, 869-469-9829/9403

Sugar Mill Real Estate, 869-469-1093, limehill@sisterisles.kn

TRANSPORT

Abba's Tours, 869-663-7155, VHF Ch 16 or 88

Bike Nevis, 869-469-9682/664-2843 F: 869-469-9176, windsurf@sisterisles.kn

City Stand, Nevis, 869-469-5621, taxis

Noel's Car Rental, T&F: 869-469-5199/1972, VHF: 16

TDC, 869-469-5690/1005, F: 869-469-1239, VHF: 18, car rentals

Strikers Car rental, 869-469-2654, strikers@sisterisles.kn

St. Kitts Sea Bridge, 869-662-7002, car ferry

Teach Tours and Taxi Service, 869-662-9022, teachtours@sisterisles.kn, good taxi driver also car rentals

Yachtsman Grill, 869-469-1382, 665-6245, Polaris, Vespa rentals

Directory

NEVIS SHOPPING

BANKING

Barclays Bank,
869-469-5467/5309,
F: 869-469-5106.

FUN SHOPS

Caribco Gifts, 869-469-1432,
F: 869-469-0072
Crafthouse Boutique,
869-469-5505
Seven Image, 869-662-6531,
**Nevis Handicrafts
Cooperative**, 869-469-1746

PROVISIONING

Horsfords Value Mart, 869-469-2626
Mansa, 869-469-8530
Nevis Bakery, 869-469-5219,
F: 869-469-0165, nevisbakery@
sisterisles.kn
Rams, 869-469-7777
Superfoods, 869-469-1267,
F: 869-469-0297
Nevis Center, (Hardware)
869-469-5600

NEVIS HOTELS & RESTAURANTS

RESTAURANTS/ ACCOMMODATION

Bananas 869-469-1891, $A-C
Cafe Des Arts, 869-667-8768, $D
Chrishi Beach Club, 869-469-5959/662-3959
Hedda@zenithnevis.com, $B-C
Coconut Grove, 869-469-1020,
coconutgrove@caribcable.com,
$A
Double Deuce, 869-469-2222,
markrobertsnevis@gmail.com,
$B-D
Four Seasons, 869-469-1111, $A
Golden Rock Inn,
869-469-3346, F: 869-469-2113,
goldenrockhotel@sisterisles.kn, $A
Hermitage Inn, 869-469-3477,
F: 869-469-2481,
contactus@hermitagenevis.com,
$A
Indian Summer, 869-469-5410,
$C-D
Lime, 869-662-9620, limetour-
skn@gmail.com, $B-C
Montpelier, 869-469-3462,
F: 869-469-2932,
info@montpeliernevis.com, $A
Mt. Nevis Hotel,
869-469-9373, mountnevis@aol.
com, $A-B

Nisbet Plantation,
869-469-9325, F: 869-469-9864,
$A
Old House Café 869-469-8499, $D
Oualie Beach Club,
869-469-9735, F: 869-469-9176,
VHF: 16, $A-B
Pinney's Beach Hotel,
869-469-5207
Sunshine's Bar and Grill, T&F:
869-469-5817, sunshines@sister-
isles.kn, $B-D
Turtle Time, 869-469-9911, turtle-
timenevis@gmail.com, $B-D
Wilma's Diner, 869-663-8010, $D
Young's Restaurant,
869-469-0800
Yachtsman Grill, 869-469-1382
665-6245, gslagon@aol.com, $B

NEVIS SCUBA DIVING

**Scuba Safaris, Oualie Beach
Club**, Nevis, 869-469-9518, info@
scubanevis.com, VHF: 16, Ellis
Chaderton

SABA

Saba numbers begin with 599. If
calling within Saba, leave off the
599 (even if using a St. Maarten
sim). If calling from abroad, dial
the exit code plus the number.
Thus, from the St. Maarten or the
USA dial 011 and the full number
given here.

SABA SERVICES

EMERGENCY/OFFICIAL

Edwards Medical Center,
599-416-3288/9,
medical emergencies
Port Authority, 599-416-3294,
VHF: 16, 11, fortbayharbor@
hotmail.com, or
travisjohnson83@hotmail.com

AIRLINES

Windward Island Airways,
599-416-2255

COMMUNICATIONS

Island Communications,
599-416-2881, US 206-350-0208, F:
416-2781, info@ICSsaba.com

MISCELLANEOUS

**Saba Marine Park and Conserva-
tion Society**, Box 18,
The Bottom, Saba, N.A., 599-416-
3295, Cell: 416-5750, VHF: 16,
info@sabapark.org

Tourist Office,
599-416-2231/2/2322, F: 599-416-
2350, tourism@sabagov.com

TRANSPORT

Taxis: Call Marine Park or Port
Office on VHF 16 when you are
still south of the island and ask
them to call one of the 15 taxis for
you, or
Garvis Hasell (taxi),
599-552-3418/416-6114
Eddie's Taxi Service,
599-416-7252/526-9089
The Edge ferry, 721-544-
2640/2631/2698, info@stmaarten-
activities.com
Dawn ferry, 599-416-2299, reser-
vations@sabactrasnport.com

SABA SHOPPING

FUN SHOPS

Every'tings,
599-416-2518, info@etsaba.com,
handicrafts
**Hellsgate Community
Cottage**, 599-416-2300, lacework
**Jobean Designs & Jobean
Forever**
T&F: 599-416-2490/9,
599-416-2638, jobean@un-
spoiledqueen.com,
Little Green Shop, 599-416-2792,
thelittlegreenshopsaba@gmail.
com, handicrafts, jewelry, casual
wear
Saba Artisans, 599-416-3260,
handicrafts
Saba Trail Shop, 599-416-2630,
The Jewel Cottage, 599-416-
6150, info@thejewelcottage.com

PROVISIONING

Big Rock Market, 599-416-2280
My Store, 599-416-3263
**Saba Self-Service
Supermarket**, 599-416-3218

SABA HOTELS AND RESTAURANTS

ACCOMMOCATION ONLY

Cottage Club, 599-416-2386,
F: 599-416-2434
Cranston's Antique Inn,
599-416-3203, F: 599-416-3469
Juliana's, 599-416-2269,
F: 599-416-2389
Saba Real Estate (apartments),
599-416-2299, F: 599-416-2415

RESTAURANTS / ACCOMMODATION

Angelina's, 599-416-3038
Bottom Bean Cafe, 599-416-3385, $D
Busy B Bakery, 599-416-2900
Brigadoon, 599-416-2380, $B-C
Chinese Place, 599-416-2353, $C
Deep End, 599-416-3438, $C-D
Ecolodge, 599-416-3888, info@ecolodge-saba.com, $C-D
Island Flavours, 599-416-5562
Lime Time, 599-416-3351, $D
Restaurant Eden, 599-416-2539, restaurant.eden@gmail.com, $A-B
Queen's Garden, 599-416-3694, info@queensaba.com, $A-B
Sea Witch Bar and Grill, 599-416-2013, $C-D
Scout's Place, 599-416-2740/2205, info@scoutsplace.com, $B-D
Swinging Door, 599-416-2506, $D
Tropics Café, 599-416-2469, $B

SABA SCUBA DIVING

Saba Deep, 599-416-3347/ 6301, VHF: 16,
Cheri Waterfield, diving@sabadeep.com, diving, dive shop, sale of dive equipment
Saba Divers, 599-416-5708, VHF: 16, mirek@sabablue.com, Miroslav and Vit
Sea Saba, 599-416-2246/ F: 599-416-2362, VHF: 16, Lynne Costenaro and John Magor, diving@seasaba.com, dive shop, sale of dive equipment

ST. BARTS

St. Barts numbers are ten digits, starting with 0590 (fixed phones) and 0690 (mobile units). Within French territories dial this ten-digit number. If you are calling from outside French territory, dial the international exit code then 590, then the full number we give but leave off the first 0.Thus, from the USA if we give 0590-27-85-78, you dial 011-590-590-27-85-78.This doubling of 590 is a little confusing, but absolutely necessary.

ST. BARTS SERVICES
EMERGENCY/OFFICIAL

Hospital de Bruyn, 0590-27-60-35, F: 27-60-35
Police, 0590-27-11-70
Fire Department, 0590-27-62-31 or just 18
Lifeboat, 0690-64-08-07
Dr. Husson, 0590-27-66-84
Doctor on call: 0590-90-13-13 (holidays/weekends)
Dentist, (Achache), 0590-52-80-32
Port Captain, 0590-27-66-97, Fax: 590-27-81-54, port.de.gustavia@wanadoo.fr
Pharmacie St. Barts, 0590-27-61-82

AIRLINES

Airport, 0590-27-6541
Air Antilles, 0590-29-74-28
Air Caraibes, 0590-87-14-80
Winair, 0590-27-61-01

CHANDLERY - FISHING GEAR

Le Shipchandler, 0590-27-86-29, F: 0590-27-85-73, VHF: 16, leship@wanadoo.fr

COMMUNICATIONS

Centre@lizes, 0590-29-89-89, F: 0590-29-81-10, centralizes971@yahoo.fr, Phone, fax, email, internet access
Port of Gustavia, 0590-27-66-97, Fax: 590 27-81-54, VHF: 16, directeur or Plaisance or commerce or secreteriat or compta @ portdegustavia.fr
mail drop, fax service, WiFi

GENERAL YACHT SERVICES

Nautica FWI, 0590-27-56-50/51, F: 590-27-56- 52. nfyachts@wanadoo.fr,
Port of Gustavia, 0590-27-66-97, VHF: 16,
St. Barth Services, 0590-27-56-26, 069650-06-25, brice@stbarth-services.com

MISCELLANEOUS

St. Barthelemy Marine Reserve, 0590-27-88-18, emergency: 0690-31-70-73, infonaturestbarth@gmail.com
St. Barts Tourist Office, 0590-27-87-27

SAILMAKERS, CANVAS, CUSHIONS

Alcatraz Sewing, 0590-52-05-98, 0690-80-99-80
West Indies Sails, 0590-27-63-89, westindies.sails@wanadoo.fr

TRANSPORT

Chez Beranger, 0590-27-89-00, F: 0590-27-80-28, chezberenger@wanadoo.fr, car and scooter rentals
Taxi Stand, 0590-27-66-31

TECHNICAL YACHT SERVICES

Boatinox, 0590-27-99-14, stainless steel work
Chez Beranger, 0590-27-89-00, F: 0590-27-71-97, chezberenger@wanadoo.fr
JCC, 0590-27-63-06, 0690-55-32-40, jcgreparateir@wandoo,fr, electrical and tool repair
Hughes Marine, 0590-27-50-70, 0690-64-95-96, info@hughesmarine.com
Kuka, 0690-58-77-59, 0590-29-74-49, VHF: 12, underwater anchor work
Le Shipchandler, 0590-27-86-29, F: 0590-27-85-73, VHF: 16, leship@wanadoo.fr rigging shop, stainless and aluminum welding and fabrication
Navy Techniques, 0690-73-97-19, mariposaboat@yahoo.fr
2-Swedes, 0690-48-55-16/41-88 -14/34-37-51, F: 0590-29-04-03, info@2swedes.com, fiberglass work, woodwork, most yacht repairs and refits

ST. BARTS SHOPPING
FUN SHOPS

Quiksilver Boardriders Club, 0590-29-69-40, F: 0590-29-60-81, quiksbh@orange.com

PROVISIONING

American Gourmet, 0590-52-38-80, 0690-81-15-96, gourmet store, yacht provisioning
Libre Service AMC, 0590-27-60-09, F: 0590-27-85-71, AMC.LS@wanadoo.fr good supermarket and liquor store, orders can be faxed in advance

Directory

La Cave de Port Franc,
0590-27-65-27,
lacaveduportfranc@hotmail.com
Segeco,
0590-27-60-10, F: 0590-27-81-34,
liquors, some foods
Tom Food,
0590-27-60-43, F: 0590-27-72-77

ST. BARTS HOTELS AND RESTAURANTS
RESTAURANTS

Eddie's, 0590-27-54-17, $B-C
La Cantina, 0590-27-55-66, $D
L'Entracte, 0590-27-70-11, $C-D
Le Repaire, 0590-27-72-48, $B
Le Select, 0590-27-86-87, $D
Maya's, 0590-27-75-73, $A
News Born, 0590-27-67-07
Pipiri Palace,
0590-27-53-20, $B-C
Santa Fe, 0590-27-61-04, $A-B

ST. BARTS SCUBA DIVING

La Bulle, Ocean Must Marina,
0590-27-62-25, 0690-73-77-85
charley.ce.line@wanadoo.fr, dive
shop, tank refills

ST. EUSTATIUS (STATIA)

Statia numbers begin with 599. If dialing from overseas, dial the exit code plus this number. Thus, from the USA dial 011 plus the 10-digit number. If calling within Statia or from another Dutch island, leave off the 599 and dial the last seven digits.

STATIA SERVICES
EMERGENCY/OFFICIAL

Emergency (all), 911
Marine Park, 599-318-2884,
VHF: 17, info@statiapark.org
Queen Beatrix Hospital,
599-318-2211
GRP Pharmacy, 599-318-3301
Port Authority, 599-318-2205,
VHF: 16, 14
Customs, 599-318-4960/ 4959/ 4947
Immigration, 599-318-2357

AIRLINES
WinAir, 599-318-2381
COMMUNICATIONS
Federal Express, 599-318-2451, courier
GENERAL & TECHNICAL YACHT SERVICES
Golden Rock Dive Center,
T&F: 599-318-2964, VHF: 16,
grdivers@gmail.com,
water available in emergency
MISCELLANEOUS
Tourist Office,
599-318-2433, F: 599-318-2324,
info@statiatourism.com
TRANSPORT
Taxi Stand, 599-318-2620
ATV rentals, 599-318-4625/1077
Ground Star rental,
599-318-2266
Hendrickson, 599-318-1442
Rainbow, 599-318-1480
STATIA SHOPPING
FUN SHOPS
Gem Gifts, 599-318-2030
Mazinga on the Bay, 599-318-3345
PROVISIONING
Duggins Supermarket,
599-318-2241
STATIA HOTELS & RESTAURANTS
Blue Bead Restaurant,
599-318-2873, $B
Cool Corner, 599-554-7989, $D
Franky's, 599-318-4948, $D
Golden Era Hotel,
599-318-2345, $B-C
King's Well Resort,
T&F: 599-318-2538, VHF: 16,
kingswellresort2000@yahoo.com,
$B-C
Ocean View, 599-318-2934, $C
Old Gin House, 599-318-2319,
info@oldginhouse.com, $A-B
Opa's, 599-318-4637, $D
STATIA SCUBA DIVING
Scubaqua Dive Statia, 599-318-5450, dive@scubaqua.com, Ingrid and Menno
Golden Rock Dive Center,
T&F: 599-318-2964, VHF: 16,
grdivers@gmail.com,
Glenn, Michele Faires

ST. KITTS
St. Kitts/Nevis phone numbers are NANP with an area code of 869, From USA or other NANP area dial 1 plus the number, within St. Kitts/Nevis just dial the last 7-digits. From overseas dial + 1 plus the number.
ST. KITTS SERVICES
EMERGENCY/OFFICIAL
General emergency, 911
Customs Boarding officer, 869-465-8121 ext 100, VHF: 16
City Drug, 869-465-2156, pharmacy
Meridian Medical, 869-465-5096
Medical Associates Dr. Kathleen Allen and partners,
869-465-5349. (Offices on Victoria Road)
AIRLINES
American Airlines,
869-465-2273
Air St. Kitts, 869-465-8571
Caribbean Aviation, 869-469-9295
Kantours, 869-465-2098,
F: 869-465-3168, VHF: 16,
travel agent
LIAT, 869-465-8200, 888-844-5428
Nevis Express, 869-469-9755
TDC Airline Service,
869-465-2286, travel agent
WinAir, 869-469-9583
CHANDLERY - FISHING GEAR
Builders Paradise, (hardware)
869-466-5488
Horsfords, (hardware)
869-465-2262
TDC, (hardware) 869-465-2988
Leeward Islands Charters,
869-465-7474, F: 869-465-7070,
sail@leewardislandscharters.com,
chart agent
COMMUNICATIONS
Federal Express, 869-465-4155
Peter.KN, 869-466-3721
UPS, 869-465-5978
GENERAL YACHT SERVICES
Christophe Harbour,
869-762-1785, 843-501-2234,
info@christopheharbour.com,
marina development

Delisle Walwyn, 869-465-2631/763-4501, VHF: 16, ship's agent

Warner's One Stop, 869-465-8630, F: 869-465-6661, laundry

Port Zante, 869-466-5021/5022, VHF: 68, portzantemarina@gmail.com, stkittsud@gmail.com, fuel dock, marina, water

Serviciz, 869-762-8130/663-8130, rickie@serviciz.com, yacht agent

St. Kitts Marine Works & Telca Marina, Reg, 869-662-8930, Bruce, 869-664-1978 bentels@hotmail.com, info@skmw.net Haul out yard, 150-ton travel lift

St. Kitts Yacht Services, 869-762-4400, info@stkittsyachtservices.com, yacht agent

Trinity Apartments, 869-465-3226/662-3098, possible laundry, speak to Wilfred Walters

MISCELLANEOUS

Caribbean Cinemas, 869-466-4777

Cap. George Fishing Charter, 869-760-3484

Brimstone Hill Fort National Park, 869-465-2609, brimstonehill@sisterisles.kn

Royal St. Kitts Golf Course, 869-465-8339, F: 869-465-4463, golfing

Royal Stables, 869-465-2222, horse riding

Scenic Railways, 869-465-7263,

Sky Safari, 869-465-4347

St. Christopher Heritage Society, 869-465-5584, schs@sisterisles.kn

St. Kitts Tourist Office, 869-465-4040,

Trinity Stables, 869-465-3226, horse riding

TRANSPORT

Avis, 869-465-5607

City Taxi Stand, 869-466-5621, Taxis

Delisle Walwyn, car rental 869-465-8449/2631, F: 869-465-1125, VHF: 16,

Gibraltar Tours and Taxi Service, 869-664-8110/465-4223, gibraltartours@msn.com

Island Spice Taxi Service, 869-664-1497, VHF: 16/68

Kittitian Taxi & Tours, 869-762-8994/663-7897, VHF: 16/68, info@

kittitiantaxiandtours.com

Leeward Islands Charters, 869-465-7474, F: 869-465-7070, sail@leewardislandscharters.com day charters

Quality Time Taxi, 869-466-5185/663-0503, Pager: 467-7027

Tatems Taxi & Tours, 869-662-1129/762-3329, tatemstaxiandtours@hotmail.com

TDC Rentals, 869-465-2991, F: 869-465-4330, tdcrent@sisterisles.kn, VHF: 18,

Unique Tours and Taxi, 869-466-5948/664-1820, VHF: 16, taxi, tours

TECHNICAL YACHT SERVICES

Fortress Marine, 869-663-4307, dougbrookes2000@yahoo.com, boatbuilders

Indigo Yachts, 869-466-1753, info@indigoyachts.com, boatyard

Ossie, 869-466-6736, machine shop

Original Boatbuilders, 869-465-1152, boatyard

Yamaha, 869-465-2511

ST. KITTS SHOPPING

BANKING

Kantours (American Express), 869-465-2098, F: 869-465-3168, VHF: 16, delwal@sisterisles.kn, American Express agency

FUN SHOPS

Ashburry's, 869-465-8175

Caribelle Batik, 869-465-6253, batikskb@sisterisles.kn, batiks

Island Hopper, 869-465-2905, F: 869-465-1887

Art Gallery Cafe, 869-765-5994, art, prints

PROVISIONING

Horsford's Value Mart, 869-465-1600, 869-465-1037 info@horsfords.com

Ram's Supermarket, 869-466-6065

ST. KITTS HOTELS & RESTAURANTS

RESTAURANTS / ACCOMMODATION

Ballahoo Bistrot, 869-465-4197, F: 869-465-7627, info@ballahoo.com, $B-C

Carombola, 869-465-9090, managers cell: 762-9617, $A-B

Belmont Hotel, Kittitian Hill, 869-465-7388, $A

Bird Rock Beach Hotel, 869-465-8914, F: 869-465-1675, brbh@sisterisles.kn, $A-B

Circus Grill, 869-465-0143, $B-C

Fisherman's Wharf, 869-465-2754, VHF: 18, $A-C

King's Palace, 869-466-3685, $C-D

Nirvana at Fairview, 869-465-3021, info@nirvanafairview.com, $A

Ottley Plantation Inn, 869-465-7234, $A

Ocean Terrace Inn (OTI), Rainbow, 869-465-2754, F: 869-465-1057, $A-B otistkitts@sisterisles.kn

Palm Court Gardens, 869-465-6060, info@amorydesigns.com, $B-D

Salt Plage, 869-466-4557, $B-C

Shipwreck, 869-764-7200, $C

Spice Mill, 869-465-6455/662-9966/662-6706, $A-C, serendipity@sisterisles.kn

Sweet Cane, 869-465-4345, murali_30@hotmail.com, $B-D

Reggae Beach Bar and Grill, 869-662-2661, gary@reggaebeachbar.com, $B-C

ST. KITTS SCUBA DIVING

Kenneth's Dive Center, 869-465-2670, F: 869-465-1950, kdcsk@yahoo.com, VHF: 16, Call early morning, between 1300 and 1400 or after 1600. Or use the cells any time: 869-667-9186/ 664-6809/ 465-2670, Kenneth Samuel

Pro Divers, 869-660-3483, prodiver@sisterisles.kn

Dive St. Kitts, 869-465-1189, dive@divestkitts.com

Directory

ST. MARTIN

French St. Martin numbers are part of the Guadeloupe exchange. They are ten digits, starting with 0590 (fixed phones) and 0690 (mobile units). Within French territories dial this ten-digit number. If you are calling from outside French territory, dial + (or the international exit code) then 590, then the full number we give but leave off the first 0. Thus, from the USA or Dutch Sint Maarten, if we give 0590-27-85-78, you dial + 590-590-27-85-78.This doubling of 590 is a little confusing, but absolutely essential.

Dutch Sint Maarten phone numbers are NANP with an area code of 721, From USA or other NANP area dial 1 plus the number, within Sint Maarten just dial the last 7-digits. From overseas dial + 1 plus the number. If your phone does not have a +, then dial 00 on the French side and 011 on the Dutch.

ST. MARTIN SERVICES
EMERGENCY/MEDICAL

Ambulance, Dutch 912 or 721-520-6262
Ambulance, French 0590-52-00-52
Central Drugstore, 721-542-2321, F: 721-542-5576
Coast Guard, 913 (special emergency number) or 545-5070
Dr. Johan Datema, or Ubbo Tjaden, Plaza Del largo, 721-544-5312, ubbotjaden@gmail.com
Emergency, 911
Simpson Bay Dental Clinic, Simpson Bay Yacht Club, 721-544-3208
Dutch side Hospital, 721-543-1111
French side Hospital, 0590-52-25-25
Friendly Island Pharmacy, 721-544-4290
Simpson Bay Pharmacy, 721-544-3653, sbp.pharmacy@gmail.com
Vet, Dr. Gary Swanston, 721-542-0111, sxmvetclinic@megatroc.com
Police, Dutch 911 or 542-2222
Police, French,

0590-87 61 55
Sint Maarten Port Authority, 721-542-2348, VHF: 12
Chief Pilot (Eddy Johnson), 721-542-2307/520-1867, sxmpilot@hotmail.com
Port Authority, Marigot 0590-87-59-06/ 87-59-06, aellis@portdu-marigot.com
Simpson Bay Lagoon Authority, 721-545-3183
SNSM (French lifeboat), VHF: 16, 0690-76-75-00, MRCC (coordinators) 0596-70-92-92
Towing, Aquatic Solutions, 721-557-2979, aquaticsxm@yahoo.com
St. Martin Sea Rescue 199, VHF: 16

AIRLINES

Air France, 721-546-7747
American Airlines, 721-545-2040
Continental, 721-546-7670
Corsair, 721-546-7660
Delta, 721-546-7616
KLM, 721-546-7747
Let's Travel, 721-542-2381
LIAT, 721-546-7675
Maduro & Sons, 721-542-3407/8, travel agent
Winair, 721-545-2568

CHANDLERY - FISHING GEAR

Boat Paint and Stuff, 0690-22-16-76, info@boatpaintstuff.com
Budget Marine, (Simpson Bay) 721-544-5577/3134, F: 721-544-4409, sales@budmar.an
Island Water World, 721-544-5310, F: 721-544-3299, VHF: 74
Island Water World, Philipsburg 721-543-7119 sales@islandwaterworld.com
Island Water World, Marigot 0590-51-32-06/0690-71-11-60, valerie@islandwaterworld.com
L'Ile Marine, (Marigot), 0590-29-08-60, F: 0590-29-08-96, lile@budgetmarine.com
Madco, (Marigot), 0590-51-05-40, F: 0590-29-43-70, madco@sadwifi.com
National Marine Suppliers, (I. de Sol), 721-544-2601/522-2070/523-3096 1-800megayacht, gbailey@nationalmarine.com
Radio Shack, 721-542-3310, F: 721-542-2497

COMMUNICATIONS

(Some businesses charge for holding mail.)
Business Point, 721-544-3315, F: 721-544-3319, hiyosxm@thebusinesspoint.com, email, internet access, mail, communications and travel
Captain Oliver's, (Oyster Pond, 97150, St. Martin, FWI) 0590-87-33-47/721-581-0790, F: 0590-87-33-47, captainolivers@domaccess.com, mail drop, phone, fax, email
Mailbox, The Palapa Center #30, Airport Blvd., St. Maarten, NA., 721-545-3890/70, F: 721-545-3893, themailbox@caribserve.net, phones, fax, email, internet, mail out, secretarial, couriers
Free WiFi on your own computer in most bars

GENERAL YACHT SERVICES

Anyway Marine, 0690-37-62-69/75-65-88, 0590-87-91-41, anyway@wanadoo.fr, yacht brokers
Anse Marcel fuel dock, 0590-87-31-94, valentin@cadisco.com
Boat Cleaning and Services, 0690-47-65-93, info@www.bc-serv.com
Bobby's Philipsburg, 721-542-2366, F: 721-542-5442, VHF: 16
Bobby's MegaYard Simpson Bay 721-544-4060, megayard@gmail.com, marina, water, fuel, haul out, dry storage, (2 yards), machining, mechanics, glass and paintwork, all kinds of repairs
Cadisco Premium Gas, 0690-77-00-87, fuel, mancel@ premiummarinegas.com
Captain Oliver's, (Oyster Pond), 0590-87-33-47/87-40-26, F: 0590-87-40-84, VHF: 67, captainolivers@domaccess.com, marina
Caribbean Yachts, 0690-76-01-00/ 0590-29-48-45, stephane@caraibes-yachts.com, brokerage,
Chantier Naval T.O.B.Y.
Time Out, (Marigot), 0590-52-02-88, F: 0590-52-99-37, timeoutboat@hotmail.com,

haul out, dry storage
Dock Maarten, 721-542-5705, Cell: 721-587-3625, F: 721-542-4940, info@dockmaarten.com, marina
DP Fuel Dock, 0590-87-58-47/0690-71-59-46
Geminga, (Marigot), 0590-29-35-52, F: 0590-29 65 36, geminga@domaccess,com, haul out, dry storage
Gas King, 721-544-3138
Gateway Marina, 721-554-5222/550-8838/554-2324, airport marina and concierge
Great House Marina, 721-571416, F: 721-543-6427, marina
Harel Yachts, 0590-29-43-85, 0690-76-22-22, 721-556-1396, herveharel@orange.fr, broker, Lagoon yacht service
Island Water World, 721-544-5310, F: 721-544-3299, VHF: 74, service@islandwaterworld.com
Inter Nett, 721-580-5642, carpet and fabric cleaning
JMC Boatyard, 721-520-3331, 0690-22-71-28, jmcmarinaandboatyard@caribserve.net, haul-out
Lagoon Marina, (Simpson B.), 721-544-2611, info@lagoon-marina.com, marina
Lagoon Marina Laundry, 721-544-3346
Marina Anse Marcel, 0590-87-31-94, F: 0590-87-33-96/ 87-30-45. VHF: 16/11, marina, water, fuel
Marina Fort St. Louis, 0590-51-11-11, F: 0590-51-11-12, VHF: 16, info@marinafortlouis.com, marina
Marina Port La Royale, 0590-87-20-43, 0690-62-90-93, F: 0590-87-55-95, VHF: 16, semregine1@wanadoo.fr, marina
Maritime School, 721-523-1209/0696-26-16-12, info@maritimeschool.net.
Moorings brokerage, 0590-87-32-55
MP Yachting, 0690-53-37-98, mpyachting@gmail.com, (Marigot), agents for Jeanneau
Must, 0590-29-17-18, 0690-40-99-95, F: 0590-29-16-65, m.u.s.t@

wanadoo.fr, yacht brokers
Porto Cupecoy, 721-545-2318, VHF: 71A/16, marina@portocupecoy.com, marina
Palapa Marina, 721-545-2735, F: 721-545-2510, VHF: 68, office@palapamarina.com, marina
Polypat, (Marigot), 0590-87-12-01, Cell: 0690-58-58-20, F: 0590-87-22-13, polypat.caraibes@gmail.com, haul out, dry storage
Portofino Marina, 721-544-5174, cell: 721-520-1588, yachtclub@caribserve.net, marina
Shrimpy's, 721-580-0861/522-5121, 0590-27-16-68, VHF: 10 shrimpysxm@gmail.com, laundry, second hand shop, hull cleaning
Simpson Bay Marina, 721-544-2309, F: 721-544-3378, VHF: 16/79A, sbm@IGYmarinas.com, marina
St. Maarten Marine Trades Assoc., 721-522-0231, www.yachtingstmaarten.com
St. Maarten Shipyard, 721-545-3740, F: 721-545-3739, stmaartenshipyard@caribserve.net, office@stmaartenshipyard.com
Sun Maintenance, 0690-74-97-14
Tender Rental, 721-599-4180, 0690-30-79-99, info@tenderrental.com
Weather Eye Yacht Sales, 721-552-6286, moreinfo@weathereyeyachts.com
Yacht Club Isle de Sol, (Simpson B.), 721-544-2408, IDS@IGYmarinas.com
Yacht Club Port de Plaisance, 721-544-4565, F: 721-544-4566, info@yachtclubportdeplaisance.com, marina
Yacht Services, 0590-52-92-38, 0690-88-88-47, 721-553-7526

MISCELLANEOUS

Inter Coiffure, 721-454-2985
La Reserve Naturelle de Saint-Martin,(French marine park), 0590-29-09-72, reservenaturelle@domaccess.com
Nature Foundation 721-542-0267, F: 721-542-0268
St. Martin Yacht Club, 721-544-2079, commodore@smyc.com

Tourist Office - Dutch side, 721-542-2337
Tourist Office - French side, 0590-87-57-23/21, F: 0590-87-56-43
Tricia Massage, 0690-50-08-60
Tri Sport, 721-545-4384, trisport@caribsurf.net, bike rentals, sales, repair

SAILMAKERS, CANVAS, CUSHIONS

SXM Sellerie, (Sandy Ground), 0690-22-11-15, laurentdemonceau@voila.fr
St. Maarten Sails, (Simpson Bay), 721-544-5231, F: 721-544-5044, admin@stmaartensails.com, sail, canvas and cushion work, agent for Quantum
Tropical Sail Loft, (Simpson Bay), 721-544-5472/553-2759 ernst@tropicalsailloft.com, sailmaker and canvas work, North Sails agent, sells fabrics and needles
Tropical Creations Upholstery, (Simpson Bay), 721-523-4424, 0690-22-50-35
Voile Caraibe (Incidences), (Sandy Ground), 0590-87-06-04, voilecaraibe.stmartin@orange.fr, sailmaker

TRANSPORT

Avis, 721-545-2847
Deep Blue, lagoon water taxi, 721-580-3314
Dollar Car Rental, 721-545-3281
Excellent Rentals, 721-545-2448
Paradise Car Rental, 721-545-3737, rent@paradisesxm.com
Tri-Sport, 721-545-4384, F: 721-545-4385, bike rentals
Taxis, (Marigot), 0590-87-56-54, Airport, 721-546-7759 (Philipsburg), 147

TECHNICAL YACHT SERVICES

Aquatic Solutions, 721-554-2979, aquaticsxm@yahoo.com
Atlantis Marine, 721-544-3788/553-7061, gsbguima@hotmail.com, electrics, electronics
Best Boat Yard, 721-580-7114/580-7607, info@bestboatyardservices. com, machining, fabrication, mechanics, hydraulics
Brokaar Marine Services, cell: 721-571416, F: 721-543-6427,

Directory

brokaar@sintmaarten.net, towing, salvage, commercial diving
Custom Fit Marine, 721-587-4546, 721-587-9621, customfitmarine@gmail.com
Caamano Marine, 721-524-0075, info@caamano-marine.com
Caraibes Diesel Services, 0590-87-03-73, 0690-38-39-75, info@caraibesdiesel.com, mechanic
Cyberman, 721-599-6662/VHF:10,
Dinghy Spot, 0690-32-82-11, dinghyspot@hotmail.com (inflatable repair)
Diesel Outfitters, (Simpson Bay), 721-556-4967, raymondlongbottom@yahoo.com, repair of all diesel engines, Perkins agent
E & MSC, 721-527-3812, 544-2912, e-msc07@yahoo.com, metal-work
Electec, 721-544-2051, F: 721-544-3641, sales@electec.info, electrical installation and repair and instrumentation, also water makers
Enertech, 721-544-2460, F: 721-544-4608, service@enertechnv.com, refrigeration & air conditioning
Five Star Yacht Consultants, 721-580-1998, consulting, dispute management, fuel polishing
FKG Rigging (Cole Bay Marine Center), 721-544-4733/5691, F: 721-544-2171, cell: 721-557-8502,VHF: 71, kevin@fkg-marine-rigging.com, dry storage, all kinds of repairs, work berths, rigging, welding & machining, rigging a specialty, large stock wire and fitting, swaging, profurl and furlex, woodworking
Havin's, 721-587-0530, F: 721-544-2293 info@havinsmarine.com, metalwork - t-top and fuel tank specialists
Island Water World, 721-544-5310, F: 721-544-3299, VHF: 74, service@islandwaterworld.com haul-out, hull repairs and painting, Evinrude sales, and OMC repairs
Kenny Awlgrip, 721-587-6942, brandehal72@gmail.com, yacht refinishing
Kiss Marine, 721-554-8171, kissmarinenv@

yahoo.com, mechanics, electrics refrigeration
L'Atelier Marine, 0690-54-27-00, leport.herve@gmail.com
Life Rafts Etc, 0690-74-43-30, info@liferaftsetc.com
Macklon Marine Refrigeration, 721-556-1453
Maintec, 721-550-5368,, maintec@sintmaarten.net, woodworking, glasswork, electrics
Maritime Solutions, 721-533-5996, maritimesoutions@gmail.com
MGS, 0590-87-07-95, 0690-56-06-37, Christian-pinho-teixira@orange.com, fabrication
MJC Fabrication, 0690-53-74-89/65-75-23, Fax: 0590-87-33-91, markcarlatempleton@yahoo.com
Necol, 721-580-8148/580-5326, andrew@necol.com, electronics
Nigel Pearman Painting, 721-523-6576, nigelpearman@yahoo.uk
Minville Marine, 0590-87-19-13, F: 0590-87-19-73, Suzuki sales and service
Paint Tech, 721-586-7187/586-7199, painttechnvsxm@yahoo.com
Palapa Shipwrights, 721-554-1584
Pascal Register, 0690-35-84-45, glasswork
Permafrost Marine Services, 721-556-3351/545-5599, VHF: 68, service@permafrostrefrigeration.com, refrigeration & air-conditioning specialists
Rob Marine, 721-554-6333, info@robmarine.net
Simpson Bay Diesel, 721-544-5397, F: 721-544-5747, direct US 727-471 8701, info@sbdiesel.com, repair of diesels, Cummins & Yamaha agent
SMbloc, 0690-25-20-34/45-45-70, smblock 971@gmail.com
Star Marine, 0590-73-05-88 glass and paintwork
SMX Marine Diesel Service, 0690-66-19-49, US: 954-260-5436, sxmdms@gmail.com
SXM Power Center, 721-544-1414, 0690-53-68-08, Yamaha agent
The Wired Sailor, 721-580-7733/527-2896, electronics, IT

Titan Marine, 721-550-2853, info@titanmarineair.com, refrigeration, ac, watermakers
TMTT, 0590-52-97-86, 721-557-1479, metal work
Yacht Rigging, 0590-29-52-82, F: 0590-29-45-15, mustyachtrigging@domaccess.com

ST. MARTIN SHOPPING
BANKING
American Express agents:
Maduro & Sons, 721-542-2678
The Windward Bank, 721-542-2313, Cash from VISA

FUN SHOPPING
Galleries Jean Jarreau, 0590-51-04-95, st.martin@galleriesjeanjarreau.com
Guavaberry, 721-542-2965, F: 721-542-4598, manager@Guavaberry.com
SXM Electronics, 721-545-2004

PROVISIONING
(Yacht agents)
Dockside Management, 721-544-4096/587-6879, US: 305-677-0055 VHF: 16, office@docksidemanagement.net, super-yacht agent
IDS Yacht Provisioning, 721-544-0200/522-3728/523-7616, info@idsprovisions.com, provisioning
International Yacht Collection, (Simpson B.), 721-544 2515/524 6006, mark@IYC.com
MegaYacht Services, 721-544-4440, Cell: 721-520-1530, harrison@megayachtservice.com
Palapa Marinas Yacht Provisioning, 721-545-5611, F: 721-545-2510, provisioning@palapamarina.com
Simpson Bay Yacht Provisioning, 721-520-3336, danny@caribserve.net
Shore Support, 721-587-0007/544-5035, 0690-75-58-08, F: 721-544-3035, simon@shoresupport.net
BWA Yachting (& Crew Network), 721-554-8918/5544-2436, F: 721-544-2496, l.frye@BWAyachting.com
Yacht Assistance, 0590-51-04-95, 0690-62-99-55, info@yachtassis-

tance.com
Yacht Chandlers, 721-581-2967/587-3506, timw@yachtchandlers.com

tance.com
Yacht Chandlers, 721-581-2967/587-3506, timw@yachtchandlers.com

PROVISIONING

Amsterdam Cheeses and Liquor, 721-581-5408, acssxm@gmail.com
Daily Extra, 721-544-2577, afoo@sintmaarten.net
Dirty Dick's Liquor Store, 0690-77-22-00
Gourmet Marche, 721-545-3055, legrandmarche.net
La Sucriere, 721-544-3530
Le Grande Marche, (Philipsburg) 721-542-4400, F: 721-542-4401, email@legrandmarche.net
Market Garden, 721-544-4436, provisioning, 721-544-4435
Sang's Supermarket, 721-542-3447, F: 721-542-3189, sangstrading@sintmaarten.net
Seascape Lobster Wholesale, 0690-35-09-36
Simpson Bay Pharmacy, 721-544-3653, F: 721-544-3654 sbp@pharmacy@gmail.com, pharmacy at Simpson Bay Yacht Club
Super U, 0590-87-92-36

ST. MARTIN HOTELS & RESTAURANTS

RESTAURANTS / ACCOMMODATION

A tasca, 721-587-0603, $B-C
Bistrot du Port, 0590-29-25-16, Marigot, $C-D
Buccaneer Bar, 721-522-9700, bernyachtmaster@yahoo.com
Calmos Cafe, 0590-29-01-85, $D, Grand Case
Captain Oliver's, 0590-87-40-26, $A-B, Oyster Pond
Castaways, 721-544-3303, $B-D, Grand Case
Chesterfields, 721-542-3484, $B-C, Philipsburg
Dinghy Dock, $D, info@dinghydockbar.com, Oyster Pond
El Rancho, 721-545-2495, $B, Simpson Bay
Fish Pot, 0590-87-50-88, $A, Grand Case
Green House, 721-542-2941, $B-C, Philipsburg
Jimbo's, $C-D, Simpson Bay

La Carambole, 0590-87-55-09, $C
El Rancho, 721-545-2495, $B, Simpson Bay
Kangaroo Court, $D, Philipsburg
Lal's Indian Cuisine, 721-587-9059, Simpson Bay, $D
L'Escapade, 0590-87-75-04, $AB, Grand Case
Escargot, T&F: 721-542-2483, $A-B, Philipsburg
Lagoonies, 721-544-3703, $C-D
La Vie en Rose, 0590-87-54-42, F: 0590-87-82-63 $A, Marigot
Le Belle Epoque, 0590-87-87-70, $C-D
Le Case a L'eau, 0690-22-78-28, maisonflottant.sxm@gmail.com 0590-87-81-79 $C-D, Marigot
Le Nadine France, 0690-88-12-90, $C-D, Oyster Pond
Le Planteur, 0590-29 53 21, $AB, Oyster Pond
Le Pressoir, 0590-87-76-62, $B, Grand Case
Mario's Bistro, 0590-87-06-36, Marigot
Mr. Busby, 721-543-6088, $D, Oyster Pond
Oyster Bay Beach Resort, 721-543-6040, info@obbr.com, Oyster Bay
Pineapple Pete, 721-544-6030, $B-C, Simpson Bay
The Bad Monkey, 0690-14-32-41, $D
Top Carrot, 721-544-3381, Simpson Bay
The Boathouse, 721-544-5409, $B-D, Simpson Bay
Tropicana, 0590-87-79-07, $C-D, Marigot
Yacht Club, 0590-87-56-65, $B-C
Zee Best, 0590 690 39 79 59, $D, Simpson Bay

ST. MARTIN SCUBA DIVING

Aquatic Adventure Diving, (Marigot) 0696-10-10-11/39-98-52
Blue Bubbles, Philipsburg, 721-542-3667/554-2502, info@bluebubblessxm.com
Dive Safaris (Simpson Bay) 721-545-2401 Cell: 721-520-8300, divesafari@hotmail.com, dive trips, dive school, hydrostatic testing and tank annual service
Ocean Explorers, Simpson Bay Lagoon, T: 721-544-5252, info@

stmaartendiving.com, dive shop plus sales of snorkeling and diving gear
Octopus, Grande Case, 0590-87-20-62, F: 0590-87-20-63
Scuba Fun, Philipsburg, 721-542-3966, contact@scubafundivecenter.com dive shop plus sales of snorkeling and diving gear
Scuba Shop, Oyster Pond, 0590-87-48-01, F: 0590-87-48-01, info@thescubashop.net, Peter Frye, excellent prices on equipment, gear rentals to charter yachts, free diving site booklet
Scuba Shop, Simpson Bay, 721-545-3213, T: 721-545-3209, info@thescubashop.net, authorized dealer, retail, rental, equipment service, gear rentals to charter yachts, free diving site booklet
Scuba Zen, Anse Marcel, 0590-87 36-13, 0690-72 87-50, pro-idc@scubazensxm.com 94/30-45-78, $B-C

INTERNATIONAL COMPANIES OF INTEREST

AB Inflatables, 239-231-4905, F: 239-231- 3389, info@ABinflatables.com
Barefoot Yacht Charters, 784-456-9526/9334, F: 784-456-9238, barebum@vincysurf.com
Budget Marine, www.budgetmarine.com
Doyle Offshore Sails, Barbados, 246-423-4600, F: 246-423-4499, doyle@sunbeach.net
Ed Hamilton & Co., 800-621-7855, 207-882-7855, F: 207-882-7851, info@edhamilton.com
Island Water World, www.islandwaterworld.com
L'Amer, (Deshaies), 0590-68-30-30, 0690-50-03-22, laurent.lelou@l-amer.fr
Sea Hawk Paints, FL, 727-523-8053, F: 727-523-7325 eñorrie@seahawkpaints.com
Sheer Rocks, 268-464-5283, reservations@sheer-rocks.com,

Directory

Anguilla's Charm at the classics

ADVERTISERS INDEX

Palm Tree, Nevis

CRUISING GUIDE TO THE VIRGIN ISLANDS

By Nancy & Simon Scott
17th Edition,
2015-2016
ISBN 978-0-944428-96-6
6 x 9, 350 pp. **$33.95**

Completely re-designed and updated style, with more Virgin Island photography and full color detailed anchorage charts, these guides have been indispensable companions for sailors and visitors to these islands since 1982. Includes a free 17 x 27 color planning chart, with aerial photos of some of the anchorages. Covers the Virgin Islands including all the U.S. and British Virgin Islands!

- GPS co-ordinates for every anchorage
- Anchoring and mooring information and fees
- Customs, immigration and National Park regulations
- Particulars on marina facilities and the amenities they offer
- Water sports-where to go and where to rent equipment
- Shore-side facilities, restaurants, beach bars, shops, provisions, internet connections

Everything you will need to help make your vacation an enjoyable and memorable experience in a concise easy-to-use format.

VIRGIN ANCHORAGES

By Nancy & Simon Scott
2012 Edition
ISBN 978-0-944428-84-9
8.5 x 11, 96 pp. **$29.95**

Virgin Anchorages features stunning color aerial photography of 46 of the most popular anchorages in the Virgin Islands. Graphic overlays aid in navigating to safe anchorages. This is an excellent companion to Cruising Guide to the Virgin Islands.

LEEWARD ANCHORAGES

By Chris Doyle
ISBN 0-944428-82-7
8.5 x 11, 91 pp **$29.95**

Leeward Anchorages shows aerial photographs of all the favorite anchorages from Anguilla through Dominica with graphic overlays to illustrate dangerous and safe passages from a bird's eye view. Carefully researched and recorded by Chris Doyle, safe passages, markers, buoys and hazards are all marked to guide you to safe, enjoyable anchorages. This is a companion book to use with The Cruising Guide to the Leeward Islands.

THE CRUISING GUIDE TO THE NORTHERN LEEWARD ISLANDS

Chris Doyle
2016-2017
ISBN 978-0-9914550-5-8
6 x 9, 288 pp
$29.95

This fourteenth edition has been split into two guides. The Cruising Guide to the Northern Leeward Islands covers the islands of Anguilla, St. Martin & Sint Maarten, Saba, Statia, St. Kitts, Nevis, Redonda, and Montserrat. This guide is an essential tool for all cruisers sailing this region. Chris Doyle spends months sailing these islands to update each edition. Included are over one hundred up-to-date color sketch charts, full color aerial photos of most anchorages, island pictures, and detailed shore-side information covering services, restaurants, provisioning, travel basics and island history. Information is linked to the author's website where you can download the GPS waypoints given in the sketch charts, learn of essential updates, print town maps, and obtain links to local weather, news, and businesses. A free 17 x 27 inch waterproof planning chart of the northern and southern Leeward Islands is now included in each edition!

THE CRUISING GUIDE TO THE SOUTHERN LEEWARD ISLANDS

Chris Doyle
2016-2017
ISBN 978-0-9914550-6-5
6 x 9, 324 pp
$29.95

This fourteenth edition has been split into two guides. The Cruising Guide to the Southern Leeward Islands covers the islands of Antigua, Barbuda, Guadeloupe, Marie Galante, the Saintes, and Dominica. This guide is an essential tool for all cruisers sailing this region. Chris Doyle spends months sailing these islands to update each edition. Included are over one hundred up-to-date color sketch charts, full color aerial photos of most anchorages, island pictures, and detailed shore-side information covering services, restaurants, provisioning, travel basics and island history. Information is linked to the author's website where you can download the GPS waypoints given in the sketch charts, learn of essential updates, print town maps, and obtain links to local weather, news, and businesses. A free 17 x 27 inch waterproof planning chart of the northern and southern Leeward Islands is now included in each edition!

www.cruisingguides.com

For more titles, charts, cookbooks and more.

SAILORS GUIDE TO THE WINDWARD ISLANDS
By Chris Doyle
17th Edition,
2015-2016
ISBN 978-0-944428-99-3
6 x 9, 430 pp. **$33.95**

Revised and updated for 2015-2016, this guide features detailed sketch charts based on the author's own surveys, and aerial photos of most anchorages. It also includes clear and concise navigational information. By far the most popular guide to the area, it covers the islands from Martinique to Grenada, with dazzling scenic photography, unsurpassed onshore information, sections on exploring, provisioning, water sports, services, restaurants and photography. Information is linked to the author's website where you can download town maps, GPS waypoints from the sketch charts, and obtain links to local weather, news and more.

CRUISING GUIDE TO VENEZUELA & BONAIRE
By Chris Doyle
2006
ISBN 0-944428-78-9
6 x 9, 290 pp. **$27.95**
This is the latest updated version of the only seriously researched guide to this area. The book includes color aerial photos of many anchorages, clear and concise navigational charts, with information on things to do and places to go while on shore. The guide is linked to the author's website where you can download updates, town maps and much more.

CRUISING GUIDE TO TRINIDAD, TOBAGO PLUS BARBADOS AND GUYANA
By Chris Doyle
2013
ISBN 978-0-944428-96-2
6 x 9, 256 pp. **$27.95**
This updated edition has been expanded to include Guyana. Including 55 sketch charts, aerial photographs, dazzling scenic photography throughout, unsurpassed onshore information with sections on exploring, provisioning, services and restaurants. The guide is linked to the author's website where you can download town maps, GPS waypoints given in the sketch charts and much more.

WINDWARD ANCHORAGES
By Chris Doyle
ISBN 0-944428-83-5
8.5 x 11, 96 pp
$29.95

Windward Anchorages is the third in the Anchorages series and a companion book to the Sailors Guide to the Windward Islands by Chris Doyle. Stunning aerial images depict anchorages from Martinique south through Dominica. These aerial images are overprinted to show the hazards to avoid, as well as, markers and buoys to guide you to the safe passages and anchorages of the Windward Islands.

WATERPROOF PLANNING CHART OF THE VIRGIN ISLANDS
COLOR WITH AERIAL PHOTOS
Color, 17 x 27 **$9.95**
Printed on two sides this new chart includes the U.S. & B.V.I. from St. Thomas to Anegada, including anchorage and mooring locations as well as GPS co-ordinates, sailing routes and distances between waypoints. The waterproof chart is excellent for the cockpit and attractive enough to hang on the wall when you get home. Designed for use with The Cruising Guide to the Virgin Islands

BUY OUR GUIDES ON OUR NEW APP!
Search for Cruising Guides Publications on Google Play or iTunes!

Cruising Guide Publications
P.O. Box 1017, Dunedin, FL 34697-1017 • phone 800-330-9542
International Orders 727-733-5322, Fax 727-734-8179

Cruising Guides

Notes

Notes

Notes